The Discovery and Conqu

A book in the series

Latin America in translation/En traducción/Em tradução

Sponsored by the Duke-University of North Carolina Joint Program in Latin American Studies

CONQVISTA

MILAGRO DE L S. S.

tiago mayor apostol de ihu cristo

en el cuzco

.S.

The Discovery and Conquest of Peru

CHRONICLES OF THE NEW WORLD ENCOUNTER

Pedro de Cieza de León

Edited and Translated by

Alexandra Parma Cook and Noble David Cook

Duke University Press Durham and London

1998

 Printed in the United States of America on acid-free paper ∞
Typeset in Dante with Centaur display by Tseng Information Systems, Inc.
Library of Congress Cataloging-in-Publication Data appear on the last printed page of this book.

The preparation of this work was made possible by a grant from the National Endowment for the Humanities, an independent federal agency.
Translation of the books in the Latin America in Translation / En Traducción / Em Tradução, a collaboration between the Duke–University of North Carolina Joint Program in Latin American Studies and the university presses of Duke and the University of North Carolina, is supported by a grant from the Andrew W. Mellon Foundation.
Translation and publication permission to print this work in the United States was granted by the Fondo Editorial de la Pontificia Universidad Católica del Perú.

Frontispiece art: Santiago the Moorslayer-Indianslayer. Felipe Guaman Poma de Ayala, *El primer nueva corónica y buen gobierno* [1613], f. 404. Courtesy Siglo Veintiuno Editores.

Those of you reading this, believe me that when I write, I would rather leave out much of what I know and pass it over than to include even a single word of what did not happen. And, good and honorable men, this you will comprehend and learn without knowing it when you see the modesty and simplicity of my style, which seeks neither verbosity nor flowery words nor other rhetoric, and only wishes to relate the truth with sincerity because I believe that good writing must be like one person conversing with another—and as one speaks and no more.

Pedro de Cieza de León *(Part Three, chapter 7)*

CONTENTS

LIST OF ILLUSTRATIONS AND MAPS

Illustrations

Maps

PROLOGUE

Pedro de Cieza de León was the first historian to write a global history of the Andes. In conveying to the reader an obligatory description of the land, and in creating a history of the Incas of Cuzco that was the earliest vision of the pre-Spanish world—analogous to the *Suma y narración de los Incas* of Juan Diez de Betanzos—Cieza offers an early and complete depiction of the Andean world, though clearly based on European precepts. *Part Three* of his history, the subject of the present translation, is a detailed narrative that initiates the story of Spanish presence in the Andes and continues in three singular books that he was able to write about the civil wars among the region's conquerors.

Cieza de León surpasses the classic definition of a chronicler. Years ago, Peruvian historian Raúl Porras Barrenechea considered him with reason among those authors who encompassed the totality of the historical experience, comparing him with, among others, Gutiérrez de Santa Clara and Garcilaso de la Vega, Pedro Pizarro and Agustín de Zárate, in addition to the general chroniclers of the Indies, such as Francisco López de Gómara or Bartolomé de las Casas. Like these writers, Cieza de León was working within a particular temporal context in his *Chronicle of Peru*, but he also depicts the events with minute detail and makes a distinction between various historical periods, far exceeding the standard criteria of his contemporaries.

Cieza de León died in Seville in 1554. During his lifetime, he was able to publish only *Part One* of his ambitious project, although copies of the following parts circulated throughout Spain. From his testament, it is clear that he wanted to send posthumously some of these to the famous friar Bartolomé de las Casas. The printing of *Part Three* had to wait until our time, whereas the remainder came out at the end of the nineteenth century. He has been called justifiably the "prince of chroniclers."

The title Cieza de León chose for his history was the *Chronicle of Peru*. The various incomplete editions incorporated diverse labels for some parts of the *Chronicle*. It is useful to remember that the titles of the Anglo-American chronicles often differed, showing a change in the author's original title or the invention of a title in cases where the manuscript lacked the original. Although the title of *Part One* of the *Chronicle*, published in Seville in 1553, is undisputed, Cieza called it at times the "Book of Foundations,"[1] alluding to a sentence in the preface of *Part One*. It was this tradition of referring to the lead theme of each part of the project as written in the preface that resulted in the changes suffered by the title of the work in its various published versions. The modern editions of *Part Two* and *Part Three* of the *Chronicle* were named by approximating the actual wishes of the author as expressed in the total scheme of the work laid out in the preface of *Part One*. William Prescott used this approach in giving a title to *Part Two* even before the manuscript's author was correctly identified.

Part Three of the *Chronicle of Peru* remained unpublished and was widely sought after, although thanks to Marcos Jiménez de la Espada it became known in the last years of the nineteenth century that a copy did exist.[2] Several years later, Jiménez de la Espada himself published fragments of it in his *Relaciones geográficas de Indias*.[3] There was much speculation regarding the location of the manuscript or of existing copies. Then, in 1946 Rafael Loredo brought chapters of the text to light; later, Carmelo Sáenz de Santa María, S.J., published the final chapters that Loredo was unable either to locate or to publish.[4] Francesca Cantù finally found a complete manuscript of *Part Three* (together with *Part Two*) in the Apostolic Library of the Vatican; she first published it in Rome and later in Lima.[5]

The present meticulous translation by Alexandra Parma Cook and Noble David Cook is based on this last edition. The Cooks do justice to the prince of the chroniclers. Now available to the English-speaking reader, this version of *Part Three* of the *Chronicle of Peru* will not only permit a better understanding of the chronicler and his work, but also put in the hands of scholars an important tool for the analysis of the Spanish invasion of the Andes.

Franklin Pease G.Y.

Notes

1 For example, Pedro de Cieza de León, *Crónica del Peru: Cuarta parte*, vol. 1, *Guerra de Las Salinas*, ed. Pedro Guibovich Pérez (Lima: Pontificia Universidad Católica del Perú, 1991), p. 390.

2 Marcos Jiménez de la Espada, ed. (*Tercero libro de las Guerras Civiles del*

Perú, el cual se llama la Guerra de Quito (Madrid: Biblioteca Hispano-Ultramarina, T. I., 1877), p. xxi) mentioned that José Sancho Rayón, editor of *Part Four* of the *Chronicle* and co-owner of a manuscript of it, owned one of *Part Three* also, of which Jiménez de la Espada obtained a copy. The same copy appears to have been used by Loredo for the incomplete editions that he published. Carmelo Sáenz de Santa María, "Los capítulos finales de la Tercera Parte de la *Crónica del Perú* de Cieza de León," *Boletín del Instituto Riva Agüero* 9 (1972–74): 35.

3 Marcos Jiménez de la Espada, ed. *Relaciones geográficas de Indias*, 2d ed. (Madrid: Ediciones Atlas, 1965), 3:157, 95.

4 Sáenz de Santa María, "Los capítulos finales," pp. 35–67.

5 Francesca Cantù, *Pedro de Cieza de León e il "descubrimiento y conquista del Perú"* (Rome: Instituto Storico Italiano per l'Età Moderna e Contemporanea, 1979). See also the preliminary study that appears in the edition published in Lima in 1987 by the Pontificia Universidad Católica del Perú.

INTRODUCTION

Biographical Sketch

The future "prince of Peruvian chroniclers" was born in the Spanish town of Llerena sometime between 1518 and 1522, most likely in 1520. He was the son of Lope de León, a minor merchant with past connections at court, and Leonor de Cazalla, whose family included merchants as well as notaries and clergymen. Pedro had an older sister, Beatriz de Cazalla, and a brother, Rodrigo, as well as two younger sisters, María and Leonor.[1]

Llerena, a picturesque town in southeastern Extremadura, lies at the center of excellent wheatlands, halfway between Cordova to the east and Seville to the south. In the sixteenth century it was one of the largest and most important towns in Extremadura. Its strong economy, based on agricultural production as well as its weekly Tuesday markets, contributed to its wealth and importance.[2] The author Luis Zapata de Chaves, a contemporary of Cieza, left a flowing account of the town:

> Llerena, a most noble place, head of the province of León in Extremadura, situated at the foot of the Sierra Morena, a happy site, with fertile soil, healthy sky, proud houses, agreeable streets, abundant beauties and filled with knights and learned men of such rare ingenuity, that one can hardly find a dunce there.[3]

Pedro de Cieza de León's early years and his education remain a mystery. What we know is based mostly on his writings. Because he left Spain when he was about thirteen years old, the age when most people began their university training, it seems unlikely that he received any formal higher education. But like other young men of similar social status in Llerena, he must have learned the basics at the local parish school or at the city's cathedral church. He therefore may have acquired some rudimentary Latin and through its study at least a familiarity with classical antiquity. In his work he makes occasional allusions to classical times and authors, though these references are comparatively few and may have been added later when he was revising his volumes.[4] Because his natural writing style is simple and direct, it leaves little space for erudite embellishments. He mentions Titus

Livy and Valerius in the dedication of *Part One* of his chronicle, and Diodoro Siculo and Cicero in the prologue; there is also an indication that he knew the *Commentaries* of Julius Caesar and Plutarch's *Lives.* In *Part One,* chapter 2, as he introduces the foundation of cities in the New World, he recalls city founders of antiquity: Rome by Romulus, Carthage by Elisa Dido, Alexandria by Alexander the Great. He was also familiar with Hannibal's crossing of the Alps to enter Italy.[5]

As a boy, Cieza traveled in Spain with his father or other merchant relatives. In his writings he often makes references to places that he visited, particularly Seville and Cordova, located not far from his home town. For example, Cieza tells us that he remembers hearing a lewd song "when I was in Cordova while still a boy" that warned of the infidelity of the abandoned wives of the men heading for Peru.[6] And he watched at Seville's wharfs when the ship *Santa María del Campo* carrying Hernando Pizarro and an unforgettable treasure horde was unloaded on 9 January 1534. He later mused: "I cannot stop thinking about those things, when I remember the opulent pieces that were seen in Seville, brought from Cajamarca, where the treasure that Atahualpa promised the Spaniards was collected."[7]

Cieza's imagination, like that of so many of his contemporaries, was fired up by this spectacle, and regardless of his youth he decided to sail to the Indies. In March 1535, assisted by his father and his uncle, one of Seville's public notaries, Alonso de Cazalla, he attempted to secure authorization from the officials of the House of Trade to travel to Tierra Firme, the mainland of South America. Pedro de Cieza is listed in the register of the "Passengers to the Indies" as authorized to sail on 2 April with Juan del Junco on Cifuentes's ship destined for Cartagena.[8] For reasons unknown, however, Cieza did not travel on that vessel but instead left on or around 3 June 1535. He appears on the list of passengers: "Pedro de León, son of Lope de León and Leonor de Cazalla, residents of Llerena, sailed for Santo Domingo in the ship of Manuel de Maya."[9]

The future explorer and chronicler was still a boy when he said farewell to his family and sailed from Seville's bustling port down the Guadalquivir River to its Atlantic mouth at Sanlúcar de Barrameda. After the ship left the coast, it most likely headed for the Canary Islands, where the fleet paused briefly to load supplies of water and last-minute provisions and to make any necessary repairs to the vessels. Their first stop in the Caribbean was at Santo Domingo on the island of Hispaniola, from there they sailed on to Tierra Firme and landed at Cartagena on the north coast of present-day Colombia. Almost from the beginning the young man participated in minor expeditions in search of riches, some of which were little more than grave-robbing episodes: "I found myself in the Cenú, that falls within the province of Cartagena, in the year 1535."[10] There he encountered his first American treasure: "I saw great quantities removed from the tombs before we went on the discovery of the Vruté under Captain Alonso de Cáceres."[11]

Cieza spent the next decade in the region, engaged in numerous expeditions.[12] He joined the *entrada* of Juan de Vadillo to explore the Gulf of Urabá, searching for a water passage to the Pacific: "I found myself in this city of San Sebastián de Buena Vista [Urabá] in the year 1536."[13] In the following year he continued with Juan de Vadillo on an expedition into the interior, and he recalled, "We were the first Spaniards to open the road from the North Sea to the South."[14] Part of their intention was to conquer the province of Abibe and to reach what is present-day Antioquia.

Young Cieza was fascinated by what he saw around him and kept notes on what he observed. He amassed firsthand information on the flora and fauna of the northern Andes during these campaigns, which provided the foundation of the natural history that makes up a large section of *Part One* of his chronicle. He later recalled:

> I traveled from this village of Urabá all the way to the city of La Plata, which are at the limits of Peru. And I would set out for all parts to see as many provinces as I could, in order to understand and record what was in each of them. Therefore from here on I will relate what I saw and what I experienced, without exaggerating or leaving out anything that I am obliged to say.[15]

Cieza often refers to personal episodes of his earlier expeditions. Years later he remembered being out on guard near a river in the mountains of Abibe and still recoiled at the thought of "the thin hairy worms, about the size of half a finger," because one of them "came down a branch of a tree and bit me on the neck, and I spent one of the worst and most painful nights in my life."[16]

The young explorer not only kept copious notes to help him remember the nature of the various peoples that he encountered, but was also involved in military activities. As he often reminds his readers, he faced many dangers and suffered great hardships—experiences that he recounts in his writings. When he was about seventeen, he made a leather breast cover out of tapir skin to protect himself against poisoned darts and arrows, which he later described, as well as the fearsome and deadly curare poison. Cieza saw himself as having "two occupations, that of writing and of following my banner and captain."[17] He constantly reminds us that he took the time to record what he had seen: "Indeed when the other soldiers rested, I tired myself writing."[18] At another time he reflects, "God is the witness of my great vigils and the little rest I have had. For this I want no other prize except that the reader should treat me as a friend, seeing the many roads and peregrinations that I have gone through to investigate the notable things of these places."[19]

The exploratory party that ascended the Cauca Valley to the seat of the chieftain Nutibara proved less viable financially than the participants had hoped, and the discovery of the province of Abibe ended with financial disaster in Cali. They had been able to amass a total of only 2,600 pesos, and of that, Cieza complains, "My part of the treasure was five and a half pesos, so that all can see what type of reward there was for such a difficult discovery as that was."[20] The expedition began with 345 footmen and 512 horsemen, along with a large number of Blacks and Indians. By the end, 96 footmen and 119 horsemen had perished: "I can affirm that in all my life I never experienced such hunger as in those days." He further laments that many of his companions were "so ill that they could not continue on such an arduous march, so they remained in the mountains awaiting a miserable death."[21]

On 14 February 1539 Cieza set out from Cali with a force under Captain Jorge Robledo to explore the Cauca and Atrato river basins. He participated in the founding of Santa Ana de los Caballeros (15 August 1539), then of the cities Ancerma and Cartago (1540) in the rich Quimbaya region, and in the following year, the expeditionaries settled in the Cartago Valley. Cieza also helped establish Antioquia (25 November 1541).[22] He later "remembered the time of the foundation, and [how] Robledo told me he wanted to give it the name of Antioch, and I responded, 'Let us hope that it does not have as many wars as that of Syria.'"[23] In order to secure his position, Robledo found it necessary to return to Spain for a royal confirmation of his conquests. It was at this time that Cieza decided to settle down in Cartago.

Shortly afterward, our chronicler was able to sort through his notes, and recalling later, "I began to write in the city of Cartago in the jurisdiction of Popayán, in the year 1541."[24] By then Cieza had spent six years traveling, exploring, observing, and jotting down what he saw and heard in the rugged and difficult terrain of northwestern Andean America. If he is to be believed, he worried whether he was up to the task. Clearly conscious of his limited education, he wondered if his undertaking would not all "be in vain, because composition of stories was granted to those of great judgment and erudition."[25] Yet, the budding author felt that what he lacked in education, he made up for in his earnest desire to describe the truth "because that is what I have tried the most, since much of what I write about, I have seen with my own eyes, being present; and I traveled through many lands and provinces in order to see it better. And what I did not see, I strove to learn about from highly credible people."[26] Another motivation for recording events was "seeing that wherever I went no one was concerned with writing anything about what was happening. And time consumes the memory of things."[27]

Cieza was one of the first Europeans in the Andean region of South America to use native informants extensively in his research, and he did so even a decade before he questioned surviving Inca record keepers, the *quipucamayos*, in Cuzco. When he told his superiors that he planned to write a history of the place and its peoples, Jorge Robledo supplied him with an interpreter: "Because my captain knew that I was curious to know the secrets of the Indians, he gave me Catalina, so that I could learn more easily."[28]

It was not until early January 1542 that Captain Robledo was able to begin the return to Spain to report on his discoveries and to secure royal authorization for what he had done. He set out from Antioquia toward Panama with a small force of ten to twelve, one of whom was Cieza. Marching over the Abibe range and descending through territories without roads, they lacked adequate food and once again suffered a great deal. Finally, after a journey of one and one-half months, they reached the port of Urabá. Here, the local official jailed Robledo, claiming that he had invaded his territory, and sent him to Spain for judgment, which fortunately was where Robledo intended to go anyway. Before leaving, Robledo convinced the official to permit Cieza to travel to the royal *audiencia* (high court) of Panama "in order to give account to the justices and president of the royal audiencia that was there. I later passed to the governance and met the Adelantado Belalcázar in the city of Cali."[29] Thus, we find Cieza in Panama in 1542, when he most likely first met and talked to those escaping Peru's civil unrest.

Cieza apparently returned quickly to Colombia, for that same year he helped found the city of Arma, on a slope leading to the Cauca River. He received an *encomienda,* under cacique Aoripana, for his efforts: "the grant of Indians for my services was granted to me within the jurisdiction of this town."[30] According to Cieza's figures, more than twenty thousand adult male warriors lived in the region. There were "large palm groves, and palm hearts were taken from some varieties, and they bore coconuts that were used for milk, and they even make a cream and lard from them, that can be used in lamps, for they burn as oil." Cieza was impressed with the fertility of the soil. Corn yielded a hundred bushels per bushel of seed, and the area could produce two crops each year. Even more important than agriculture for Cieza and his compatriots, however, were the "large deposits of gold in the big river a league from the city . . . , if one sends a Black, there is not a day that he will not produce two or three ducats for his master. In time this will become one of the richest lands in the Indies."[31]

Captain Jorge Robledo returned to the Indies from Spain, under Miguel Díaz de Armendáriz, with title of marshal and governorship of Antioquia, Arma, and Cartago.[32] Robledo intended to place Sebastián de Belalcázar under his authority, but on the night of 4 October 1546 the conqueror of Quito turned the tables on Robledo at a place called Lomo de Pozo. That site had witnessed numerous Indian massacres, and Cieza found the irony: "by some secret judgment of God it was determined that he [Robledo] should die in this spot."[33] After a quick trial, Robledo—who "was so much liked for his goodness to us, that we looked upon him as a father"—was executed, along with two of his supporters. Their corpses were placed in a thatched native house, which was set on fire to prevent the Indians from eating them.[34]

Fortunately, Cieza was not there at the time. "I wanted to go with him [Robledo], but he asked me to remain in the town [Arma] to supply things that might be necessary. He wrote me from Pozo to send him the arms that he had left in the town, and some ammunition, which was done."[35] A group of Belalcázar's men entered Arma, plundering, and Cieza complained: "They took some Indian women from me, and because one of them fled from the person she thought was going to take her, he came up to me with great arrogance, and putting a daggar to my chest, demanded the Indian that he wanted for himself."[36] Robledo's death, the sacking of his estate, and the theft of his native women caused Cieza to leave Colombia, abandoning his *repartimiento* (grant) of Indians and his hacienda at Arma, as well as the mines he had exploited.

By the time Cieza left Colombia he had been composing his history for about five years and had compiled an extensive record. He faced numerous problems writing, and indeed, one wonders how he managed at all to produce such massive work. Paper and ink were scarce and expensive; he once complained that "a sheet of paper was sold at thirty pesos in Cali."[37] The logistics of carrying hundreds of sheets of paper as a footman, engaged in rapid marches and dangerous skirmishes, seem incredible. He was generally lucky in preventing losses, but once, at the battle of Jaquijahuana—the last great engagement of the Peruvian civil wars—Cieza lost important documents and notebooks, which he much regretted.

In the second half of 1546 we find Cieza in Popayán, along with many others who were heeding the call of the royal authorities to join and march southward to defeat the uprising of Gonzalo Pizarro in Peru. The Peruvian *encomenderos* refused to accept the New Laws issued in Spain in 1542 that severely curbed their privileges. When a new and intransigent viceroy arrived to enforce the legislation, many rallied around Gonzalo Pizarro to fight the hated laws and its executor. The Pizarrists defeated and killed Viceroy Blasco Núñez Vela at the Battle of Añaquito, near Quito, in January 1546. By the middle of the year, settlers further north, in Colombia, had ample information on the turmoil to the south. For Colombian settlers, who had not found the riches of El Dorado that they had expected, the uprising provided a propitious opportunity to take part in the reconquest of Peru from rebel forces. For those who proved themselves worthy in defending royal claims, there was hope of reward at the cost of the confiscated Indians and estates of the rebels.

The Popayán contingent served under Belalcázar, and, like many others, Cieza would be forced to shift alliances in order to survive. By now he was a horseman. His first personal contact with what had been part of the Inca Empire came at Pasto, around April 1547 as he crossed the Angasmayo River at the stone bridge of Ruminchaca. The Belalcázar cavalry moved southward in the highlands, using at first the Inca highway. At Tomebamba (Cuenca) they shifted to the coast to San Miguel de Piura. They intended to unite with the forces coming by sea with Licentiate Pedro de la Gasca, who had been sent from Spain by the Council of the Indies to defeat the Peruvian rebels and restore order. Again, Cieza the soldier coexisted with Cieza the chronicler, as he diligently took notes on the cities and countryside they passed through and which he then included in *Part One* of his work.

In August 1547 they arrived in Tumbez, where the royalist forces under Pedro de la Gasca had concentrated only a month earlier. Therefore, they decided to march in four separate columns to unite at Jauja in the central Peruvian highlands. Belalcázar marched back into the highlands using the Inca highway, but Cieza joined the main body of the Gasca forces, moving southward along the coast toward Lima, the City of the Kings. He later recalled, "I passed through it [the Pacasmayo Valley] in the month of September 1548 [*sic,* 1547], to join the other soldiers who had come down from the jurisdiction of Popayán with the camp of Your Majesty."[38] He had time on the trek to inspect the fortress and Temple of Paramonga, which he wrote about in detail. The group continued to Lima, entering it in early December. It was at this time that Cieza surveyed the great Temple of Pachacamac in the Lurín Valley.

A group of about one hundred horsemen, including Cieza, led by Captain Palomino, took the road from Pachacamac to Huarochirí and quickly climbed to the 5,000-meter snowy passes to cross over the coastal section of the Andean cordillera. He would go on to write, "Those who read this book and who have been in Peru will remember the road which goes from Lima to Jauja by the rugged mountains of Huarochirí and through the snowcapped peaks of Pariacaca; those who have heard about it will know if what they saw is greater than what I write."[39] They then descended, crossing the suspension bridge over the Mantaro River, and entered the city of Jauja, where the king's forces under Gasca were assembling. Marching southward, the combined forces arrived at Huamanga (Ayacucho), then continued the march southward. Cieza carefully observed and later described in detail the Inca religious center of Vilcashuaman.

Continuing on, Pedro de la Gasca's forces finally crossed the Pampas River over a great suspension bridge—"so strong that horses can gallop over it as though they were crossing the bridge of Alcántara, or of Cordova."[40] They waited on reinforcements at Andahuaylas, where on 2 February Belalcázar caught up with the main camp. Gasca was now moving closer to Cuzco. Gonzalo Pizarro's men had blocked access to the city by cutting four important suspension bridges. A new bridge was constructed by the Indians on a bend of the Apurímac River at Cotabamba. Cieza developed a friendship there with Pedro Alonso Carrasco, who was helping to oversee the project. Carrasco, one of the early Spanish settlers of Cuzco, and a "great friend" of both Francisco and Juan Pizarro, though not of Gonzalo Pizarro anymore, became one of Cieza's informants.[41]

By 9 April 1548, the royal forces had crossed the river and were assembled on the great plain of Jaquijahuana, not far to the west of Cuzco. The battle was somewhat of an anticlimax because Gonzalo Pizarro's men, realizing that their cause was lost, crossed over to the side of the royalists. When the rebel army disintegrated, Gonzalo Pizarro and his chief captain, Francisco de Carvajal, were quickly captured and executed—their body parts were displayed prominently in Lima and Cuzco to dissuade others from ever challenging royal authority. Cieza, on the side of the king, emerged unharmed, but he lost some notebooks and papers in the melee.

One of Gasca's clerks was Pedro López de Cazalla, Cieza's first cousin on his mother's side. López de Cazalla had been in Peru from the time of Francisco Pizarro and had acted as secretary for both him and Governor Cristóbal Vaca de Castro. It is probable that with hints from Cieza's well-positioned cousin, President Gasca was alerted to Cieza's burgeoning chronicle of the events he was witnessing. President Gasca must have been impressed by young Cieza's capabilities and may have appointed him the official chronicler of the events in Peru. Later, correctly or not, Cieza referred to himself as "the first chronicler of the Indies." Gasca, perhaps now accompanied by Cieza on the march back to the coast, arrived in Lima on 17 September 1548. There he permitted Cieza to review the correspondence of various people during the Gonzalo Pizarro revolt: "Being in [Lima] . . . I saw the letters of Gonzalo Pizarro. . . . I remember there were so many that three secretaries, continuously reading to President La Gasca, did not finish for four days."[42] Perhaps he too joined in the reading of the letters that were so incriminating for many of the Peruvian settlers. He copied those that he needed and used them extensively in his history.

By early 1549 the young historian secured orders from Gasca authorizing local officials and others to provide him with information on the realm and its past. In 1549 Cieza set out "to visit Charcas and the provinces and cities that there are in that land, carrying letters from President Gasca to all the *corregidores,* asking them to assist me in learning and finding out the most noteworthy things about the provinces."[43] Unfortunately, the original letters have not been located. It is clear from internal evidence that he did have access to Gasca, who was also interested in describing Peru, and had prepared a report that he sent to the king.[44] Gasca was preoccupied with making certain that his own deeds as the pacifier of Peru were recorded in the best light and was almost obsessed with collection of records to document his role for posterity. Cieza claims that he had access to these papers as well, and much later, as he neared the end of composing the *War of Quito,* he wrote:

> And those who read this must know that Licentiate Gasca, from the time he left Spain, until the time he returned, had a wonderful method to make certain that things were not forgotten, and at night he would write in notebooks that he had for this purpose all the things that had happened that day, and thus over the days and months and years he recorded with much veracity all that had happened. And as I knew he had such a full and accurate account of the events, I made it a point to gain access to his notebooks and to make a copy of them, which I have in my possession.[45]

Clearly, Cieza had a good relationship with the much older Pedro de la Gasca. Rather than being an officially appointed chronicler, he secured the patronage of Gasca, who would shortly be named bishop of Palencia.[46]

Cieza again took the highway through Huarochirí, then continued southward, realizing that he needed to see firsthand the area to the south of Cuzco. He carefully described ruins, flora and fauna, and especially the people whom he encountered; left a detailed account of Lake Titicaca, the highest navigable lake on the globe at 3,810 meters; studied the ruins of the monumental pre-Inca site of Tiahuanaco near the south shore of Lake Titicaca; and traveled into southern Charcas (modern Bolivia), taking testimony from various "old conquistadors"—such as Juan Vargas, Captain Juan Ladrillero, General Pedro de Hinojosa, Captain Pedro Anzures—men whose testimony he believed was reliable. He reached the area of Potosí, where a great mountain of silver ore was discovered just a few years before he arrived. His description of Potosí in the published *Part One,* along with the woodcut based on his sketch, fueled the imagination of generations of Europeans who searched for riches in the vastness of the Americas.

In 1550 Cieza was back in Cuzco, where the corregidor, Captain Juan de Saavedra, assisted the young researcher in his attempts to interview the remaining Inca quipucamayos and high officials about the Andean past. Cieza settled down in Cuzco, the ancient capital of Tawantinsuyu, and "with the best translators and interpreters that could be found, I asked these Inca lords what type of people they were and of which nation."[47] The Spanish had entered Cuzco only fifteen years earlier, and plenty of survivors of the conquest could answer the young man's questions about their ancestors as well as about the more recent past. These informants were also an invaluable source for *Part Three,* where Cieza wanted to balance the account of the Spanish actions by also presenting the native point of view of the European invasion. He was able to interview, among others, Cayu Tupac Yupanqui, a descendant of Huayna Capac. He was also the first European to establish an Andean chronology of two parts: Inca and pre-Inca. He had discerned that highly developed peoples had existed in the Andes long before the Inca expansion: the Tiahuanaco south of Lake Titicaca provided him an obvious example. But he viewed the Incas as civilizing agents. Almost sixty years later, as the Inca Garcilaso de la Vega prepared the *Royal Commentaries of the Incas,* he mined Cieza's printed *Part One* in his description of the Andean past.

Cieza returned to Lima in July 1550 to present the manuscript to his sponsors. "Most of what I have written was seen by Dr. Bravo de Saravia and the licenciate Hernando de Santillán, judges of the Royal Audiencia of the City of the Kings."[48] At the same time, Cieza began preparations for a return to Spain. He also planned to marry. An agreement to wed Isabel López de Abreu—daughter of Juan de Llerena, a merchant in Seville originally from Trigueros, and his wife María de Abreu—was worked out and signed on 19 August 1550 in Lima by Isabel's brother, Pedro López de Abreu. López de Abreu, also a merchant, had secured power from his father before leaving Spain to arrange a suitable marriage for his sister. Such proxy marriages were not uncommon in the period; moreover, a flurry of arranged marriages took place in Peru in the early 1550s because all holders of encomiendas were required by Charles V to be married or forfeit their Indians. The bride's dowry, some four thousand gold crowns, was to be transferred to the groom when he reached Seville. Cieza would contribute two thousand crowns as *arras*, as his part of the agreement. At the same time, Pedro López de Abreu was left in charge of Cieza's Peruvian estate. On 11 September Cieza gave powers to three residents of Llerena returning to Spain to represent him in finalizing the agreement when they reached Seville. There is no indication if the couple knew each other personally, but Isabel would have been about only five years old when Cieza left Spain.[49]

Cieza then collected his approximately eight thousand manuscript pages and put the final touches on *Part One* that he "had completed writing originally in the City of the Kings, in the kingdom of Peru, on the eighth day of the month of September of the year 1550. At the time its author was thirty-two years old, having spent seventeen of them in these Indies. Signed Pedro de Cieza. God be Praised."[50]

There is no direct information on Cieza's return voyage. He probably left Lima's port of Callao toward the end of 1550 and sailed north to Panama. The swift northward flow of the Humboldt Current and the prevailing winds normally allowed for a reasonably good and quick voyage. From Panama he would have traveled overland, using mules to transport his manuscripts and any other goods, and then waited at Nombre de Dios for a ship to take him to Spain. The usual sailing route was via the straits between Cuba and Florida, then northward with the assistance of the Gulf Stream. They would pass Bermuda, then swing eastward, and continue toward Spain's coast. Cieza probably reached Seville in the summer months of 1551.

Not long after he arrived, Pedro and Isabel cemented their bond because on 11 August 1551, two thousand gold ducats were transferred to Cieza, along with a promissory note for fifteen hundred ducats in kind—consisting of clothing, jewels, furnishings, and slaves—to be given within eight days. In a separate document Cieza provided the arras, or the customary groom's marriage gift, for his bride. Cieza's mother had died while he was away, so the formal ceremony was probably witnessed by his father, his brother Rodrigo (by then a priest), and some relatives, the Cazallas. The couple decided to live in Seville and took a centrally located house on the *calle de las Armas* (now Alfonso XII) in the parish of San Vicente. Pedro then went about the work of finding a printer and an illustrator and began the time-consuming and difficult process of securing the proper authorizations for the manuscript to be printed.

Early in 1552 Cieza returned to Llerena for the baptism (6 January) of his nephew, Juan, son of his sister María Alvarez. His brother, Rodrigo de Cieza, was also there, acting as godfather. While in Llerena the chronicler met Luis Zapata de Chaves, who had recently returned from Flanders with the future Philip II. Zapata's father had been a member of the Royal Guard and saw to it several years earlier that the young Luis was placed in the service of Prince Philip as a page. By the time Cieza and Zapata met and conversed in Llerena, Zapata was a well-respected author and would later gain fame with *Carlo Famoso* and *El Libro de Cetrería*. It has been suggested that after talking to Zapata and perhaps using Zapata's connections, Cieza decided to go to court to secure direct permission from Philip for the printing of his manuscripts.[51]

Cieza presented *Part One* to Prince Philip in Toledo in 1552. The Council of the Indies approved the text on 11 August 1552.[52] The full authorization to print, good for fifteen years, came from the Crown when the court was at Monzón, in Aragon, on 14 September 1552. The contract between the author and the Sevillian printer Martín de Montesdoca of the parish of San Martín was signed on Wednesday, 26 October 1552. Cieza originally required the printing to be finished within two months, but that deadline was extended to three. A run of 1,050 copies was to be issued from the press; the type of paper, print type, and the price for the author were all stipulated in the agreement. Montesdoca completed his work on 15 March 1553. Later, Cieza's will reveals the nature of the distribution of the first volume: Juan de Espinosa, a bookseller in Medina del Campo, had received 130 copies; Juan

Sánchez de Andrada in Toledo sold 30; Diego Gutiérrez de los Ríos in Cordova received 8; the bookstore of Juan Canalla in Seville had more than 100 copies of the text; and a number of smaller consignments were made, including one to the Indies. One book dealer originally from Villalón, who had a shop next to the church of the Magdalena in Seville, had 15 copies.[53]

Part One became almost immediately popular. During 1554, a total of three printings were completed at Antwerp. The first was done by Steelsius in the printshop of Jean de Laet. The second printing was similar to the first, but included a letter by Jean Beller on geography. The third edition was that of Martin Nutius—smaller in size and containing the same style plates.[54]

But the appearance and popularity of the printed book was bittersweet. In May of 1554 Cieza's young wife died; nothing is known of the cause of Isabel's rather sudden death. She was buried in the church of San Vicente, and her estate included a "purple velvet gown . . . with satin sleeves and gold braid . . . a braid-trimmed skirt of crimson satin . . . the coffer in which [Cieza] kept her jewels . . . and the slave Beatriz which was hers." Cieza was not well either, and shortly after Isabel died, he signed his own will before several witnesses on 23 June 1554, and a codicil was prepared less than a week later, on 28 June. Within a few days, on 2 July 1554, Pedro de Cieza de León, the intrepid historian-soldier, was dead. He was buried in Seville in the church of San Vicente alongside his wife, and the fate of his unfinished work rested with the executors of his last wishes.[55]

Cieza at times felt overwhelmed by the work that he set out to do and worried that he might die before he completed the task. Near the end of his narrative of the *War of Chupas*, which he was finalizing in Seville, he compared the finishing of the massive work to the challenges he had so often faced in the Indies:

> Thus I find myself, as I often was in the conquests I was engaged in, climbing up a mountain so high and rugged that the summit seems to be in the highest clouds . . . and when I was halfway up the slope, I found myself so fatigued that it was difficult to imagine myself at the top. And looking below it seemed to me that the profound valleys descended into an abyss. And lacking strength I asked for God's help to

> continue. And looking at the things that I have written since the year [15]23 to the present, how much has already been written and how much still remains until it is concluded, I face more toil than in the mountains. Because if I want to conclude what has been started, I fall short, and if I want to proceed, my judgment is so weak and my mind so feeble, that I do not know how I can do it. But observing, as the philosopher says, that men have to undertake great things and high subjects, since the common ones are the work of all, and asking God to give me strength, and invoking help from his most sacred Mother, I will go ahead and end the work, or death will end my life.[56]

Several days before he died, perhaps remembering items he had left out of the original will, Cieza filed a minor codicil. His father-in-law, Juan de Llerena, was encharged to execute the will. Most provisions dealt with the masses for the souls of the deceased and of family members, as well as with the gifts normally distributed at the time of mourning, but Cieza also provided a list of his wife's clothing to be donated for the Virgin of the principal church of Castilleja de la Cuesta, where his brother Rodrigo was cleric. He mentions the beautiful veils, headdresses, and the neck ruffles Isabel had worn that were to be presented to whatever images of the Virgin in the city Cieza's executors might find fitting. Minor gifts were also given to Catalina Martín, who lived in Cieza's household, and to muleteer Juan Gonzalo from the village of Fuente for a settling of accounts because, earlier, Cieza had loaned Juan a small sum.[57] On 8 August 1554 the will was opened and read before interested parties—including the surviving siblings of the deceased, as well as his father—in Seville by the notary Antonio de Cazalla, Cieza's uncle.[58]

Not unlike others who had held Indian grants, Cieza made provision in his testament for the Amerindian. In the 1550s substantial efforts had been made by a number of ecclesiastics, including Bartolomé de las Casas and Domingo de Santo Tomás, to see to it that those Christians who had harmed the Native American, should provide some form of restitution. Many encomenderos in the Andean area during these years, fearing the perdition of their souls, atoned through either cash or products or prayers for the souls of the Indian men and women who had served them. In his will Cieza admitted that he had caused them harm while he was involved in various expeditions and participated in raids on Indian villages. He ordered masses to be said "for the souls of the Indian men and women in the lands and places where I have been in the Indies who are now in purgatory."[59]

Out of concern for his own soul he provided funds for the enlargement of the convent of Nuestra Señora de los Remedios in Llerena, which was probably located near his home, most likely on Altozano de Camargo Street (now Gazul de Uclés). He also bequeathed beds and bed clothing to three hospitals in Llerena. More gifts of his wife's clothing and jewels were provided—some for the adornment of the image of the Virgin in the monastery of La Concepción in the city, some for the convent of Los Remedios. Other articles of his wife's possessions were donated to the churches of Trigueros in the Huelva district, the home of her father, and to the church of San Vicente in Seville.

The chaplaincy of the couple was in the church of San Vicente in Seville, where most of the cash donations to the church went. Juan de Llerena acted as overseer of the chaplaincy until his own death in 1580. In his will Cieza's father-in-law passed the supervision to "the oldest son of Doña María my granddaughter, the daughter of Joan Caton and my daughter Doña Beatriz."[60] Cieza also provided for a pension in the original will for his aging father. After the estate was settled, the remainder was to be amassed and sold for purchase of *censos de quitar* (bonds) of the town of Llerena. Cieza's brother Rodrigo was given the task of overseeing this settlement and of making certain their father received the interest income from the censos; any excess beyond what was necessary for the adequate sustenance of his father was to be divided equally by Pedro's living siblings.[61]

The Manuscripts

Cieza's testament reflects his continuing concern for the preservation and dissemination of his work. *Part One* of his monumental history had already been printed in Seville and Antwerp and was proving a success. But because *Parts Two, Three,* and *Four,* the bulk of his life's work, were still in manuscript form, Cieza included a provision in the will:

> I order that another book which I wrote that contains the chronicle of the Incas [*Part Two*], and the discovery and conquest of Peru [*Part Three*], that if any one of my executors wishes to print it, he take it and enjoy the profits of the publication. If they do not wish it, I order it to be sent to the Bishop of Chiapas [Bartolomé de las Casas] at the court, and that they give it to him with the charge of publishing it.[62]

It is interesting that Cieza may have viewed *Parts Two* and *Three* as an entity separate from the texts about the civil wars. Cieza knew well the work and voice of Bartolomé de las Casas, the "Defender of the Indians," and he might have met him in Seville in 1552. Certainly, in the text of his manuscripts Cieza frequently takes a position with regard to the Amerindian that can be classified as Lascasian.[63]

Cieza was concerned that his history of the civil wars might damage many reputations, that passions were still too inflamed to permit immediate publication. He noted that if the manuscript were "printed now it might cause some scandal and some people might resent what is contained therein, because the events in those wars took place only recently." Cieza therefore ordered his executors to "take the three books and reports, all of which are in my desk, and remove the said letters and other writings that may be in this desk, leaving only the aforesaid three books and reports and anything else pertaining to them." He went on to insist "that they close and seal this desk and place another two small locks on it." To insure that the contents would be safe, Cieza further ordered that "the locked desk be taken to the monastery of Las Cuevas, or any other monastery my executors think fit." This transfer was to take place under the watchful eye of a notary. Once the desk was deposited, Cieza wanted "the keys to remain in the possession of my executors, one key for each." The desk was to stay locked "until fifteen years after my death, during which time no one is to look inside."[64]

Not only was Cieza concerned about saving the reputations of people he knew, but he also wanted to make certain the text would see the light of day. He authorized his executors to turn over the manuscript and papers to "some expert to see and correct and to remove from it what he thinks superfluous, without adding anything to what has been written." Cieza allowed the future editor to complete his work: "As regards what still has to be written, in accordance with the reports which are in my desk, he may proceed as he thinks fit." Wanting to ensure that there would be no confusion as to who wrote what, he insisted that whoever finished the writing clearly state "the point to which he found it written and where he himself began to write." Cieza concluded that "in this manner he can print it, protecting the honor and reputation of all, so that no one is hurt or defamed, and he may benefit from the profits of the publication."[65]

As often is the case, Cieza's plans did not materialize. *Part Two,* the history of the Incas intended for Bartolomé de las Casas, was appropriated in Seville by Inquisitor Licentiate Andrés Gasco. Only a royal order forced the inquisitor to send the manuscript to the Council of the Indies. Philip II wrote to Gasco from Monzón on 29 November 1563: "I am informed that you have two books written by the hand of one Pedro de Cieza . . . that deal with matters of Peru . . . that have not been seen or examined or granted the necessary authorization for distribution." The king ordered the inquisitor to turn the books over to the Council of the Indies "as soon as you have perused this," and so that there would be no misunderstanding as to the length of time necessary for the perusal, he added: "I demand that you send the said books with all diligence and speed."[66]

Cieza's brother and executor, Rodrigo de Cieza, then priest of Castilleja de la Cuesta, sent a series of petitions to the Council of the Indies beginning 19 October 1568. At this point the manuscripts were in the possession of the heirs of the royal cosmographer Alonso de Santa Cruz, but Rodrigo de Cieza insisted that they be turned over to him. Apparently, his demand produced no results, for on 29 January 1578 and again on 15 February he requested the council to return the manuscripts.[67] Rodrigo argued that they had been encharged to him and were rightfully his. He also pointed out that his brother had served many years in Peru and was ordered by Pedro de la Gasca to write "all that took place during the discovery . . . and in the wars that there were."[68] Rodrigo complained that the books were taken from his brother, who had been forced to go to court to recuperate them but died while trying to get them back. An official of the council ordered that they be found and brought to the council.

The manuscripts also passed through the hands of the royal chronicler Juan Páez de Castro and after his death ended up in the Library of the Escorial. The chroniclers Alonso de Santa Cruz and Juan López de Velasco may also have secured copies of the manuscripts, or parts of them.[69] Antonio de Herrera y Tordesillas, who had been named the official historian of Spain in 1596, set out to write a massive history of that nation's discoveries, which resulted in the multivolume *Historia general de los hechos de los castellanos en las Islas y Tierra Firme del Mar Océano* (Madrid, 1601–15). Such a substantial undertaking required extensive sources, and Herrera was given Cieza's papers from the Cámara Real "in order to write the history of the Indies. It had been written by Pedro de Cieza, chronicler of those parts, by order of President Gasca, and it comes approved by the Royal Chancellery of the City of the Kings." Herrera acknowledged taking possession of the manuscripts: "by the truth I sign my name in Valladolid on 7 July 1603. Antonio de Herrera."[70]

Thick, bound bundles of manuscript pages were removed and unceremoniously lifted, almost line by line, by the royal historian, though not always accurately. Herrera did admit that he found the work useful: "This Pedro de Cieza is the one who wrote the history of the provinces of Quito and Popayán, with much punctiliousness, although he had less luck than others in compensation for his work."[71] Herrera's plagiarism was not an uncommon practice at the time; authors freely borrowed from others and rarely acknowledged their debt. Herrera's deed proves useful today in allowing us to see what Cieza's last chapters of *Part Three,* missing from the Vatican manuscript, might have contained.

At least one contemporary—none other than one of the "old conquistadors," Pedro Pizarro—attacked the integrity of Cieza's work. Around 1570, following the prodding of Viceroy Francisco de Toledo, Pizarro penned in Arequipa a long narrative near the end of his life. He probably had access to the published texts of Agustín de Zárate and Gonzalo Fernández de Oviedo y Valdés, as well as to Cieza's *Part One.* Pizarro excused himself from writing extensively about the battles during the rebellion of Gonzalo Pizarro—"although I was in all of them at the service of His Majesty"—because he knew that other chroniclers had dealt with them, "taking advantage of the people involved in two ways. First, to secure information on what had happened, and second, to ask if they were interested in being put in the chronicle, collecting from 200 to 300 ducats to put them prominently in what they were writing." He contemptuously added, "they say that a Cieza did this in a chronicle that he wanted to do from hearsay, and I think from very little observation, because in truth, being one of the first to enter this kingdom, I do not know him."[72] Sixteenth-century historians were not bashful when it came to defaming their competition. Cieza himself took shots at López de Gómara, Hernán Cortés's secretary and the author of a popular history: "Into these errors fall all those who write on the basis of reports and folders of documents, without ever seeing or understanding the land about which they write."[73] It is possible that Pedro Pizarro disliked Cieza because he had been under Gasca's protection, and Pizarro had been treated shabbily by the president.[74]

Cieza de León's original intent was to publish a four-part history of Peru. *Part One,* the only section printed during the author's lifetime, was a geographical and ethnological account of South America's Andean region. He often referred to it as "The Book of the Foundations" because he also included the establishment of the cities that he described. *Part Two,* "The Realm of the Incas," was a history of the Incas; *Part Three* was the account of the Spanish discovery and conquest of the realm; and the massive *Part Four,* made up of five book-length manuscripts, examined the civil wars among the Spanish settlers. Each "book" was titled after the major battles fought during this turbulent period: Salinas (1538), Chupas (1542), Quito (1546), Huarina (1547), and Jaquijahuana (1548). It appears, however, that Cieza died before he was able to complete the last two "books"; as he noted in his will, "I wrote a book, I say three books, of the civil wars in Peru."[75]

Cieza intended to write another narrative, one in which he would have expanded on the early European exploration of Colombia's northeast, including a close description of the many expeditions in which he had also taken part. In his account of the discovery of the Uruté under Captain Alonso de Cáceres, while remembering the many hardships, he hinted that he was working on another history: "as the readers will see in a book I have begun, of what occurred in the provinces contiguous to the Ocean Sea."[76]

The Missing Manuscript

The fate of *Part Three* of Cieza's chronicle prior to its discovery by the Italian historian Francesca Cantù in the Vatican Library in the 1970s is difficult to trace. According to Cieza's wishes, the manuscript of *Part Two* and *Part Three* was either to be published by his executors or to be sent to Bartolomé de las Casas. There is no indication that Las Casas ever received any such papers. It seems also that Cieza himself may have sent *Part Three* with a note to an unknown person: "And this notebook, after it is read, bring it and take another; and if you wish that of the Incas, take it also."[77] The recipient of this note and manuscript was probably Juan Páez de Castro, whose great library became part of the royal collection at the Escorial. "A chronicle of the Indies of Pedro de León, in three parts"[78] does figure in the inventory of the time, and it seems that Páez de Castro made a copy of the manuscript Cieza loaned him, a copy that may have been the text used by Herrera and others. Nevertheless, the manuscript's trail ends in Spain, and the next positive clue to the whereabouts of Cieza's account of the conquest of Peru is in a 1655 catalog of the extensive library of the peripatetic Queen Christina of Sweden.

In 1655 Queen Christina, who had abdicated a year earlier, was on her way to Rome. One of the reasons for the queen's surprising decision to renounce her crown was her conversion to Catholicism, a religion prohibited to a reigning Swedish monarch. Throughout her life, Christina was a great patroness of the arts, and her library constantly grew with new acquisitions. An original catalog of her collection from 1650 did not contain any Spanish work dealing with Peru, but it appears that sometime before 1655 the queen's diligent agent, Nicolaas Heinsius, acquired for her in Antwerp an anonymous manuscript entitled *Historia del Regno de Peru.* That year a new catalog was compiled, and it included what is clearly Cieza's *Part Two* and *Part Three.*

The question remains: how and when did the manuscript leave Seville and reach Antwerp? There is a strong possibility that either Cieza himself or perhaps his brother Rodrigo sent it to Antwerp in order to negotiate a printing of these volumes because they had a greater chance of publication there following the commercial success of *Part One.* Perhaps the failure to obtain the proper license, as well as Cieza's death, hindered a successful outcome of contracting a publisher for the rest of his work. The manuscript entrusted to the printers in Antwerp must have been misplaced, to languish forgotten for a hundred years. When the handwritten texts were finally sold, the author was no longer remembered, but obviously the content intrigued the buyer.

Queen Christina died in Rome in 1689 and her library, which included *Historia Peruana unius anni. Hispanice,* was sold to the future Pope Alexander VII, who eventually donated his collection to the Vatican Archive. The adventures of the manuscript, which began in the Americas in the sixteenth century, did not end there, however. During the Napoleonic wars, the French occupied Rome, and as in many other parts of the world, the foreign forces could not resist taking souvenirs back to their homeland. Thus, five hundred manuscripts were transferred from the Vatican Library to the Bibliothèque Nationale in Paris, among them the "anonymous" *Peruviani Regni Historiam.* Indeed, the first page of the Vatican manuscript contains a stamp of the Paris library. Following Napoleon's defeat, the stolen manuscripts were returned to Rome, where Cieza's *Part Three* remained hidden from scholars who had been searching for it in vain until Francesca Cantù brought it to light and published it in 1979. The first published version appeared in Rome more than four hundred years after its author entrusted his heirs with its printing.[79]

Other early copies of *Part Three* may have existed, though their whereabouts remain a mystery. *Part Two* and *Part Four* of Cieza's chronicle were published in the latter part of the nineteenth century; *Part Three,* however, was missing. Marcos Jiménez de la Espada (1877) claimed that José Sancho Rayón, who had published *Part Four,* had in his possession a copy of *Part Three* and had been kind enough to allow Jiménez de la Espada to secure a copy (p. xxi). In 1964, historiographer Francisco Esteve Barba verified that he believed that Rayón's heirs held the manuscript of *Part Three.*[80] Yet another copy may have existed in Spain: Raúl Porras Barrenechea wrote that in 1908 Pablo Patrón had affirmed that the heirs of editor Justo Zaragoza had the manuscript in their possession and that Jiménez de la Espada had made a copy. Historian Antonio Ballesteros affirmed the codex was in the Library of the Conde de Heredia Espinola. However, after Porras Barrenechea diligently and with substantial effort reviewed the catalog and interviewed the librarian, he was unable to locate the manuscript.

Another rumor alleged that the heirs of Jiménez de la Espada had sold it to Archer M. Huntington and that it became part of the collection of the Hispanic Society of America in New York City. This is false; they have two early printed versions of *Part One,* and manuscript copies of the three extant books of *Part Four.*[81] One of the nineteenth-century Spanish copies may have ended up in the United States in the hands of a private collector.[82] Rafael Loredo located sections of *Part Three* among the papers of Jiménez de la Espada and began publishing a series of chapters in the journal *Mercurio Peruano* in 1946.[83]

The importance of the work of Pedro de Cieza de León has long been recognized. In 1877 Marcos Jiménez de la Espada called Cieza "the most excellent of the Peruvian chroniclers, and perhaps the Indies" (p. xi). Clements R. Markham affirmed that Cieza was "the most trustworthy of all the old writers of Peru" (1883, p. xxvi; 1913, p. ix). Bailey W. Diffie concluded that "Added to his acute powers of observation is a transparent honesty that has survived the test of time ever better than that of Bernal Díaz. . . . For those who wish to understand Inca society Cieza's works are indispensable and should be the first read."[84] Miguel Maticorena suggested rightly that Cieza was "the most authoritative of the South American chroniclers."[85] Philip Ainsworth Means may have done Cieza an injustice when he wrote, "Pedro de Cieza de León is one of the two most important chroniclers of Peru, his sole equal being the Inca Garcilaso de la Vega."[86] The Inca, who wrote more than a half century after Cieza and relied on his own faded memory and that of others, as well as on printed and manuscript sources, is not nearly as trustworthy or objective as Cieza de León. Guillermo Lohmann Villena believes that Cieza "was so close to the events, and was so extremely careful in the search for and examination of the documents, that what one loses by the fact he was not physically present, one gains in the possibility of approaching the level of an historian who studies, analyzes, and offers to the reader what he considers most probable; and we find him so careful, that we give him our complete confidence."[87]

Certainly, Cieza's keen observations and vivid descriptions of events, places, and human interaction form an indispensable source for our understanding of the initial encounter of European and Native

American peoples on South America's west coast. He wrote with a directness and simplicity that are refreshing in an age of artifice. He was interested in detail and explanation. He found good as well as evil in the deeds of both the Europeans and the Amerindians. He looked below the surface of the superficial for hidden relationships, and if what happened around him seemed at times unjust, as a pious man he was fully confident that justice would ultimately prevail. Cieza not only observed and recorded events around him, but diligently interviewed eyewitnesses, tried to get both sides of the story, and whenever pertinent documents were available to him, carefully perused them. It is precisely because he researched the subject and strove for balance that Pedro de Cieza de León was not just a prince of chroniclers, but a historian.

The Translation

In translating Cieza's narrative we have tried to remain faithful to the simple and straightforward style that characterizes his work. He stated more than once throughout *Part Three,* and elsewhere, that he wanted his writing to be clear so it would not confuse the reader. He was fully aware of the complexity of the subject he was dealing with, particularly when he needed to cover events that were occurring simultaneously. Although Cieza's texts have been used and analyzed by successive generations of scholars, he himself was not aiming at the erudite elite. Even his references to classical antiquity are limited to those that most of his contemporaries would have understood. He wrote for what we would call today the general public, wanting to reach the average reader and tell the world the story of what he considered one of the most spectacular events of all times.

Our translation of *Part Three* reflects Cieza's desire to reach the general reader. We tried to convey the author's style and the flavor of the sixteenth century, but without an archaic and unintelligible voice. In order to keep the narrative clear and concise, we modernized the punctuation, breaking up sometimes page-long sentences and in rare instances the lengthier paragraphs. We also modernized the spelling of names of people and places, guided primarily by the work of Franklin Pease, James Lockhart, and John Hemming. Tracing and finding the modern equivalents for some geographical terms proved a time-consuming task. The basis for our translation was the edition published by the Catholic University of Peru in Lima and edited by Francesca Cantù, the *Crónica del Perú: Tercera parte* (Lima: Universidad Católica, 1989). Kurt Baldinger's glossary helped us define obscure words. We corrected occasional typographical errors on the basis of two other editions of *Part Three:* one edited by Carmelo Sáenz de Santa María, Cieza's *Obras completas,* vol. 1 (Madrid: CSIC, 1984); the other edited by Mario A. Valotta, *Descubrimiento y conquista del Perú* (Madrid: Grupo Cultural Zero, 1984).

The Spanish text of the Vatican *Part Three* is not a polished, final copy. There is evidence, both in the margins and between lines, that the author was making corrections throughout. Whenever appropriate in the English version, we have indicated in the notes the words that have been substituted. Sometimes we added names or key words in brackets in order to clarify the narrative. Finally, it is important to remember that Cieza de León was a European observer using terminology familiar to him and any sixteenth-century Spaniard. Therefore, some of the terms he employed may not coincide with our present understanding of the Andean world. Nevertheless, a translator has a duty to the author to use his terminology, not what seems more appropriate to us today. Whenever necessary, we have alerted the reader to this fact in the notes. For example, although there were no sheep in the Americas before the Europeans arrived, Cieza consistently uses the word *sheep* throughout his manuscript when he is referring to llamas or alpacas. He also uses the name "City of the Kings" to refer to Lima throughout most of his manuscript. We have noted these two correlations in only the first few chapters of Cieza's narrative rather than every time these terms appear in the translation as a whole.

Two dictionaries were invaluable in our endeavor. For the early modern Spanish, the 1611 work of Sebastián de Covarrubias Orozco, *Tesoro de la lengua castellana o española* (Madrid: Editorial Castalia, 1994), proved more than a dictionary, for it opens a window into Spanish society of the time. And for the meaning of Quechua terms, the dictionary later prepared (printed in Valladolid in 1560) by one of Cieza's informants, Domingo de Santo Tomás, *Grammática o arte de la lengua general de los indios de los reynos del Perú* (facsimile edition,

Madrid: Ediciones de Cultura Hispánica, 1994), provides the key to unlock the secrets of the Andean world.

The Vatican manuscript of *Part Three* is incomplete. Two folios in the center of the manuscript, and two or three at the end, are missing; it is also bound together with *Part Two,* in folios 1–132 (that is, in error *Part Three* preceded *Part Two* in the binding), under the heading <Reginensi, Latini 951>. Furthermore, the final chapters are missing. The extant *Part Three* does not cover the principal actions of the uprising led by Manco Inca, but only hints at the preparations for it, and Almagro is still in Chile when the last chapter ends, leaving the reader hanging in the middle of the narrative. In his *Part One* dedicatory to Philip II, Cieza outlines each part of his chronicle. In his synopsis of *Part Three* he states that he intended to end that part with the full description of the native uprising in Cuzco and the return there of Diego de Almagro from Chile.[88]

Antonio Herrera y Tordesillas seems to have had these chapters available when he wrote his massive history. The missing events are covered in chapters 4–7 of "Book Eight of Decade Five," and in chapter 1 and half of 2 of "Book Two of the Sixth Decade." Carmelo Sáenz de Santa María, who prepared the three-volume *Obras completas* of Cieza, completes the Cieza narrative of *Part Three* with these particular Herrera y Tordesillas chapters. In order to finish the full account of the discovery and conquest of Peru, we have included here a translation of Herrera y Tordesillas's pertinent chapters.[89]

This project, as others, would not have been possible without the confidence and support of John Jay TePaske. We appreciate and have learned from the generous comments of Franklin Pease G.Y. and two anonymous readers; their suggestions were invaluable as we prepared the final version of the text. We thank also the National Endowment for the Humanities, which recognized the significance of Pedro de Cieza de León's history for a modern understanding of the European penetration of the Americas and helped bring the text to the English-speaking audience.

Alexandra Parma Cook and Noble David Cook

Notes

1 There was probably another girl, mentioned in Cieza's will, who died in infancy. Beatriz married Pedro de Cazorla, a merchant; they had seven children. Pedro's brother, Rodrigo de Cieza, was a cleric in Castilleja de la Cuesta. María (who called herself Alvarez) married Lorenzo Hernández Viscaíno; they had six children. Leonor married Luis Zapata del Bosque, and they had a daughter. See Luis José Garrain Villa, *Llerena en el siglo XVI: La emigración a las Indias* (Madrid: Junta de Extremadura, 1991), pp. 63–84.

2 Garrain Villa, *Llerena*, pp. 16–19.

3 From *Libro de Cetrería;* cited by Garrain Villa, *Llerena,* p. 22. Zapata also wrote *Carlo Famoso* and *Miscelanea.*

4 Franklin Pease G.Y., "Introducción" to Pedro de Cieza de León, *Crónica del Perú: Primera parte* (Lima: Universidad Católica, 1986), pp. xxi–xxii. Unless otherwise noted, subsequent references to the *Primera parte* will be cited as *Part One. Part Two* will refer to Francesca Cantù's edition, *Crónica del Perú: Segunda parte* (Lima: Universidad Católica, 1985). Quotations from Cieza's work are our own translations unless otherwise noted.

5 *Part One,* chapter 37.

6 *Part Three,* chapter 79.

7 *Part One,* chapter 94.

8 Victor W. von Hagen, ed., "Introduction" to Pedro de Cieza de León, *The Incas of Pedro Cieza de León,* trans. Harriet de Onis (Norman: University of Oklahoma Press, 1959), p. xxxv. The original document is in the Archivo General de Indias (hereafter AGI), Contratación, leg. 5536, book 3, folio 168, 2 April 1535.

9 Garrain Villa, *Llerena,* p. 67; the sailing references are from AGI, Contratación, leg. 5536, folios 168 and 251.

10 *Part One,* chapter 62.

11 *Part One,* chapter 14.

12 Information on this period comes largely from the evidence provided in Cieza's writings.

13 *Part One,* chapter 9.

14 *Part One,* chapter 9.

15 *Part One,* chapter 1.

16 *Part One,* chapter 7.

17 *Part One,* preface.

18 *Part One,* preface.

19 *Part Four: Chupas,* chapter 38.

20 *Part Four: Salinas,* chapter 80.

21 *Part One,* chapters 10 and 15.

22 Garrain Villa, *Llerena,* p. 68.

23 *Part Four: Quito,* chapter 99.

24 *Part One,* chapter 121.

25 *Part One,* preface.

26 *Part One,* preface.

27 *Part One,* preface.

28 *Part Four: Chupas,* chapter 3. Catalina was one of three native translators used by the force; the other two were Barbola and Antona.

29 *Part Four: Quito,* chapter 99; see also Mario A. Valotta, "Introducción," to Pedro de Cieza de León, *Descubrimiento y conquista del Perú* (Madrid: Zero, 1984), pp. 23–24.

30 *Part One,* chapter 17; Valotta, "Introducción," p. 24.

31 *Part One,* chapters 17 and 18.

32 Valotta, "Introducción," p. 25.

33 *Part Four: Quito,* chapter 194.

34 Robledo's widow, María de Carvajal, resolutely pressed for justice. Finally, in 1550 Belalcázar was ordered back to Spain to face charges. He became ill and died in Cartagena in 1551 at the age of 75. See von Hagen, "Introduction," p. xlvi.

35 *Part Four: Quito,* chapter 194.

36 *Part Four: Quito,* chapter 195.

37 *Part One,* chapter 26.

38 *Part One,* chapter 68.

39 *Part Two,* chapter 15.

40 *Part One,* chapter 89.

41 *Part Two,* chapter 46; *Part One,* chapter 64; see also *Part Three,* chapter 83 for a biographical sketch of Carrasco.

42 Von Hagen, "Introduction," p. liv.

43 *Part One,* chapter 95.

44 The manuscript of the Description of Peru was sent to Willem Van Male (Malleaus), secretary to Charles V. It is in the National Library of Austria, and there are two recent editions: Josep M. Barnadas, *Descripción del Perú, 1553* (Caracas: Universidad Católica Andrés Bello, 1976); and Juan Freile Granizo and Julio Estrada Ycaza, "Descripción del Perú," *Revista del Archivo Histórico de Guayas* 9 (1976): 35–58.

45 *Part Four: Quito,* chapter 234.

46 We concur with Pease on this evaluation of the relationship between Cieza and Gasca. See Pease's "Introducción," *Part One,* pp. xxvii–xxix.

47 *Part Two,* chapter 6.

48 *Part Two,* chapter 74.

49 Valotta, "Introducción," p. 31.

50 *Part One,* chapter 121. According to this information, Cieza would have been fifteen years old when he arrived in the New World, yet he has also indicated other ages, between thirteen and fifteen.

51 Garrain Villa, *Llerena,* p. 70.

52 Valotta, "Introducción," p. 32.

53 See Miguel Maticorena Estrada, "Contrato para la primera edición de Sevilla," in Pease, *Part One,* p. xlviii. The original is in the Archivo de Protocolos in Seville, Oficio XI. Francisco Romano, Libro II de 1552, 2036v–2037v. The notaries Cristóbal de Ayala and Agustín de Buiza signed the contract.

54 Cantù, "Prólogo," *Part Two,* p. xii.

55 One can only speculate on the cause of Cieza and Isabel's deaths. The proximity of their deaths suggests a common cause—an infection, perhaps typhus, which was all too common in Spain at the time, or any of a number of endemic diseases prevalent in Seville. Another likely cause of death for a young woman of twenty-seven would be associated with childbirth, but there is no mention of a pregnancy in the records to date.

56 *Part Four: Chupas,* chapter 89.

57 Garrain Villa, *Llerena,* pp. 248–49.

58 Garrain Villa, *Llerena,* p. 65; from the Archivo de Protocolos de Sevilla, Oficio XV, vol. 2, fol. 234.

59 Garrain Villa, *Llerena,* p. 72; Luis José Garrain Villa, "Algunos apuntes sobre el testamento de Pedro Cieza de León," *Coloquios Históricos de Extremadura,* no. 18 (Cáceres: Institución Cultural "el Broncense," 1991), p. 101.

60 Garrain Villa, *Llerena,* p. 75.

61 Garrain Villa, "Algunos apuntes," pp. 101–2.

62 Garrain Villa, "Algunos apuntes," pp. 99–100.

63 Miguel Maticorena Estrada, "Cieza de León en Sevilla y su muerte en 1554: Documentos," *Anuario de Estudios Americanos* 12 (1955): 630, 669; and Pease, "Introducción," p. xvii.

64 Garrain Villa, *Llerena,* p. 80.

65 Garrain Villa, *Llerena,* p. 80.

66 Valotta, "Introducción," p. 46; AGI, Indiferente General, 425.

67 Garrain Villa, *Llerena,* p. 81.

68 Cantù, "Prólogo" to *Crónica del Perú: Tercera parte* (Lima: Universidad Católica, 1989), hereafter cited as *Part Three,* p. xxx; AGI, Indiferente General, 1086.

69 Cantù, "Prólogo," *Part Two,* p. xiv.

70 Pease, "Introducción," *Part One*, p. xxvi (based on Marcos Jiménez de la Espada [1877], pp. cii–ciii).

71 von Hagen, "Introduction," p. lxxvii. Francesca Cantù, "Apéndice. Pedro de Cieza de León y Antonio de Herrera: Elementos para una comparación," *Part Three*, pp. xciii–ciii.

72 Pedro Pizarro, *Relación del descubrimiento y conquista del Perú* [1571], ed. Guillermo Lohmann Villena (Lima: Universidad Católica, 1978), chapter 28.

73 *Part Two*, chapter 22.

74 Pease, "Introducción," p. xxix; Lohmann Villena, "Consideraciones preliminares," in Pizarro, *Relación*, pp. i–xiv.

75 Maticorena Estrada, "Cieza," pp. 661–74.

76 *Part Four: Quito*, chapter 43; Pease ("Introducción," p. xxii) notes that there is no other indication of this manuscript.

77 Cantù, "Prólogo," *Part Three*, p. xxxi. This is part of a short note that appears in the top margin of folio 1 of the Vatican *Part Three*. Francesca Cantù not only discovered the missing manuscript but was able to trace its whereabouts. Our text is based largely on her investigation.

78 Cantù, "Prólogo," *Part Three*, p. xxxii.

79 Cantù, "Prólogo," *Part Three*, pp. xxiv–xli; Carmelo Sáenz de Santa María, "Introducción General," *Pedro de Cieza de León: Obras completas* (Madrid: CSIC, 1984), 1:viii. For the first edition of *Part Three*, see Francesca Cantù, *Pedro de Cieza de León e il "descubrimiento y conquista del Perú"* (Rome: Instituto Storico Italiano, 1979).

80 Francisco Esteve Barba, *Historiografía indiana* (Madrid: Editorial Gredos, 1964), p. 417.

81 In his "Introducción" to *Part One* Pease has done an excellent job of sleuthing to try to trace down all the rumors (pp. xvi–xvii).

82 It was offered at the Librería de Estanislao Rodríguez, Calle San Bernardo, Madrid, then appeared in the John Howell Bookstore in San Francisco before being sold. See Pease, "Nota de los editores," *Part Three*, p. viii.

83 Carmelo Sáenz de Santa María found the original manuscript used by Loredo in the papers of Jiménez de la Espada, "Los capítulos finales de la Tercera Parte de la *Crónica del Perú* de Pedro de Cieza de León," *Boletín del Instituto Riva-Agüero* 9 (1972–74): 35–67.

84 Bailey W. Diffie, *Latin-American Civilization: Colonial Period* (Harrisburg, Pa.: Stackpole Sons, 1945), p. 519.

85 Maticorena Estrada, "Cieza," p. 615.

86 Philip Ainsworth Means, *Biblioteca Andina* (Detroit: Blane Ethridge Books, 1973), p. 349.

87 Guillermo Lohmann Villena, "Prólogo," in Sáenz de Santa María, *Obras completas,* p. vi.

88 *Part One,* p. 10.

89 Sáenz de Santa María, "Introducción," *Obras completas,* p. xvii.

I

About the discovery of Peru

When I lifted the pen to tell men[1] of today and tomorrow about the conquest and discovery that our Spaniards made in Peru when they won it, I could not but reflect that I was treating the highest matter that one can write about in the universe regarding worldly things. What I mean to say is, where have men seen what they see today, fleets entering loaded with gold and silver as if it were iron? Or where was it known or read that so much wealth could come from one kingdom? So much and so great is it that Spain is full of these treasures, and her cities are populated by many rich *peruleros*[2] who have left there. Furthermore, with all the money they have carried back, they have caused things to become more expensive in this kingdom, as those who have contemplated it well know.[3] Not only has Spain become expensive, but all of Europe has changed, and the merchandise and all commerce have prices other than they had. Prices have risen so much in Spain that if it continues as it has, I do not know how high prices will rise or how men will be able to live.[4] *fol. 1*

And, that I would write about a land where to spend a human life, a land so extensive, so plentiful, and so abundant, and where there is neither snow nor forest, that it cannot be improved upon, as I already noted in *[Part] One*.[5] And that God could have permitted something so great would be hidden from the world for so many years and such a long time, and not known by men, yet that it would be found and discovered and won, all in the time of Emperor Charles, who[6] had such need of its help because of the wars that had taken place in Germany against the Lutherans and [because of] other most important expeditions.[7] I am certain that all this sphere of the Indies, which is so large, had been discovered in times of much wealth. Furthermore, if the royal officials wanted to take the time to see from the *quintos*[8] what the treasure that had come from Peru added up to, it alone would be worth more than all the others put together, and not by a little, but by much.

One reads that in Spain, in eight hundred and twenty-two before the birth of Christ, the Pyrenees mountains were engulfed in flames so that the Phoenicians and those from Marseilles took many ships

PARTE PRIMERA
Dela chronica del Peru. Que tracta la demarcacion de ſus prouincias: la deſcripcion dellas. Las fundaciones de las nueuas ciudades. Los ritos y coſtumbres de los indios. Y otras coſas eſtrañas dignas de ſer ſabidas. Fecha por Pedro d Cieça de Leon vezino de Seuilla.
1553.
Con priuillegio Real.

1. Title page. Pedro de Cieza de León's *Primera Parte* (Seville, 1553). Courtesy of the Jay I. Kislak Foundation, Miami Lakes, Florida.

loaded with silver and gold, and then[9] there was much silver in Andalusia. And we also know that in Churabón in time [blank] there was so much silver that it was taken for granted. And when Salomon embellished the temple with vessels and riches, a lot was spent for it. Aside from all this, we know that in the Levant there are regions rich in gold and silver.[10] But none of these things can equal or compare to *fol. 1v* [the wealth] of Peru because counting what was in Cajamarca when the ransom [was collected] for Atahualpa, and what was later divided in Jauja and in Cuzco, and what else there was in the kingdom, it is such a great sum that I, although I could, do not dare to state it. But if one wanted to build another temple[11] with it, it would be more opulent than the one of Cuzco and as none that has existed in the world. All that had been taken from Peru is nothing compared with what is lost in the land, buried in tombs of kings and of *caciques*[12] and in the temples. The Indians themselves know it and acknowledge it. Indeed, after everything that they took from Huaylas, Porco, Caravaya, Chile, and from the Cañari, who will count the gold that arrived in Spain from these places? And if we encounter such difficulties with this, what will we say of the peak of Potosí,[13] where as far as I know, ever since they have been extracting silver there and without knowing how much the Indians had taken, more than twenty-five million pesos of gold, all in silver, have come out? And they will always extract this metal as long as there are men willing to search for it.

Now I will begin the delicate writing to relate the end of the war between the brothers Huascar and Atahualpa and how thirteen Christians almost miraculously discovered it [Peru], and then proceeded to win it in a war where no more than 160 fought.[14] And how later events evolved from one thing to another so that in Peru there was so much dissent, so many wars among our [men], conducted in such a harsh manner, and they were so cruel one with another that Sila and Mario[15] and the other usurpers pale in comparison. Many of the incidents related in this discourse would cause disbelief had there not been witnesses, so that in dealing with Peru it is unnecessary to talk about Italy or Lombardy or any other land,[16] even if it were more bellicose, because what so few people have done can only be compared to itself. During these altercations many died, and many who had been forgotten came to be captains and became so wealthy that some—

[even] one alone—had more income than the greatest lord of Spain, except for the king.[17]

Notes

1 the world

2 A term used in Spain for those who became rich in Peru and returned to their homeland.

3 Cieza had settled in Seville after returning from the Indies and witnessed firsthand its explosive growth made possible in part by New World treasures. For studies of Seville of the period, see Ruth Pike, *Aristocrats and Traders: Sevillian Society in the Sixteenth Century* (Ithaca: Cornell University Press, 1972); Mary Elizabeth Perry, *Gender and Disorder in Early Modern Seville* (Princeton: Princeton University Press, 1990); and Perry, *Crime and Society in Early Modern Seville* (Hanover: University Press of New England, 1980).

4 American bullion was a contributing factor in the general rise in prices in Europe during the period. The classic statement on the subject is Earl Jefferson Hamilton's *American Treasure and the Price Revolution in Spain, 1501–1650* (Cambridge: Harvard University Press, 1934). See also David R. Ringrose, *Madrid and the Spanish Economy, 1560–1850* (Berkeley: University of California Press, 1983).

5 *Part One* describes the peoples, places, and natural resources of the region from Panama to Chile.

6 when

7 Early on Cieza notes the impact the American wealth had on Spain's foreign policy. Its wars in defense of Catholicism would not have been possible without the treasures extracted from the Indies.

8 The royal fifth *(quinto)* is the tax paid to the Crown on all precious metals. See Peter Bakewell, "Mining in Colonial Spanish America," in *The Cambridge History of Latin America*, ed. Leslie Bethell (New York: Cambridge University Press, 1984), 2:105–52.

9 they say

10 Carlos Aranibar, Franklin Pease, and others suggest that some references to the Latin scholars in various volumes were added after Cieza returned to Seville. The mention of Churabón followed by a blank space in the text indicates the ongoing and preliminary nature of *Part Three* of the chronicle. See Franklin Pease's introduction to Pedro de Cieza de León, *Crónica del Perú: Primera parte*, 2d rev. ed. (Lima: Universidad Católica del Perú, 1986), pp. xxi–xxii.

11 the pilars

12 Cieza uses the term for "chief" normally used in the Antilles and applied elsewhere in the Indies, rather than the Andean word, *kuraka.*

13 Virtually a mountain of silver ore, one of the richest to ever be discovered, Potosí came to symbolize the wealth of the Indies, leading to the popular saying, "It is worth a Potosí." Cieza describes the mine and the city that rose on its slopes in *Part One,* chapters 109–110.

14 There were 168 men at Cajamarca according to James Lockhart, *Men of Cajamarca* (Austin: University of Texas Press, 1972), p. xiii.

15 Roman dictators Lucius Cornelius Sulla (Felix) (138–78 B.C.) and General Caius Marius (155?–86 B.C.). Both are examined by Plutarch.

16 Mention of Italy would have stirred Cieza's Iberian contemporaries. Naples, falling to the opportunistic foreign policy of Ferdinand, was conquered largely by Castilian troops under Gonzalo de Córdoba in the opening years of the century. Many of the men who participated in the Peruvian venture earned their first military experience in the Italian campaigns. See John Lynch, *Spain under the Habsburgs,* 2 vols. (New York: Oxford University Press, 1964).

17 Cieza noted in the margin, "And I do not think that I have exaggerated too much."

II

About how Governor Pedrarias named Francisco Pizarro captain of the South Sea and how he left Panama for the discovery

fol. 2 Following Alonso de Hojeda and Nicuesa, Pedrarias de Avila came as governor, and he remained in the city of Darién for some time.[1] As Panama and the kingdom of Tierra Firme were being settled, and as the Adelantado Vasco Núñez de Balboa and the pilot Pedro Miguel, according to some son of Juan de la Cosa,[2] first discovered the South Sea, there was discussion of exploring the lands of the said South Sea. The chronicler Gonzalo Fernández de Oviedo, who was a royal official in Darién, wrote most elegantly and well about those times; indeed, he was present there and saw most of it. Although I was able to obtain some information and could write something about the subject, I will proceed to the multitude of things that I have to do, and refer the reader to what Oviedo writes, where he will see it quite long and copious.[3]

Therefore, I say[4] [that] at the time that Darién was being settled there were two men [among] the Spaniards present there—one named Francisco Pizarro, who was at first a captain of Alonso de Hojeda, and Diego de Almagro. They were people on whom the governors often relied, because they were enterprising and steady and would persevere in any task. They became *vecinos*[5] of the city of Panama during the distribution of Indians made by Governor Pedrarias. The two were partners even in their Indians and property.[6]

It happened that Pedrarias sent Captain Zaera to the island of Hispaniola to try to bring some people[7] and horses to settle in the province of Nicaragua before Gil González Dávila could do it because [Pedrarias] learned that [González Dávila] had been exploring there in order to settle it. Nicolás de Ribera,[8] vecino of the City of the Kings (Lima), who is a contemporary of that time and one of the thirteen who discovered Peru, informed me that he knew that when Zaera arrived in the city of Santo Domingo, he contracted one Juan

Basurto to come to Panama, where Pedrarias would make him his captain-general in order that he could settle and explore the province of Nicaragua.[9]

Basurto, anxious to undertake that expedition, came to Tierra Firme with Zaera, and they brought some people and horses. In the meantime, Governor Pedrarias had given the commission for the said *fol. 2v* expedition to Captain Francisco Hernández. Juan Basurto resented it, and Pedrarias was aware of it. In order that his journey would not be in vain, [Pedrarias] negotiated with him that because Francisco Hernández had been confirmed in the post, and [Basurto] could not go to Nicaragua now, instead, he should go exploring with some ships in the South Sea because there were great expectations of finding prosperous land.

They say that Juan Basurto accepted the post that Pedrarias gave him. In order to make the expedition more to his liking, he decided to return to Santo Domingo to bring additional people and horses because in those times the kingdom of Tierra Firme lacked provisions. He left with great haste to embark from Nombre de Dios, where death intercepted his design and called him to account for his life's journey.

They learned in Panama about the death of this Basurto and how he was going to do what has been written. Francisco Pizarro and Diego de Almagro were living in the same city, and they were partners there, along with Hernando de Luque, a cleric.[10] Half in jest they talked about that expedition and how much Adelantado Vasco Núñez de Balboa wished to undertake it and to discover what existed in the southern part. Pizarro revealed to his companions his desire to risk his person and property in order to undertake that expedition. He prodded Almagro, pointing out that without taking chances men can never achieve their goals. They decided to request the venture for the said Francisco Pizarro. And thus, those who know it and are still alive state that they went to Pedrarias and petitioned him for the command of the discovery. Following long discussions, Pedrarias granted it to them with the provision that they form a partnership with him so that he could have a share in whatever profits there might be. The partners were satisfied, and all four formed a partnership whereby after the expenses were covered, all the gold and silver and other booty would be

2. Foundation of Panama. Pedro de Cieza de León's *Primera Parte* (Seville, 1553), p. 2r. Courtesy of the Jay I. Kislak Foundation, Miami Lakes, Florida.

divided equally between them without one taking more than another. Pedrarias then named Pizarro his captain so that in the name of the emperor he would undertake the aforesaid expedition.

The news spread around Panama and most of the vecinos were laughing, considering them crazy because they wanted to spend their *fol. 3* money in exploring mangroves and *ceburocos*.[11] But this talk did not prevent them from seeking money to outfit the expedition, and they purchased a ship that was in the harbor, which was said to be one of those that Vasco Núñez procured from one Pedro Gregorio. They took as pilot—as far as I know—one whose name was Hernán Peñate. They hastened to equip the ship with sails and rigging and everything else necessary for the voyage.[12] They tried to recruit some of the people who were in the region. They collected eighty Spaniards, more or less, of whom Salcedo[13] went as standard bearer, Nicolás de Ribera as treasurer, and Juan Carvallo[14] as inspector. After they finished putting on the ship everything that was necessary, they boarded four horses that were available and no more. The people embarked, and Francisco Pizarro, after taking leave of Pedrarias and his partners, did the same.

Notes

1 a few days. In 1508 the Council of Burgos authorized two major expeditions for mainland Tierra Firme. Alonso de Hojeda was to explore to the east of the Gulf of Urabá, and Diego de Nicuesa the western territory called Veragua. The two parties began exploration and settlement in early 1510. In the spring of that year the Hojeda party constructed the fort of San Sebastián de Urabá. Following lack of food, terrible weather, and constant strife with the Indians, Hojeda's forces shrunk considerably, forcing him to return to Hispaniola for reinforcements. The fort was left under the command of Francisco Pizarro. According to some, Hojeda ended his career as a conquistador at this point and entered a monastery. After several weeks, the starving Pizarro group left. The complex background of the Tierra Firme period is well described by Carl Ortwin Sauer, *The Early Spanish Main* (Berkeley: University of California Press, 1966), pp. 168–77, 218–37.

2 Juan de la Cosa, a Biscayan cartographer and pilot, was active in overseas exploration from the time of Columbus. In 1500 he prepared a map, one of the first to show both the Old World and the New World. See Sauer, *Early Spanish Main,* pp. 18, n. 44, 116–19, 161–72.

3 Gonzalo Fernández de Oviedo y Valdés (1478–1557) was born in Madrid and fought in the French and Italian campaigns. In 1514 he joined the Pedrarias Dávila expedition to Castilla del Oro and subsequently traveled around Nicaragua and settled in Santo Domingo, though he made frequent trips back to Spain. He published a description of the American flora and fauna in Toledo in 1526; then in 1535 in Seville he published the first part of his major historical account. Between 1536 and 1546, he completed the second and third parts of his history, including excellent and detailed information on Peru's conquest and the Almagro expedition to Chile. He was in Spain from 1546 to 1549, reporting on the civil wars in Peru. Oviedo's history is long and copious, as Cieza notes, and filled with allusions to classical texts, although they are often inaccurate. It is full of embellishments, unlike Cieza's straightforward and direct narrative, and Oviedo is biased, choosing heroes

and villains. He met Pizarro and Almagro in Darién and referred to the former as a "bastard son of a gentleman squire." See Oviedo's *Natural History of the West Indies*, trans. Sterling A. Stoudemire (Chapel Hill: University of North Carolina Press, 1959). On Oviedo's career, see James C. Murray, *Spanish Chroniclers of the Indies: Sixteenth Century* (New York: Twayne Publishers, 1994), pp. 100–108; see also David A. Brading, *The First America: The Spanish Monarchy, Creole Patriots, and the Liberal State, 1492–1867* (New York: Cambridge University Press, 1991), pp. 31–44.

4 for Francisco Pizarro having so much

5 A legal resident of a city, with political rights and status, and normally owning property. Many people resided in the colonial towns and cities, but only a part of them were vecinos.

6 Cieza glosses over Pizarro's earlier career. An illegitimate son of hidalgo Gonzalo Pizarro and a peasant woman, Francisca González, he was born around 1478 in Trujillo, Extremadura. He grew up with his mother's family and received no formal education. He entered the army as a young man and may have served in Italy. In 1502 he joined the expedition of Governor Nicolás de Ovando to the island of Hispaniola. He participated in the exploration of the Gulf of Urabá, and helped in the foundation of Darién. In 1513 he was with Balboa on the "discovery" of the Pacific Ocean and was later responsible for his capture under orders of Governor Pedrarias Dávila. He became one of the founders of the city of Panama (1519). From this base he served in numerous minor expeditions and received a grant of Indians (encomienda) for his services. He acted briefly as lieutenant governor, chief magistrate, and member of the city council of Panama. See Lockhart, *Men of Cajamarca*, pp. 135–57.

7 Cieza consistently refers to the participants of the expeditions as simply people *(gente)*; only rarely does he use the term soldiers *(gente de guerra* or *soldados)*. Although they carried weapons and fought when necessary, most of these men were not professional soldiers.

8 Nicolás de Ribera the Elder was one of Cieza's principal informants, especially for the early period. Ribera was born about 1487 in Olvera, Andalusia. He was an eyewitness to many of the events that Cieza describes in *Part Three*. Ribera was one of the founders of Lima and became its first mayor in 1535. He served at least five times as town councillor and was given a life appointment by the emperor in 1537. During the civil wars he maintained close links to the rebels, but ultimately joined royalist forces under Pedro de la Gasca at Jauja. He died in 1563. See Manuel de Mendiburu, *Diccionario histórico biográfico del Perú* (Lima: Imprenta Gil, 1934), 9:382–421; José de la Riva Agüero, *El primer alcalde de Lima Nicolás de Ribera el Viejo y su posteridad* (Lima: Imprenta Gil, 1935).

9 discover the provinces that were in the sea of

10 father. Hernando de Luque, a priest-entrepreneur, was never an equal partner in the venture. He was born in Olvera, Andalusia, and left for the Indies in 1514 with the first bishop of Darién, Friar Juan de Quevedo. He was made *maestrescuela* of the newly erected cathedral, a much sought out post, which included the teaching of divinity. After the city of Panama was founded, Luque was named curate and vicar of the cathedral parish. He was appointed bishop of Tumbez on 26 July 1529 and named "Protector of the Indians of Peru." He died before the capture of Atahualpa at Cajamarca. See Lockhart, *Men of Cajamarca*, pp. 70–73, and Mendiburu, *Diccionario*, 7:122–25.

11 Cieza used a Caribbean term for a rugged terrain or a rocky island.

12 the expedition

13 Born at Cazalegas near Talavera de la Reina around 1492, Juan de Salcedo was on Pizarro's first expedition. In 1528 he was a captain under Pedrarias Dávila in Nicaragua, but returned to Spain in July 1533, dissatisfied with the treasure allotment at Cajamarca. Salcedo was still living in 1554. See Lockhart, *Men of Cajamarca*, pp. 189–90.

14 Juan Carvallo was probably also a member of the first expedition. In 1528 he lived in Panama, where he prepared a report to the Crown, which is unfortunately lost. The following year he went to Nicaragua. See José Antonio del Busto Duthurburu, *Diccionario histórico biográfico de los conquistadores del Perú* (Lima: Studium, 1986), 1:350.

III

About how Captain Francisco Pizarro left to explore the coast of the South Sea and why that kingdom was called Peru

Francisco Pizarro, along with the Spanish Christians who accompanied him, embarked and left the port of the city of Panama in the middle of the month of November of the year of Our Lord fifteen hundred and twenty-three.[1] Diego de Almagro remained in the city to procure people and anything else necessary for the conquest in order to send succor to his partner.

When Pizarro left Panama on his ship, they traveled until they arrived at the Pearl Islands,[2] where they landed and took on provisions of water, firewood, and grass for the horses. From there they proceeded until they reached a port that they named *de Piñas*[3] (Pinecones) because so many [pinetrees] were growing nearby. All the Spaniards disembarked with their captain so that no one was left on the vessel except the sailors. They decided to penetrate further inland in search of provisions to outfit the ship, believing that they would find them in the territory of a cacique named Beruquete or Peruquete.

For three days they followed a river upstream with great hardship because they walked through frightful forests. The terrain along the course of the river was so thickly overgrown that it was difficult to walk. They arrived at the foot of a great mountain range. They climbed it although they were already worn out from previous hardships, the little they had to eat, and from sleeping on damp ground in the forests, as well as having to carry on their shoulders their swords and shields along with their backpacks. Indeed, they became so tired that one Christian named Morales died from pure exhaustion and weakness.

The Indians who inhabited those forests were aware of the arrival
fol. 3v of the Spaniards. Because they had already heard about some others [Spaniards],[4] that they were very cruel, they did not want to wait for them. Rather, they abandoned their houses made of wood and straw or palm fronds and hid in the thicket of the forest, where they were

safe.[5] The Spaniards had reached some small houses, which they said were those of the cacique Peruquete, where they found nothing but some maize and those roots that [the Indians] eat.[6] The old Spaniards say that the kingdom of Peru was named for this village or chief called Peruquete and not for a river because none exists of such name.[7]

Because the Christians neither saw any Indians or found provisions or anything else that they had expected, they were dejected and shocked to see such poor land. It seemed to them that hell could not be worse, and commending themselves to God, they and their captain patiently retraced their path, returning to where they had left the ship. They reached the seashore worn-out and covered with mud, and most of them barefoot, with their feet raw from the sharp thorns in the forests and from the river rocks. They then embarked, and as best as they could, they navigated westwardly, continuing their exploration. Within a few days they landed in a port, which they later named *de la Hambre* (Hunger), where they provisioned themselves with water and firewood.

They departed from this port and sailed for ten days, but they lacked provisions so that each person was given no more than two ears or spikes of maize to eat for the entire day. They also had little water because they carried only a few casks, and they did not eat any meat or any other refreshment because it was all gone. They all felt dejected, and some were cursing themselves for having left Panama, where food was already plentiful. Pizarro, who had suffered many hardships and currish hungers in his life, encouraged his companions, telling them to confide in God, that He would provide them with sustenance and good land. After conferring together, they returned to the port they had left and named it de la Hambre[8] because they entered it so famished.

Because of the hardships they endured, the Spaniards were very thin and yellow looking,[9] so that they found it distressing to look at one another. The land before them was hellish because even the birds and the beasts shied away from living there. They saw only thick underbrush and mangroves. Water came down from the heavens, and there was water always covering the land. The sun was so obscured by dense clouds that they could not see its brilliance for several days. And thus they found themselves trapped in those forests, expecting nothing but death because if they wanted to return to Panama, they

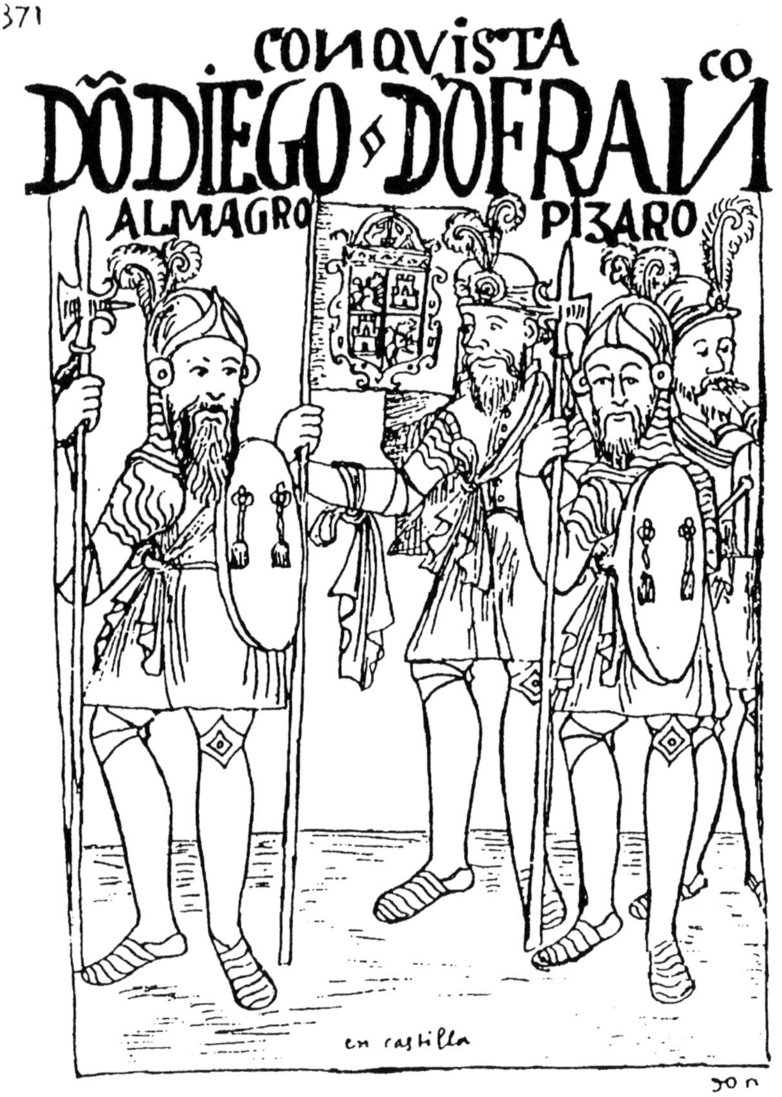

3. Francisco Pizarro and Diego de Almagro. Felipe Guaman Poma de Ayala, *El primer nueva corónica y buen gobierno*, 3 vols., ed. Rolena Adorno and John V. Murra (Mexico City: Siglo Veintiuno, 1980), f. 371. Courtesy of Siglo Veintiuno Editores.

lacked provisions, unless they killed the horses. Because there were among them men of good judgment who wished to see an end to the expedition, it was decided that some of them should sail to the Pearl Islands to secure provisions. And after they discussed it, they carried it out, although neither those who went had any food to take with them, nor did any remain for the rest of them. *fol. 4*

Notes

1 It was 1524. It is difficult to date with certainty many of the events. Peruvian historian, José Antonio del Busto Duthurburu, who has devoted most of his scholarly career to the period of conquest, states that they left Panama on 13 September 1524, on board a small vessel, the *Santiago.* But Busto (*Historia general del Perú: Descubrimiento y conquista* [Lima: Studium, 1978], p. 32) rarely cites his sources. Nevertheless, his dates are usually accurate.
2 The archipelago of the Pearl Islands lies southeast of Panama in the Gulf of Panama.
3 The Puerto de Piñas is near the contemporary boundary between Panama and Colombia.
4 of the Spaniards
5 that the Spaniards would not reach them, but they had already
6 It is unclear which of the South American tuberous crops Cieza had in mind. If close to the coast at this latitude, the roots he mentions may have been yucca or sweet potatoes.
7 Cieza's version of the origin of the name Peru is one of many. The Viru River on Peru's north coast, just south of Chan Chan and the Moche Valley, is another possible origin, but Cieza rejected it. The Viru is unlikely to have been the source, for the Spanish could not have learned the name of the valley until later. Documents as early as 1526 use the term referring to a cacique's territory on the Pacific coast of Panama near the border of modern Colombia.
8 Busto places it north of Cabo Corrientes.
9 Those nearing death were commonly characterized by a yellowish, waxy complexion. As Sebastián Covarrubias notes in his early seventeenth-century dictionary, "yellow *[amarillo]* among all the colors is the most infelicitous, because it is the color of death, and of a long and serious illness." (*Tesoro de la lengua Castellana o española* [1611, Madrid: Editorial Castalia, 1994]).

IV

About how Montenegro[1] and several Spaniards returned in the ship to the Pearl Islands to get provisions without bringing anything to eat except a dry cowhide and some bitter palmettos, and about the hardship and hunger endured by Pizarro and those who remained with him

When the captain and his companions decided that the ship would return to the Pearl Islands for some supplies—indeed they needed them very much—they did not know how those who were to go would sustain themselves during the journey. There was no maize or anything else to eat, and to search for it on land was useless because the Indians lived in the forests between raging rivers and marshes. And after contemplating and carefully considering, they found no other solution to prevent them all from perishing except for the ship to set sail, and those who had to go would take with them a very dry and hard cowhide to eat, one that was on that very ship. They chose from among them Montenegro to carry out the aforesaid. In addition to the hide, they cut some bitter palmettos near the coast. I ate some of them in the forest of Caramanta[2] when we were exploring with the Licentiate Juan de Badillo.

Montenegro promised that if God granted him a good journey, he would try to return shortly to relieve their need. They cut up the hide into pieces, and after soaking it in water all day and all night, they cooked it and ate it with the palmettos. Commending themselves to God, they set out on their voyage to the Pearl Islands.

When the ship left, the captain and his companions searched for food among those mangroves, wishing to come upon some settlement. But the weary men found only trees of thousands of varieties and many thorns and thistles, mosquitoes and other things, all of which caused pain and none made them content.

fol. 4v Because the hunger was wearing them down, they cut some of those bitter palmettos, and in the forest they found some reeds with fruit similar to acorns that smelled almost like garlic, and being hungry they ate them. Some days they caught fish on the coast. They stayed alive with difficulty, wishing more than life itself to once again see the ship in which Montenegro left, with fresh provisions. Furthermore, because they were in such need and the hardship was so great, the land so unhealthy and gloomy, and it rained most of the time, they became so ill that more than twenty Spaniards died. In addition, others were stricken, and they all were so thin that it was pitiful to look at them.

Pizarro had the spirit worthy of the man that he was, and he did not despair at what he was seeing; instead, he himself searched for some fish, striving to strengthen the [men]. He encouraged them so they would not become dispirited, telling them that they would soon see the ship approaching in which Montenegro had gone. They built some huts that we call *ranchos* here, where they sheltered themselves from the water.

Being in this state, they say that a beach appeared in view at the end of what must have been a distance of eight leagues. One Christian named Lobato told the captain that he thought that some of them should go there, and perhaps they would find something to eat, because where they were they could expect nothing but death. The captain liked what this Lobato said, and he along with those who were most fit headed there with their swords and bucklers.[3] The rest of the Spaniards remained in the camp they had set up. And when they left for the beach, they went on until they reached it, and there it pleased God that they found a great quantity of coconuts and saw certain Indians. In order to capture some of them, the Spaniards moved quickly, but the Indians sensed their coming and began to flee. Nicolás de Ribera told me that they saw one of those Indians jump into the water, and it was incredible because he swam what must have been more than six[4] leagues without stopping, and they saw him swimming until nightfall when they lost sight of him.

Most of the Indians who fled went into some marshes. The Spaniards caught two of them, and the rest headed toward a surging river where they had their canoes. And just like those who escape a crossbow shot, they went happy at not having been captured by the Spaniards, who astonished them in being able to endure such suffering. It is said that they were wondering why [the Spaniards] did not

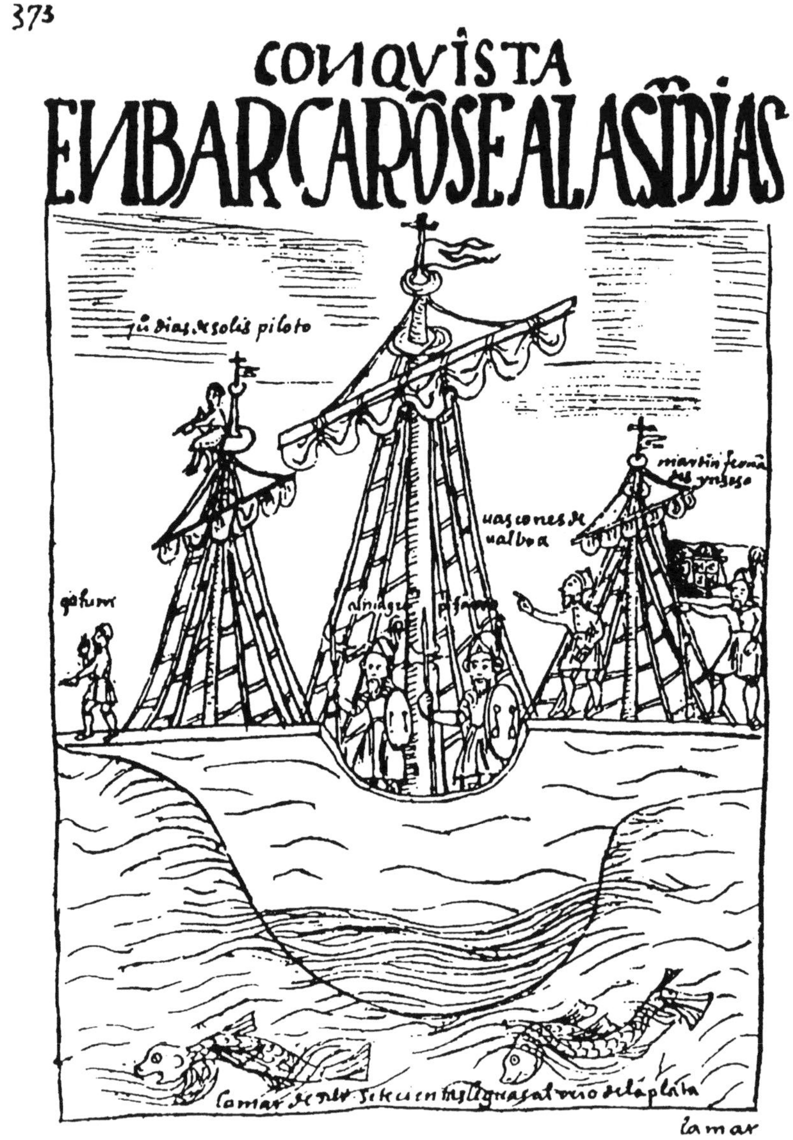

4. The ship of discovery. Felipe Guaman Poma de Ayala, *El primer nueva corónica y buen gobierno,* 3 vols., ed. Rolena Adorno and John V. Murra (Mexico City: Siglo Veintiuno, 1980), f. 373. Courtesy of Siglo Veintiuno Editores.

clear away the brambles and sow some seed and eat from that instead of looking for what [the Indians] had in order to take it from them by force. These and other things that the Indians say became known from them themselves, when they were captured by the Spaniards. I say this because I want to always explain everything to the reader. *fol. 5* These Indians carried bows and arrows with such a malignant plant[5] that one Indian among them who was wounded with an arrow died within three or four hours. In this undertaking the Spaniards found one *fanega*[6] of maize, which was divided among them.

Notes

1 Gil de Montenegro.

2 Within the jurisdiction of Popayán in southern highland Colombia; see Marcos Jiménez de la Espada, ed., *Relaciones geográficas de Indias: Perú* (Madrid: Atlas, 1965), 2:332.

3 A small, round shield commonly used by Spanish soldiers in the sixteenth century.

4 eight leagues

5 Various plant poisons were used. One of the more popular was prepared from a vine, *strychnos toxifera.* See Julian H. Steward and Louis C. Faron, *Native Peoples of South America* (New York: McGraw-Hill, 1959), pp. 296–97.

6 A fanega is a solid measure equal to approximately one and one-half bushels or fifty-eight liters, but may vary according to time and place.

V

About how Montenegro arrived at the Pearl Islands and how he returned with the succor

Montenegro and those who were on the ship sailed until they reached the Pearl Islands, weak from the hunger they had suffered. When they arrived, they ate and rested, keeping in mind they had to return quickly to relieve those who had remained with Captain Francisco Pizarro. They then loaded the ship with a good supply of maize, meat, bananas, and other fruits and roots, and with all this they returned to where they had left the Christians. They arrived while the captain and some of the men had gone out for what has been described in the previous chapter. The pleasure and exhilaration they all felt when they saw the ship can hardly be exaggerated. They valued more the little sustenance being brought by it than all the gold in the world. Thus, before the ship reached port, those who had been sick rose up as if they were cured.

After going around for several days on the beach where they had found the coconuts and in the surrounding woods, and realizing that they would not find any settlement and that the inland was infernal and full of marshes and rivers, Captain Francisco Pizarro decided to return with his companions to the camp where the others had remained. On the way they met a joyful Spaniard who was coming to tell them about the safe arrival of the ship. He was carrying in a backpack three loaves of bread for the captain and four oranges.[1] When they comprehended what had happened, the captain and those who were with him were no less delighted than the others had been. They thanked the Lord for remembering them at a time of such hardship. Pizarro divided the loaves and the four oranges among all of them without himself eating more than any of the others. They became as invigorated as if each had eaten an entire capon.

They then hurried back with him until they reached the camp
fol. 5v where everyone was merry, and Montenegro reported to the captain what had happened during the voyage. Everyone ate what came on the ship while conversing about what they had gone through until

then. They say that twenty-seven Spaniards were missing, who had died from hunger.

The captain and those who survived embarked on the ship, determined to sail along the western coastal stretch where they hoped to encounter a good, fertile, and prosperous land. And after they embarked, they sailed and landed in a port, which they named Port Candelaria because they had arrived there on the day of Our Lady of the Candelaria.[2] They noticed some pathways here and there, but the land was worse than the one they had left. It was full of mangroves, and it was such a frightful forest that it seemed to reach the clouds and so dense that all one could see were roots and trees, because the forest here is different than in Spain. In addition, the rain was so frequent and heavy that they could not even walk. Because most of the shirts they wore were made of coarse linen, their clothes were rotting, and their hats and caps were falling to pieces. There was powerful thunder, and lightning bolts were flashing, as those who have gone along that coast have seen. It was so cloudy that there were many days when they could not see the sun, and even when it came out, the forest was so dense that they were always half in darkness. The mosquitoes molested them because clearly where there are many, they are a great nuisance. It happened to me many times that while it was raining and thundering in the middle of the night, I walked out of a tent in the valley and drenched in water I climbed up to the hills just to escape them. The long-beaked *[zancudos]* mosquitoes are particularly bad, and many have died from their bite.[3]

In some parts of those forests there are many natives; in other parts, only a few. Since the land is so vast, they can easily spread out because they do not have villages close together, nor are they as civilized as others. Rather, they cohabit with their wives and children among those brambles, and they cut the forest on the slopes and sow their maize and other foodstuffs. They all learned and were aware of the ship's movement along the coast, and they knew that the Spaniards were disembarking in the ports, and those who were close to the sea hid without daring to wait for them.

Notes

1 The Spanish were remarkably quick in transplanting their favorite plants and animals. Oviedo, for example, said he planted orange trees in Darién, which would have been around 1514.

2 Candlemas, or the second day of February. Port Candelaria was located on the Pacific coast of modern Colombia, north of Cabo Corrientes.

3 Linda A. Newson describes the devastation caused by mosquitoes and other insects. See "Old World Epidemics in Early Colonial Ecuador," in Noble David Cook and W. George Lovell, eds., *"Secret Judgments of God": Old World Disease in Colonial Spanish America* (Norman: University of Oklahoma Press, 1992), pp. 102–4; and Linda A. Newson, *Life and Death in Early Colonial Ecuador* (Norman: University of Oklahoma Press, 1995), pp. 144–54.

VI

About how the captain and the Spaniards came upon an Indian village where they found some gold, how they landed in Pueblo Quemado and from there sent a ship to Panama, and what else happened

Francisco Pizarro and his companions noticed that there were pathways through those forests. They decided to follow one of them to *fol. 6* see if it led to any settlement so that they could capture some Indians from whom they could learn about the land that they were in. And so they took their swords and bucklers and went two leagues inland, or a little more, where they came upon a small village. They saw not one Indian because they all had fled, but they found plenty of maize and roots and hog meat[1] and came upon six hundred pesos of pure gold in jewelry. In the pots that they found in the Indians' fire, some human feet and hands could be seen among the meat that they took out to eat.[2] Therefore, it was believed that the inhabitants of that region were Caribs. They also had bows and arrows with the poison that they make from plants. The Spaniards ate what they found in that place and decided to return to the sea to embark because they were unable to capture any of the natives of that land.

Having boarded the ship,[3] they coasted until they reached a village they named *Pueblo Quemado*.[4] With everyone's agreement they decided to go inland to see if they could get to a village and capture some Indians because they saw paths among the mangroves, and it was obvious that there must be people; indeed, they seemed well trodden. They were not mistaken because there were many people in that place, and they all had been forewarned about [the Spaniards'] movements in the land, and they hid their women and valuables.

Our Spaniards followed one of those paths, and after a little more than one league they came upon a deserted village because the Indians, as has been told, had abandoned it. They found a large quantity of maize and many fields of maize and those other tasty roots that [the Indians] eat, and quite a few of the *pixivaes*[5] palms, which are

very good. This village, according to their custom, sat well fortified at the peak of some slopes or mountain ridges so that it resembled a fortress. Since they found so many provisions in that village, the captain as well as all the Spaniards concluded that it would be advantageous for all of them to take shelter in it because it was so strong and so well provisioned with food. They would also send the ship to Panama to bring Spanish reinforcements and to be repaired; indeed, it was so damaged that it was taking on water in many places. Be-
fol. 6v cause it seemed to them a good decision, the captain ordered that Gil de Montenegro, along with the swiftest and most nimble Spaniards, should search for some Indians throughout the forests in the huts that they had made, which we call *rancherías* here, so they could go on the ship and help pump. Everyone was needed because there were few sailors and the ship was taking on water.

The natives of that region had met and discussed the arrival of the Spaniards and that it was very humiliating to be fleeing their villages in fear because there were so few of them. Therefore, they decided to face any affront or danger that was coming their way in order to expel [the Spaniards] from their land or kill them if they refused to leave. And they vilified them, saying that they were vagabonds who did not work and roamed from place to place. They said even more, as several of those who were captured by the Spaniards later confessed. Having made this decision, they posted themselves as sentries and watchmen around the village that the Spaniards were staying in to find out if any of them would leave and what they planned to do. When Gil de Montenegro left the village along with the Spaniards chosen to go with him on the raid to capture the Indians to pump on the ship, the Indians who were on the lookout sent warning to the place where the assembly was with the said resolve. Although the natives who formed the league still intended to kill the Spaniards or to expel them from their land, they strangely feared them, though there were barely sixty able-bodied men. This fear penetrated many, and yet they were on their own soil, and they knew and understood it. I do not know what else to attribute it to other than that Almighty God has at times and situations permitted the Spaniards to achieve such great and dubious deeds, because unless He clouded the mind of the Indians, they could have defeated them with just a few puffs or handfuls of soil. I do not believe that He permitted it because of their merits, but that it pleased

Him to defend their honor and because they had their good name. But, as we have seen, He punished mightily with an arm of vengeance many of them for not recognizing such great favor.

But because the *montañeses*[6] already had their usual weapons, and they saw the Christians separated, they rejoiced at the division and planned to attack Montenegro and kill those who were with him, and then go to where the captain was and do the same thing. Indeed, they believed that if they succeeded with the first, the rest would be easy to do. Thus, they attacked our men, their faces and bodies—because they are nude—covered with the concoction that they spread on. It is what we call *bixa,*[7] which is like red ochre, and another that is yellow. Others had painted themselves with a bixa that is like turpentine—and I once had a poultice made of it put on me. They looked like demons and howled loudly according to their custom because that is how they fight. They attacked the Spaniards, who although they were so few in number and saw so many enemies before them, did not become fainthearted. Instead, they commended themselves to God and His powerful Mother, and they seized their swords and slashed the Indians they could reach, while Montenegro, their leader, was telling them not to put much stock in them. The Indians strove to kill them, and they shot their darts at them, but they did not dare to come too close for fear of the swords. *fol. 7*

One Christian named Pedro Vizcaíno killed and wounded several Indians, but then they inflicted such wounds on him that he later died from them. And during one charge they killed two more Spaniards and wounded others. Those who survived defended themselves so well that when the Indians realized that for the three that they had killed there were many more casualties of their own, they were astonished that human beings could be so brave. They conferred again and decided to leave these men and instead attack those who had stayed behind. [Those Spaniards] had become ill, which was the reason why they had not gone with those who had caused [the Indians] so much harm. Furthermore, there were fewer of those whom they wanted to attack than those whom they were leaving.

Notes

1 The Spanish referred to peccaries as *puercos,* or hogs; it might also have been the meat of tapirs; see Steward and Faron, *Native Peoples,* p. 46.

2 The Choco of the northwest Pacific coast of Colombia, as well as their immediate neighbors to the south, ate monkeys. Perhaps the Spaniards erred in this case, and what they saw were monkey hands and feet. See David B. Stout, "The Choco," and John Murra, "The Cayapa and Colorado," in Julian Steward, ed., *Handbook of South American Indians,* 7 vols., Bureau of American Ethnology Bulletins, no. 143 (Washington, D.C., 1946–59), 4:269–76, 277–91.

3 having embarked

4 *Pueblo Quemado* literally means "Burned Village" and was located near Cabo Corrientes, Colombia.

5 *Guilielma utilis,* the easily identifiable palm, frequently provided sustenance when other foods were unavailable. It probably originated in South America and was used extensively in the Caribbean basin.

6 Garcilaso de la Vega refers to montañeses not necessarily as the people from mountainous northwestern Spain, but as savages. It is this meaning that Cieza seems to imply. See Garcilaso de la Vega, El Inca, *Royal Commentaries of the Incas and General History of Peru,* trans. Harold V. Livermore (Austin: University of Texas Press, 1966), pp. 607–8.

7 *Bixa orellana* is a small Indian plum tree native to tropical America. A reddish yellow dye, or *annatto,* is made from the pulp around the seeds of the *Bixa orellana.*

VII

About how the Indians attacked the Spaniards and the difficulty the captain was in and how the Indians fled

After making the decision to attack the captain and the other Christians who had remained with him, the Indians struck. They arrived with great clamor and howls to where the Christians had been too careless to think that the Indians would come and assail them. But seeing the shots of darts and arrows they showered them with, they charged with their swords and bucklers. The captain went ahead of them, encouraging and emboldening them so they would disregard the large number of enemies they were fighting. Commending themselves to the Lord, and calling out to the apostle Santiago,[1] they resisted the Indians with great effort. The captain feared that the Indians might have killed the Christians who had gone exploring, but because the Indians had left them, they were trying to return to the camp as quickly as they could in order to join the rest of their companions.[2] *fol. 7v*

The Indians were intent on accomplishing their goal to kill the Christians. The Christians, seeing what was happening, fought bravely, but they received many blows from the Indians. Two Spaniards died, and twenty were wounded, some of them seriously. And it pleased God that the Spaniards who had gone with Montenegro arrived because had they been delayed any further, without a doubt they, as well as the others, would have been in peril. But when they united, they regained their spirit and fended off the Indians. The captain showed great valor, and on that day he had plenty, as he fought courageously with sword and buckler. The Indians realized that he was the one who was inflicting most harm on them, and wanting to kill him, many charged at him in a throng, wounding him. They were wearing him out so much that although he had always been unrelenting in a fight, they forced him to roll down a slope. Thinking that they had killed him, some of them descended, filled with joy, in order to despoil him and take his weapons. But he was so adept and alert that when he reached a more level ground, he stood up with his sword high, determined to avenge his own death before the Indians could kill him. And he struck the first ones who arrived, killing one or two of them.

The Spaniards had seen what happened to their captain, and furious at the Indians, they launched out against them, forcing them to run away, howling and groaning. The Indians were astonished to see that the Spaniards could fight with such force in silence and concluded that there must be something divine about them. Some[3] Spaniards went to the aid of Francisco Pizarro, whom they found in the difficulties I had mentioned. He was wounded and they carried him up and treated his wounds as well as all the others who were injured. For them there was only the refreshment that the reader can imagine, and to have had some oil to burn[4] their wounds would have been indeed a great thing.

fol. 8 The captain saw what had happened to them and that they had been unable to send the ship that was damaged and was taking in water in many places to Panama for succor. Consulting with his companions, they all decided to leave that place. Indeed, they were in danger because there were many Indians, whereas most of [the Spaniards] were wounded and all were very thin, and the land was poor and full of hardship. And they all agreed to embark and land at Chochama,[5] from where they would send the ship to Panama. They embarked as quickly as they could and returned to Chochama. On the way they missed Diego de Almagro, who had left Panama with succor, as I will tell later.

Francisco Pizarro and his companions decided to send the ship from there back to Panama for what has been said. The treasurer, Nicolás de Ribera, would sail on it with the gold that they had to give account of to the governor because they had good news of what lay ahead. And so it was done. All the provisions that were on the ship remained behind so they could eat and overcome the said hardships because the land was unhealthy, full of forests, and it continuously rained and thundered as has been said. It is never cold, but the land is very humid.

Ribera and those on the vessel sailed until they reached the Pearl Islands, where they learned that Almagro had gone in a ship searching for them. Because the Christians who had remained in Chochama would be happy to learn such news, they sent a canoe with the message to the captain. The ship arrived in Panama, and Nicolás de Ribera and those who sailed in it reported to Pedrarias what had happened to them since they entered the land of the Cacique Peruquete.

In Panama everyone wanted to know how Pizarro and his companions fared in the discovery, and they were horrified when they heard what they had endured in the mangroves.

Pedrarias was distressed that so many Spaniards had died, and he blamed Pizarro because he had persisted in the discovery. Induced by some malevolent people who always take pleasure in slandering those who do well, Pedrarias announced that he would like to send [Pizarro] an associate, with equal power, so the exploration could proceed without so many casualties. They say it was for this or other reasons that Pedrarias wanted to send Francisco Pizarro an associate. *fol. 8v* But when his partner, the maestrescuela Don Hernando de Luque, learned about it, he told Pedrarias that what he was planning was unjust and that he was poorly repaying Francisco Pizarro all that he had suffered and spent in the king's service. He admonished him for many other things, pleading with him not to order any changes until he saw the final outcome of the expedition. [Pedrarias] accepted the arguments presented by the maestrescuela, did not decree anything, and agreed to outfit the ship. What I have written was related to me by this Nicolás de Ribera,[6] who is alive today and resides in this land and has Indians in the City of the Kings,[7] where he is a vecino.

Those of you reading this, believe me that when I write, I would rather leave out much of what I know and pass it over than to include even a single word of what did not happen. And, good and honorable men, this you will comprehend and learn without knowing it when you see the modesty and simplicity of my style, which seeks neither verbosity nor flowery words nor other rhetoric,[8] and only wishes to relate the truth with sincerity because I believe that good writing must be like one person conversing with another—and as one speaks and no more. Pardon me if I have dwelled on this because it will serve for what will come, without having to repeat these things. And with that, I will return to the task before me.

Notes

1 Santiago (Saint James) was frequently evoked during the conquest of the New World. The battle cry dates back to the Spanish reconquest from the Moors. In the Andes, Santiago quickly became identified with the force of

lightning, or Illapa. An entire issue of *Historia y Cultura* (Bolivia) 23 (1994) is dedicated to the cult of Santiago.

2 Christians

3 Some were taken captive

4 Cauterize.

5 In the manuscript Cieza wrote "Chicama" (a valley in the Trujillo district), which is wrong and misleading. The correct place is Chochama, which lies southeast of the Pearl Islands in the Gulf of San Miguel. See Mary W. Helms, *Ancient Panama: Chiefs in Search of Power* (Austin: University of Texas Press, 1979), pp. 63–65.

6 See chapter 2.

7 Lima.

8 This remark seems a direct jab at Oviedo. See chapter 2.

VIII

About how Diego de Almagro left Panama with people and succor in search of his partner, and about how they injured his eye and how he[1] was united with him

As has been written, Captain Francisco Pizarro had left Panama with his people. Diego de Almagro and Father Luque furnished another ship and recruited people so that Almagro himself could go to search for him with that succor. And, because Almagro was so diligent and meticulous, he arranged it quickly. He petitioned Pedrarias for a license and left Panama before Ribera, the treasurer, had arrived. Furthermore, nothing was known about the circumstances of Francisco Pizarro or what God had done with him. Some say that Almagro took this time sixty-four men from Panama; others say seventy; it is not important.

They embarked in the port and sailed up the coast[2] in search of the Christians, who were in Chochama passing their time. The wounded were recovering, and the healthy were searching for what they needed. Some died from illness, and others were bloated,[3] and some were eaten by caymen in the rivers when they crossed from one *fol. 9* side to the other. The mosquitoes bothered them considerably.

When Diego de Almagro had left Panama, they set their course up the western coast to search for the Christians because they were not sure where they might be. As they skirted the coast, they landed in a boat in all the ports that they encountered, without omitting any. Because they had not run into them, they traveled until they reached the port of Pueblo Quemado, where Pizarro and his companions first had been. In the ports that they had seen, it was clear from the machete cuts and pieces of hemp shoes and other things that [the Christians] had been there.

In this Pueblo Quemado Almagro decided to go with fifty Spaniards into the village to see what was there. The natives had heavily fortified it with a palisade in order to defend themselves from the Christians if they came back again. They knew very well where Pizarro was and about the arrival of Almagro. They all assembled with their leaders, determined to kill those who by plundering, driving them out of their houses, and capturing their women and children had been causing their deaths. Almagro and his companions saw the fortification of the village and realized that there were warriors inside. But they did not even consider retreating; instead, they decided to attack the village and gain the stronghold. However—according to some who affirm it as the truth—when they approached, the outcry, the clamor, and yelling of the Indians frightened and intimidated certain Spaniards who were there—most of whom were natives from around Sayago[4]—that seeing the fierce countenance of the Indians and their cries, they were ready to flee in pure terror.

Almagro and his followers attacked the Indians, who had just started to shoot darts and arrows, threatening them with death because they had entered their land uninvited and without being owed anything. The Spaniards shrugged off their threats and shouts, and assailed them in silence, as is customary with them when they fight, and they killed and wounded many of them. They pressed them so hard that in spite of everything they won the palisade. But first, one of the Indians threw a rod at Almagro, and he aimed so well that he hit him in the eye and injured it. They furthermore affirm that other Indians advanced against him, and if it were not for a black slave, they would have killed him. He did not falter, even though he was so badly wounded, nor did he cease fulfilling his duty until all the Indians fled. His men, sad that such misfortune occurred, carried him to a house *fol. 9v* and put him in a bed they were able to make for him out of branches. He was quickly treated as best as could be done, and they remained in that land until his eye was cured, although his vision was not as good as before. When he was well, they embarked, cursing the land they were leaving behind and the men who lived there, saying that it seemed more a devil's playground than a human settlement. They set sail from that place, following a course up the coast, yet they did not come upon the Christians. They landed in the ports to see if they could find any traces, and because they did not encounter anything, they suspected that they all must be dead; after all, neither they nor the ship appeared.

Dismayed, they sailed until they reached the mouth of the San Juan River.[5] They found some villages on both banks of the river, and it seemed to be a better land than any they had seen. The Indians of that coast and river were startled when they saw the ship. They could not imagine what it was and became terrified. There were also some who knew what it was, and they were not pleased to see it, given what they had heard. But because Almagro had gone as far as the San Juan River without running into his partner or a sign of him or the ship, he decided not to go any further. Instead, he would return to Panama; he was convinced without any doubt that Francisco Pizarro and those who had left with him were all dead. And that is what they did with great sadness, and only landed when they arrived at the Pearl Islands, where as soon as they disembarked, they learned how Ribera had returned to Panama with the ship and that Pizarro and his companions were in Chochama, where they had remained when the ship departed.

When they heard this news they were elated, and they again set sail and went to the port of Chochama, where all were happily reunited. Those on land related the great hardships they had endured and how many had died, and subsequently those from the ship told them how much they had been searching for them and how they had gone as far as the San Juan River. Francisco Pizarro and his companions showed great sorrow that Almagro had lost an eye.

Now that the two partners—Francisco Pizarro and Diego de Almagro—were together, they discussed many issues relating to the discovery. They were distressed because they never left mangroves and forests, and they feared it might all be like that, but because they had already begun and were in debt, it would not be expedient to give up; it was better to continue and in that risk their lives. They agreed that Almagro would go back to Panama to repair the ships and return with *fol. 10* more people in order to proceed with the exploration. And what they agreed to, they carried out, unloading all the provisions that were on the ship.

Notes

1 what else happened until the ones were united with the others

2 Technically, they were sailing south and therefore "down the coast." But because they went against a strong current, they always said "up the coast" when sailing from Panama south; while on the return voyage from Peru to

Panama, going with the current, they said that they sailed "down the coast." See Garcilaso de la Vega, *Royal Commentaries*, p. 21, n. 1.

3 Malnutrition in its final stages is characterized by severe bloating of the abdominal area.

4 A territory in the province of Zamora in Spain.

5 The San Juan River empties into the Pacific Ocean not far north of present Buenaventura, Colombia.

IX

About how Diego de Almagro returned to Panama, where he found that Pedrarias was recruiting people for Nicaragua, and what happened to him as well as his partner, Captain Francisco Pizarro

Because it had been agreed that Diego de Almagro would return to Panama for what has been related, Francisco Pizarro with all the people went ahead with what they had to do—that is, to wander among those rivers and mangroves, where there were few people because the Indians have their villages beyond the mountains to the north, and the rest to the west. And if there were any Indians near those rivers, when they learned that the Spaniards were in the land, which was so large and forested, they dispersed so as not to fall into their hands, hiding in the dense woods. Nevertheless, some of those men and women were taken, and [the Spaniards] learned from them about where they were. Because that coast is so unhealthy and their hardships were so great, everyday some Spaniards died, and others were swelling up like wineskins. They were continually tormented by mosquitoes, and several of them had their legs ulcerated. They were all always wet from crossing the rivers and marshes and from being caught in the severe and heavy rainstorms.

With such sad existence, many passed their time reproaching themselves because they had been so easily enticed only to endure such hardship and misery. Pizarro was always encouraging them with heartening and cheerful words, admonishing them to suffer with patience[1] because nothing good and profitable was gained lightly and easily. Furthermore, he told them that when Almagro returned with the succor, they would all go exploring together, by sea or on land. In this way they lived with the hope of what they expected to find while suffering the existing adversity.

When Diego de Almagro parted from Francisco Pizarro, he returned to Panama, where he learned that Pedrarias, furious at his captain, Francisco Hernández, was recruiting people to go and pun-

ish him for certain acts of sedition in the province of Nicaragua. After [Almagro] disembarked, he went to talk to [Pedrarias] and to report where Francisco Pizarro was staying and how much they had suffered
fol. 10v among those rivers and mangroves, although they wanted to endure it all, hoping that soon they would encounter a land with many people and riches. [Almagro] would return to bring again succor and people.

They say that the governor listened coldly to what Almagro was telling him and that it became known that he was resolved not to permit any more people to leave Panama. Almagro, who learned of it, went back to talk to him about the purpose of his coming. Because [Pedrarias] did not give him the permission to recruit people, he made some requests and complaints regarding the issue, which worked, because Pedrarias did not impede what he had said he opposed. Thus, Almagro and his partner, Father Luque, were quickly repairing the ships and recruiting people, and everyone was calling the land Peru because of what has been said earlier. Some from that era say that this time Pedrarias wanted to send an associate to Francisco Pizarro and to name another captain so that together they would make the discovery—also, that when Almagro and Father Luque found out about it, they tried to counter it, and achieved that Diego de Almagro was given the power and title of captain and that both were his. Others say that Pedrarias did not plan to give such captaincy, but that Almagro had his information, seeing that [Pedrarias] was to go to Nicaragua and there existed a writ for a captain. I cannot affirm which of those is certain, but I do know that for the power to command, a father will deny a son and a son the father.

From this trip to Panama, Diego de Almagro returned with the title of captain to where his partner had remained, bringing two ships and two canoes with people and the other things necessary for the expedition, and the pilot, Bartolomé Ruiz,[2] who had often served, went with him. With these people, ships, and canoes Almagro went in search of Pizarro. When they saw each other, it is said with certainty that Pizarro was irritated that Almagro had obtained the title of captain, believing that it was Almagro's doing and not Pedrarias's. But because the time was inopportune for imagining enemies, he suppressed his anger, though he did not forget it. And the said title of Captain Diego de Almagro was publicly read. [Almagro] had also justified himself to his partner—and he could be right—[saying] that he took the post so that it would not be given to a stranger because had it been otherwise, it would have been an affront to both of them. Furthermore, he did not want to oppose anything that [Pizarro] commanded and ordered.

Now that they found themselves with many men and several horses, they decided to explore by sea because on land, especially where they were, it was so difficult given the dense mangroves, as well as the many rivers full of fierce caymen and also the mosquitoes that tormented them so much. And with this agreement, they all went to the ships to embark. *fol. 11*

Notes

1 with good spirit

2 Ruiz was born in Moguer, Andalusia. He was probably in Panama when Pizarro returned from the first expedition and may have participated in earlier voyages. He died around the time when Almagro and Pizarro were reunited in Cajamarca in April 1533. His son Martín Yáñez de Estrada, also of Moguer, was a notary in Tumbez. See Mendiburu, *Diccionario,* 9:487–92.

X

About how Pizarro and Almagro journeyed as far as the San Juan River, where it was agreed that the pilot, Bartolomé Ruiz, would explore along the western coast and Almagro would return for more people[1]

After the Spanish Christians embarked with their captains to begin exploring along the coast ahead, they weighed the anchors, and with the sails hoisted, they departed. They sailed until they reached a river that they called Cartagena, near the San Juan River. They say that some Spaniards, with their swords and bucklers, landed in the canoes that they had brought. And finding themselves unexpectedly in an Indian village on the banks of the San Juan River, they took the amount of fifteen thousand *castellanos,* more or less, of base gold, and they found provisions and seized some captives. With that they returned to the ships, joyful and delighted that they were beginning to enter a land rich in gold and sustenance. But they were still distressed to see that the land was so full of rivers and marshes with mosquitoes, and that the forests were so large and frightening that in some parts it seemed that their branches, being so tall, were hiding in the clouds. They decided to land to see what was there and if they could find more gold, which is the aim of those of us who come from Spain to these Indies, whereas giving these people the news of our sacred religion should be placed above all else.

Those from the ships landed in the canoes; the Indians led them to understand that the region was mountainous, as they could see, *fol. 11v* but that further on there was another land and another people. They wanted to go in order to see if inland they would encounter level plains, which is what they wished for. Furthermore, there are so many rivers that it is impossible to travel other than on water, and that is what the natives usually do in the canoes. They are all nude and live in large wooden huts,[2] seventy by seventy, and more and less, with their wives and children, and they are separated from each other. They obtain in many parts a quantity of fine and base gold. I have written more about this in my *Part One.* [The Spaniards] realized that because of the many rivers it was impossible to explore inland, and when they all concurred on that, they decided that the Spaniards and Captain Francisco Pizarro would remain there because there were maize and roots[3] to eat, and they had the canoes to go from one part to another. Diego de Almagro would return to Panama with the gold that had been found in order to recruit more people. The pilot, Bartolomé Ruiz, would navigate along the coast as far as he could in order to see what land would appear. And that is what was done. Almagro left for Panama and Bartolomé Ruiz to explore the coast.

Those who remained with Pizarro wandered among those rivers, quite wet from the continuous rain and the water from the rivers. They found only some of the aforesaid wooden huts, and they had maize, yucca, sweet potatoes, and palms, which was not half bad.[4] But the mosquitoes would not leave them alone, and because there were always some ill people, several of them died. The captain suffered so much during this discovery that it would not suffice to possess the necessary audacity in my writing or to exaggerate it in order to come close in my description, and when I consider it, my hand trembles as I reach this point. I will move on, leaving it for someone more competent, although I will say that only Spaniards could have endured what these men went through. They can compare themselves only to each other and not to people from another nation.

While exploring the coast, the pilot, Bartolomé Ruiz, sailed until he reached Gallo Island,[5] which they say he found populated and the Indians on the verge of war because of the warning they had passed to each other that there were Spaniards in their lands. From there he continued until he discovered the bay that they named San Mateo.[6] He saw on the river a large village full of people who were astonished to see the ship and were watching it, believing it fell from the sky, but *fol. 12*
were unable to guess what it might be.

The ship proceeded on its voyage and explored as far as what they call Coaque.[7] Sailing further ahead on the western course, they sighted a lateen sail[8] approaching on the high sea. It was so large that they believed it was a caravel, something they thought was very unusual. Because the vessel did not stop, they realized it was a balsa, and bearing down on it, they took it. There were five Indian men on it and two boys with three women, who became prisoners on the ship. Using signs [the Spaniards] asked them where they were from and what land lay ahead; and with the same signs they responded that they were natives of Tumbez, which was the truth. They showed them spun wool and raw wool that came from sheep,[9] which they described through gesturing, and they said that there were so many of them that they covered the fields. They often named Huayna Capac and Cuzco,[10] where there was much gold and silver. They said so much about this and other things that the Christians who were on the ship thought they mocked them because the Indians always lie about many things that they relate. But these [Indians] told the truth about everything.

Bartolomé Ruiz, the pilot, treated them well, pleased to be bringing such people of good reason and who wore clothes so that Pizarro could question them. And sailing further ahead, he explored until the point of Pasado,[11] where he decided to return to where the captain had remained. When he arrived, he disembarked with the Indians. The captain received him well, pleased with the news he was bringing about what he had discovered. The Indians remained firm in what they had described, and for the Spaniards who were with Pizarro it was a joy to see and hear them.

Notes

1 and what else happened

2 Cieza uses the Taino word *caney.*

3 and other things

4 These staples, along with the white potato from the Andes, revolutionized Old World diets. Yucca, also known as manioc and cassava, is a tuber ideal for tropical climates with high rainfall. It requires little care and can be harvested as needed. After the root is ground—and in the case of the bitter variety, the poison is squeezed out—it produces a white starch that can be used to prepare porridge, varieties of bread, and even chicha beer. See Alfred W. Crosby, *The Columbian Exchange: Biological and Cultural Consequences of 1492* (Westport: Greenwood Press, 1972).

5 It literally means Rooster's Island and is located across the bay from Tumaco in the department of Nariño on the southwest coast of modern Colombia.

6 San Mateo Bay is by the mouth of the Esmeraldas River in northern Ecuador.

7 About 150 kilometers south from San Mateo Bay.

8 A lateen is a triangular sail.

9 By "sheep" Cieza means llamas or alpacas. There were no sheep in the Americas before the Europeans arrived. The Spaniards, however, called the native domesticated camelidae *sheep* because they provided a similar raw material: wool. Cieza consistently uses the word *sheep* when he is referring to llamas or alpacas.

10 *Cuzco* and *Huayna Capac* would be the words the Spanish could distinguish: Cuzco, the great capital of the Inca Empire, and Huayna Capac, the last ruler of a united realm, who was still alive at this point.

11 They had just passed the equator, hence Cabo Pasado, before Ruiz turned northward to report to Pizarro. Cabo Pasado is about fifty kilometers south of the equator on the Ecuadorian coast.

XI

How when the Spaniards went in canoes looking for provisions, all the Spaniards who went with their Captain Varela in one of the canoes were killed by the Indians

During the time that Diego de Almagro had returned to Panama for people and succor in order to proceed with the discovery, the captain and his companions had decided to explore those rivers. They were continually dying, and the Spaniards and others were becoming ill, and while they were crossing the rivers, the caymen were feeding on them to satiation. The ill continued to die, and those who were *fol. 12v* healthy cursed life, wishing to die so they would not be where they were. The captain reassured them, telling them that when Almagro came, they would all go to the land that the Indians captured on the balsas had told them about. They did not want to hear about it, and neither did they believe the Indians when they pondered those things. Because they lacked provisions, it was necessary to go and search for them; indeed, they had nothing to eat. They chose some to go in the canoes and named one of them as their leader. The rest remained with the captain in the huts they had built.

The Indians of those rivers found it troublesome to have the Spaniards in their land. They congregated many times to discuss killing them. They did not dare to attack them openly because they feared them and were afraid of their crossbows and swords. Instead, they resolved to do some great deed on the rivers when [the Spaniards] went out in their canoes, as they sometimes did, and kill as many as they could. When the canoes went out, one of them, with fourteen Spanish Christians and their leader named Varela, went ahead of the others in a raging river that they took upstream more than a league in search of provisions. Everything was full of mangroves and thick undergrowth, with large swamps from the unending water. In that region the rivers are like the tides of the South Sea, which is different from the ocean, and everyday they ebb and flow. Because it was low tide, the river receded so much that the canoe ran aground.[1] The Indians saw them coming, and because the one that ran aground had been ahead of the others, they joyfully descended downriver, painted with ochre and in full regalia, in more than thirty small canoes, in order to kill those who were in the large one.

The Christians saw them coming, but they had no chance to fight or to reach solid ground, so they commended themselves to God and awaited what would happen. The Indians, with the usual yell and cry, came close and surrounded them and shot all the arrows that they could at them. Because the mark was sure and not far, they hit where they aimed. The Spaniards were very unfortunate: at one end they *fol. 13* found themselves surrounded by Indians, the land was distant, and the water too shallow for the canoe to move; also, the other canoes had run aground. Unable to resist the shots of the Indians, they were all killed. The Indians, feeling great joy, stripped them until they were left in the nude. And because the water was beginning to rise, the other canoes could come up the river and see the damage the Indians had done, which greatly distressed them. Without separating from each other in the canoes, in spite of the Indians, they took all the necessary provisions in the villages that they came across. With that and the canoe in which the Christians had been killed, because it was too large for the Indians to take, they returned to where they had left the captain. When he learned of their misfortune, he felt great sorrow.

Note

1 The low-lying mangrove swamps along this coast extend several kilometers inland, and at low tide large flats are exposed, with only a handful of small navigable channels. The tidal range from mean high to low along this section is +4.36 meters to −1.12 meters; by contrast, the variation at Cartagena in the Caribbean is only +0.64 meters to −.45 meters. Cieza's observations on the difference in tides between the two bodies of water is correct. This sharp variation explains why the river can literally "rage" upstream with the incoming tide. See *Atlas básico de Colombia* (Bogotá: Instituto Geográfico "Agustín Codazzi," 1978), p. 42.

XII

About how Pedro de los Ríos came as governor to Tierra Firme and what Almagro did in Panama until he returned with people

Pedrarias Dávila had gone to Nicaragua, where he cut off the head of Captain Francisco Hernández, according to what the chronicler Gonzalo Hernández de Oviedo has written. The emperor sent from Spain as his governor of Tierra Firme a knight from Cordova named Pedro de los Ríos.[1] He arrived in Panama while Almagro was exploring with Pizarro, his partner, and he was received in his post by the city government and accepted as governor by those who were in the province. This understood, and returning to our subject, I say that I have already related how Diego de Almagro left Captain Pizarro with the Spaniards at the San Juan River and returned to Panama. When he arrived at Taboga Island,[2] he learned that Pedro de los Ríos was in the city as governor. It distressed him because he believed it would interfere with recruiting people from the land. He did not want to put into port until he found out from his partner, Father Luque, what he thought about all this. He quickly sent a messenger, writing to Luque about his arrival and why he had come, the gold he was bringing, and where he had left the Spaniards, as well as other things. He wrote another letter to Pedro de los Ríos, saying almost the same thing. It went with the letter to his partner, the maestrescuela, so that he would give it to [the governor] if it were appropriate or destroy it if it might be harmful.

fol. 13v But when the cleric Luque saw the letters, he spoke to Pedro de los Ríos, giving him the letter Almagro had sent him. [Ríos] replied[3] that it distressed him that so many Spaniards had died in that conquest. He promised to give as much support as he could because it was a service to God and the king. He ordered that Diego de Almagro should come to Panama, and [Almagro] was informed about it, and he entered the port of that city with his ship; all were saying that they had come from Peru. The governor came out to the shore with some knights to receive him. Almagro related to him at length everything that had happened and how they hoped they would discover a prosperous and densely populated land. When Pedro de los Ríos learned this, he confirmed the posts that Pizarro and Almagro had received from Pedrarias. He ordered that they be given the writ and allowed them to recruit people. Diego de Almagro collected with great difficulties and troubles up to forty Spaniards from among those who had arrived from Spain because at that time not as many came as nowadays. With these people and six horses, as well as fresh provisions that he could get of salt beef, hemp sandals and shirts, caps, things for the apothecary, and more of what was needed for those who were destitute, he again left Panama.

In the meantime, Francisco Pizarro and his companions wandered as usual through the rivers and mangroves, eaten by mosquitoes, suffering intolerable hardships and misfortunes, and detesting being in such hell. They all wanted to return to Panama, but since they still felt fear and shame, they did not dare to do it against their captain's will; furthermore, in a poor land there is no disloyalty. And where there is wealth, those very riches contradict virtue so that everything gives way to avarice, and to have money, murders are committed, and they pillage and do all that you have seen happening these years in this kingdom. When they stood around in little groups and talked, the Spaniards were muttering that Pizarro held them by force. He was aware of it but overlooked it because they were right, and one who is starving cannot be helped except with a feast. He awaited his partner with a great desire to see him. Not many days passed before they sighted the ship. Those who came in it disembarked, and the seamen were horrified to see the ones on land so yellow and thin.

Notes

1 Pedro de los Ríos was named governor of Castilla del Oro by Charles V in 1525. He was absent in Nicaragua for a period, but in 1527 was back in Panama and had completed his tenure as governor by 1529, when Licentiate Antonio de la Gama arrived to administer his *residencia,* a legal review of his term in office. See Mendiburu, *Diccionario,* 9:354–57.

2 Cieza refers here to a group of islands that, according to Oviedo, lie just a little more than a league off the shore of Panama. Between May and Au-

gust and November and February, large numbers of fish were taken for sale in Panama as the needlefish *(Agujas paladares)* came to shore to lay their eggs and larger fish followed to feed on them. See Gonzalo Fernández de Oviedo y Valdés, *Historia general y natural de las Indias,* ed. Juan Pérea de Tudela Bueso, 5 vols. (Madrid: Atlas, 1959), 5:9.

3 to Father Luque

XIII

About how the captains and the Spaniards embarked and sailed to Atacames,[1] *and what happened to them*

After[2] Diego de Almagro reunited with Captain Francisco Pizarro, as has been described in the previous chapter, they decided that all those who had arrived and those who were there before would embark and try to find the land that the Indians captured in the balsa by Bartolomé Ruiz had told them about. They tried to teach [the Indians] our language as quickly as possible so they would be able to respond to what they were asked and would become interpreters.[3] When they embarked, they traveled until they arrived at Gallo Island, where they stayed fifteen days recuperating from their previous hardships. When this period passed, they set out with the ships and canoes along the coast and a great river that emptied into the sea. Pizarro, who was in a canoe, wanted to enter it and explore there, but the canoe capsized on a bar between the sea and the river. The other canoe did not run such a great risk. The captain was in[4] it and saw the Spaniards swimming from the one that had been lost, and the canoe rushed to pick them up. They rescued all of them, except five who drowned. *fol. 14*

Leaving such a dangerous place, they withdrew to the ships and traveled as far as San Mateo Bay, where all of them went ashore. They brought out the horses and went toward Atacames with them; because the land was full of mangroves and rivers, they had not needed them before. They wished very much to encounter some man or woman from that region in order to get information about it. The horsemen spotted an Indian a good distance away, and eager to capture some, they rode full speed to seize him. But he sensed a trap and frightened of the horses, he fled with such swiftness that those who were following him were astonished. And[5] fearing to become captive in the power of the Spaniards, whose reputation of cruelty had been spreading, and eager not to lose his freedom, he ran with great audacity. One of the horsemen told me that his arrival and the Indian falling to the ground, losing his breath and vigor, and his soul expiring, occurred all at once.

The Spaniards did not cease marching—suffering more than be- *fol. 14v* fore because of the large number of mosquitoes. There were so many that in order to flee their onslaught, the men threw themselves in the sand, burying themselves up to their chins. It is a contagious scourge, this of the mosquitoes, and everyday Spaniards were dying from it and from other illnesses that afflicted them. A little further from that place they captured three or four Indians. They said, mostly by signs, what there was in that land. The journey by sea and by land proceeded until they reached the village of Atacames, where they found plenty of maize and other foods that the people here eat.

The natives of the land knew very well what was happening and how at sea there were ships and that white, bearded men were coming on land, who had horses that ran like the wind. They were asking each other, "What were they striving for or searching for; for what reason were they stealing from them the gold they found, and why were they capturing their women and were doing the same to them?" They increasingly abhorred them, and many formed a league to kill them.

The Spaniards, delighted with all the maize that they had found, ate leisurely because where there is want, if men have maize, they do not feel it; indeed, a very good honey can be made from it, as those who have made it know, and as thick as they want, because I have made some when I was there. And they have bread and wine and vinegar, so that with this and with the herbs that can always be found, and not lacking salt, those active in exploration would call themselves lucky.[6]

Some of the Indians came out into view, fearful because they have little courage, but they wished for an opportunity to safely cause some harm. Some of the Spaniards went out with bucklers and swords, not taking more than two horses, and they set upon the Indians. But they did not dare to wait, and regardless how quickly they darted into the sea, the spears were stained with the blood of several of them. Fearing such people, [the Indians] did not want to enter into previous tricks—I mean these because others were gathering troops
fol. 15 to attack the Christians, who were there more than eight days. And one day they heard a shot fired from the ships. Believing that a great horde of Indians was attacking them, the captain wanted to return to the bay. But after he discussed it with Almagro, it was not done because he commanded some Spaniards to take a hillock that was nearby in order to survey what was happening. And all it was were

fifteen or twenty large vixens, and because they had seen them from afar, they believed they were Indians. One of the horsemen went to investigate, and when he realized what it was, he informed them. And since all of them had left the camp, they were thirsty because there was no river or lake of the many that abound in other parts. To relieve the need, Pizarro ordered the horsemen to go and bring all the gourds that they had filled with water.[7]

Slightly more than two hundred natives had assembled in order to wage war against the Spaniards because they were in their land without reason or justice and against their will. Those who had ridden the horses saw [the Indians] as they were returning to the bay and decided to attack them. The Indians awaited them—to their own detriment—because eight were left dead in the field and three were captured; the rest fled, frightened of the horses. The Spaniards went with the water to where their companions, weak from thirst, waited for them. They all went to the bay where they found provisions, and they stayed there nine days. During that time they often discussed what they should do, and most were in favor of everybody returning to Panama in order to recuperate and recruit more people resolved to explore what lay ahead.

Almagro contradicted them, arguing that they were wrong to say that it would be expedient to return to Panama. Indeed, in returning poor, they would be begging for food for the love of God, and those with debts would be in jail. It was much better to remain where there were provisions and let the ships go to Panama for succor rather than to forsake the land. Some say that Pizarro was so distressed by the enormous hardships that he suffered while exploring that he then wished what had never been known in him, which was to return to Panama. He told Diego de Almagro that he was opposed to returning to Panama because he was always coming and going with the ships and never lacked provisions or suffered the excessive hardship that they had suffered. To that, Almagro replied that he would gladly remain with the people and that [Pizarro] should go to Panama for succor. And they had a heated exchange about this, so that friendship and brotherhood turned to animosity, and they reached for their swords and bucklers, determined to harm one another. But the pilot, Bar- *fol. 15v*
tolomé Ruiz, and Nicolás de Ribera and others intervened and pulled them apart, and mediating between them, they reconciled them, and

they embraced. Forgetting the passion, Captain Pizarro said that he would remain with the men wherever was best and that Almagro should return to Panama for succor. This[8] over, they left there, and they passed by the river in the bay to look at some villages that were visible to see if it would be advisable to stay in them or if they should search for another place.

Notes

1 Cieza wrote "Tacámez." Atacames is located on the Ecuadorian coast, between the mouth of the Esmeraldas River and Cape San Francisco. The Bay of Atacames may have had a total population of between eleven thousand and fifteen thousand at time of contact, which explains the stiff resistance; see Newson, *Life and Death,* pp. 67–9.

2 Captain

3 The capture of young men to be trained as interpreters was a policy well elaborated in the Caribbean.

4 in one of those that

5 the Indian

6 The Spanish often took by either barter or plunder what they needed for subsistence. In areas inhabited by hunters, fishers, and gatherers, with no stored surpluses of foodstuffs, the explorers faced more difficulties. By the time of the conquest of Peru, an ample contingent of seasoned colonists already understood the richness of American agricultural products and how to consume them.

7 Gourds were domesticated early and were used for a variety of purposes in Andean South America; see Edward P. Lanning, *Peru before the Incas* (Englewood Cliffs, N.J.: Prentice-Hall, 1967).

8 Cieza noted in the margin that "Nicolás de Ribera also informed me about this, who is of."

XIV

About how all the Spaniards wanted to return to Panama and could not, and how Diego de Almagro departed with the ships while Pizarro remained on Gallo Island, and about the couplet that they sent to Governor Pedro de los Ríos

The Spaniards had passed the river, but the land they saw did not please them because it was very rainy and too overgrown by forest. The rivers were full of Indian houses,[1] and there were enough of them to kill those [Spaniards] who remained. That was the reason why they sailed up the coast until they arrived at Tempula,[2] which they called Santiago, where there is a raging river. They stayed there eight to ten days, but were afraid of the Indians and quickly left that land. All of them spoke ill of Pizarro and Almagro, saying that they held them captive without allowing them to leave those mangroves; they all wanted to go. The captains tried to distract them with promising words, reassuring them with hope of what lay ahead, but most saw their exhortations as cumbersome, rather than cause for joy.

With these things they returned to San Mateo Bay, where they again deliberated on where would be the safest place for them to remain while Almagro went to Panama and came back for them. After many considerations it was agreed that Captain Pizarro would remain on Gallo Island until succor arrived. Most of the Spaniards repeated again that it would be best if all of them returned instead of perishing miserably where they did not even have sacred ground for burial. But their importunities played no part because God permitted that at that time the grandeur of Peru would be discovered.

Almagro prepared to go, taking great care to seize any letters, for *fol. 16* he knew that they were full of complaints about his partner and about him because they were persisting in the exploration. He embarked on one ship and departed. The other one took the men to Gallo Island, where they would stay. There were altogether a little more

5. Men on an island. Pedro de Cieza de León's *Primera Parte* (Seville, 1553), p. 65v. Courtesy of the Jay I. Kislak Foundation, Miami Lakes, Florida.

than eighty Spaniards because the rest had already died. At the end of the first month that they had been on Gallo Island, Captain Pizarro decided that the other ship would also go to Panama. The inspector, Carvallo, would go in it so it could be repaired, and he would come back in the one that carried Almagro. They contend that because the Spaniards were so disgruntled, some of them wrote letters to Governor Pedro de los Ríos, begging him to liberate them from their present captivity. Notwithstanding that Francisco Pizarro tried to ensure that no letters were sent, some did go. And they say that Doña Catalina de Saavedra, the governor's wife, had sent a request for some balls of cotton yarn—because she had been told that there was much of it in that region—and that one Spaniard sent in one of the clews a couplet that said:

To the Lord Governor.
Look it well over,
There goes the herder
While here remains the butcher.[3]

Yet, others have also stated that this couplet went in Almagro's ship among the letters for the governor. There was also a Spaniard named Loboto who went on Almagro's ship and who had been sent by the men to secure that they be set free so they could forsake those mangrove swamps. And he was able to leave because he was Almagro's friend; otherwise, he could not have gone.

After the ships departed, as has been said, Francisco Pizarro remained with the Spaniards on Gallo Island. The island Indians did not want such neighbors, and they preferred to leave them their houses and land rather than to remain among them. They crossed to the mainland, complaining about the interlopers, referring to the Spaniards. There were not many provisions on the island. So much water poured from the sky that it normally rained most of the time. The thick cloudiness permeated the heavens and the air space below so that the sun provided little brightness. Thus, they did not see in the heavens the serenity that comforts and gladdens men, but only darkness and the sound of thunder along with the great flashing of lightning. Mosquitoes multiply abundantly in these conditions, and because the natives were gone, they all swarmed at the unfortunate *fol. 16v* men who had remained alone on the island. Many were half naked, without anything to cover themselves with. Since they were soaking wet and in those forests and on poor pathways, part[4] of them died because even without all this punishment they were already dying of hunger and could find almost nothing to eat. With reason, some said that death would be the end of suffering. Certainly there were times when I had endured such a life during similar explorations that I had wished for it. The readers should consider what these [men] experienced, although it is one thing to talk about it and another to feel it.

Francisco Pizarro realized their need for food and discussed with his companions that it would be useful to make a boat and cross to the mainland to search for maize. For the common good, they put it into effect, and although it took a great effort, they finished it. Several Spaniards crossed to the mainland, and they returned loaded with maize, and thus they sustained themselves for several days.

Notes

1 The term Cieza uses is again the Taino word, *caneyes*. In this region the houses were round and made of light supporting timbers with a covering of canes.

2 Cieza contemplated two spellings for Tempula, both incorrect: "Tenpula" and "Tenpulla." At the site of the present Tempula River, this event probably took place near the end of July 1527; see Busto, *Historia general*, p. 39.

3 "A señor governador. Miraldo bien por entero; allá va el recojedor y acá queda el carniçero." This couplet marks one of the dramatic events to take place during the discovery of Peru; notice of this derogatory couplet appeared in virtually every later account.

4 many

XV

About how when Diego de Almagro arrived in Panama, Governor Pedro de los Ríos, distressed by the death of so many people, did not allow him to recruit more. And how [Ríos] sent Juan Tafur to set free the Spaniards, and what Pizarro did with the letters his partners had sent him

When Diego de Almagro left on the ship, as has been said, he proceeded on his voyage to Panama, where he arrived shortly. When Governor Pedro de los Ríos learned why he had come, he was not pleased. First, he expressed concern because so many Spaniards had died in that land without reaping any benefits from all the hardship they had endured and continued to endure. He said with resolve that he would find a solution to prevent the harm from continuing. Diego de Almagro pointed out how much they had spent and what they owed, and how they had great reports on what lay ahead. [The governor] and all the others laughed at [Almagro], saying that in the land of Peruquete,[1] "What could there be, but good rivers and plenty of mangroves?"

The maestrescuela, Don Hernando de Luque, attempted with all his force to convince Pedro de los Ríos not to hamper Pizarro's discovery. Neither he nor Almagro succeeded because Pedro de los Ríos wanted to send for the Spaniards, although in the end, and with great difficulty, they did obtain [a concession] from him. If twenty of the Spaniards who were involved in the conquest wanted to follow Francisco Pizarro of their own free will, he would grant licence for one ship to proceed with the discovery along the same coast, but they would have to be back in Panama within six months. And if they could not gather twenty, and only ten men joined, he would give the same licence. It was clear that Pedro de los Ríos did this in order to be done with Luque and Almagro because it was well known that he told Juan Tafur, who was the one carrying the order, to strive that no Christian remain in those forests. *fol. 17*

When this was decreed, Almagro and Father Luque were greatly dismayed, assessing the enterprise from the beginning, how much they had worked and spent, how much they owed, and how little they had to repay it.[2] They decided to write to Pizarro, urging him not to return to Panama, even in the face of death. Indeed, if he did not discover something that was good, they would be lost and dishonored forever. Juan Tafur left with the ships and sailed until he arrived at Gallo Island, at the same time that [the Spaniards there] had brought the load of maize in the boat.[3]

Notes

1 For "Peruquete" see chapter 3.

2 The exact nature of the partnership of the principal venturers has been examined carefully by Lockhart, *Men of Cajamarca*, pp. 70–77.

3 According to Busto (*Historia general*, p. 39), Tafur arrived near the end of September 1527.

XVI

About how Juan Tafur arrived where the Christians were and how they were set free, all of them wanting to return, except thirteen; and they and Pizarro remained

Juan Tafur arrived with the ships at Gallo Island. When the Spaniards who were with Captain Francisco Pizarro realized why he had come, they wept from joy. It seemed to them that they were leaving a worse captivity than that of Egypt.[1] They bestowed many blessings on the governor for showing them such favor. [Tafur] presented the order, and it was obeyed, though Pizarro was dismayed when he saw that all wanted to leave. Taking into account what his partners had written him, he resolved to persevere in his quest, trusting that God would give him the courage and the means to carry it out. With quiet demeanor he told his companions that by virtue of the order that had come from Panama they could return and that the choice was in their *fol. 17v* hands. If he had not allowed them to leave, it was because they would be compensated if they discovered good land; furthermore, he considered returning poor to Panama harder than trying to escape death because they would face difficulties. And he told them further that he took satisfaction in one thing: if they had suffered hardship and hunger, he had not avoided suffering either; on the contrary, he was always in the lead, as all had seen. Therefore, he was begging them to examine and reconsider their options and to follow him, taking a sea route to discover what there was. After all, the Indians that Bartolomé Ruiz had seized said such marvelous things about the land ahead.[2]

Although the captain said these and other things to his companions, they did not want to hear it; rather, they urged Juan Tafur to return to Panama and deliver them from those forests. Only thirteen—out of compassion they felt for [Pizarro] and because they did not want to go back to Panama—said that they would accompany him and would live or die with him. Because God permitted Francisco Pizarro to discover Peru with these thirteen, as will be told later, I will name them all.[3] I say their names are: Cristóbal de Peralta,[4] Nicolás de Ribera,[5] Pedro de Candia,[6] Domingo de Soraluce,[7] Francisco de

Cuéllar,[8] Alonso de Molina,[9] Pedro Halcón,[10] García de Jarén,[11] Antón de Carrión,[12] Alonso Briceño,[13] Martín de Paz, and Juan de la Torre.[14] These men willingly offered to remain with Pizarro, who was elated, thanking God for it since it pleased Him to put the steadfastness into their hearts.

[Pizarro] asked Juan Tafur to give him one of the ships as the governor had ordered so that he and those who wanted to follow him could explore what lay ahead. Tafur did not want to give the ship, which was a further vexation for the troubled Pizarro. It was useless to demand it or to protest or to beg, or even to talk of profits and make great promises so that [Tafur] would let him keep one of the ships. And as [Pizarro] realized it, exasperated, he told him to be off and that he would remain with that handful [of men] until they sent him a ship from Panama. Tafur did not believe that so few men would want to stay among the Indians because it was more foolish than courageous, and he replied that he would go in due time. After this
fol. 18 the captain spoke with those who were to stay with him to determine the safest place to wait, without fear of the Indians, until a ship was sent from Panama. They had discussed it and considered it well and agreed to remain on Gorgona Island. Even though it was a poor land, it was uninhabited; it had water, and with the maize that they had they could spend several days there. [Pizarro] wrote to his partners about the situation he was in and how important it was to send him a ship with all speed in order to discover the land that the Indians who had been captured on the balsa had told them about. He also wrote to the governor, expressing displeasure with what he had decreed. They embarked, while Pizarro remained on Gorgona with those already named, along with some Indian men and women.[15] They say Juan Tafur acted so badly that he did not even allow them to unload the maize they were to be left with and that they threw it ashore because they were in such a hurry. There, much of it rotted. [Tafur] wanted to take with him the Indians from Tumbez that Pizarro had as interpreters, but in the end he gave them to him, and Ribera went to get them from the ship that they were on.

Juan Tafur and the Spaniards went back to Panama after Francisco Pizarro had begged the pilot, Bartolomé Ruiz, to return on the ship that would come. And he remained on Gorgona with his thirteen companions.

Notes

1 The events of the captivity of the Jews in Egypt was something that most sixteenth-century Spaniards knew well and could easily relate to.

2 This event was told and retold by subsequent authors, with much embellishment. The most often quoted version is that of El Inca Garcilaso de la Vega, whose text approaches epic quality: "He took his sword in hand and with its tip traced a line on the sand, facing toward Peru, the direction of his hopes, and turning his face to them said: Gentlemen, this line stands for the labor, hunger, thirst and toil, the wounds and sickness, and all the other dangers and tribulations that have to be met in this conquest, and that one has to face until life ends. Those who have the spirit to endure and vanquish them in such a heroic undertaking, should cross the line as a sign and demonstration of the valor of their spirit, and to give testimony and certify that they are my loyal companions." See *Los Comentarios Reales de los Incas*, 4 vols., ed. Horacio H. Urteaga (Lima: Imprenta Gil, 1943), 3:270–71. Cieza's much more authentic version shows a more careful and deliberate Pizarro compared to Garcilaso de la Vega's flamboyant figure.

3 Cieza lists twelve, not thirteen. The missing person is Gonzalo Martín de Trujillo, who figures in Cieza's narrative in the following chapter. He was dead by the time of the ransom of Atahualpa; see Busto, *Historia general*, p. 41.

4 Peralta was reportedly an hidalgo from the city of Baeza; see Busto, *Historia general*, p. 41.

5 See chapter 2.

6 Born on the island of Crete, he would later play an important part in the conquest due to his metalworking skills. The major elements of his career are outlined in chapter 21.

7 Cieza uses "Soria Lucina" rather than "Soraluce." According to James Lockhart (*Spanish Peru, 1532–1560: A Colonial Society* [Madison: University of Wisconsin Press, 1968], pp. 78–79) and Busto (*Historia general*, p. 41), he was a Basque merchant born in Vergara. He secured a major fortune in the venture, but was dead before early 1537.

8 He may have been born in Cuéllar (Busto, *Diccionario*, 1:409–410). He was with Pizarro in Panama by 1524. After Gallo Island, he continued with the others to Tumbez and Santa. In 1528 he testified in Panama in favor of several colleagues. He was confirmed town councillor, but disappears from view in 1529.

9 From Ubeda, according to Busto, *Historia general*, p. 41.

10 From Cazalla de la Sierra, north of Seville; see Busto, *Historia general,* p. 41.

11 Cieza calls him "García de Jerez." Busto identifies him as "Jarén, Utrera merchant and slaver of Nicaraguan Indians" (*Historia general,* p. 41).

12 From Carrión de los Condes, he was in Panama by 1522 and participated in the first and second expeditions. He was in Panama in 1528, acting as a witness for García de Jarén and Pedro de Candia, then seems to disappear; see Busto, *Diccionario,* 1:348–49.

13 Briceño was born in Benavente about 1506. He reached Nicaragua by 1525 and participated in Pizarro's second and third expeditions. Briceño and Candia were the only ones of "the thirteen" to be at Cajamarca. Following the distribution of Atahualpa's ransom, he returned to Spain and probably went back to Benavente. See Lockhart, *Men of Cajamarca,* pp. 215–16; Busto, *Diccionario,* 1:69–70.

14 Born in Villagarcía near Llerena, Cieza's hometown, around 1479, Torre came to the Indies about 1516. His father had been one of the original settlers of Hispaniola and Puerto Rico. He went with Pizarro on his second and third voyage, and remained in San Miguel after it was founded. He eventually settled in Arequipa and held a lucrative encomienda. He died in 1580. Archivo General de Indias, Seville, Lima 144; Justicia 471; Patronato 124, ramo 4.

15 These Native Americans are not included in the list of the "famous," nor do we know their exact number.

XVII

About how Captain Francisco Pizarro remained on the deserted island and of the many things he and his companions endured, and about the arrival of the ships in Panama

Those who have seen Gorgona Island, as I have, will not be astonished how much I stress what the Spaniards endured, and that is without saying anything about its dense vegetation and the heavens always ready to pour rain on it. In the Ocean Sea, between the Indies and the Terceras,[1] there is an island that they call Bermuda. It is famous because in its vicinity sailors are continually tormented, and they flee from there as if from pestilence. In the South Sea, Gorgona has the reputation of being neither land nor an island, but the apparition of hell. Yet, Francisco Pizarro wanted to stay in a place he knew to be so terrible because he believed it was safer than Gallo Island or the main- *fol. 18v* land. The hardships they suffered there were in the extreme because rain, thunder, and lightning are continuous. The sun peeks out rarely, and it is a wonder when the clouds break so that the stars can be seen in the heavens. There are enough mosquitoes to wage war on all the Turk's men.[2] There are no people, nor would there be any reason for them to populate such wretched land. There are many forests, and they are just as thick as they are frightening. As to what surrounds this island and its degrees, I already have written about in *Part One*.[3]

Without losing faith in their effort [and] as well as they could, the Spaniards built ranchos, which are what we call huts here, in order to protect themselves from the rain. From a ceiba tree[4] they made a small canoe, in which the captain with one of his companions went to catch fish so that on some days all could eat. Other times he went with his crossbow and killed what we call *guadaquinajes*,[5] which are larger than hares, and their meat is just as good. And they say that one day he alone with his crossbow killed ten of these. Thus, they were filled with great forbearance, and [Pizarro] kept unfailingly providing food for his companions. Such was his tenacity that he did it with just

the crossbow and the canoe, without ever complaining about the rain or about never being able to dry off or having to listen to the continuous noise of the mosquitoes. Martín de Trujillo[6] and Peralta were ill on this island; the guadaquinajes sufficiently cured them so that they could eat. They found a fruit on that island that almost resembled a chestnut. It is so beneficial to purge with that only one is enough, and no other rhubarb is necessary. One of the Spaniards ate two, and he was so purged that it would make a mockery out of a fast.[7] They saw another forest fruit similar to small grapes; they ate some, and they were very tasty. Among the rocks and the concavities of the rocks on the island coast they caught fish, and often they came across monstrously large snakes, but they were quite harmless. There are also huge monkeys and small mottled cats[8] and other strange beasts worthy of being seen. Born in the highlands of the island, rivers of ex-
fol. 19 cellent water flow downward. One can see every month of the year during full moon that at day's end, as the sun is setting, an infinite number of what we call needlefish come to this island through some of its concavities to lay eggs on the shore.

The Spaniards gleefully waited for them with clubs and killed as many as they wanted, and they fished many snappers, sharks, and they also found shellfish, which it pleased God was sufficient to sustain them, along with the maize that they had left over, so that they never lacked food. Every morning they thanked God and at night likewise, saying the Ave Maria and other prayers as Christians, whom God wished to protect from so many dangers. Through the prayers they knew the feast days and were able to keep track of Fridays and Sundays. With this I will leave them to pass their days until the ship returns for them, and I will tell how Juan Tafur arrived with the other Christians in Tierra Firme, which they called Castilla del Oro.[9]

Notes

1 The Azores. One of the principal islands of the group retains the Portuguese name, Terceira.

2 Charles V engaged Spanish troops against the Turks several times. The Turk in question is Suleiman the Magnificent, the sultan of the Ottoman

Empire between 1520 and 1566. For a synopsis of Charles V's policy toward the Ottoman Empire, see Lynch, *Spain under the Habsburgs,* 1:85–90.

3 See chapter 3.

4 A tropical silk-cotton tree.

5 Cieza refers here to capybaras, the largest rodents along the shores of rivers and lakes throughout South America.

6 Trujillo, whom Cieza omitted from his list of the thirteen at Gallo Island, does appear here.

7 The root of an Asian species of rhubarb, the *Rheum officinale,* was a commonly used purgative, an integral part of sixteenth-century Spanish pharmacopoeia. See Mercedes Fernández-Carrión and José Luis Valverde, *Farmacia y sociedad en Sevilla en el siglo XVI* (Sevilla: Biblioteca de Temas Sevillanos, 1985). In *Historia medicinal de las cosas que traen de nuestras Indias occidentales que sirven en medicina* [1574], facs. ed. (Seville: Padilla Libros, 1988), Nicolás Monardes wrote that he had received from Tierra Firme "a piece of root called there 'ruybarbo' " (f. 100r) similar in purgative qualities to the Asian variety. Covarrubias extolled the root's curative powers: it purges bile and phlegm, moderates the stomach, helps the liver and spleen, cleanses the blood, resolves jaundice and dropsy, eliminates high fevers, and slows hemorrhage (*Tesoro de la lengua*).

8 Perhaps an ocelot or one of the varieties of the *Margary trigina.*

9 It literally means "Golden Castile." Sauer (*Early Spanish Main,* p. 247) provides the earliest notice of the term in a royal order of 1513, naming Pedrarias Dávila governor of a "land which until now has been called Tierra Firme and we now order that it shall be called Castilla del Oro." It was the southern littoral of the Caribbean, from roughly the southern part of the Yucatan to the Gulf of Paria.

XVIII

About how Juan Tafur arrived in Panama and how one ship returned to Gorgona to Captain Francisco Pizarro

Juan Tafur and the Christians who had embarked on the ships left Captain Francisco Pizarro on the island, and they sailed until they arrived in Panama, where Governor Pedro de los Ríos was. [The governor] was distressed when he learned that Francisco Pizarro had remained on Gorgona with so few Spaniards. He said that if they should die or if the Indians came to kill them, it would be their own fault since they refused to come on the ships with Juan Tafur.

Those who did come related so many sorrowful stories about the hardship and hunger they had suffered that it was very painful to listen to them. Father Luque and Diego de Almagro read the letters from their partner Francisco Pizarro and shed many tears of compassion for him. They were determined to send a ship quickly so that he could either proceed with the discovery or return to Panama. They went to the governor to request a licence for it, expounding to him important reasons for doing it. He replied that he neither wanted to grant such licence nor allow a ship to leave Panama. Almagro vehemently protested, declaring that there was no justice in it because they had suffered and spent so much in the discovery, and he refused to allow a ship to go and bring back those who had remained on the island. Given these and other things that Almagro said, the governor
fol. 19v acknowledged that he was right and issued the licence for the ship to go. The two partners rejoiced and quickly loaded many provisions on one of the ships in the port. When it was ready for the voyage, they returned to the governor to tell him to inspect the shipment because they wanted to send it off. They say that he regretted that he had granted the licence[1] and responded that he would send someone to inspect the ship, register it, and report to him if it was in a condition to sail. But he secretly told one[2] Juan de Castañeda to go along with a carpenter named Hernando to see the ship and to say that it was unfit to sail or leave port until they repaired it. But they say that Castañeda, comporting himself as a Christian, acted better than Pedro de los Ríos had ordered because his inspection helped and did not harm

anything. Rather, Pedro de los Ríos himself soon sent for Diego de Almagro and told him that the ship should sail with God's blessing in search of the captain, as long as they fulfilled the order signed by him. The substance of it was that they could sail for up to six months, and after that they would come to Panama to report what they had done or else face the penalties he had set.

This done, the maestrescuela, Don Hernando de Luque, and Diego de Almagro wrote joyful letters to the captain, saying how well he had demonstrated his great courage since he dared to stay with so few people in such a desolate and wretched land. Furthermore, they had worked hard to send him the ship because the governor was impeding it. Therefore, he should attempt to reach the Tumbez region that the Indians had told them of; after all, the ship was being piloted by Bartolomé Ruiz, who was the one who captured them on the balsa. After they wrote him of these and other things, Bartolomé Ruiz left with the ship, without taking any more men than the sailors, and he sailed swiftly in the direction of Gorgona.

The captain and the Spaniards who had stayed passed their days with the difficulties described in the previous chapter, eating the shellfish and fish they had caught and the maize that they had left over, awaiting the ship as if it were the salvation of their souls. They longed for it so much that they fancied the small clouds forming far at sea was it. When they realized that it was not coming so long after the *fol. 20* ships had left them, they were dismayed and weary, and became determined to build rafts in order to return to Panama down the coast. Having agreed to this, they saw, well at sea, the ship approaching one day. Some thought it was a log, others that it was something else, and because they had yearned for it so long, even when they recognized a sail, they did not believe it. But as it came closer, the sails whitened, and they realized that it was what they had longed for, and they became ecstatic and could not speak from the excitement. And it entered the port of the island at the noon hour.[3] The pilot, Bartolomé Ruiz, then disembarked with some sailors, and they all embraced one another with delight. Those from the land told those who had come by sea what they had gone through on the island; likewise, [the sailors] related what happened to them during the voyage, as is normally done.

Notes

1 A similar change of heart took place a decade earlier when Governor Diego Velásquez of Cuba, fearing a challenge to his authority, decided that he had made a mistake choosing Hernán Cortés to lead an expedition to explore the mainland.

2 a carpenter named

3 The group had been stranded about six months; Ruiz's rescue ship reached them in March 1528. See Busto, *Historia general,* p. 41.

XIX

About how Captain Francisco Pizarro and his companions left the island and what they did

After the ship arrived at Gorgona, as has been related, and Francisco Pizarro had seen the letters from his partners, he and those who were with him discussed that because sufficient provisions had come on the ship, it would be best for all the Indian men and women who were in their service to remain on that island with their baggage, which was not much, and care for the three[1] Spaniards who were most feeble. This idea was approved by everyone, and Peralta, Trujillo, and Paz remained; they, along with everything else, were to be picked up by the ship on its return. The Indians from Tumbez came along because they already knew how to speak [Spanish], and it would be inadvisable to go without having them as interpreters. The captain and the others embarked and sailed directly west and up the coast.[2] It pleased God to grant them such good weather that after they sailed for twenty days, they detected an island across from Tumbez and near Puná, which they named Santa Clara. Because they needed firewood *fol. 20v* and water, they landed there to take on provisions.

There are no settlements on that island, but it was held as sacred in that district, and occasionally [the Indians] made great sacrifices there, presenting the offering of the *capacocha*.[3] The demon, who with God's permission so dominated these people, was seen by the priests. They worshiped several idols or stones. When the Indians from Tumbez who traveled on the ship saw the islet, they recognized it and joyfully told the captain how close they were to their own land. Having lowered the small boat, the captain and several Spaniards went ashore, and they came across the *huaca*[4] where [the Indians] worshipped, which was their stone idol—slightly larger than a man's head, tapered, with a sharp point. They saw a great sample of the wealth of the land ahead of them because they found many small gold and silver pieces shaped as hands or a woman's breasts or heads, and a large silver vessel—which was the first that was taken—that could hold an *arroba*[5] of water, as well as some pieces of wool, which are their marvellously sumptuous and beautiful *mantas*.[6] When

6. Customs of the Indians. Pedro de Cieza de León's *Primera Parte* (Seville, 1553), p. 10v. Courtesy of the Jay I. Kislak Foundation, Miami Lakes, Florida.

the Spaniards saw and got these things, they were as happy as can be imagined. Pizarro lamented for those who had gone with Juan Tafur because by not coming with him, they then would miss taking part in such a great wordly event. They withdrew to the ship and listened to the Indians from Tumbez telling them that what they had found on that island was nothing compared to what there was in the other large settlements of their land.

Another day, as they sailed along their route, at the hour of the nones,[7] they saw a balsa approaching by sea, so large that it resembled a ship. They overtook it with their ship and captured fifteen or twenty Indians who were traveling in it, dressed in mantas, shirts, and war garb; within a short while they saw four other balsas with people.

They asked the Indians who were in the one they had captured where they were going and where they were from. They replied that they were from Tumbez and that they had left to wage war on those from Puná, who were their enemies, which the interpreters [the Spaniards] *fol. 21* had brought with them affirmed. When [the Spaniards] came next to the other balsas, they captured them along with the Indians who were in them, making them understand that they were not detaining them in order to hold them captive or to imprison them, but so that they could go together with [Pizarro] to Tumbez. They were happy to hear this, and they marveled at the ship and its instruments and how white and bearded the Spaniards were.

The pilot, Bartolomé Ruiz, was approaching land, and when [the Spaniards] realized that there were neither forests nor mosquitoes,[8] they thanked God for it. When they arrived on the beach of Tumbez, they anchored, and the captain told the Indians captured on the balsas that they should know he did not come to wage war or to cause them any offense or harm, but to get to know them in order to have them as friends and companions. They should go with God's speed to their land and tell all this to their caciques. With their balsas and everything that they carried on them, without missing anything, the Indians went on shore, telling the captain that they would relate this to their lords and that they would return quickly for them as he ordered. The Indians from Tumbez were able to tell the Indians all this that was said to them and other things, and to respond to their questions because they had spent so many days with [the Spaniards] that they had learned a large part of our language.

Notes

1 two

2 They sailed south; they went against the strong currents—hence, "up" the coast.

3 A capacocha is any solemn ritual procession; for variations in the ritual, see Sabine MacCormack, *Religion in the Andes: Vision and Imagination in Early Colonial Peru* (Princeton: Princeton University Press, 1991).

4 Huaca is a Quechua term referring to a spiritual object, force, or place and can be a rock, a mountain, lake, or spring—in fact, any natural unusual

object. In the Andean world, the word is still used to distinguish the pre-Christian religious connotation from the Christian.

5 As a measure of weight, the arroba was approximately twenty-five pounds; the liquid measure varied by region and time.

6 Woven cloths of cotton or wool fiber, the mantas were a major item in the Andean economy. Various types of wool were used. The coarse, plain-colored *abasca* mantas made of alpaca fibers were the most common. The fine *cumbi,* made often of vicuña, and of brilliant hue, were prized items for reciprocal exchange and sacrifice. See John Victor Murra, *The Economic Organization of the Inka State* (Greenwich: JAI Press, 1980), pp. 65–84.

7 The fifth of the seven canonical hours, corresponding to three P.M.

8 They had finally reached the north coast of present Peru, where the climate shifts from tropical to semiarid and, not much farther to the south, a true desert.

XX

About how the Indians who left the ship reported about the Spaniards, which those from the land marveled at, and how they sent them provisions and water and other things

When the natives of the mainland saw the ship approaching on the sea, they were astounded because they were seeing something they had never seen or heard about before. They did not know what to say about it. They saw at the same time how they put into port and dropped the anchors, and how the Indians captured on the balsas—according to what had been related—descended from the ship. They [the Indians of the balsas] did not stop until they arrived before[1] their lord, in whose presence and that of many people who had gathered they related how they went on the sea and encountered a ship with some white men, who were attired and had large beards. According *fol. 21v* to what certain Indians—their compatriots, brought as interpreters—told them, [the white men] were searching for lands because many of them were traveling in other ships by sea, and these had left from an island where they had stayed many days.[2] They spoke to their lord about what they heard from the Indians who had come with the Spaniards and about what they themselves saw and heard. They were quite astonished, believing that such people were sent by God's hand and that it would be proper to give them a warm reception. Then ten or twelve balsas were prepared—replete with food and fruit, many jugs of water and *chicha*,[3] and fish and a lamb[4] that the virgins of the temple[5] gave to take to them. The Indians went to the ship with all this without any guile or malice, but rather with joy and pleasure to see such people.

The captain received it gratefully and with a loving attitude; he and his companions were delighted when they saw the lamb among what they had brought them. Among the Indians was an *orejón*,[6] one of those with the deputy who resided there, who said to the captain that they could safely come on land without being harmed and provision themselves with water and whatever they needed. The captain replied that he had no misgivings about trusting people who seemed so rational. Then a sailor named Bocanegra[7] went in a small boat and, along with the Indians who helped him, filled twenty casks with water; as I said, the natives were helping him to do it. When the orejón saw the Christians, he took them for very rational people since they were not causing any harm, but rather gave of what they had brought. After he saw the ship and its equipment, he thought it expedient to send an official report about those people to Quito to King Huayna Capac, his lord. He looked at and asked so much that the Spaniards were astonished to see such a sagacious and knowing Indian, who—as well as he could through the Indians serving as interpreters—asked the captain where they were from, what land they had come from, and what were they looking for, or what their purpose was in going by sea and land without stopping. Francisco Pizarro replied that they had come from Spain, where they were native, and that in that land there was a great and powerful king named Don Carlos,[8] whose vassals and servants they were, and many others because he ruled large territories. They had left to explore these parts, as they could see, and to place what they found under the authority of that king, but, primarily and *fol. 22* above all things, to let them know that the idols they worshipped were false and the sacrifices they made were without foundation. And in order to save themselves they had to become Christians and believe in the God that [the Spaniards] worshipped, who was in heaven and was called Jesus Christ, because those who did not worship him and obey his commandments would go to hell, a dark place and full of fire. Those who knowing the truth take him as God—the only Lord of the heaven, sea, and earth, along with the rest that has been created—will be dwellers in heaven, where they will remain forever.

Captain Francisco Pizarro told these and many other things to that orejón, so much that he was astounded hearing them. He was on the ship from morning to the hour of vespers.[9] The captain ordered that they should give him food and drink of our wine, and he gazed at that brew, which seemed to him better and tastier than theirs. When he was leaving, the captain gave him an iron axe, which strangely pleased him, esteeming it more than if they had given him one hundred times more gold than it weighed. And he further gave him a few pearls and three pieces of chalcedony; for the *cacique principal*[10] he gave one sow, one boar, four hens, and one rooster.[11] With this the orejón left, and as he was going, he asked the captain to permit two or three Christians to come with him because [the Indians] would take pleasure in seeing them. The captain ordered Alonso de Molina and one Black to go.[12]

When the cacique saw the presents, he appreciated them more than I can express, and all came to see the sow and the boar and the hens, delighting in hearing the rooster crow. But all that was nothing compared to the commotion created by the Black man. Because they saw that he was black, they looked at him over and over again, and made him wash to see if his blackness was color or some kind of applied confection. But he laughed, showing his white teeth, as some came to see him and then others, so many that they did not even give him time to eat. They looked at the Spaniard, [noting] how he had a beard and was white. They asked him many things, but he understood nothing. The children, the old, and the women—all looked at them with great merriment. Alonso de Molina saw many buildings and notable things in Tumbez. Both he and the Black were well served with food. The latter walked here and there wherever they wanted to see him, as something so new and by them never seen before. Alonso de Molina saw the fortress of Tumbez, irrigation channels, many planted fields, and fruits and some sheep.[13] Many Indian women—very beautiful and well attired, dressed according to their fashion—came to talk to him. They all gave him fruits and whatever they had to take to the ship. They used signs to ask where [the Spaniards] were going and *fol. 22v*
where had they come from. He replied in the same manner. Among those Indian women who were talking to him there was a very beautiful lady, and she told him to stay with them and that they would give him as wife one from among them, whichever one he would wish. Alonso de Molina asked the cacique, lord of that land, permission to leave, and he gave it to him, sending with him many provisions for the captain. And when he arrived at the ship, he was so overwhelmed by what he had seen that he did not relate anything. He said that the houses were of stone, and that before he spoke to the lord, he passed through three gates where they had gatekeepers who guarded them, and that they served him in cups of silver and gold.

The captain gave many thanks to God our Lord for it. He complained about the Spaniards who had returned [to Panama] and Pedro de los Ríos because he made it happen. In truth, he was deceiving himself because if he had come with [all of] them and tried to wage war for money, [the Indians] would have easily killed them because Huayna Capac was alive and there were no divisions like those [Pizarro] later found when he returned. If they wanted to convert with kind words the people they had found so gentle and peaceful, then those who had returned were not necessary because those who were with him [Pizarro] sufficed. But matters of the Indies are the judgments of God, coming from His profound wisdom, and He knows why He permitted what happened.

Notes

1 in the presence of

2 The peoples of the north Andean coast had encountered "foreigners" before, especially people from the upper Amazon basin and from the coastal lowlands north of the Gulf of Guayaquil.

3 Beer, generally made from corn, although yucca could be used also.

4 Llama or alpaca.

5 This is the first mention of the *mamaconas,* or the "virgins" of the temple, who reminded the Europeans of Christian nuns. These young women, selected from each province and chosen for their perfection and skill, served many functions: in temple ceremonies and sacrifices, in the preparation of chicha and the weaving of the finest cumbi cloth, and as concubines of the Inca or elite males. See Irene Silverblatt, *Moon, Sun, and Witches: Gender Ideologies and Class in Inca and Colonial Peru* (Princeton: Princeton University Press, 1987), pp. 81–108.

6 Spaniards called officials of the Inca *ayllu* (lineage) or of the provincial elite orejones (large ears) because of the large ear plugs they wore.

7 Andrés de Bocanegra.

8 Holy Roman Emperor Charles V (1516–58), the grandson of Ferdinand and Isabela, ruled a realm that combined the crowns of Castile and Aragon, Burgundy, and the Habsburg empire. He was one of the most powerful monarchs of sixteenth-century Europe and the leader of the secular arm of the Counter-Reformation.

9 Evening.

10 The head chief of an administrative or ethnic entity. In the Andes he often had one or more secondary leaders under him.

11 The gift of animals is interesting considering the Spaniards had so recently complained of starvation. They did carry livestock on board, and pigs and chickens were particularly hardy. In the Caribbean, the Spaniards often

left some of these animals on deserted islands, hoping to return later to collect their offspring as food to supply new expeditions.

12 There were numerous Black slaves in Panama in the 1520s, and many participated in the Peruvian venture. A slave had saved the life of Diego de Almagro. As Lockhart points out, the records are remarkably silent regarding the sure participation of Blacks in the conquest. Juan García, a Black from Old Castile, acted as crier and piper; mulatto horseman Miguel Ruiz (his mother was a slave) from Seville received a double share of treasure at Cajamarca. See Lockhart, *Men of Cajamarca*, pp. 35–36, and Frederick P. Bowser, *The African Slave in Colonial Peru, 1524–1650* (Stanford: Stanford University Press, 1974), p. 4.

13 Camelidae.

XXI

About how the captain ordered Pedro de Candia[1] *to go and see whether what Alonso de Molina said he saw in the land of Tumbez was true*

Among the things Alonso de Molina told the captain that he had seen was a fortress that seemed to be very strong because it had six or seven walls, and there were many riches inside. When Pizarro learned about these things, he considered them so remarkable that he did not entirely believe in them. He thought of sending Pedro de Candia, who was quite ingenious, to see whether what Molina and the Black had said was true and to trace the land and ascertain where it would be easy to enter when, if it pleased God, they returned. Pedro de Candia was delighted to do this and soon departed.

fol. 23 As always, the Indians were on the beach, and they went with him until they brought him into the presence of the lord of Tumbez, who was accompanied by many of his Indians. He and they were surprised to see Pedro de Candia's stature, and they begged him to discharge an arquebus that he carried because he had done it on the ship several times in the presence of some Indians, which was the reason why the others knew about it. In order to please them, he placed the fuse, and aiming at a thick board that was near there, he hit it and shot through it as if it were a melon. When the arquebus discharged, many of the Indians fell to the ground, and others screamed, and they judged the Christian as very brave because of his stature and for discharging those shots. Some say that the lord of Tumbez ordered that they should bring a lion and a tiger[2] they had there to see if Candia could defend himself from them or if they would kill him. They brought them and set them loose on Candia, who, having the arquebus loaded, fired it, and more Indians than before fell to the ground in fright. And without the Indians, the animals came to him as gentle as if they were lambs, as Candia told it. The cacique ordered them returned to where they had been. He asked Candia for the arquebus and poured many cups of their maize wine into the barrel, saying: "Take it, drink, since[3] one makes such great noise with you that you are similar to the thunder of the heavens."[4] And he ordered Pedro de Candia to sit down. They gave him plenty to eat and asked him many things about what they wanted to know. He answered what he could to make them understand. He saw the fortress. The mamaconas, who are the sacred virgins, wanted to see him, and they sent to beg the ruler to bring him there. Thus it was done. They were extremely pleased to see Candia. They were skilled in working with wool, of which they made fine cloth, and they were in the service of the temple.[5] Most of them were beautiful, and all were very affectionate.

Because Pedro de Candia had seen the fortress and the other things *fol. 23v* that the captain had ordered, he asked permission of the lord to return to the ship. He gave it to him, ordering that balsas with plenty of maize, fish, and fruit go along. And to the captain he sent with Candia a beautiful ram and quite a fat lamb.[6] When he was back on the ship, Candia told the captain so many things that what Alonso de Molina said was nothing in comparison. [Candia] said that he saw silver vessels and many silversmiths working, and that on some walls of the temple there were gold and silver sheets, and that the women they called of the Sun[7] were very beautiful. The Spaniards were ecstatic to hear so many things, hoping with God's help to enjoy their share of it.

We learned that a messenger went from Tumbez with all speed to Quito to King Huayna Capac to report all this and to inform about the kind of people [the strangers] were and the nature of the ship. But they say that when the news arrived, [Huayna Capac] was already dead. Yet, it is also affirmed that he was not, but that later, after he ordered them to bring to him one of the Christians who had wished to remain among the Indians, he died. Be it the one or the other because it all counts for the same; it is considered certain that [Huayna Capac] died the same year and time that Francisco Pizarro arrived on the coast of his land.[8] The time that [Pizarro] spent in the mangroves, Huayna Capac had spent doing great things in Quito. And as everything is arranged and ordered by divine permission and disposition, it pleased God that while Huayna Capac reigned and lived, although pagan, the Spaniards would not enter his land, and that [the Spaniards] would wander together close to Panama, as they did, until He decided and it pleased Him to guide them in the way and manner that has been related. This is what written works are for, and for that they must serve: that men can learn about events truthfully, and also

7. Indians speaking with the demon. Pedro de Cieza de León's *Primera Parte* (Seville, 1553), p. 17r. Courtesy of the Jay I. Kislak Foundation, Miami Lakes, Florida.

that they contemplate and heed how God arranges things, and what is done is not what they intend, but rather what pleases Him.

Notes

1 Pedro de Candia, considered one of the largest men in Peru, was born in Crete about 1494. An artillery specialist, he fought against the Turks and participated in the Italian campaigns, fighting in the battles of Oran, Tripoli, and Pavia. He married in Villalpando (Zamora), and later joined the expedition of Governor Pedro de los Ríos to Tierra Firme in 1526. In Peru he took an Inca princess as concubine, and their son was a friend of the mestizo

chronicler, El Inca Garcilaso de la Vega. He was killed in 1542 at the end of the Battle of Chupas by Diego de Almargo the Younger, who accused him of treachery. See Lockhart, *Men of Cajamarca,* pp. 129–33, and Busto, *Diccionario,* 1:312–15.

2 Probably a puma and a jaguar.

3 because you are so valiant

4 The cacique was making an offering of chicha to propitiate Illapa, the force of "lightning, or the thunderbolt." See MacCormack, *Religion in the Andes,* p. 286.

5 For a good description of the weaving of cloth, especially the finest cumbi, see Murra, *Economic Organization,* pp. 65–84.

6 Camelidae.

7 Mamaconas.

8 There is much debate regarding the exact date of Huayna Capac's death, but it seems the Inca died, probably of smallpox, sometime between 1525 and 1531. Cieza suggests here it must have been after the end of the Tumbez reconnaissance—that is, after April 1528. See John Rowe, "La fecha de la muerte de Wayna Qhapaq," *Histórica* 2(1) (1978): 83–88; and Mariusz S. Ziolkowski, "Las cometas de Atawallpa: Acerca del papel de las profecías en la política del estado Inca," *Anthropologica* 6(6) (1988): 85–110.

XXII

About how Captain Francisco Pizarro continued the discovery and what happened to him

fol. 24 When Pedro de Candia told them what he had seen, the captain and the Spaniards desired even more to see the land that they had discovered. But because they were so few, there were not enough of them to explore on land or to take any action; they waited until—God willing—they could act with strength. In order to fully attain what there was, they decided to proceed ahead in the ship. Thus, unfurling the sails, they left that place, bringing along a boy [the Indians] had given them to point out to them the port of Paita.[1] And as they were sailing, they discovered the port of Tangarará[2] and reached a small island with large rocks, where they heard frightful snorting and roaring. Some [Spaniards] jumped into a small boat, and when they went to see what it was, they found that it came from an infinite number of sea lions,[3] of whom there are many and very large ones along that coast. They returned to the ship and sailed until they arrived at a point that they named Aguja.[4] Further on, they entered a port that they named Santa Cruz because they entered it on that day.[5]

Along the entire coast of the land that we call Peru, [the news] had spread that the Spaniards were sailing on a ship, that they were white and bearded, and that they did not harm, rob, or kill, but rather gave of what they were carrying and were very pious and humane and other things that [the Indians] had judged from what they had seen in them. This reputation was more an exaggeration than real. But because men, even if they are barbarous, delight in seeing things, no matter how strange and unbelievable they are, there were many who wished to see the Spaniards and their ship and the Black and the arquebus being fired. While [the Spaniards] were in the place that I mentioned, some balsas with Indians went to where they were, carrying a lot of fish, fruit, and other provisions to give them. The captain received everything gratefully, ordering that the Indians on the balsas be given some combs and fish hooks and Castilian beads. Along with those Indians came a chief, who said to the captain that a lady lived in that land whom they called La Capullana,[6] and when she heard the tales about him and his companions, she had a great wish to see them. Therefore, he bid him to come ashore, and they would be well provisioned with whatever they might need. The captain replied that he appreciated very much what he had told him on behalf of that lady and that he would return shortly, and to please her he would come on land to see her. With that, the Indians returned, and the ship departed. *fol. 24v*

Because the south wind was blocking them, they tacked for more than fifteen days; in truth, the east wind seldom prevails in those parts. They lacked firewood, and since they were close to the coast, they landed in order to supply themselves with it. The anchors were not even lowered or the sails furled when many balsas with fish and other food and fruit for them appeared next to the ship. The captain ordered Alonso de Molina to go ashore with the Indians who had come on the balsas in order to bring firewood for the ship. As [Molina] was returning with the provisions, the sea changed so much that the waves rose high, and the sea was swelled, so he could not reach [the ship]. The captain waited three days to take him on. But fearing that the cables might break and the ship wreck on the coast, they weighed the anchors to leave, believing that the Christians would be safe with the Indians since they showed such good will and so little malice.

They sailed from there until they arrived in Collique, which lies between Tangarará and Chimu,[7] places where the cities of San Miguel and Trujillo were founded.[8] The Indians came out joyously to receive them, bringing them the food from their land to eat; they provided them with water and firewood, and they gave them five sheep.[9] A sailor named Bocanegra,[10] seeing such fine land, left the ship with the Indians. He sent word with them to the captain to release him [from duty] and not to wait for him because he wanted to remain among such good people as were those Indians. The captain ordered Juan de la Torre to go and find out if it was true. He returned to the ship, confirming to the captain how well and happy [Bocanegra] was, without any desire to return to the ship because the Indians, delighted[11] when they heard him say that he wanted to remain among them, took him on their shoulders seated in a litter and carried him inland. Juan de la Torre saw herds of sheep, large fields, and many irrigation channels, green and so beautiful, and the land appeared so cheerful that there was nothing to compare it with.[12] And those animals that the Indians call what I related in my *Part One*,[13] the Spaniards called sheep because they saw that they had wool and were so gentle and domestic.

fol. 25 They left there, and the captain sailed on his course, exploring until he arrived at Santa, with great desire to discover the city of Chincha, about which the Indians had related great things.[14] But when he arrived where I say, the Spaniards themselves told him he should return to Panama to get people with whom they could settle and rule the land, which undoubtedly was the best and the richest in the world, as they had seen from the sample. It seemed a good idea to Francisco Pizarro, and because he could not wait to be back with the power of the Spaniards, he ordered the ship to set forth to where they had come from, having discovered at that time the entire coast as far as Santa.[15]

Notes

1 On the north Peruvian coast due west of modern Piura.

2 By the Chira River, Tangarará provided the original site for the Spanish town of San Miguel. It was later shifted to Piura, further inland. See Germán Stiglich, *Diccionario geográfico del Perú*, 2 vols. (Lima: Torres Aguirre, 1922), 2:1034.

3 There may have been seals also because both were prevalent at certain latitudes of the Pacific coast of America, and their numbers were so vast that the sound was probably deafening.

4 Aguja literally means "needle." Today it is called Punta Negra, and it lies south of the Bay of Sechura. Beyond the point, the Spanish would begin to navigate in a more southeasterly direction.

5 Holy Cross, September 14.

6 Along this part of Peru's north coast, female chieftains of ethnic entities were called capullanas and were common. Silverblatt (*Moon, Sun, and Witches*, p. 151) notes how quickly they lost their power under Spanish colonial administration.

7 Cieza refers here to the modern Lambayeque Valley, which had been under the domination of the Chimu, until they were conquered by the Incas. See Rogger Ravines, ed., *Chanchan, metropoli Chimu* (Lima: Instituto de Estudios Peruanos, 1980), pp. 32–35.

8 San Miguel was founded near Tangarará in 1532 and was transferred to a

site named Piura further from the coast. Trujillo was established in February 1535.

9 Camelidae.

10 Andrés de Bocanegra.

11 joyous

12 Andean people were excellent hydraulic experts. Some aqueducts on the desert north coast were more than sixty kilometers in length, and mountainsides were frequently terraced. See Paul Kosok, *Life, Land, and Water in Ancient Peru* (New York: Long Island University Press, 1965).

13 In chapter 3 of *Part One* Cieza indeed describes the Andean camelidae, both the domestic llamas and alpacas, as well as the wild vicuñas and guanacos. Yet, in the current text he consistently refers to them as sheep (*ovejas*).

14 Cieza explains why in *Part One*, chapter 74: "This valley is one of the best in all of Peru; it is beautiful to see its trees, irrigation channels, and how much fruit there is everywhere." Chincha Valley was also heavily populated.

15 They began the return trip approximately 3 May 1528. See Busto, *Historia general*, pp. 43–44.

XXIII

About how Captain Francisco Pizarro turned around and landed in some Indian villages, where[1] things went well for him, and what else happened to him[2]

Alonso de Molina—the Spaniard who had not been able to board the ship because of the storm, as has been told in the previous chapter—had remained with the Indians. They took him to a *cacica*[3] of a part of that land, where he was well treated and looked after without being vexed or harmed. Instead, they never left him alone, asking him all they wanted to know. The captain, returning with the ship, sailed until they reached the port that they had named Santa Cruz, and [they] came in so late that it was already three hours into darkness. The Indians saw the ship, as did Alonso de Molina. They quickly prepared a balsa, and even though it was already so dark, the Christian and several Indians went to the ship, and they were well received by the captain and his companions. The lady Capullana invited them to land in a port that was further north, where they would be well looked after by her. The captain replied that he would be delighted to
fol. 25v do it. Alonso de Molina related the many things that he had seen. He praised the fertility of the soil, said that it did not rain and that with irrigation water they cultivated their fields in many parts of the coast and that they told a great deal about Cuzco and Huayna Capac.

While conversing about these things, they arrived in the said port where they anchored in order to disembark. Many balsas with provisions and five sheep came, sent by the aforesaid lady. She sent to tell the captain to trust her word and to come ashore without hesitation, but that she first wanted to assure herself of them and go to their ship, where she would see all of them. She would leave hostages with them so that they could stay on land without fear for as long as they wanted to. The captain was extremely pleased with these good arguments that the cacica relayed to him. He thanked God because it had pleased Him that such a land was discovered; indeed, it would be His holy faith planted and the gospel preached among all those people, who possessed such good reason and understanding. And he ordered four Spaniards to disembark. They were Nicolás de Ribera, who is the only one of them still alive in the year that I am writing what you are reading; Francisco de Cuéllar,[4] Halcón,[5] and the same Alonso de Molina who first had remained among [the Indians]. Halcón wore a gold net with a cap and a medallion, and a velvet jacket and black breeches. Furthermore, he displayed his sword and dagger in such a way that he appeared more a soldier from Italy than an explorer of mangroves. They went directly to the cacica, who along with her Indians rejoiced and according to their custom gave them a grand welcome with many gifts. Then [the Indians] offered them food, and in order to honor them, [the cacica] herself rose up and gave them a drink from a cup, saying that this was the custom of treating guests in that land.[6] Halcón, the one with the jacket and medallion, liked the cacica and gazed at her.[7] When they finished eating, this lady said she would like to see the captain and talk him into coming on land to refresh himself because clearly he must be weary of the sea. The Christians replied that he would come in due time. In the meantime, the more Halcón looked at her, the deeper he fell in love.

When they arrived on the ship, the captain warmly welcomed her, *fol. 26*
as well as all the Indians who came with her, ordering all the Spaniards to treat them with respect. With much grace and fine words the lady told the captain that because she, a woman, had dared to enter his ship, he, a man and a captain, should not refuse to come ashore. But for his security she wanted to leave five chiefs on the ship as hostages. The captain replied that he had not disembarked because he had sent his men and because he had come with so few, but since she insisted, he would do it without wanting other hostages than her word. La Capullana, very pleased when she heard this, thanked him, and after she saw the ship and its rigging, she returned to her land; Halcón never took his eyes off of her, the whole time sighing and moaning. Then another day in the morning, before the sun appeared, there were more than fifty balsas with many Indians around the ship in order to receive the captain. In one of them came twelve chiefs, who boarded the ship. They told the captain that when he disembarked, they would remain until he returned because it was proper to do it this way, for he was going among foreign people. The captain replied that he did not believe they were treacherous; rather, he took them for brothers and would entrust his person to any of them. Al-

though he strongly insisted that they should all disembark, he did not succeed because they remained and stayed on the ship until they saw him on [the balsa], with only the sailors remaining [on board].

The captain and the pilot, Bartolomé Ruiz, left along with the others. The cacica with many chiefs and Indians came out to receive them, very orderly, with green branches and ears of maize. They had made a great bower with seats for all the Spaniards together, whereas the Indians were somewhat apart from them, and they faced each other. When the food was ready, they gave them a lot of fish and meat to eat, prepared in various ways, with many fruits and their traditional wine and bread.[8] When they finished eating, in order to further entertain the captain, the chief Indians who were there with their wives danced and sang according to their custom. The captain was elated to see that they were so knowledgeable and civilized. He wished to be in Castilla del Oro in order to organize a return with enough people to subjugate them and secure their conversion.

Notes

1 he was well received

2 until he entered the second time in

3 A female chief.

4 See chapter 16.

5 Probably Pedro Halcón.

6 It is still customary in the Andes to pass around a large glass (*kero*)—at that time made of silver or gold or hardwood—filled with chicha.

7 The following was crossed out in the manuscript: "because aside from the avarice that keeps us here, lust plays a large part in why so many had been as bad as."

8 The "wine" Cieza refers to would have been chicha. The fruits he describes in *Part One,* chapter 66: cucumbers, guayavas, guavas, avocados, guanavanas, caymitos, and pineapples. He includes also "bread" made from either maize or yucca.

XXIV

About how the captain took possession of those lands and what else he did until he left them

After he ate, pleased with those lords who had gathered to honor him, *fol. 26v*
Captain Francisco Pizarro spoke to them through the interpreters. He told them how much they distinguished him with the honors they bestowed on him and that he was confident[1] God would someday repay them; at present, given the affection he felt for them, he would like to inform them about something very propitious for them. They should forget their fallacious beliefs and the useless sacrifices they made because it was only expedient to honor and serve God with sacrifices of good deeds and not with the shedding of blood of either men or animals. He declared that the Sun they worshiped as god was no more than an object created to illuminate and preserve the world, and that God Almighty had his seat in the most prominent place in the heavens, and that the Christians worshiped this God, whom they call Jesus Christ. Further, if they did the same, He would grant them heaven's glory, and if they refused, He would cast them into hell forevermore. He concluded by telling them that he would try to return quickly and would bring priests who would baptize them and preach to them the word of the holy gospel. And then he told them that they should know they were all to acknowledge as their lord and king the one who was that of Spain and of many other kingdoms and realms.[2] Further, as a sign of obedience they should raise a banner that he placed in their hands, which the Indians took and raised three times—laughing, taking everything that [Pizarro] had told them for a joke because they did not believe that there could be another lord in the world as great and powerful as Huayna Capac. But since what he was asking them did not cost them anything, they agreed with the captain on everything, laughing at what he was saying.[3]

After this, the captain said farewell to the Indians in order to return to the ship. And when he went in a balsa, it overturned in such a way that he almost drowned. When he boarded the ship, he retired to one of its beds.[4] When Halcón realized that he was parting from the cacica, he went to plead with [Pizarro] to leave him behind in that

8. Huayna Capac in the conquest of Quito. Felipe Guaman Poma de Ayala, *El primer nueva corónica y buen gobierno,* 3 vols., ed. Rolena Adorno and John V. Murra (Mexico City: Siglo Veintiuno, 1980), f. 333. Courtesy of Siglo Veintiuno Editores.

land among the Indians. [Pizarro] did not want to because [Halcón] was foolish and could not change [the Indians]. Halcón was so upset by this that he lost his mind and went mad, shouting loudly: "Now, now, you rogues, this land is mine and of my brother the king, and you have usurped it from me!" And he went after them with a broken sword. The pilot, Bartolomé Ruiz, struck him with an oar, and he fell to the ground; they placed him below deck and chained him. *fol. 27*

Returning with the ship the same way that they had come, they reached another port on the coast, where they encountered many Indians in balsas, joyously greeting them. And as the ship anchored, they approached it with great gifts that the caciques were sending the captain. One of the Indians arrived with a sword and a silver vessel, which were lost in the port where the captain had fallen into the water. But the Indians had searched for it so much and so diligently that they found it, and they sent it to him by land, and it arrived. At this time, the nobles of that region went to the ship with some caciques, delighted to see it anchored in their port. They spoke with the captain, pleading with him that because he had disembarked in the land of their neighbors, he should do the same in theirs because they would leave as hostages anyone of them that [the captain] ordered. He answered that he did not want any of them to remain on the ship, but [wanted] to go out, as they commanded, in order to please them because his wish was to make them all content. The chiefs were well satisfied when they heard this and remained so until they returned to land. There they ordered preparation of provisions to feed [the Spaniards] and to make a bower like the one where they had first stayed.

Francisco Pizarro was astonished when he saw so much reason in those people and how they were dressed and how well the chiefs carried themselves. In the morning he went ashore, where he was received the same way the others had done; thus, they gave him and his companions food. Because there were many chiefs together, he delivered another speech about how they would benefit from abandoning their idols and rites, taking our faith, and worshiping God, our Redeemer and the Lord Jesus Christ. And that they should understand they would soon become subjects of the Emperor Charles, king of Spain, and he made them raise the banner no more or less than the others. But they also took it as a joke and laughed heartily at what they were hearing. When he wanted to retire to the ship, he asked each of the chiefs who were there to turn over to him a boy to learn the language, so they could speak it when they returned. They gave him a lad whom they named Felipillo and another whom they called *fol. 27v* Don Martín.[5] A Spanish sailor named Ginés asked the captain permission to remain among the Indians, as did Alonso de Molina, who said that he wanted to remain in Tumbez until, God willing, [Pizarro] returned with people to settle that land. Francisco Pizarro commended to the Indians Ginés, who remained among them; they replied that they would look after him.

After this [Pizarro] departed, and when he embarked, he headed in the direction of Tumbez. When the ship reached Cabo Blanco, he disembarked to take possession in the name of the emperor; and as he went to do it in a canoe, he almost was lost because it was small and it capsized. When he found himself on the coast, he said in the presence of those who were with him: "Be my witnesses as I take possession of this land with all else that has been discovered by us for the emperor, our lord, and for the royal crown of Castile." As he said this, he gave several knocks, placing his mark as is normally done.[6] He returned to the ship, and they sailed until they arrived at the beach of Tumbez, where many chiefs and caciques awaited them; some of them came in balsas, bringing refreshments. The captain spoke to them as he had done to the others and told them that in order for them to know that his affection was real and that of a friend, he wanted to leave a Christian with them so that they could explain to him their language and have him among them. They were overjoyed to learn this, and promised to look after [the Christian] and protect him, as he would see when he returned. Thus, Alonso de Molina and his group remained in Tumbez.

About these Christians some say that within several days all three came together, and that when [the Indians] took two of them to Quito to King Huayna Capac, they learned that he was dead and [the Indians] killed [the Christians]. Others say that they were lascivious with women and that [the Indians] loathed them so much that they killed them. The most certain, and what I believe, is what I have also heard, and that is that [the Christians] joined those from Tumbez in the war against those from Puná, where after the three Christians fought a great deal, those from Tumbez were defeated, and because [the Christians] could not flee as easily, the enemy caught up with them and killed them. Certainly, had there remained wise men or religious who would have striven to improve the souls of those infidels, there is no doubt that God would have been with them. But they were young and inexperienced men, brought up at sea, and they could have gone astray so much that the Indians would have killed them as they say or as has been related.

Because the captain had talked with those from Tumbez about *fol. 28* what has been said and learned from them the great things they related about Chincha, he departed, loading first some sheep that the Indians gave them, which the captain ordered to be preserved and maintained to carry as a sample. He did not want to stop at the island of Puná. While they were passing the point that they named Santa Elena, many chiefs gathered to see the captain and talk to him. They believed that the Christians were favored by God and were His because they thus sailed on the sea although there were so few of them, and when they saw the ship, they went out to it. They spoke to Francisco Pizarro, saying that they all were delighted to see that [the Spaniards] were so kind and such real friends and that they should stop in their land, where they would be cared for. The captain did not want to leave the ship, but to please them he ordered that they anchor. And when those who had come on the ship returned to land, they reported to the others how they had seen the captain, and they decided to make him a present of what they most valued—mantas made of their wool and cotton, and some small beads made of bone, which they call *chaquira*,[7] a great ransom. Well now, they could have used as the ship's ballast what there was in that land, but since the captain had ordered them to refrain from asking about gold or silver, or from paying any attention to it regardless how much of it they saw, [the Indians] did not give them any. But more than thirty chiefs came aboard the ship, and each one, as a sign of love and goodwill, gave [Pizarro] a manta and put a string of the said chaquira around his neck, and they placed the mantas over his back because that is their custom. With the noise that the Indians made, Halcón climbed on deck, first asking permission since he had his shackles, and looking toward the captain he shouted: "Who has ever seen an ass as covered with beads and as saddled as this one?" This he said to him, and he shouted to the Indians, saying that the Christians had usurped the kingdom from him and that they were worthless traitors. The captain indicated to them that he was mad and thanked them for the gift, and when they wished to leave, he asked them to give them a boy to learn the language; they did, and he later died in Spain.

They sailed from here, and in Puerto Viejo many balsas with provisions came out; all were delighted to see and talk with the Spaniards. And they left him another boy, whom they named Don Juan.[8] They did not disembark again or stop until Gorgona, where they had left the Spaniards, and they rejoiced, although they found the one called Trujillo dead. They embraced the rest of them and told them
fol. 28v about what they had seen and what they had discovered. After they all retired to the ship, they set sail, determined not to stop until they reached Panama.

Notes

1 hoped

2 Charles V.

3 Cieza's consistent recounting of the importance of conversion to Francisco Pizarro tempers some of the more critical evaluations that he was nothing more than a gold seeker. Cieza indicates on several occasions in the text that the extension of Christianity was one of the motivating factors in Pizarro's complex makeup.

4 cabin

5 Felipillo and Martinillo became famous interpreters, finally for different camps—Felipillo with the Almagrists and Martinillo with the Pizarros. Martinillo, from Poechos, was about fourteen when his uncle, the cacique Maizavilca, gave him to Pizarro. See José Antonio del Busto Duthurburu, *La hueste perulera* (Lima: Universidad Católica del Perú, 1981), pp. 307–26.

6 Such ritualized acts of taking possession were important elements in the Europeans' attempt to establish their "rights" in new lands. See Patricia Seed, *Ceremonies of Possession in Europe's Conquest of the New World, 1492–1640* (Cambridge: Cambridge University Press, 1995).

7 These prized beads could be of reed sea shells, stone, or even gold or silver; the Spaniards soon found a good market in the import of glass beads. The origin of the word may be Circum-Caribbean to Panama. Newson (*Life and Death*, pp. 30–35) provides a useful account of their importance in the northern Andes.

8 He may also have died in Spain. According to Busto (*Hueste perulera*, pp. 322–23), there is no mention of him during the third expedition.

XXV

How Pizarro arrived in Panama, where he tried to negotiate with Pedro de los Ríos to grant him people to return with, but because it did not happen, he decided to go to Spain

From Gorgona Island Captain Francisco Pizarro sailed without stopping until he reached the city of Panama, where he was received with honors by the governor and all its vecinos. As can be imagined, his partners were overjoyed to see him. They gave thanks to God our Lord because it pleased Him that at the end of so many hardships they would discover such a great land. They marvelled at the sheep, seeing their size, and they esteemed their wool because such fine cloth could be made from it, and they praised the colors of the dyes as perfect.[1] They believed that because they found that vessel and the other sample on the islet, in the cities and large villages there would have to be much silver and gold. And as often happens with similar novelties, in the city there was talk of nothing else than Peru. They praised Pizarro for his perseverance because his hardship and need were not enough to discourage him or make him lose the will to accomplish what he was striving for. For eight days he was secluded and did not appear in public. During those days, he and his partners discussed how to proceed with the discovery and conquest of Peru.

They decided to ask Pedro de los Ríos to allow them to take people and horses; after all, the greatest part of the gain would be his. They encharged Don Hernando de Luque to make the proposal, which was done in the presence of the other partners because Pizarro came out [of seclusion], and they both went with him to visit the governor. When they were alone with him, Luque spoke, indicating how much Pizarro and Almagro had endured in Darién and how they always acted as the king's servants. The same had been true in Tierra Firme, where he had governed at the time of Pedrarias, who, knowing that everything they said was true, had given them the command of the South Sea. There they had suffered the hardships that he knew *fol. 29*
about, and it was evident because Francisco Pizarro reached such extreme [conditions] that his companions abandoned him, leaving him

on Gorgona, an unhealthy land, populated by mosquitoes and snakes. From there, with the ship that he and Diego de Almagro had sent him, it pleased God that he discovered the land that they had heard about. From there they brought the samples everyone had seen, and Francisco Pizarro was willing to return quickly to that excellent and plentiful land. Therefore, because he was the governor of Castilla del Oro, he should allow them to recruit people, and he should favor the conquest and should send to ask His Majesty to grant it, for it was believed that he would acquiesce. Pedro de los Ríos replied abjectly that if he could, he would do what they asked, but that one should not depopulate his province to go and conquer new lands, nor should more die than had already died for the bait they were dangling—sheep and a sample of gold and silver. After this and other discussions between the governor and the three partners, they took leave of him, saddened by the lack of support they were finding for the conquest of the land that they had discovered.

They debated a great deal as to what they should do in order to carry out their plan. They decided to send an envoy to Spain who would inform His Majesty on their behalf and ask him for a grant of governance and *adelantamiento*[2] for them, as well as a bishopric for their partner, the maestrescuela, who was the one who urged the most that they send an envoy; and thus they settled it. But Diego de Almagro spoke to Pizarro, in front of Luque, saying that since he had possessed the fortitude to have spent more than four years among the mangroves and rivers of the coast, suffering such hunger and hardship never heard or seen by men before, he should board a ship and go to Spain himself and fall at the feet of the emperor so that he would give him grants to govern the land because it would be different from negotiating through an envoy, who after all was a third person. Listening to his partner, Pizarro recovered his spirits. He said that [Almagro] was right and that if he had some money to expend, his going would be much better for all of them than sending someone. The maestrescuela, Luque—pondering it further, and knowing that power does not tolerate equality and that everyone wanted it
fol. 29v mostly for himself— opposed Almagro's view with plenty of reasons and repeated that they should send the dispatches with Licentiate Corral.[3] Pizarro remained silent at Luque's proposition, giving them to understand that he would go along with whatever they arranged.

But Diego de Almagro, having gotten into his head what he had said, persevered and repeated it in such a way that his opinion prevailed. But first,[4] Don Hernando de Luque said, "Pray[5] to God, sons, that you do not rob the benediction from one another; I still say that as far as both of you are concerned, the most agreeable would be that you go together to negotiate or send a person to do it for you." But because Almagro was so vehement regarding Pizarro's going, it was concluded that Pizarro would negotiate the governorship for himself, for Almagro the post of adelantado, for Father Luque the bishopric, and for Bartolomé Ruiz the high constableship. In addition, he was to ask for advantageous grants for those of the thirteen who were with him in the discovery and were still alive. Francisco Pizarro gave his word to carry this out, saying that he wanted everything for them. But you will see further ahead what later happened.

I remember that while I was in Peru looking in the archives of the cities where their founding papers and other old contracts are kept, in the City of the Kings[6] I came across a[7] document the subchanter had in his power, where one could read some lines that said what Almagro and Father Luque told Pizarro: "You must negotiate what we have agreed upon, which you are to do without any evil, deceit or cunning."

Notes

1 The wool was woven in its natural color or dyed. A variety of colors were employed, and the dyes were obtained from both plant and animal materials. Different shades of blue were produced from leaves of native shrubs; the most common source for red was the cochineal insect; and for yellow, the bark of the false pepper tree *(Chinus mollis)* was used. Colors were mixed to obtain other colors, and most dyes included ingredients that remain a mystery. See Raoul D'Harcourt, *Textiles of Ancient Peru and Their Techniques* (Seattle: University of Washington Press, 1977), pp. 5–6.

2 The adelantado was an advance agent with full powers of governing. The office, or adelantamiento, which has its origin in the reconquest of the Iberian Peninsula, was normally granted to the head of any important expedition. See, C. H. Haring, *The Spanish Empire in America* (New York: Oxford University Press, 1947), pp. 19–22.

3 Licentiate Diego de Corral held an encomienda in Darién. He died in

1532. See Raúl Porras Barrenechea, ed., *Cartas del Perú (1524–1543)* (Lima: Sociedad de Bibliofilos Peruanos, 1959), pp. 30, 41.

4 still

5 that I, my judgment

6 Lima.

7 an old

XXVI

About how Captain Francisco Pizarro went to Spain to report to the emperor about the land he had discovered, and what Almagro did in Tierra Firme

Francisco Pizarro had full confidence in Diego de Almagro, and thus he encharged him with obtaining money with which he could go to Spain, so he would have at least something to spend wherever he went. Although they had property, it was encumbered, and they owed thousands in debts; nevertheless, Almagro was very tenacious, as those who were acquainted with him know. He was crippled and could not walk, but he went around the city carried in a chair on *fol. 30* the shoulders of slaves, seeking money[1] from among his friends. He amassed all he could, which was one thousand five hundred castellanos, very little money with which to go and request such a great enterprise, but in those years there were not the thousands that we see nowadays. With that and the sample [of treasure] they had found on the islet, Pizarro made ready for Spain, taking the sheep they had brought to lend credence to his argument and some of the Indians that they were given as interpreters. He went to Nombre de Dios, where he later embarked for Spain.[2]

After [Pizarro] left, Almagro did not desist; instead he decided to send a ship to the jurisdiction of Nicaragua, which at that time was under the control of Pedrarias Dávila. Almagro had paid off [Pedrarias] with the profit due to him according to the partnership originally formed; or to be precise, [Almagro] excluded him for one thousand five hundred castellanos—very little interest for how much [Pedrarias] lost, which was so much that even today he would have had his share. Nicolás de Ribera boarded the ship that went to Nicaragua so that he could speak as an eyewitness about what existed there [Peru]. Almagro wrote to Pedrarias and his other friends. Pedrarias was in León, a city in that province, which was where he learned the news. He complained about Almagro because he had removed him from the partnership. He said he would do nothing for him, but for Pizarro and Luque he would do what he could.

There were in Nicaragua important men—among them Hernando de Soto,[3] Hernán Ponce,[4] and company—who had rigging for building ships. From Ribera they learned about Peru and the city of Tumbez. They saw the sheep and some mantas, and they resolved to build ships or to finish the two they were constructing, and to enter into a partnership with Pedrarias to go and settle the land. But these partners were cunning because they were trying to go without a commission, [believing that] once they were there, [the governance] would be theirs. Pedrarias wanted to give them an associate who would have jurisdiction there on his behalf, but they would not agree to it. The pilot, Bartolomé Ruiz, and Ribera[5] secretly talked with Hernán Ponce about how someone should go to Panama to wait until Pizarro returned from Spain with the governance; with him, [Ponce] could *fol. 30v* make an arrangement to his benefit and honor. Hernán Ponce promised that he or one of his companions would do it. With that, the pilot, Bartolomé Ruiz, and Ribera said farewell to the governor in order to return to Tierra Firme.[6] They suspected that Pedrarias wanted to take their ship to send it along with others to settle Peru. And when they wanted to sail, the governor sent a constable to confiscate the ship and to inspect it because he was very troubled about having given them permission. But neither he nor the constable were able to detain them. Instead, they left and took with them, according to what I have been told, another ship that was there because there was no fit rig the governor could send after them. And they reached Chira, where they found another constable who ordered them, under severe penalties, not to go to Panama. But when they left there, they sailed on until they entered its port, where they spoke with Diego de Almagro, reporting to him what had happened to them. Almagro feared that Pedrarias or Hernán Ponce and Hernando de Soto might enter the land of Peru and occupy it while his partner went to Spain and returned with the governance.

Notes

1 that he could

2 Probably at the beginning of September 1528; see Busto, *Historia general,* p. 46.

3 Hernando de Soto was born about 1498 in Jerez de Badajoz. In 1513–14 he participated with Pedrarias in exploring the Isthmian region and was a captain in a 1520 expedition to Veragua under Gaspar de Espinosa. In 1524 he joined Francisco Hernández de Córdoba's conquest of Nicaragua. Although he held an encomienda and public office in the city of León, around 1529–30 he became interested in Peru. With the profits from his activities in Central America and Peru he returned to Spain in 1536, secured the Order of Santiago, and in 1537 was granted the right to conquer Florida, largely at his own cost. See Lockhart, *Men of Cajamarca*, pp. 190–201, and Charles Hudson, *Knights of Spain, Warriors of the Sun: Hernando de Soto and the South's Ancient Chiefdoms* (Athens: University of Georgia Press, 1997).

4 Hernán Ponce de León, from Talavera de la Reina, was a partner in the conquest of Nicaragua in 1524, where he received a rich encomienda and was a city councilman. After his involvement in Peru he went to Panama in 1539, requesting an administrative review of Pizarro, and in 1540, he was in Spain. See Lockhart, *Men of Cajamarca*, pp. 192–93, 197; Mendiburu, *Diccionario*, 9:196–98; and Porras Barrenechea, *Cartas del Perú*, pp. 356, 373, 390.

5 Nicolás de Ribera.

6 to the ship

XXVII

About how Captain Francisco Pizarro arrived in Spain and was given the governance of Peru

When Captain Francisco Pizarro embarked in the port of Nombre de Dios, he traveled until he arrived in Spain. And after he reached Seville, he departed for court, while the news spread throughout Spain of how they had discovered such a large and wealthy land. Everybody gaped at the sheep that he brought, and since Pedro de Candia, who went with him, had seen Tumbez, he described it. They did not believe it, saying that it was a ruse to trick those who might want to go there into believing that there were stone houses and so much gold. They sometimes interrupted Pedro de Candia's discourse with their arguments in such a way that they silenced him.

When Pizarro reached the court, he presented himself before the [members] of the Council of the Indies because they govern the Indies by mandate from the king.[1] He informed them how much he and his partners had suffered and spent; he told them about what he saw in the land that he had discovered and about the reports he had. They *fol. 31* listened to him carefully and were distressed by their hardships. They consulted with the king, and [Pizarro] was easily awarded the governance, and other grants were extended to him. It was said that he secured the most and the best solely for himself, without remembering how much his partner had suffered and deserved. Thus, when Almagro found out that he was not bringing him the adelantamiento, he was extremely angry. In order that the truth of this business can be seen without going around canvassing for opinions, I will put here verbatim some clauses taken from the agreement that was made with [Pizarro], as is evident from the original that I had in my power for a few days, in this City of the Kings.[3] It reads:

> The Queen.[2] As for you, Captain Francisco Pizarro, vecino of Tierra Firme called Castilla del Oro, by you and in the name of the venerable father Don Hernando de Luque, maestrescuela and provisor of the church of Darién, a vacant seat in the said Castilla del Oro, and of Captain Diego de Almagro, vecino of the city of Panama, you reported to

us that you and your said partners, wishing to serve us and in the best interests of our royal crown—it could have been five years ago, more or less—that with the permission and the decree of Pedrarias Dávila, who was our governor and captain general of the said Tierra Firme, you took the command of conquering, discovering, pacifying, and settling along the coast of the South Sea of the said land in the east, at your cost and that of your said partners, all that you could in those parts. And you built two ships and a brigantine for it on the said coast, so that in this—in having to carry the rigging and supplies necessary for the trip and the fleet from Nombre de Dios, which is on the north coast, to the other south coast, with men and other necessary things for the said trip, and to turn to make the said fleet over again—you spent a great sum of gold pesos. And you went to make and you made the said discovery, where you suffered many dangers and hardships. Because of that, all your people who were with you left you on a deserted island with only thirteen men who did not want to leave you. And with them and with the succor of the ship and the people given to you by Captain Diego de Almagro, you left the island, and you discovered the lands and provinces of Peru and the city of Tumbez, in which you and your *fol. 31v* partners spent more than thirty thousand gold pesos. And because of the desire that you have to serve us, you would like to continue the said conquest and settlement at your cost and upkeep so that at no time are we obligated to pay you or satisfy the expenses that you might have in it, except what was granted to you in this agreement. You supplicated and asked me for a grant that would order you be entrusted with the conquest of the said lands and that I should bestow the grants on you with the conditions herein contained,[3] regarding which I ordered the following treaty and agreement to be made with you:[4]

First, I give permission and authority to you, the said Captain Francisco Pizarro, that for us and in our name and in that of the royal crown of Castile, you may continue the said discovery and conquest and settlement of the province of Peru up to two hundred leagues of land along the same coast. These two hundred leagues begin from a village that in the language of the Indians is called Tempula, later named Santiago by you, until the village of Chincha is reached—which could be the said two hundred leagues of coast, more or less.

Item, understanding that you are the executor in the service of God Our Lord and ours, and to honor your person and to benefit you

9. Llamas. Pedro de Cieza de León's *Primera Parte* (Seville, 1553), p. 124v. Courtesy of the Jay I. Kislak Foundation, Miami Lakes, Florida.

and grant you favor, we promise to make you our governor and captain general of all the province of Peru, lands [and] villages that are at present and will be later within the entire two hundred leagues, for all the days of your life, with the salary of seven hundred twenty-five thousand maravedis each year, counted from the day that you set sail from these our kingdoms to continue the said settlement and conquest. This should be paid to you from the income and interests belonging to us in the said land that you would thus settle. From this salary each year you are to pay a mayor[5] and ten shield bearers and thirty foot soldiers and one doctor and one apothecary. This salary will be paid to you by our officials of the said land.

fol. 32 Further, we grant you the title of our adelantado of the said province

> of Peru as well as the office of high constable of the same, all this for the days of your life.

It appears that Francisco Pizarro obtained these offices for himself without remembering either Almagro or the pilot who had helped him so much and took part in the discovery. This is what is included in the agreement for them, it seems, because as it continues, it says further:

> Also, it is our grant, respecting the good life and doctrine of the person of the said Don Hernando de Luque, to present him to our Holy Father as bishop of the city of Tumbez, which is in the said province and government of Peru, with the boundaries that will be indicated by us with apostolic authority. In the meantime, until the bulls reach us, we make him universal protector of all the Indians of the said province, with the salary of one thousand ducats each year, paid from our income in the said land; in the interim there are ecclesiastical tithes from which it can be paid.
>
> Also, we confer to the said Captain Diego de Almagro, the lieutenancy of the fortress that is and lies in the city of Tumbez, which is in the said province of Peru, with the salary of one hundred thousand maravedis each year, with more than two hundred maravedis each year to defray expenses—all paid from the income of the said land. These he will enjoy from the day that you, the said Francisco Pizarro, arrive in the said land, even though the said Captain Almagro might remain in Panama or another place that suits him. And we make him an hidalgo so that he can enjoy the honors and privileges that other hidalgos can and should enjoy in all the Indies, islands, and mainland of the Ocean Sea.

In another clause it says that the thirteen who were with the Governor Don Francisco Pizarro in the discovery should become prominent hidalgos, with a known seat in those parts, and those among them who are hidalgos should become knights of the Golden Spurs. The agreement concludes with another section where it appears that it was issued in Toledo on the twenty-sixth of July of fifteen hundred and twenty-nine.[6] It is signed by the queen and by Juan Vázquez, her secretary, and marked with the signatures of the [members] of the Royal Council of the Indies.[7]

When the agreement was concluded, [Pizarro] was given the instructions with the working orders, and his royal provisions sealed with the royal seal, and other favors and grants. With this he departed from the court, leaving behind hope of success in the land where he wanted to go, and went to Trujillo, which is his homeland.

Notes

1 The Council of the Indies was formed in 1524 and at first met wherever the king held court. In prestige it ranked below only the Council of Castile, and its functions covered almost all aspects of administration. In consultation with the monarch it appointed colonial secular and ecclesiastical officials, from the viceroy to town officers. It created law, issued regulations governing trade, supervised ecclesiastical affairs through royal patronage, and acted as a court. Most of its senior officials were university trained, many having studied law. See Mark A. Burkholder and Lyman L. Johnson, *Colonial Latin America,* 2d ed. (New York: Oxford University Press, 1994), pp. 72–74.

2 It is not clear whether the queen who signed this agreement was Juana the Mad, the mother of Charles V, who often figures in official documents, or Charles's wife, Isabel of Portugal. Porras Barrenechea and Rafael Varón believe it was Empress Isabel. See Rafael Varón Gabai, *Francisco Pizarro and His Brothers: The Illusion of Power in Sixteenth-Century Peru,* trans. Javier Flores Espinosa (Norman: University of Oklahoma Press, 1997), pp. 38, 62.

3 incorporated

4 it seems that for asking for the grants

5 *Alcalde mayor.*

6 two

7 A series of documents were issued at Toledo from 15 May 1529 to 24 August of the same year, covering various aspects of the proposed expedition. For copies of the complete texts, see Raúl Porras Barrenechea, *Cedulario del Perú, siglos XVI, XVII, y XVIII* (Lima: Torres Aguirre, 1948), 1:3–66.

XXVIII

About how the Governor Don Francisco Pizarro returned to Tierra Firme, having first sent certain Spaniards in a ship to report on what he had negotiated

The governor stayed only briefly in his homeland because first, he had little money to spend, and second, he could not wait to be back in the land that he had discovered.[1] Alonso Riquelme, treasurer; García de Salcedo, inspector; and Francisco Navarro, accountant, went as officials of the Royal Treasury.[2] Pizarro tried to recruit people, but because they saw his poverty, they did not believe that there were any riches where he wanted to take them. He took along his four brothers: the principal one was Hernando Pizarro, a good man with great sense of honor, who was the legitimate son of Captain Gonzalo Pizarro, father of all of them; Juan Pizarro and Gonzalo Pizarro, his paternal brothers, bastards because only Hernando Pizarro was legitimate; and Francisco Martín de Alcántara, his maternal brother.[3] He recruited some people, though only a few. In order to let it be known in Tierra Firme that [the agreement] was already dispatched and en route, he directed that fifteen or twenty Spaniards should sail ahead. They arrived at Nombre de Dios and told about it. The governor, facing dire necessities and hardships because of his lack of money, made preparations as best as he could and came to Sanlúcar,[4] where he departed on [blank] of the month [blank] of the year [blank] of [blank],[5] and they sailed, returning to the Indies.[6] *fol. 32v*

Captain Diego de Almagro learned from the recent arrivals that Francisco Pizarro was returning as governor of the land that they named New Castile and that he had obtained the position of adelantado for himself. He publicly complained about his partner—that he had left only to come back as a lord without remembering the one who had made it all possible. He further said that Pizarro gave him a shabby recompense for everything that he had done for him and that [Almagro] did not need to complain about the king because had he [Almagro] gone before [the king], he would not have paid [Pizarro] with the mayoralty of Tumbez. Furthermore, when Pizarro returned, not one man of those who had gone with him would enter his [Almagro's] house, nor would he spend any more than he had already expended. Don Hernando de Luque told him that it was his fault because he had so ardently pressed for Pizarro's trip to Spain and had ignored his advice that a person who would treat them equitably should go to negotiate. And even though he had heard about it, he should calm down, for there was no reason to believe everything they said. They say that the bishop-elect Don Hernando de Luque was unable to calm him down; instead, [Almagro] went to the mines. When Luque saw this, he obtained a cash loan with which he paid the passage charges for those who, as I say, had come ahead.

fol. 33 When Nicolás de Ribera went under [Luque's] orders to Nombre de Dios to do it, Almagro was so annoyed, as has been said, that there was no reasonable thing anyone could say to him that might mollify him. The bishop-elect Don Hernando de Luque wrote him letters, exhorting him to come to Panama because everything that Pizarro had negotiated was for all of them; after all, he did have a partnership with him. In addition, he wrote to give him the satisfaction of knowing what they were saying regarding Pizarro's adelantamiento—that it was a mockery. With these letters and with what he had been told by Nicolás de Ribera—who had come by on his return from Nombre de Dios—[Almagro] lost some of his fury and wrote to the bishop-elect to recruit and equip men, and that in the meantime he was going to Panama. He arrived there before too many days went by and spoke amiably to those who had come. And so that his partner would find some work finished before he arrived, he sent carpenters to cut wood at the river they call Lagartos in order to repair the ships that were damaged from past voyages.

The pilot, Bartolomé Ruiz, also complained about Francisco Pizarro because he had not negotiated for him the staff of the high constable, having promised and sworn to it.[7] He said that had he not been on the ship and taken the Tumbez Indians on the balsa, [Pizarro] would not have been as hopeful on Gorgona as he had been to shortly discover what those Indians had described. In Tierra Firme, Captain Diego de Almagro tried to recruit some people for the conquest of Peru that was to be undertaken and to get provisions so that those coming from Spain would have food. The news of how the emperor had granted the government of Peru to Francisco Pizarro reached

Nicaragua. Many, in order to participate in the conquest, awaited the news of his arrival in Tierra Firme; and on Hispaniola and in many other parts of the Indies this news had spread.[8]

Notes

1 Pizarro's activities in Spain have been partially traced by Raúl Porras Barrenechea, "Dos documentos esenciales sobre Francisco Pizarro y la conquista del Perú," *Revista Histórica* 17 (1948):9–95; see also Varón, *Pizarro and His Brothers*, pp. 38–40.

2 Porras Barrenechea published copies of the royal appointments of the treasurer Riquelme (Toledo, 24 May 1529), the accountant Navarro (Toledo, 15 May 1529), and the inspector Salcedo (Toledo, 24 May 1529) in *Cedulario del Perú*, 1:3–7.

3 The Pizarro siblings met different fates following the conquest period. Hernando was jailed in 1541 at the castle La Mota in Spain. While there, he controlled the family's fortunes. In 1551 he married his niece, Francisco's mestiza daughter, and after his release in 1561, they lived in the palace he built in Trujillo. He died in 1578. Juan Pizarro was killed in 1536 during the Indian uprising of Manco Inca; Gonzalo Pizarro was executed in 1548 after losing the Battle of Jaquijahuana, thus ending his revolt against royal authority. Martín de Alcántara fell defending Francisco Pizarro at the time of his assassination in Lima on 26 June 1541. See Lockhart, *Men of Cajamarca*, pp. 157, 168–89; María Rostworowski de Diez Canseco, *Doña Francisca Pizarro: Una ilustre mestiza 1534–1598* (Lima: Instituto de Estudios Peruanos, 1989); and Varón, *Pizarro and His Brothers*.

4 Sanlúcar de Barrameda.

5 Cieza wrote in the margin of the manuscript: "To the vicar general, one has to write to Hernando Pizarro if he remembers the day, month, and year when they left Sanlúcar; I have to remember and request it." Hernando Pizarro was imprisoned at La Mota from June 1541 to May 1561. Cieza could have checked the departure records at the House of Trade in Seville to determine the date.

6 They probably left in January 1530, though the exact day remains unknown. Francisco Pizarro did not collect enough men to satisfy the Crown authorization, but Gonzalo, remaining in Sanlúcar, convinced royal inspectors who had come to examine the ship's register that most had left with Francisco. Hernando departed with two ships and joined Francisco in the Canaries before continuing on to Tierra Firme. See José Antonio del Busto

Duthurburu, *Francisco Pizarro: El Marqués Gobernador* (Madrid: Ediciones Rialp, 1966), pp. 48–49.

7 Francisco Pizarro himself was appointed high constable *(alguacil mayor)*, whereas Ruiz was named the pilot general of the South Sea. See Porras Barrenechea, *Cedulario del Perú*, 1:42.

8 There was a close commercial and political link between Nicaragua and the Peruvian venture. Furthermore, many service Indians from Nicaragua participated in the conquest of Peru. See David R. Radell, "The Indian Slave Trade and Population of Nicaragua during the Sixteenth Century," in William M. Denevan, ed., *The Native Population of the Americas in 1492*, 2d ed. (Madison: University of Wisconsin Press, 1992), pp. 67–76; and Lockhart, *Spanish Peru*, pp. 199–205.

XXIX

About how the Governor Don Francisco Pizarro arrived at Nombre de Dios and what occurred between him and Diego de Almagro; and how in Panama they renewed their friendship and formed a new partnership

I have related previously how the Governor Don Francisco Pizarro embarked in the port of Sanlúcar de Barrameda. From there, after going ashore in various ports, he arrived in the city of Nombre de Dios. In those days the houses were built of wood and straw, but now it is another matter. Because more gold and silver leaves from that port than any other that I know of in the world, and fleets loaded with all types of merchandise come in, the town has been refined, and the houses are tiled and embellished with beams and wood paneling.

The governor brought three ships, and in them came 125 Spaniards. Diego de Almagro soon found out because he was there in Panama. He then left for Nombre de Dios, where he and the governor met. *fol. 33v* They spoke amicably in public, as did [Pizarro's] brothers with him. I learned as certain that afterwards it became known that when they were alone, Diego de Almagro complained to his partner of how badly he had behaved toward him. After all, he [Almagro] had always treated him well; he had procured for him the command of the discovery and sustained him by sending and bringing him people as much as he could. If [Pizarro] had suffered hardships there, one cannot say that he himself was living in comfort—after all, he had lost one eye and remained even today crippled. And, it was because of his letters that [Pizarro] stayed in Gorgona, where he had sent him the ship used to discover the wealthy land. He [Almagro] had worked in all this and solicited what [Pizarro] was aware of. Indeed, even the trip to Spain; it was he who had insisted that [Pizarro] should go, and he had obtained the money for his expenses, believing that [Pizarro] would negotiate what he had stated and sworn and promised him and the bishop-elect. All of this turned out differently because [Pizarro] had come back as governor and adelantado, and for him [Almagro] he had brought the mayoralty of Tumbez with one hundred thousand maravedies of salary—more laughable than anything else. But he consoled himself with the knowledge that he had served well a most Christian prince, who without a doubt—indeed he was confident that consistent with his mercy and kindness—would reward him. I also heard that to this the governor replied somewhat angrily that it was not necessary to remind him of the past; indeed, he knew it full well and was aware of it. Furthermore, he had reported in Spain about [Almagro's] acts and solicited the adelantamiento for him, but they refused to do it—not because they were unaware of who he was, but rather because a joint governance was never granted, nor was it tolerated because it would be bad government. The territory of Peru was so vast there was governance for both of them and for others; furthermore, what he [Pizarro] was bringing was also [Almagro's] because he had a share in everything, and his desire was that [Almagro] should command and govern as he wished. Almagro, resentful of what [Pizarro] said to him, replied that he should show him the petition so he could see if their answer was as he related it. But neither did he show it, nor did Almagro give up his grievance, although they spoke and treated each other as before. [Almagro] returned to Panama to prepare the ships. Pizarro did the same. He was received with great honors by all the vecinos because they liked and loved him very much.

Some have said, and it was well known among all those of that time—many of whom remain alive—that when Almagro saw Hernando
fol. 34 Pizarro and his prestige, he feared him and failed to get along with him. Consequently, from then on Hernando Pizarro held him in little regard and did not like his dealings. In this, some fault Hernando Pizarro and others Diego de Almagro, of whom they say that because he was bitter and all were in his pay, he did not satiate their appetites and treated them as Blacks. Others deny this and say that he was the beginning, the middle, and the end of making possible what happened in Peru.

Those of you who wish to understand this business, ask Pizarro's friends about it, and to swear to you a hundred times[1] that what is said about Almagro is true and it is in all certain. Then do the same with those who were Almagro's [friends], and not only will they say that the Pizarros were ungrateful to him and that it is true what is said about him, but they will also swear to it.[2] It is a difficult task for someone who wants to write the truth, for they all relate the evident, which according to my understanding is that they all erred and were duplicitous and negotiated with cunning, be it Pizarro or Almagro or any of them.

But because Almagro was so despised for aiding his partner to be able shortly to leave Panama, he wanted to negotiate a certain partnership with some vecinos of the city, whose names were Alvaro de Guijo and the accountant, Alonso de Cáceres. But Licentiate Espinosa, who was at the time in Tierra Firme, and the bishop-elect and other honorable men mediated between them and convinced him to come to terms [with Pizarro], and they formed a new partnership with another agreement. Its substance was that the governor would leave to Diego de Almagro the area he had in Taboga and that he could not seek any favors for himself or any of his brothers until [Almagro] asked the emperor for a governance that would begin where Pizarro's ended. Further, all the gold, silver, stones, repartimientos, *naborías*,[3] and slaves, along with any other goods or property, would belong to both of them and to the bishop-elect, Don Hernando de Luque. After they reached this agreement and new contract, Diego de Almagro obtained money, and they paid the freights and the expenses that the governor had incurred. At this time Hernán Ponce[4] was in Panama.

Notes

1 over the gospel

2 swear it over a consecrated altar

3 A term from the Caribbean meaning "service Indians." Although naborías were not legally slaves, they were bound to serve.

4 In the left margin of the manuscript one finds: "known from Hernán Ponce." Ponce de León had arrived from Nicaragua with two ships laden with Indian slaves to be sold in Panama.

XXX

About how Governor Don Francisco Pizarro left Panama and Captain Diego de Almagro stayed there, and how Pizarro entered Coaque

fol. 34v By virtue of the new agreement and partnership between Pizarro and Almagro, the expedition was dispatched better than was thought possible because Almagro knew how to provide the necessities, procuring victuals and all the rest needed for it. They decided that the governor should then set out, and after landing in the part of Peru that seemed suitable, he should await the succor that would follow, which was why Almagro had to remain in Panama. People and horses would come from Nicaragua; they believed that they would also come from other regions and that they would all suffice to master the land no matter how large it might be. After Pizarro and Almagro discussed what would be most expedient in this and other matters, Pizarro left Panama with three equipped ships.[1] Some 180 Spaniards went in them, and his brothers embarked with him, as well as Cristóbal de Mena, Diego Maldonado, Juan Alonso de Badajoz, Juan de Escobar, Diego Palomino, Francisco de Lucena, Pedro de los Ríos, Melchor Palomino, Juan Gutiérrez de Valladolid, Blas de Atienza, Francisco Martín Albarrán, Francisco Lobo, Juan de Trujillo, Hernando Carrasco, Diego de Agüero, García Martín Narváez, Juan de Padilla, and many others, up to the said number. Thirty-six horses went, a great force in a war here because without them one could not subjugate so many peoples. They carried many bucklers for when they might engage in combat, made in our manner—which is not bad, but advantageous—from staves of the wine casks that come from Spain. They are strong, and the arrow or dart that goes through would have to be shot by a powerful arm; that seldom happens.

The governor went ahead until he arrived at the Pearl Islands, where he waited until everyone came. When all united, he left there determined not to do what he had done the first time, which was to go through those mangroves within sight, but to enter a harbor beyond the forests, in the land that he had discovered. All were exhuberant because they believed that in a short time they would return to Spain with great riches. Some saw this desire fulfilled, and others died in poverty. Navigating the sea, they stayed on course, and the weather helped them in such a way that within five days, according *fol. 35* to the reports of some who were there, they sighted[2] land, where they later put into port, and they recognized that it was the bay they call San Mateo.[3] Pizarro and his men discussed what they should do to succeed from the beginning in the enormous enterprise they were undertaking.

Following a thorough debate, it was decided on [Pizarro's] proposal that the Spaniards and the horses should proceed on land along the coast and that the ships would go by sea. The plan was put into effect; the people set out from there, and they went on facing hardships because in that land there are rivers and marshes to traverse.[4] At last, one morning they arrived in a principal town called Coaque, where they found great spoils because the Indians, although they had learned about the Spaniards, did not hide their property or flee into the forests. The reason was their imprudence, rather than willingness, because they believed that the Spaniards would not pillage or assault the peaceful and that they did not owe [the Spaniards] anything and had not offended them at any time. Instead, they thought that they would enjoy each other and have their banquets, as happened when Pizarro was first involved in the discovery. When they realized the deception, many fled; it is said that [the Spaniards] took more than twenty thousand castellanos and many fine emeralds, which at that time were worth a great treasure any place, but because those who were there had seen few, they were unfamiliar with them. Most of [the emeralds] were lost because of a remark by a friar there named Fray Reginaldo, who said that the emerald was harder than steel and could not be broken; thus, believing that they were striking glass, they shattered with hammers most of the stones that they took.[5]

When the Indians watched these things, they were astonished by such people; they stared at the horses, which they later believed to be immortal, if those who tell us this are not fooling. The native lord of this town, terrified and shocked, hid in his house, cursing such bad guests who had visited him. Pizarro and his men installed themselves in the town; and because they had captured several Indians, the governor asked them about the cacique. Because he learned

from them where he was hiding, he was very pleased to have secured them. He ordered that they should go get him and bring him into his presence, and thus it was done. [The cacique] appeared before him, shaking, and he excused himself through the interpreters, saying that he had not been hiding, nor was he in a stranger's house, but his own. When he saw[6] that they had entered the town without his authority and taken what he and his Indians had, and fearing that they
fol. 35v might kill him, he did not come to see them. To this Pizarro replied that he should feel secure and order the Indians to return to their houses because he [Pizarro] wanted neither captives nor to take their land. Further, [the cacique] had erred in failing to come to meet him and offer peace because it would have prevented the Spaniards from taking the gold and the other things that they took from them. But he should be assured that he would order that no more harm came to him. He treated the cacique well so that they would not dislike or hate [the Christians]. Thus, the lord of the town returned to his house and ordered the Indians to come with their wives and supply the Christians with the provisions that they had most of. But they bothered and offended the natives so much that when they saw how they scorned them and ruined and robbed them, they took to the forests and left them their houses. And they did it with such design that although they went to look for them, they encountered only a few.[7]

Notes

1 Pizarro left on one ship on 20 January 1531. The second vessel commanded by Cristóbal de Mena was to set sail early in February. See Busto, *Pizarro,* p. 53.

2 recognized

3 They reached the Bay of San Mateo thirteen days after leaving Panama, or early in the first week of February 1531; see Busto, *Pizarro,* p. 53.

4 Cieza glosses over this slow southward trek. From Atacámes they passed through Cancebí, finding ceramics and fish nets. Then they entered Quiximíes, where with difficulty they crossed a river; beyond this point they encountered more dense mangroves. Fortunately, Ruiz and his ship caught up to the group with supplies. See Busto, *Pizarro,* pp. 53–54.

5 Friar Reginaldo de Pedraza, the leader of the six Dominicans who accompanied Pizarro on this expedition, hid some of the emeralds in his

clothes. He returned to Panama to escape the plague of verrugas rampant in Coaque, but on the isthmus the friar became feverish and died. The emeralds were discovered sewn into the lining of his habit. See Busto, *Pizarro*, pp. 55–56, and Lockhart, *Men of Cajamarca*, p. 202.

6 knew

7 Coaque had perhaps four hundred residences and a modest fortification; see Busto, *Pizarro*, p. 55.

XXXI

About how Pizarro decided to send ships to Panama and Nicaragua with the gold that was found, and how some Christians came to join him,[1] and about how many became ill

Within a few days of the governor's arrival to Coaque it was decided with the agreement of Hernando Pizarro and the other leaders there that the ships should return to Panama and Nicaragua so that the Spaniards and horses that would have been recruited there could come. Thus, [Pizarro] wrote to his partner, Diego de Almagro, about everything that had hitherto occurred. On the two ships that went to Panama he sent most of the opulent and beautiful gold pieces taken in Coaque. He ordered the remainder to be taken to Nicaragua on another ship under the command of one Bartolomé de Aguilar.[2] Pizarro wrote letters to his friends, advising them to hasten to come because he had great news of the land ahead and that it was ruled by one lord who was very powerful.

As the ships left, the governor and the Christians remained in Coaque, an unhealthy land near the equinoctial line. Our people endured great hardships there because they stayed more than seven months, and it befell some of them that they would go to bed at night healthy and at sunrise be swollen up and even dead. Others were crippled and their limbs shrunken for twenty or more days before they recovered. Besides this, most of them erupted with such bad and ugly boils[3] above their eyes, as those[4] who survived from that time know.[5]

Because they did not know how to cure such a contagious disease, some cut [the boils], and they bled so much that only a few of those who did this escaped death. With all this travail they did not lack maize, or some fruit and native roots, but they were deprived of eating meat or fish for many days because they had none. They eagerly awaited the ships, and when they did not come, they were distressed by their delay. But because some were crippled, and others had boils, and all of them were weary of eating nothing but maize, they resolved to leave there for a better land. After the move had already been discussed, they saw a ship approaching on the sea, which made them all rejoice; they believed that this would not be the only ship coming. It came fully loaded with provisions and refreshments for the Spaniards. There were thirteen horses and several Spaniards, among them Alonso Riquelme, treasurer, and García de Salcedo, inspector; Antonio Navarro, accountant; Jerónimo de Aliaga, Gonzalo Farfán, Melchor Verdugo, Pedro Díaz, and others. When they disembarked, they were well received by Pizarro and those who were with him. They gave him letters they were carrying from Diego de Almagro, the bishop-elect, and other people who wrote to him. Several days later they set out from there, marching along the coast until they arrived at the village of Pasado. The considerable reputation of the Spaniards had already spread among the Indians—very different from what they had originally thought and believed: that they were holy people, not disposed to kill or steal or do harm, but were friendly and peaceful toward them. Whereas now, according to those from that time who are still around, they say that [the Spaniards] were cruel people without justice or truth because they went from land to land like thieves, pillaging and killing those who had not offended them, and that they brought large horses who ran like the wind and swords that cut anything within reach, and they said the same about lances. Some of them believed it, and others said it could not be so bad and waited to see with their own eyes the truth about the new people who had entered their realm. They kept sending notices about everything to the representatives of the Incas, who passed the information to Cuzco and Quito and everywhere.[6]

Against the advice of many of his followers, the lord of this village [Pasado] peacefully awaited the governor with his Indians in order to win his goodwill so that he would treat him as a friend and not plunder his village as if he were an enemy. Pizarro was pleased, and praising his intention, he pledged that the Christians would always honor him; they did not kill or plunder those who gave obedience to the king of Castile and wished to form an alliance with them. But he warned him not to feign his friendship, and [the lord] answered that he was in his land and with his acceptance. Thus, the Indians served the Christians, something they know how to do well because they were made to serve their own king and those who are in the land with his mandate. I was told, and it is true, that because the Christians needed native women to grind and make bread for them, the governor kept the peace and alliance accorded with the cacique. With this agreement he exchanged for seventeen Indians an emerald as large as a dove's egg, believing it was worthless, but it was worth a great treasure. After that Pizarro left well regarded by those of that region.

Notes

1 and about what they did

2 Bartolomé García de Aguilar was from Trujillo and joined the Pizarros during the third voyage. He became chief constable in San Miguel and settled there permanently. He died during the Gonzalo Pizarro revolt and was declared a traitor. The Crown tried to sequester his substantial estate. See Busto, *Diccionario,* 1:26–27.

3 These diseases are probably two forms of *Bartonellosis* (Carrion's disease as either Oroya fever or *Verruga peruana*). Oroya fever killed more quickly, coming with fever and anemia, and had a mortality rate from 10 to 40 percent. The *Verruga peruana* began with pain in the muscles, bones, and joints, followed by large nodules or boils in the shape of nuts. The joint pain would account for the crippling effect, though the mortality rate was lower. See Newson, *Life and Death,* pp. 144–47.

4 some of those

5 Folios 36r–v and 37r–v (cfr. supra) are missing in the manuscript. The editors of the Peruvian edition on which this translation is based have substituted them with the text published by Rafael Loredo, "Tercera parte de la *Crónica del Perú," Mercurio Peruano* (Lima) 340 (1955): 467–71.

6 Messages were swiftly carried in a relay system from one part of the realm to another by messengers called *chasquis.* With the roadway network of the Incas, news could be passed, mostly orally, over an expanse of hundreds of kilometers.

XXXII

About how [Pizarro] proceeded on his march, and [the Indians] killed two of his Christians, and Belalcázar arrived with other Christians from Nicaragua, and what else happened

Don Francisco Pizarro yearned to reach the fine land that lay beyond Tumbez, and he regretted that he had put into port so far back. God, Our Lord, allowed it thus because if he had gone all at once where he wanted to, without the people who had joined him [blank], there is no doubt that [the Indians] would have easily killed them. But because at its beginning no enterprise can be completely understood until it unfolds, Pizarro was thus unaware that ahead of him great armies were assembled and that fortunately they were fighting one another as enemies.[1] Having taken leave of the chief of the village, he departed in friendship, proceeding until he arrived in the Bay of Caráquez.[2] Because it was very wide, they could not cross it, but they went up to where the river that enters into it flows out, and they easily passed through and entered the village of an Indian woman whose husband had died a few days earlier. There was novelty in the spirit of those Indians because in secret they greatly insulted the Spaniards, but in public, fearing them and their horses, they showed their good side in spite of what was done, as they say. In their meetings and gatherings they discussed in what manner and with what artifice they would kill [the Spaniards]; they attempted several times to go out all together and kill them, but when they realized that the time had come to act, they became cowardly and lost their courage. They themselves tell us all of this to this day. They did not deal any further with the business of inflicting harm for their sake on the Spaniards, who were dwelling in the aforesaid village. One of them, named Santiago, went out on horseback about three or four shots of a crossbow away to obtain something that they needed. The Indians saw him, and because he was distracted, a band of them attacked him and killed him. Before this, [the Spaniards] had learned from our [Indians] that the [enemy]

Indians had evil intentions, and even though the governor tried to win their friendship with kind words, it failed. Angrily he ordered Cristóbal de Mena[3] to go with several Spaniards and try to capture those who had anything to do with it. When they returned from the campaign, another Spaniard strayed slightly from the path, and he was also killed because underneath this friendship they were really enemies. Pizarro resented this and issued a complaint against the Indians of that region because they killed his [men], although neither he nor they had done any harm or given offense to them. Enraged by this, he ordered horsemen to penetrate with the iron points of their lances the first ones they encountered. Several of them were killed in this way. And one chief whom they seized was brought before [Pizarro], who spoke to him through interpreters, complaining that his kin had killed two of his Christians, who had not harmed them or taken any of them captive or prisoner. The chief replied that those who did that were crazy and that they should order his release so that he could punish them. When Pizarro heard his good reasoning, he ordered one Indian to be brought, who had been captured and had been with those who killed one of the Christians. The cacique spoke to him harshly, saying that as punishment for his wickedness he would be hanged. And so they put him on a pole, and he neither spoke nor excused himself; rather he indicated that he gave little importance to life and that he was happy to die. The chief was released, and Pizarro spoke to him gently and lovingly, appealing to him not to abandon their lands or rise up in war and that they had good friends in the Christians.

Afterwards they marched ahead to the province of Puerto Viejo, where the Indians preserve great shrines, and in some places ugly figures with indecent members were seen, which they worship. But because the chiefs were involved in the wars fought between Atahualpa and Huascar, no army was mobilized with the strength to kill the Christians. Instead, they decided to show them good will and provide them with what was available in their region because [the Christians] were just passing through to where they obviously would be killed since there were so few of them. And so they welcomed Pizarro, expressing joy about his coming, and he ordered that peace be kept with the friends, and no harm or injury be given to them. They provided food and whatever service they could without receiving payment for it. But because in war it is difficult to keep soldiers well disciplined, certain offenses were committed, which Pizarro did not punish. He spent fifteen days in that land. He learned about a small ship that had left Nicaragua and that Sebastián de Belalcázar[4] and other Christians and several horses were coming by land; he was pleased about that. And within a few days Belalcázar and Morgovejo de Quiñones,[5] Juan de Porras,[6] Francisco de Fuentes,[7] Diego Prieto,[8] Rodrigo Núñez,[9] Alonso Beltrán,[10] and others—up to thirty—arrived; there were twelve horses. They were well received by the governor and those who were with him.

Notes

1 Cieza is referring to what the Europeans saw as the fratricidal strife between Atahualpa and Huascar, following the death of their father, the Inca Huayna Capac. This divisive civil war played a major role in the success of the Spanish conquest. For an Andean viewpoint, see Franklin Pease G.Y., *Los últimos Incas del Cuzco* (Madrid: Alianza América, 1991).

2 Cieza spells it "Guaraques"; the bay is not far north of Puerto Viejo and Manta.

3 Mena was born in Ciudad Real and came to the Indies around the mid-1520s; he was encomendero and town councillor in Granada, Nicaragua. He supplied horses and slaves for the Peruvian venture and sent fresh recruits from Panama in 1531. For the Pizarros, his main liability was his friendship with Almagro. His shares at Cajamarca were insulting, smaller than that of any other horseman. He returned to Spain in 1533 with his manuscript history of events in Peru (published anonymously in Seville in 1534). See Lockhart, *Men of Cajamarca*, pp. 133–35.

4 Sometimes a variant spelling, "Benalcázar," is used. In 1522, while in Panama, he stated that he was from the town of Belalcázar, and he normally used that spelling, as does Cieza. Belalcázar was illiterate and came from a humble family. His original surname was Moyano, but he preferred to use the name of his birthplace. He was encomendero in Panama in 1522, participated in the conquest of Nicaragua, and later held office there. See Lockhart, *Men of Cajamarca*, p. 128.

5 See chapter 52.

6 Juan de Porras was born in Seville about 1501. He was in Hispaniola in 1523 and participated in the conquest of Honduras the following year. After Cajamarca, he returned to Seville by late 1535 and received a coat of arms for his services. Like Cieza, he settled with his wife in the parish of San Vicente

and still lived there as late as 1562. See Lockhart, *Men of Cajamarca,* pp. 238–39; and Busto, *Hueste perulera,* pp. 29–36.

7 Francisco de Fuentes, probably from Seville, arrived in Darién in 1520 and participated in the conquest of Nicaragua, where he received an encomienda. According to his service report he came to Peru with Soto, not Belalcázar. He received a town lot in Lima in 1535, but moved on to be a founder and town official of Trujillo and later of Chachapoyas. He died in 1560, and his will suggests he made substantial restitution to his Indians. See Lockhart, *Men of Cajamarca,* pp. 322–24; and Busto, *Hueste perulera,* pp. 203–18.

8 This name could be an error and may really refer to Alonso Preto, who did come from Nicaragua with Belalcázar and was at Cajamarca; see Lockhart, *Men of Cajamarca,* p. 407 n.

9 Rodrigo Núñez was born in Extremadura about 1500 and came to the Indies with Pedrarias in 1514. He was involved in the conquest of Veragua, Honduras, and Nicaragua, and received an encomienda in León in the 1520s. He had a colorful career in Peru, and his support of Diego de Almagro the Younger resulted in his execution by enraged Pizarrists in 1544. See Lockhart, *Men of Cajamarca,* pp. 334–37; and Busto, *Hueste perulera,* pp. 11–22.

10 Actually Hernando Beltrán. Born in Andalusia about 1496, Beltrán was a sailor involved with expeditions to the Pearl Islands and Nicaragua. His participation in the Peruvian venture was rewarded with a substantial share at Cajamarca, and with it he returned to Spain in 1535. He settled in Seville's maritime district, Triana, where he was still alive in 1546. See Busto, *Diccionario,* 1:233–34; and Lockhart, *Men of Cajamarca,* pp. 399–400.

XXXIII

About how the governor proceeded on his march and there was great discontent[1] among the Spaniards, and about how messengers came from Puná, [saying] that the islanders were determined to kill our men

The Christians did not take a step anywhere in the land without notice about it being sent to Atahualpa[2]—who had already by this time taken the fringe[3]—about how [the Spaniards] commanded by force and with goodwill on the coast and the land where our [people] were, and [the Indians] appealed to him as their lord. They say that it disturbed [Atahualpa] to learn about it and that he and some people from his army considered launching against the Christians. But so many of his brother's captains with large companies were coming to wage war against him that he abandoned repulsing Pizarro. He considered the other war more important, because when they told him there were so few [Spaniards], he laughed, saying to leave them, that they would serve him as *yanaconas*.[4] And because he was very smart, he sent certain orejones to go in disguise and find out what was being said about those people. For that reason, no one was sent by the Inca to defend their land when the Spaniards came. Furthermore, not all the natives where they were passing through were there; instead, chieftains and many of them were absent because they were in the camps of the Incas.

The rumor of how the Spaniards wanted to rule over them and take *fol. 38* away their land had spread in all directions. Those from Puná, a rich and populous island near the mainland, as I related in *Part One,* were very powerful and always used cunning. They believed they could kill the Spaniards by using deceit if they came to their island, and they laughed at those from Tumbez, their enemies, because when Pizarro was exploring with the thirteen the year before, they had praised him so much. In the meantime, Pizarro was coming with his men, marching until they arrived at the Point of Santa Elena, a well-known place to those of us who have been in this land. The Spaniards were dis-

10. Rites and sacrifices of the Indians. Pedro de Cieza de León's *Primera Parte* (Seville, 1553), p. 22r. Courtesy of the Jay I. Kislak Foundation, Miami Lakes, Florida.

pleased with what they saw, and they did not believe what Pizarro, Candia, and the others said that they had seen. This is the result of our ebullient condition—we want to see everything immediately—and those men thought too much time had already passed without their having encountered any of the jars and vessels that they would later see. And they asked why they were being taken any further when what they were seeing was so poor, and [urged] that they should return to settle in Puerto Viejo. Pizarro reassured them, animating them to go on, telling them that if they returned to settle where they said, the Indians would think they were running away and would attack them, and they would be in danger. With what the governor said, they proceeded on their journey, discontented and even lacking some things. [Pizarro] ordered Diego de Agüero[5] and Quincoces[6] to go further along the coast and reconnoiter the Bay of Guayaquil. They explored what was necessary and returned to Pizarro, telling him that he should cross over to Puná because there was so little sea between the island and the mainland.

When the chiefs of the island learned that the Christians were so close and wanted to come to their island, they wanted to have the upper hand. They sent messengers who were instructed in what they should say, which was to invite [the Spaniards] to cross over and enjoy themselves with them, and they would be well received and cared for by them. And so that they could cross without difficulties, they would send many balsas in which they and their horses could come. All the time they had contrived, according to what was said, that those bringing them would untie the ropes on the sea so that all would die in the water at the same time and hour. Because Pizarro was unaware of the deed that they planned, he readily replied to the messengers, promising alliance and peace with the islanders, saying that our men would do no harm there. With this, they went back, and Tumbalá, the chief lord, was overjoyed to hear it. He then ordered construction of many balsas, and they were so diligent and content with all this that the interpreters learned about their design, according to what is affirmed. They found out about it from someone who underestimated revealing such a secret to them because they were natives. They listened, concealing their feelings and without betraying alarm, and because as *fol. 38v* interpreters they had been exempted from work and treated so well, they did not want to lose such a position, so they secretly reported to Pizarro what they had found out. He thanked them profusely, promising them that he would care for them as his children, and they would be treated as such. Unperturbed, he ordered that no Spaniard should cross over to the island without his command. His brother, Captain Hernando Pizarro, had remained behind with some people, and the governor wished that they would come. Noticing that the Christians were reticent to cross, those from Puná feared that they might have been warned of their design, the one that has been told. In order to be sure, Tumbalá crossed over to them, and with great pretense asked Pizarro why was it that he was not crossing over with the Christians as had been agreed earlier. Pizarro answered, revealing what he knew, that it was because they were so cunning and crafty; although neither he nor the Christians vexed or harmed him or entered his island, [Tumbalá] had made a pact to kill them in such an ugly manner. Further, he should know that God Almighty was with them and sheltered them and delivered them from their lies and treachery. The Indian lord answered—excusing himself more emphatically than is usual with them—that it was a lie someone had told him in order to ingratiate himself because he never thought of or was accustomed to killing his guests and friends. And so that [Pizarro] could see that it was[7] as he was saying, he begged him that he himself should get on one of the balsas, and he would see how discourteous all his [people] were to believe what they were saying. When Pizarro saw the cacique speak so earnestly and with so little discomposure, he believed that what [the interpreters] had told him must have been their own invention because in truth they grumble a lot. He ordered his men to cross very cautiously.

The islanders received them well and fully provisioned them with what they had—having, as some relate with certainty, a vile design against the Spaniards, who stayed there more than three months. Others defend the Indians because they say our people made themselves absolute lords over what did not belong to them, and that, along with other things that soldiers tend to commit, was the reason why they were all so despised by the Indians of Puná, who would have rather died than witness what they saw.[8]

Notes

1 Given the context of the arguments that follow, the transcription of the original is inaccurate. It should read "gran descontento," not "grande contento."

2 Again, the chasquis, specially trained runners working as relay teams, kept the Inca informed.

3 "To take the fringe" means to assume the leadership. The Inca ceremony is simple, as Cieza describes it in *Part Two,* chapter 10: the *llautu*—a multicolored braid, about one inch wide—is placed on the head and wrapped approximately four times around the forehead. At the center, there is a four-inch-wide fringe, which reached the eyes, with red tassles held by gold tubes.

Sometimes at the top the llautu had a six-inch stick with a pompon and three feathers. See John Howland Rowe, "Inca Culture at the Time of the Spanish Conquest," in *Handbook of South American Indians,* 7 vols., ed. Julian H. Steward, Bureau of American Ethnology Bulletins, no. 143 (Washington, D.C., 1946–59), 2:235, 258.

4 Servants or retainers of the Inca.

5 Agüero was born about 1511 in Deleitosa near Trujillo. Pizarro recruited him in 1529. He was standard bearer at Cajamarca, and active at Jauja and Cuzco, and a founder of Lima and its councillor until his death. He was one of the first to visit Collao and see Lake Titicaca. In 1538 he married the daughter of the governor of Pánuco in Mexico, Doña Luisa de Garay. He died in Lima in 1544, but left a dynasty that continues to the present. See Lockhart, *Men of Cajamarca,* pp. 209–12.

6 Juan de Quincoces was born in Hermosilla in Burgos and joined the Peruvian venture in Panama in 1531. He had strong commercial connections with Burgos merchants and ultimately settled in Lima, where he became a town councillor. He died in 1536 or 1537, perhaps a victim of the native uprising. See Lockhart, *Men of Cajamarca,* pp. 310–11.

7 a lie

8 such a thing

XXXIV

About how those of the island still planned to kill the Spaniards, and Tumbalá was imprisoned, and how the islanders fought with our men

The Spanish Christians remained on Puná during the said time. They were well served by the Indians, who thoroughly detested them because they realized and knew that they were striving to become their lords. It seemed to them that they were of a different stripe from the Incas, whom they had served. Furthermore, many of their enemies, supported by the Spaniards, had come from Tumbez and stayed on *fol. 39* their island in spite of them. They made great sacrifices to their gods, and those who were appointed for it even spoke with the demon in order to get his advice. They did not know where or how to find a way to kill those whom they so despised. Hernando Pizarro had not arrived to join his brother. It is well-known that following much dispute and debate, Tumbalá, the chief lord, and his allies and confederates decided to kill the Christians by using a trap. They let them know that they wanted to have a royal hunt, which they call *chaco*[1]—and it is truly something to see—and that while they [the Spaniards] would be watching the animals dying as a novelty, [the Indians] would seize hidden weapons and attack and kill them.

They all were excited to do this deed, and so they say that some of them invited Hernando Pizarro to see the said hunt, or another similar one, and that he replied that he might do it to please them. But having been warned by one Indian, he rushed to join his brother, whom Tumbalá had invited to be present with the Christians in the chaco, which they wanted to hold to please them and make them content. He answered that he was glad. Traditionally, no Indian in this land ever revealed a secret entrusted by his lord. They lost this custom, along with other good ones, when the Spaniards arrived in their land. Thus, after Tumbalá and the others arranged what has been written, one of them did reveal the secret, telling it to Felipillo, who then related it to Pizarro, who was horrified that the Indians wanted him dead although he had done them no harm. He did not want to give up going [to the chaco], nor did he entirely believe the words of the interpreter. But he ordered the Spaniards—those on foot as well as those on horses—to go prepared for war rather than to watch the hunt. They did so with great gusto.

Many people gathered in the designated place. When [the Indians] noticed the circumspection of our men and their silence, they suspected what it could be, and thus with pain in their souls they began the hunt according to their custom. It was amazing in what strange [manner] countless large deer along with other animals were taken, which were divided among the Christians.

They told me that the treasurer, Alonso Riquelme, and Hernando Pizarro had such a quarrel that Riquelme, very upset, boarded a ship, announcing that he was returning to Spain to report to the king about everything that happened. Don Francisco Pizarro learned about it and was distressed. He ordered Juan Alonso de Badajoz to get some Spaniards for him, with whom he returned all the way to *fol. 39v* the Point of Santa Elena, where he caught up with [Riquelme] and brought him back and reconciled him with his brother. The Indians who were in league and had contrived to kill the Spaniards were not pacified; when they met, holding cups of their wine[2] in their hands, they asked why they should look for an opportunity to kill them—that it was shameful, and that instead they should all come out openly to do it because there were so few [Spaniards], and that once they acted, it would be much easier than they thought. Many on the mainland were informed regarding this deed, and everyone believed that it was for common relief and general benefit to kill those intruders who, because they did not work, wanted to go on pillaging as they had been doing. And although this double-dealing was going on, [the Indians] were not remiss in serving them; rather, they were more diligent than before. Nevertheless, I learned that while Pizarro was dividing certain gold given to him as gifts by the villages that he passed through after Coaque, and while speaking with Jerónimo de Aliaga[3] and Blas de Atienza,[4] one of the interpreters arrived and revealed to him everything that was happening. Having learned this and having been informed of how Tumbalá and other chiefs were meeting and discussing it,[5] he ordered that everyone should be ready for what might come and that those who were necessary should go and seize Tumbalá, along with the other caciques that they find with him, and bring them to him. Because [the Indians] were unable to escape, they captured those that they found, amounting to sixteen, all chieftains and Tumbalá among them. They were taken to Pizarro's quarters, and he asked them angrily through the interpreters why were they so cunning, trying in so many ways to kill him and his men although they had not taken their property or women or anything else other than what they had willingly given them to eat. All this he had overlooked in past occasions, having been informed about it all, because he wanted to leave their island in their good graces and keep them as his friends and allies. But they loathed him and have forced them to openly wage war against them as enemy traitors, and the punishment would begin with them as the principal instigators of it.[6]

When he said that and other things, he ordered that Tumbalá should be carefully watched; because he was a chief, [Pizarro] did not want him to die. The others were delivered into the hands of those of Tumbez, their enemies, who killed them with great cruelty, although they had committed no other crime than wanting to defend their land from those who wanted to usurp it;[7] and they did not believe this to *fol. 40* be a sin. The league was assembled to attack the Spaniards, and more than five hundred Indians went out on orders of their elders, most of them with strong, sharp palm rods. They knew that the chiefs had been killed and that Tumbalá was imprisoned, and it alarmed them. In their language they called upon their gods to help them against the Christians, whom they cursed many times because they had entered their lands and strove to destroy them. In the meantime, the governor and his men were in a fighting spirit, although he believed that because Tumbalá was in his power, his people would not dare to attack. But when the Indians were spotted, the Spaniards attacked them, mounted on their horses with their lances in hand, not wanting to return them to the lance bucket. They were so resentful of the Spaniards that they began to hurl shots with the strength that some have in their arms. The horsemen were already upon them, as well as the shield bearers; they killed many Indians, and more were wounded by lance and sword. They could not endure against the ability of the masters in combat, and thus those who were left, giving frightened howls, fled in great fear. Hernando Pizarro had entered among them, and they wounded his horse in such a way that it later died. Pizarro ordered it thrown into a deep cavern that was there, and they blocked it so that the Indians of Tumbez would not believe that they had the power to kill horses.

While those of Puná were engaged in this conflict with the Christians, those of Tumbez robbed indiscriminately; moreover, they were destroying and wrecking because of ancient hate and enmity. And to please them even further, Pizarro ordered that more than four hundred of their compatriots whom those of Puná had held captive be delivered to them. Yet, secretly those of Tumbez disliked the Christians as much as did those of Puná, believing that what had befallen their neighbors would befall them also.

Notes

1 Cieza describes the hunt in *Part Two,* chapter 16. Several thousand men might participate, creating a large circle around the game—deer, guanaco, and others—then closing in until it was possible to join arms and create a natural corral. The animals were taken for wool or meat sometimes prepared as sun dried *charqui.*

2 Chicha.

3 Aliaga was born in Segovia in 1508 and was a notary by profession. When he was sixteen, he sailed for the Indies, and was active in the settlement of Castilla del Oro. He joined Pizarro's third expedition and participated in all the major events of the conquest, also acting as a notary—executing various documents, including powers of attorny, sales bills, and loans. He always remained loyal to the Crown and was well rewarded for it. He settled in Lima, married, and fathered both legitimate and illegitimate mestizo children. He left for Spain to report to Charles V in 1550. While he was there, his wife died, and he married the daughter of the count of Paredes. He remained in Spain and died at the count's palace at Villapalacios in 1569. His dynasty would continue to play a role in Lima affairs into the twentieth century. See Lockhart, *Men of Cajamarca,* pp. 258–62; and Busto, *Diccionario,* 1:56–58.

4 Probably born in Segovia about 1489, Atienza was with Balboa and Pizarro during the discovery of the Pacific. He helped found Panama and received an encomienda there. He participated in the first and third voyages,

and remained in San Miguel as the main force marched to Cajamarca. He was a founder and first alcalde of Trujillo, where he received another Indian grant. He last appears in Lima about 1552. See Busto, *Diccionario,* 1:170–72.

5 when Pizarro learned about it

6 of the war

7 by killing them

XXXV

About how those of Puná and their allies fought a battle with the Christians, in which [the Indians] were defeated, and what else happened

More than three thousand five hundred men were assembled, all with their weapons, awaiting Tumbalá and the other lords and chiefs who had been killed, as has been told earlier. When those who fled the fray joined them, they told them what had happened and that the Spaniards had treated their elders inhumanely because they handed them over to those of Tumbez, who then beheaded all of them. Further, that Tumbalá was in the power of the Christians, with whom they had fought out of desperation when they saw such a thing, and *fol. 40v* that many of their companions had died. When the islanders heard this, they uttered such screams and wails that they could be heard far away. They complained about their fate and their gods for allowing the Christians, being so few, to be powerful enough to kill so many. They asked each other why they were doing it. They denounced the Incas because although they had such fierce enemies in their land, they fought a war amongst themselves and allowed what was occurring. They decided to either die on the battlefield as good men, or avenge with the death of the Spaniards their chiefs and caciques, who were killed by those of Tumbez. Thus, they ordered in their hasty fury that seven hundred archers go in their balsas to attack the ship in the harbor, and all the rest of them decided to draw near the Spaniards and fight a battle with them. Thus, they marched in their squadrons with their captains and leaders going before them.

Pizarro believed himself secure because he had Tumbalá in his power, but they soon heard the clamor of the warriors. Those in the balsas had reached the ship, but those who were on it positioned the sails in such a way that they protected themselves from the shots of the darts and arrows. The rest of them arrived within sight of the Spaniards [who were on land], of whom three or four greedy ones had strayed to look for gold among the dead. Two of them were sighted by the Indians and cruelly killed. In the meantime, Pizarro encour-

aged his people with the words of the valiant captain that he was, and of great fortitude. The horses were placed in position, as well as the shield bearers, and they awaited the Indians, who attacked from three directions with determination and great boldness. Our men mingled among them, lancing with lances and slashing with swords those islanders and their allies—so many that the field was full of blood. When they saw so many die and fall wounded, they fled, vexed and very frightened. After having tried everything possible to succeed in their design, they did no more harm than to wound two Spaniards and three horses. Those who went against the ship had the same fate because they withdrew without having any impact, and it appeared to them that what they had seen went against all reason: that so few men could prevail against the thousands of them. They saw it as an absurdity, and thus they tormented themselves, calling the dead
fol. 41 fortunate. Those who survived the battle and the others who had remained fortified themselves in some small hills that extended near to where the Spaniards were.

Pizarro ordered that the wounded and the horses be treated, exhorting everyone to be alert and that no one out of greed for gold should leave his lodgings. The Indians who were in the hills came out a few times, giving the cry that they usually give; shooting many darts and other shots, they returned to where they felt safe. When Pizarro saw that so many Indians had died and would die in that war, and distressed by the perdition of their souls—because it is well known that all would end up in hell—he called the interpreters, and with the great sadness that he felt, he told Tumbalá: "Why did you cause so much evil? Indeed, it is because of you that so much harm has come to the island. Being free, you strove for my death and that of the Christians in every possible way. God has delivered us from your intrigues; I ordered your capture to secure you, and I did not want to kill you because of your dignity as a lord. There is no will on your part to order your men to put down their arms and to desire our friendship; you have already seen what it means to want to be our enemies; the experience resulted in your harm. Be assured that you will have to give an account of the dead to God, which is another and more important business." And so that the harm would not continue, he admonished him in God's name and demanded that he send messengers to order the Indians to put down their arms and go to their houses, populating the villages with their women and children, "because I promise not to wage war, or to allow pillaging or any wrong to be done to them." Tumbalá responded with few words: much was said about him that was a lie, and he saw his land plundered and dissipated, and his enemies, those of Tumbez, were going about in it, a lamentable thing. But to please [Pizarro], he would send someone to plead with and order the Indians to put down their arms and to come in alliance and friendship.

Pizarro was delighted because he wished to conquer without bloodshed. The messenger went to the Indians, but when they heard what Tumbalá had ordered, they became angry at him, saying that wild beasts would not make them accept peace with someone who had caused them so much harm. Messengers came and went several times, but nothing was concluded, which angered Pizarro. He ordered Juan Pizarro, his brother, and Sebastián de Belalcázar to go with some *fol. 41v* people to the island and to wage war against the islanders because they were so obstinate in their evil designs. It was done as he had ordered. But the Indians went into the frightening marshes that exist in those parts and into other strong places where they were secure from being harmed. Those [Spaniards] who had gone found seven sheep; they killed them and quartered them for food. And after they destroyed all they could on the island, they returned to join Pizarro.

At this time, while the Spaniards were engaged in these disputes with those of Puná, Hernando de Soto arrived with people and horses from Nicaragua. He and they were well received by the governor. He did not give [Soto] the rank of general because Hernando Pizarro held it, and it would have been bad to remove it from him; without much ado, he named him captain. Soto hid how he felt about it. When Hernando de Soto had come with the said people, Pizarro decided to leave Puná because the natives were so rebellious, and to go to Tumbez, the land of his friends and where he believed they would be well lodged and provisioned because up to then, those of Tumbez owed much to the Spaniards, and the Spaniards owed them nothing.[1]

Note

1 The Spanish arrived at Puná around Christmas of 1531; sometime in April of the new year they set sail southward for Tumbez. See Busto, *Historia general*, pp. 52–54.

XXXVI

About how those of Tumbez held secret councils [to discuss] whether they would remain friendly with the Christians or come out against them as enemies, and how they killed two Spaniards, having decided to kill all of them if they could

The chiefs from Tumbez and many of their Indians had been with the Spaniards in Puná, where Francisco Pizarro delivered to them more than six hundred people, men and women whom the islanders had held captive, and he permitted the harm [those from Tumbez] did—which was considerable—without interfering, believing that they had faithful friends in them for what lay ahead; and they themselves had openly said and proclaimed it. But when they realized that Pizarro and his men wanted to leave the island to come directly to their land, they feared to receive such people. Sometimes they thought that it would be good to continue without a hint of deceit the friendship that had been forged. But, believing that [the Spaniards] would rule their land, various opinions were expressed, affirming that those who had shown support for them would be severely punished and killed by the Inca. Moreover, the Spaniards did not proclaim friendship of equals; rather, they would command and rule essentially at will, and that is *fol. 42* how it appeared because they held them in such low regard. So while the Spaniards were at the point of crossing from the island to Tumbez, [the Indians] held assemblies and secret councils, heedful that no notice of it reached our people. And after they thought it over and discussed it, they arrived at an agreement to try with all their power to kill the Spaniards, although they realized they might lose their lives.

Pizarro was completely unaware of this because he trusted their word that they would be his friends. Therefore, some Christians decided to get in the balsas to leave the island for Tumbez with part of the horses and baggage, and the rest would go on the ships by sea. Captain Hernando de Soto got onto a balsa with two or three Spaniards, and Captain Cristóbal de Mena boarded another one, and one named Hurtado with another youngster, Alonso de Toro's brother,[1] embarked on another balsa. And they began their journey, while the Indians had already decided on the said design. This Hurtado and the other boy arrived ahead of everybody else. They encountered many of those from Tumbez along the coast, who called to them with deceit and great pretense as if they wanted to take them to their lodgings. Because the poor wretches were careless and without any suspicion, they went to where they were calling them. Then with great cruelty their eyes were gouged, and while they were still alive, the barbarians cut off their limbs. They had some pots ready on a great fire, and they put them inside, and they expired in this torment. The aggressors were determined to get their hands on Captain Soto[2] to do the same that they had done with the others. When Soto arrived on the beach, the Indians who were at the helm of the balsa were natives of Tumbez itself, and they learned what had happened. They could not conceal it because [the Indians] are fickle; instead, they joyfully jumped on land, which alarmed Soto. They were cautiously coming to kill him, but when they learned that only a few Christians had arrived, they thought that it might be better to postpone the death of those who were already in their port until more would come.

Soto and those who were with him did not sleep that night. The next day Pizarro and the rest of the Spaniards arrived. When the Tumbezinos saw him and them, they were afraid—although they were many—to come out and carry out their plan. And when their fury turned to phlegm and courage to cowardice, they wanted to leave without having to hear the snorting of the horses. They said that their sins were great because their gods not only had forgotten and for-
fol. 42v saken them, but were helping the Christians, who although so few, would overcome them. Their spirits cowered to flee and leave them the land.

And because it is convenient for the clarity of my writing to finish relating the dissensions and wars of the two brothers, Huascar and Atahualpa, I will leave this event at this stage and will briefly attempt to conclude what I say and then I will return to it.[3]

Notes

1 Three Toros, from Trujillo, came to Peru. The eldest Hernando was a squire of Hernando Pizarro. Alonso, a footman, was at Cajamarca and settled in Cuzco, receiving an encomienda there. He defended the city during the Indian uprising of 1536–37. During Gonzalo Pizarro's revolt he was his camp master, but was replaced by Francisco de Carvajal. He was killed in 1546 by his enraged father-in-law for refusing to give up an Inca concubine. See Lockhart, *Men of Cajamarca*, pp. 357–60.

2 and the others

3 The following remark appears in the margin: "this chapter and the following [that is, the two that deal with the war between Huascar and Atahualpa] should be placed after Pizarro founded San Miguel." Following the author's direction we will postpone these two chapters, pointing out the change in foliation in due time.

XXXVII

How Pizarro, having arrived in Tumbez, wanted to punish the Indians for killing the two Christians, and what else happened

fol. 45 When Pizarro learned that those of Tumbez, whom he had honored *fol. 45v* so much, had done such great villainy as to raise arms in order to attack and kill the two Christians so dreadfully, he denounced them and called them traitors. He ordered the people on the ships to disembark and stay in two strong dwellings or forts there—he and Soto with Belalcázar and a portion of the people in one, and Captain Hernando Pizarro and his brothers with Captain Cristóbal de Mena and the rest of the Spaniards in the other. Those of Tumbez had left for secret places of the valley. Pizarro, because he now hated them, wanted to punish the death of the two Christians. Therefore, he ordered several of his captains to go out with the necessary people to plunder the land, trying to capture any Indian men and women they could find. Horrified that the Tumbezinos had killed two Christians, those who went did not lack will to hurt them, and it was nothing to them to kill one hundred or a thousand Indians.

They found few or none, but they pillaged what they could, sheep as well as other things, and with that they returned to the camp. But Pizarro's fury had not passed, and he ordered Captain Soto to go with the Spaniards and cross the river because the Indians must have crossed over to that part. Soto left and crossed the river; he killed some Indians and captured more, although there were only a few because they were within a quagmire of marshes. When those of Tumbez saw how incensed the Spaniards were because they wanted to wage war against them, and because [the Spaniards] were at ease in their land, and Atahualpa neither sent anyone nor came against [the Spaniards], they contemplated what would be best for them. They agreed to beg pardon for what had happened and to offer peace without any guile, because otherwise [the Spaniards] would destroy and pillage their valley; such calamity would be difficult for them to behold. They sent the best suited of them as messengers to negotiate peace in the name of all of them.

They appeared in Pizarro's presence, and they asked him in the name of the Sun, a god they worshiped, to have mercy on them, imploring his favor with loud wails, promising that those of Tumbez would have perpetual alliance with the Spaniards without any artifice. Pizarro believed that although those of Tumbez made peace in order not to be killed or captured or have their valley plundered, it would be beneficial to conclude it with them, even though it might last only a short time; after all, he needed them to give him guides and to help carry their baggage and for other purposes. Thus, he told the messengers to return to the caciques and tell them that just as there was courage in the Spaniards to wage war, there was mercy to grant peace, but they should beware not to break it with treachery. He promised it because he was fond of them for the hospitality they had shown him when he and the thirteen were exploring and because it would not please him if they or others were destroyed. When their messengers told the caciques and the chiefs of Tumbez what Pizarro had answered, they appeared before him, and they thanked him for *fol. 46* how well he was treating them. After he renewed his alliance with those of Tumbez, as has been said, he asked about the road ahead—what the nature of it was and if there were settlements or not. They answered the truth: on the plains there were large sandy areas lacking grass for the horses and water, and in the highlands there were steep crags of live rock and great amounts of snow. But he did not believe it because one always gives little credence to what the Indians say.[1]

Many of the Spaniards grumbled about the land because they had so little confidence in what lay ahead. They became dejected. There were some among them who asked permission to return to Nicaragua or Panama. Pizarro granted it, asking only that they leave their weapons and horses. He ordered that some should go along the coast to see what the nature of the land was. They returned, affirming that there was nothing except cacti and carob trees—and only in a few places because everything was sand—and they were saying that the good and well-settled [land] was what they had left behind in Puerto Viejo. Pizarro was certain that great provinces existed in the land, and he encouraged his companions to persevere and suffer until God

11. The Inca ruler. Pedro de Cieza de León's *Primera Parte* (Seville, 1553), p. 46r. Courtesy of the Jay I. Kislak Foundation, Miami Lakes, Florida.

granted them. He consulted with Hernando Pizarro, Hernando de Soto, Cristóbal de Mena, and other leaders, indicating that because those of Tumbez appeared to be friends, it might be a good idea to leave the sick Christians along with part of the baggage in one fortress in order to climb into the highlands with less difficulty. It was approved wholeheartedly by everyone. Thus, they put many provisions in the fortress, and in order to have water they dug a well.

Up to twenty-five Spaniards, among them the royal officials and Francisco Martín de Alcántara, remained in Tumbez. Pizarro named the accountant Antonio Navarro[2] captain and justice. Before this, Francisco Martín de Alcántara and certain other Spaniards had gone out toward the highlands, and they saw several of the royal highways that pass through there; they came back to report. They say that because two Franciscan friars could not immediately see lands [and dobloons] of gold[3] they wanted permission to return to Nicaragua—something for which they have to give a good account to God, because if they had wanted to preach and convert, there was a need that the reader can understand.[4] And four other Spaniards even asked Pizarro for permission to remain there because he wanted to leave Tumbez, saying that they did not want to end their lives within marshes and in misfortune. He granted it to them freely, saying that he would not take anyone against his will, nor would he cease forging ahead, even if only his brothers and he might see it through.

The orejón whom Atahualpa had sent from Cajamarca[5] had come, disguised to where the Christians were, and they thought that he was one of the Indians who were serving them. He counted how many [Spaniards] there were, and he did the same with the horses. He returned to report to the one who had sent him. From what he had seen, he believed that if many assembled, it would be easy for them to kill all of [the Christians] because there were so few; and that is what he affirmed.

Notes

1 Here Cieza outlines the principal geographical regions of Peru: the coastal desert strip, where it almost never rains, the Andean highlands, with snow-covered and glaciated peaks, and the upper Amazon rain forest.

2 Navarro was named accountant for the Pizarro expedition by the agreements of Toledo on 15 May 1529. He was active, witnessing the founding of precious metals and noting down quantities taken at Puná, San Miguel, Cajamarca, Cuzco, and Jauja from December 1532 to July 1534. On 11 March 1535 four ships arrived in Seville, and aboard the San Miguel was Antonio Navarro. See Noble David Cook, "Los libros de cargo del tesorero del Alonso Riquelme con el rescate de Atahualpa," *Humanidades* (Lima) 2 (1968): 41–88; Porras Barrenechea, *Cartas del Perú (1524–1543)* (Lima: Sociedad de Bibliofilos Peruanos, 1959), pp. 184–85; and *Cedulario del Perú*, pp. 5–6.

3 The words "jars and dobloons of gold" ("las tinajas y doblones de oro") had been modified by the author, but given some discoloration, they are illegible. The *doblón* is an old Spanish coin whose value varied, but in the 1530s was substantial.

4 The conflicting and obscure history of the early Franciscans in Peru can

be traced best in Antonine Tibesar, *Franciscan Beginnings in Colonial Peru* (Washington, D.C.: Academy of American Franciscan History, 1953), pp. 3–22.

5 This passage, which refers to descriptions in chapter 40, comes in advance here because of the postponement of the two chapters concerning the war between Huascar and Atahualpa. See note 1, chapter 36.

XXXVIII

About how Pizarro left Tumbez and arrived at Solana,[1] *from where Soto and Belalcázar left with people for the highlands, and how the city of San Miguel was founded*

Pizarro was given great notices of Cuzco, Vilcas,[2] and Pachacamac,[3] where it was said there were large buildings of the kings, many of which were coated with gold and silver. That is what he told his men to animate them as they were leaving Tumbez, where the royal officials had remained with the others who were mentioned. [Pizarro] went through those plains with considerable hardship because the abundant sand tired those going on foot. And as there was so much sun and no shade, and no other water than what they were carrying in some gourds, they became worn out and very fatigued. They went on in this manner until they found a deserted royal house and water, which greatly comforted them, and they and the horses refreshed themselves. They departed from there a short distance, and they saw the river and the beautiful and cheerful valley through which the wide highway of the Incas passed. I have written extensively about these highways and buildings in *Part One;* therefore, I will reiterate nothing of it because it is a bother for the one who writes and even more so for the one who reads.[4] *fol. 46v*

The natives of the valley had received news of the Spaniards passing through and how detrimental it was for those who wanted to oppose them. Fearing their horses and the slashing of the swords they decided that it would be safer to be friendly with them, even if it were feigned, than to wait until they were captured and robbed. Thus, what they decided, they put into effect, and the chiefs went out to talk to Pizarro, who treated them honorably. He commanded that under imposition of penalty no impudent one should go and molest or injure those who, coming in peace, had concluded an alliance with them. And he asked the natives to furnish provisions so that the Christians would not destroy their crops and pillage their lands. They were happy to do it, and without showing that they were bothered, they provided them with what they had. Pizarro realized that there were abundant resources in that valley for them to stay several days. He consulted with his brother, Hernando Pizarro, and the other captains and decided that Soto,[5] with some horsemen and shield bearers, *fol. 47* should go and explore in the eastern territory, because the Indians assured him of the grandeur of the towns in the highlands.

Soto and those who went with him left, taking along guides who knew the land. They went until they reached what they call Cajas,[6] a province in the highlands. They saw large buildings, many herds of sheep and rams; they found small pieces of pure gold, which pleased them the most; and there were so many provisions that it amazed them. When the highlanders learned that the Christians had entered their land, they said that they were mad because some were in one place and others were somewhere else. Great rumors spread about them; [the Indians] charged that they were cruel, arrogant, lecherous, idle, and other things that they fancied. They were in Atahualpa's camps; the *mitimaes*[7] and many of the natives who were there discussed killing them, and thus a good throng of them, carrying strong ropes to tie them up, attacked Soto. They thought that they were *pacos*[8] who would easily let themselves be captured; they call a certain family of their sheep "pacos." Soto and those who were with him confronted the Indians, of whom they killed[9] many, and [the Indians] wounded one Christian named Jiménez. The one who wounded him paid for it because, slashing him with the sword, they hacked him to pieces. The Indians, terrified, showed such cowardice that, lacking the spirit with which they had entered the battle or *guazábara*,[10] they turned around and began to flee. Some were captured. Soto and the Christians, after looting all they could, returned to where they had left Pizarro, who already had sent for the Spaniards who had stayed in Tumbez. When Soto saw the royal highway that they call of Huayna Capac, which passes through the highlands, he was amazed when he observed the way it had been built. When they joined the Spaniards, they reported to the governor what they had seen. The imprisoned Indians related much about the wars that went on between Huascar and Atahualpa; they said [Atahualpa] was on his way to Cajamarca.

With this news and what they had seen, our men were overjoyed; they believed more and more what the Indians had been telling them. When Pizarro realized that they were already entering the bountiful land and that the Indians were describing large cities and provinces far ahead, he decided to establish a new settlement of Christians because it would be beneficial to leave within those valleys some town in place. Because they had gone up to the Tangarará Valley, he founded there the city of San Miguel and made the division of the district that would be expedient there. In the book of foundations[11] I have written extensively concerning this city, to which I refer the reader, and if he has not seen it, to see it if he wishes. The Spaniards who *fol. 47v* were the weakest and the officials of the king remained there as vecinos. The accountant Navarro became lieutenant governor.[12] With the rest of the people, who were 160 Spaniards, [Pizarro] decided to proceed ahead.[13]

Notes

1 Probably Sullana, on the Chira River about sixty kilometers inland and thirty kilometers north of modern Piura.

2 Cieza describes Vilcas in *Part One,* chapter 89. Lying beyond Huamanga (Ayacucho), it was approximately halfway between Quito and Chile. It was a massive place, with a finely wrought stone Temple of the Sun, and many open plazas, one in the shape of an amphitheater, for religious ceremonies. Its storehouses held large amounts of cloth and other goods, which suggests a large population.

3 Located in the next river valley south of Lima, the great temple at Pachacamac continues to impress visitors, even after being quarried by treasure seekers ever since Captain Rodrigo Orgoños and Francisco de Godoy first cut into its side, as described by Cieza in *Part One,* chapter 72.

4 In *Part One,* chapter 40, Cieza describes this section of the Inca highway as being some fifteen feet wide, protected by a strong wall roughly the height of a man. Wherever water was available, the road was shaded.

5 and Belalcázar

6 Cajas was about 150 kilometers to the east of modern Piura.

7 In this case, mitimaes are those Indians who had been sent by the Inca to colonize outside their own ethnic entity.

8 Alpacas.

9 and wounded

10 Here, Cieza may again use an Antillean word, meaning roughly "a tumultuous skirmish."

11 *Part One,* chapter 59. San Miguel was founded 15 July 1532.

12 Navarro was in Cajamarca by 10 May 1533; see Cook, "Libros de cargo," p. 60.

13 At the end of the chapter Cieza wrote in the margin: "Here needs to go the stay of Atahualpa in Cajamarca." See also note 3, chapter 36.

XXXIX

About how when the people who escaped from the battle were collected, Huascar's captains made more exhortations, and a third battle was fought in the Jauja Valley, which was very bloody; and about how Atahualpa remained in Cajamarca

I remember well that I concluded *Part Two*[1] by dealing with the Incas in the battle that Atahualpa fought against the captains of Huascar, his brother, in the province of Paltas, and where Atahualpa was victorious following the death of many men. And now at the time of the current narrative, when Pizarro and his men came to Tumbez, Atahualpa was pursuing his enemies, enjoying the trophy of his victories. He knew day by day, and even hour by hour, everything that had happened to the Spaniards, and the war they had in Puná. He wondered how they could have prevailed, being so few against so many, who were impeding their movements in the land. He attributed it to the weakness of his people and not the strength of ours, but he did not want to abandon his claim to take action. He acted guided by God because his understanding was blind to what was best for him. He sent orders that they should not show [the Spaniards] any favor in their villages, and he and his people departed from the Paltas.

Huanca Auqui,[2] Inca Roca,[3] Urco Huaranca,[4] and the other captains of King Huascar quickly got away from the enemy as they fled the battle. And yet, many of those who had escaped went to look for them, joining them to loyally die with them in the service of Huascar, the true Inca, and not permit the bastard [Atahualpa] to secure that rank. It was blindness on both sides because by divine permission and arrangement their rule was ending, and neither one of them would reign; instead, it would be people so strange and different from their spirit as was Spain from Peru and Peru from Spain fifty years ago.

The news of the battle went to Cuzco, and the old Indians who had been with Huascar told me that when he learned that his enemy had *fol. 43*

12. The palace in Tomebamba. Pedro de Cieza de León's *Primera Parte* (Seville, 1553), p. 55v. Courtesy of the Jay I. Kislak Foundation, Miami Lakes, Florida.

emerged victorious, he was so incensed that he was determined to hang himself and made great exclamations to his gods. His advisers exhorted him to stop weeping and to order a new mobilization of people to bring on the ruin of Atahualpa. That is what he did, and the news swept all the way to Chile.

They also discussed what the Christians had done since they had entered Coaque and until they had left Puná. They did not contemplate any opposition to [the Spaniards], nor did they believe it would be a difficult task because it was Atahualpa whom they feared and detested. He, overjoyed by the previous victories, earned such esteem that many came to support him who did not think that they would.

He displayed great arrogance, and all of Peru seemed a small realm to him. He feigned a thousand deliriums affirming them as the truth, that the Sun supported him and even spoke. There was no lack of those who believed it, stubbornly maintaining that he was saying the truth. He marched toward Cuzco, placing the provinces that he passed through under his rule and leaving behind deputies and governors chosen by him.[5] They say that he was very cruel and excessive, killing many whom he hated because they were Huascar's followers. Thus, he went on until he arrived in Cajamarca, where news reached him about how Pizarro had crossed to Tumbez and that each day he was joined by Christians and horses coming by sea.

They relate in this province that [Atahualpa] conferred with the principal captains and leaders who had come with him about what should be done. After pondering it over well, they all agreed that Atahualpa should remain in Cajamarca and not advance in person for two reasons. The main one was that those of Tomebamba and many of those bordering on Quito and other lands of the Chachapoyas, Huancachupachos, and the Incas of the lowlands appeared to be his friends only out of fear, not out of love, and they were faithful to Huascar. If they saw him near Cuzco, they would all join together and attack him from the rear; thus, he would face death or perdition. The other [reason] was that it was said those bearded idlers did not plant, but went *fol. 43v* from place to place eating and stealing whatever they found. There were so few of them, but with the horses they brought, they were so strong that they were able to do what they had done, and they could enter into the highlands and occupy some province there or form an alliance with his enemy, which would cause him greater danger. To remedy one and the other it was necessary to remain in Cajamarca with a force of people strong enough for whatever might occur and for Chalcuchima and Quizquiz and other captains to return to Cuzco and try to end the war by killing Huascar.

In the meantime, Huanca Auqui and the other captains had marched until they arrived in the Jauja Valley, where they found Huascar's order that they should again engage Atahualpa in battle. Many Huancas, Yauyos, Chancas, Yungas, Chachapoyas, Huancachupachos and other nations[6] united because to succeed and rectify everything, they assembled a strong army, all of them with their weapons, and they wished that fortune would be more favorable to them than it had been up to then so that they could punish Atahualpa and those who supported him. They agree that there were one hundred thirty thousand men who assembled on Huascar's side. And, as I have also said before, Chalcuchima and Quizquiz left Cajamarca with the other captains and people. Those who informed me about it were the captains who saw it all with their own eyes and were present in the battles, and because they know how many there were from the large account they have of it, better than by lists, they affirm that one hundred forty thousand warriors came, not counting those who were serving and carrying baggage.[7] Hence, you see the great calamity of that time in Peru and how apparent it is that God permitted the entry of the Spaniards[8] at a time of such upheaval never before seen by those born there. The hatred these Indians had for each other was already great; no friendship or any fief[9] were maintained, nor did they honor religion in order to loyally keep the faith owed to their king, as had been arranged by their ancestors. They did not take heed that those who had been born closer to the Tagus than the Apurímac[10] were at their heels in order to take the supreme lordship of their provinces and that royal authority would rest in Don Carlos, emperor of all Romans.

fol. 44 Following some incidents between both armies, they came closer to each other, all fired up for battle, so that they came into view in the same valley, where each captain roused his people. Then they began to yell loudly and howl at each other because those from here often expend their voices into the wind, and they played many kettledrums and shell trumpets[11] and other of their instruments. They insulted each other, which they know how to do well; those of Huascar asked why they were following a usurper, a son of a low woman; they[12] responded to the tune that Atahualpa was the true king and Huascar not worthy to be one because he enjoyed such delights in Cuzco, surrounded by women and concubines. All were in squadrons, and at the arranged time they fought one another—constantly humming, which made it sound as if there were more than were there. The ground was already full of the dead, and the soil had turned the color of blood. Chalcuchima was wise and well versed in war; he fought with Abante,[13] Huascar's captain, and captured him and succeeded so well that after many Huascareños had died and been wounded, by some divine secret, they were defeated and fled with all speed. They continued to pursue them, which caused more harm because of those who died or were captured. The dead on both sides, according to what they themselves say, were more than forty thousand men; and some affirm that this number exceeded sixty, but I always follow the most credible, which in my judgment would be the former. Many were estimated wounded. They also relate that with the exhilaration over the victory, they were careless with regard to Abante so that he fled and joined the others who had escaped from the battle, which they call of Jauja.

Notes

1 Chapter 74.

2 One of Huascar's brothers. Cieza spells the name "Guancaunque."

3 Cieza's spelling is "Ingoroca."

4 Cieza spells it "Urcoguaranga."

5 Throughout, Cieza uses the European term *province,* which is inaccurate in the Andean context. Andean rulers held power over people rather than land.

6 Cieza refers to the various ethnic entities as nations, again using familiar European terminology.

7 Although the Andeans did not write in the European sense, they did keep extensive records, using knotted string devices they called *quipus.* These decimal-based quipus—in which the type of knot, color of string, and placement on the cord indicate objects and quantities recorded—were excellent tools for manipulation of statistical data. See Rowe, "Inca Culture," 2:325–27; and Murra, *Economic Organization,* pp. 109–10.

8 in Peru

9 Cieza again resorts to familiar European terminology not applicable in the context of the Andean structure.

10 Cieza is referring to the principal rivers that cross the core of Castile and Tawantinsuyu respectively.

11 The *pututo,* made of the large conch shell *Strombus galeatus.*

12 those of Atahualpa

13 Cieza spells this name "Avante."

XL

About how there was another battle between them, and Huascar left Cuzco and was seized through deception

Huanca Auqui assembled with the other captains and the people who had escaped from the battle in a place[1] that they say is called Huarachaca, where they halted and rapidly notified the Inca [Huascar] in Cuzco about what had happened. He became filled with dread; he did not want to fool himself, but made sacrifices in accordance with his paganism. He ordered the orejones and chiefs—the nobility of Cuzco—to gather together, and the mitimaes to come with their garrisons and other people from Condesuyu and Collasuyu[2] so that they would go out on his behalf and try to preserve the authority
fol. 44v that was being usurped from him. Therefore, using loyal messengers he notified his captain-general, exhorting him in his friendship and placing his honor and position into his hands and the gods' favor. The news of this event also went to Cajamarca, where Atahualpa rested, and he became as elated as his brother had become dejected.

In the Jauja Valley there was much devastation when Atahualpa's people plundered it, as they did in other lands they passed through. Chalcuchima proceeded on his way to Cuzco. And Huanca Auqui again assembled a great army and wanted to await the enemy. It was to his misfortune because they say that in the battle the wretch was defeated following the deaths of more than twenty thousand men. Huascar came with large companies, sitting in a litter so opulent that what they relate about the gold and precious stones of which it was made is incredible. Orejones of his lineage carried him on their shoulders, but he was so dejected that he spoke little and wanted to be seen in public less than what was usual[3] in those times. Chalcuchima and his men marched victoriously, and they say that when he learned that the Inca [Huascar] had left Cuzco with such a large company, he was apprehensive and sent messengers to him; they were to attempt to capture[4] him using a ruse. Those who went acted in such a way and assured him with such words that he believed them and when he left the Apurímac River with part of his people to place under his command the army of his enemy, they had him so entrapped that they seized him. Others relate that they fought a battle, and he was captured then. And some suggest that Chalcuchima and Quizquiz entered Cuzco and that they captured Huascar within the city itself. Each one can believe[5] what he wishes. As for me, I am convinced that he was captured at Apurímac, a famous river in this kingdom in the pass they call Cotabamba. They treated him so inhumanely that it it is pitiful to tell about it. They insulted him with ignominious words. They plundered his depository; they dishonored his principal women; they killed many innocents who had not sinned; and they ordered the people of Cuzco to obey Atahualpa as lord from then on, and accepting him as Inca, they should give him their obedience. The news of this singular event spread in all directions.

With this that I learned thanks to my endeavor and curiosity about the altercations between these lords,[6] I want to return to what was happening to the Spaniards because it is time to do that. When they *fol. 45* left Puná for Tumbez, [the Indians] went to Cajamarca to tell Atahualpa how much harm [the Spaniards] had caused all of them and how they plundered whatever they found and took it, using them against their will, taking their women as concubines and their children as captives. Moreover, they had proclaimed that they would gain the entire land and remove it from its lord. Furthermore, they related that when [the Spaniards] heard that they worshiped the Sun and their other gods, they joked about it, and they demonstrated it more clearly when they violated their huacas, considering them as something to joke about. And [the Spaniards] all confessed that they had one god whom they worshiped, whom they affirmed to be the only lord Creator of the heaven and earth, and that they obeyed a very great king. Atahualpa learned about it more extensively at this time than before because those of Tumbez informed him, and they knew it very well for two reasons. First, because they had the Christians among them who had wanted to stay when Pizarro first came and from whom they learned a lot. Second, because many of them were with Pizarro in Puná—a time when they had no other care than to rob[7] their enemies and to learn what the Spaniards were thinking and planning to do, which the interpreters told them[8] because they had been in Spain and in Panama, where they had learned and seen much of what they told their compatriots. Further, those of Tumbez told Atahualpa about the size and speed of the horses, how brave the

13. Indians worshiping a stone as god. Pedro de Cieza de León's *Primera Parte* (Seville, 1553), p. 63r. Courtesy of the Jay I. Kislak Foundation, Miami Lakes, Florida.

Spaniards were, and how they fought with lance, sword, and buckler. When Atahualpa heard this, he began to think more about the situation than he did until then, even though when they told him that they did not reach even two hundred men, he indicated that it was absurd to think that they would be engaged for nothing. At that point he ordered nothing more than that an orejón, his kin, go in disguise to the camp of the Christians and learn their intentions and their ways, and that he should quickly return to inform him.

Notes

1 a village
2 Of the four parts of Tawantinsuyu, Condesuyu extended in the direction of today's Arequipa, and Collasuyu lay in the direction from Cuzco through Lake Titicaca and beyond.
3 was necessary. With up to forty thousand men, Chalcuchima marched quickly, hoping to defeat them in fact
4 and kill
5 what suits me
6 Cieza learned the details of the recent fratricidal strife in Cuzco (*Part One,* chapter 74).
7 from those of Puná
8 Probably Felipillo and Martinillo.

XLI

About how Pizarro set out from the new settlement he had established in order to ascend into the highlands in search of Atahualpa

It was well-known to the Spaniards that Atahualpa, a most powerful lord, was in Cajamarca with large companies of men. They were not troubled by such news, but they wished to have more Spaniards and horses backing them. They trusted that God Almighty would be with them. When the Indians of those valleys learned that those people had settled in their land, it greatly distressed them because they would have preferred not to have such neighbors. They held several secret discussions about waging war on them, but their plan did not come to pass. Pizarro spoke to many chieftains, admonishing them not to break the peace, and he ordered the Spaniards to treat them well. He also sent the necessary messages on the ships to Diego de Almagro that [Almagro's] appointment as marshal had already arrived.[1]

He left the city of San Miguel with his people, marching through those cool valleys, where—as they had been informed—they found large buildings, many storehouses with provisions of all kinds, and the highway built as I related in *Part One*. The Yungas[2] served them, supplying them with what they needed. When the Spaniards regarded such beautiful land, they praised God an infinite number of times. They had collected a quantity of gold, but not much. In the Collique Valley they encountered four orejones, Atahualpa's retainers. They were waiting to see Christians, and thus they appeared before Pizarro without any fear. He received them well, treating them as eminent men. He told them not to be afraid or leave, and he promised not to molest them or detain them; rather, he was pleased with their visit and information. They praised Pizarro's gentleness and his virtue, more as a precaution because they were there for no other reason than to observe and sniff around so that they could quickly
fol. 48 go up to inform their lord, Atahualpa. But they told Pizarro that they were Atahualpa's servants and that they were there collecting tributes owed to him, and they did not wish to leave there until they could

be of service to [the Spaniards] in anything they ordered. Pizarro, seeing that they possessed such reason, asked them about Atahualpa and why they were waging war. They replied that in the past years Huayna Capac, a great lord and the father of Atahualpa and Huascar, had died and that the two fought over ruling the entire realm, and that there were many battles from which Atahualpa had emerged the victor. Pizarro further asked them how many people Atahualpa had. They replied that he had many, and if he wanted to summon them, they would be countless.

When he learned these and other things from the orejones, he gave them permission to go and retire to their houses. Because they were smart, they had found out from the interpreters what they could. Having learned how many horses and Christians were there or had remained in Tangarará, and pretending that they were going to their lodgings, they took to the road, and they went until they arrived in Cajamarca. There they related to Atahualpa in detail what had happened to them with the Christians and that those who were coming along the coast numbered no more than 160. Atahualpa was astonished that so few men could have such courage. He toyed with ideas in his mind, but no decision was reached. He sent an order to Chalcuchima to place security around Huascar, his brother, and to come to him with the prisoner; it is believed it was to execute him in his presence.

Some mitimaes went to the provinces to recruit people to come and join Atahualpa. It is well-known among many of the orejones that when one orejón—the one who had gone on Atahualpa's orders to see the Christians—saw that [Atahualpa] wanted to prepare and mobilize people, he exclaimed with great presumption, being very drunk, that he should not fear 160 tired and leg-weary men who were coming against him just because they brought those huge dogs—he was referring to the horses. And that they should give him four or five thousand warriors, and he would bring them to him all tied up. They say further that because of what this one said, they became merry, heartily laughing, declaring that the Christians would serve Atahualpa as yanaconas—which is the name of a perpetual servant or captive.

Pizarro was coming, and he learned about the large companies that were with Atahualpa. He implored divine favor because if such help was lacking, they would bury them and their horses with mere handfuls of dirt. He encouraged his companions, saying that they should *fol. 48v* trust in God without fearing the force that they said Atahualpa had. All were in good spirits. Thus, after they passed through the valleys and plains, they came to where it was convenient to climb up to the highlands, which they did, and always having guides and being informed of what lay ahead, they approached Cajamarca. When they began to ascend the mountains, some of the Christians murmured about Pizarro: why was he putting himself into the enemy's hands with so few people? It would have been better to wait in the plains than to wander around the highlands where the horses were useless. Although Pizarro was aware of it, he pretended that he knew nothing.

Notes

1 this done

2 Cieza uses the word *yungas* to refer to warm, humid, and productive valleys and points out in *Part One,* chapter 43, that the term also referred to the Yungas, the peoples of the coastal valleys of Peru.

XLII

About how Atahualpa was informed how near he was to the Spaniards, and about the council he held, and how he sent messengers to Pizarro that he should not cease marching

News of the Christians was continually being passed to the great lord Atahualpa. When he learned that they were less than two days away from Cajamarca, he feared their audacity. He ordered the captains of the mitimaes and the chief lords to gather and discuss what they should do regarding the Christians because they were stealthily coming closer, acting as usurpers. Although they were not natives and had not been harmed, they had pillaged whatever they found, considering it theirs. And according to what was learned from them, they strove to rule the land, so if they were to seize it, clearly many of their kin would come by sea aboard the ships they use. Because the harm they were causing was general, it was expedient that all think about it and decide what they should do. Those of them who are alive, which are many, state that they talked a long time about this matter, and at one time they said that the best would be to attack and crush them, killing them all because there were so few. At other times [they said] that it was madness to take heed of 160 men and to fear them so much, that it would be better to let them reach Cajamarca, where they would tie all of them up and take revenge on them. It was a great enterprise, and God's work and His power are apparent in clouding the mind of the Indians so that they did not attack the Christians because without fighting or anything other than setting upon them all at once in a throng, they would have taken them all, especially the way they came over the highlands. And the enterprise was guided in a way that was advantageous to vanquishing the Indians, as they did.

Atahualpa and his men decided not to attack them, but instead to *fol. 49* await them in Cajamarca as they were and to go with their message to the captain who was with them. Thus, fifteen or twenty Indians left Cajamarca, accompanying the ambassadors. They took a ridiculous gift of some small baskets of fruit, ten or twelve ducks poorly roasted and with their feathers on, and three or four quarters of a sheep so overroasted that they were worthless. Some say that with these Atahualpa sent word to Pizarro to hasten and come to Cajamarca, where he was awaiting him, and they would all amuse themselves. Others relate that instead he angrily sent to tell[1] him they should immediately leave his land and return to him all the gold, silver, stones, women, men, and everything else they had stolen because they were not theirs, and if they refused, he would kill them all. Pizarro joyfully received the gift and honored the messengers, to whom he gave some of what he had. He replied to Atahualpa, admonishing him to show kindness to the Christians and that he would arrive[2] in Cajamarca, where they would talk and get to know one another, something he wished for very much because they had told him that he was a great lord. The messengers returned, telling [Atahualpa] that the Christians were already very close. They again discussed what they should do, but they did not change their first plan, other than that when he [Pizarro] came near the valley of Cajamarca, Rumiñavi would go out with six thousand warriors to capture those who might flee from them because they already believed they had [the Spaniards] in their power.

After the Indians had left, Pizarro discussed in detail the message and gifts that Atahualpa had sent them.[3] [The Spaniards] marched cautiously. They had neither battles, nor did anything remarkable happen to them because all the people[4] were assembled in Cajamarca. Because they moved quickly, they arrived within sight of the villages of the valley. The service Indian men and women wept for them, saying that soon those who were with Atahualpa would kill them. The Spaniards saw Atahualpa's army sitting on hillsides with so many tents that it seemed like a city. To the advantage of our men and to [the Indians'] perdition, when [Atahualpa] learned that [the Spaniards] were so close to him, he left them the royal lodgings of Cajamarca, while he moved to others near where the tents were seen. He did this in order to seize all of them there and to wage war on them by surrounding them. Thus, the Spaniards fully discovered Cajamarca, a large province and about which they say great things, and they entered it in the *fol. 49v* middle of the month of November[5] of the year of the Lord fifteen hundred and thirty-two.[6]

Notes

1 notify
2 go
3 they guessed that
4 warriors
5 they entered it on the eve of the Holy Cross of May
6 Midday of 15 November. See Lockhart, *Men of Cajamarca,* p. 10; and Busto, *Historia general,* p. 67.

XLIII

About how Pizarro and the Spaniards took up quarters in Cajamarca, and how Soto went to Atahualpa's camp, and what else happened

Although there was such a large army at Cajamarca, one could see their lovely fields, slopes, and valleys—how they were sown and well cultivated because they retained and assiduously observed the laws of their elders, which mandated that they should eat from the deposits without destroying the fields.[1] The villages were filled with supplies of precious cloth and other riches, and many herds of sheep. The royal residences were surrounded by a wall, not very tall, and there was a large triangular plaza. [The Spaniards] found no people of importance, except some women, the oldest ones. As they had been ordered, they set up quarters so they could stay together.

The Indians rejoiced to see them so close; they called them crazy for their audacity. Pizarro believed that it would be useful to send someone to survey the entire enemy camp. Thus, he ordered Soto and twenty-four horsemen to go see it and even to tell the great Lord Atahualpa on his behalf that they should regard each other as and be friends; he took Felipillo with him as interpreter. Shortly after Soto left, the governor thought that it was inopportune to send so few people because if there were some mishap, they would be lost. Therefore, he ordered General Hernando Pizarro to go out with several horsemen as rearguard to Soto, who was already close to the camp of the Inca. They observed the many Indians who were stationed in every direction. Near them was a marsh or a somewhat wide and muddy stream. Soto rode full speed ahead and easily crossed it, which astonished the Indians. Atahualpa's people were arranged according to their custom: those with bows were together, those with clubs also, and those who had other weapons, in the same order. Soto passed
fol. 50 by the squadrons of Indians, asking for Atahualpa—who, although he knew about his coming, did not want to leave his royal lodging, where he was attended by many lords and principal captains.

When Soto arrived with the interpreter at the door of the palace, the guards gave warning; he answered to let them know what they wanted. Soto said he wanted to see Atahualpa and to give him his message. [Atahualpa] emerged with noble courage and such solemnity, which well illustrated his rank. He was not alarmed when he saw either the horse or the Christian. He sat down in his opulent seat. He spoke in a low voice, asking what Soto sought and what he wanted to tell him. Soto replied that Pizarro had sent him to see and greet him on his behalf and that he regretted that [Atahualpa] had not awaited him in the residences. And that he begged him to come and dine with him, and if not, to come another day to eat because he wished to meet him and to inform him about his coming and why he was in that land. Soto said this and other things without dismounting—neither he nor anyone who had accompanied him. Atahualpa understood well what was said to him. He did not answer,[2] but spoke to one of his captains that he should tell [Soto] to return and tell his captain that he would be with him another day because it was already late and thus he could not go then. Soto again asked if he had more to tell him because he would give Pizarro that answer. He replied in the same manner that he would go with his people in squadrons and armed, but that [the Spaniards] should not feel uneasy or be afraid. In the meantime, Hernando Pizarro arrived and discussed some issues with Atahualpa, and he replied to what he and Soto had talked about—that [the Indians] should go in good time according to [Atahualpa's] will and he should know that the Christians were not frightened by seeing many people. Following this, Soto took the reins of his horse in front of Atahualpa, so he would learn what it was, and he made him move his hind legs and fence with his front legs, and he came so close to Atahualpa that the snorts of the horse blew the fringe on his forehead, the crown of the reign. Atahualpa did not stir, nor did his face betray any excitement; rather, he was so serene and looked as calm as if he had spent his whole life taming colts. But there were some among his people, more than forty, who became so frightened that *fol. 50v* they scattered in all directions. After the Christians returned to Cajamarca, Atahualpa became furious over the cowardice of his people because they had fled like that when they saw a horse wriggle. He ordered that they should appear before him and he said: "What do you think? These are nothing but animals who are born in the land of those who bring them, just like sheep and rams are in yours. Why did

14. Hernando Pizarro approaches Atahualpa at the baths of Cajamarca. Felipe Guaman Poma de Ayala, *El primer nueva corónica y buen gobierno,* 3 vols., ed. Rolena Adorno and John V. Murra (Mexico City: Siglo Veintiuno, 1980), f. 382. Courtesy of Siglo Veintiuno Editores.

you run away from them? You will pay with your lives for the affront I have received on your account." And they were then killed, without any of them remaining alive.

Arriving to where Pizarro was, his brother and Soto related what had happened to them. They said that Atahualpa had the appearance of a great prince and acted as such. There were many people with him, all of them well armed, and he had the will to wage war, not to make peace. Some of the Spaniards were apprehensive because for every one of them there were more than four hundred [Indian] men. Pizarro encouraged them with soothing words, saying that they should trust in God because it is certain that everything that happens below and above heaven is arranged by His will. Moreover, he rejoiced that so many people were together because they would be easier thrown into confusion and even defeated. [The Spaniards] made sure to keep a careful watch, making their rounds and vigils.

The Indians also had their sentries, and as if our men were already fleeing, Rumiñavi came out, as had been ordered, with the people already mentioned, loaded with *ayllus*—which are weapons of knots and strings[3] used with certain skill for capture—to take up position on the road so that none of [the Spaniards] could escape. Atahualpa made his sacrifices, and they even repeated their conversations with the demon with whom they all speak. All this was useless if God permitted what was done and had it thus arranged. When it was daytime, they made many fires and smoke signals around Atahualpa's large camp. They all ate because that is what they do, and Atahualpa decided to come closer to Cajamarca, where the Christians implored God to deliver them from [the Indians'] hands and power.

Notes

1 Cieza is pointing out how different the Inca army was from the Europeans, who traditionally pillaged and destroyed fields in order to provision their armies. Excavations of Huánuco Pampa indicate the massive amounts of products—such as freeze-dried potatoes (*chuño*), maize, and cloth—that were regularly stored by order of the Inca. See Craig Morris and D. E. Thompson, *Huánuco Pampa—An Inca City and Its Hinterland* (London: Thames and Hudson, 1985).

2 to Soto

3 The ayllu was usually made of three knotted strings, with stone balls at the ends. These were spun rapidly, then released so they would entrap the legs of a running animal, thus felling it. They are similar to the bolas of the Pampas of Argentina, which were used in the hunt for guanaco. The ayllu can down a galloping horse as easily as it does an alpaca and is also effective against humans.

XLIV

About what Atahualpa told his people before they moved from where they were, and how one of the Christians came to talk to him

Atahualpa was very proud. It seemed to him impossible that anything *fol. 51* could occur that would prevent him from killing and capturing the Christians because they were more than [one hundred][1] seventy thousand warriors against them. He had seen the horses. He said that they did not eat men, so why should they be afraid of them? Nevertheless, he ordered the principal lords[2] and the captains and commanders to assemble. Because the Incas were very wise and rational and conducted long debates in their meetings, and [because] Atahualpa had followed warfare since his childhood, he offered them an orchestrated speech, full of pauses, admonishing them to act valiantly against the enemy. After all, there were many among them who had been in the war with his father and had enjoyed great victories, conquering many nations, as they knew and were well aware of. Because that was certain and they realized the daring of those one hundred and some foreigners in coming into the land pillaging and burning and appearing to be the example of complete cruelty, they should thus all go with one heart and will and seize them in order to make a solemn sacrifice of the horses—in which their strength lay—and to take them as slaves. To ensure that none of them could flee or escape being killed or captured, he had left them the principal lodgings of Cajamarca. He planned to subtly deceive them so that safely and without danger they could succeed in what was so important to them by pretending[3] with the captain who was with them that it would be convenient if the Christians and horses stayed hidden in the houses and he[4] [Pizarro] should await him in the plaza with some unarmed men. [Atahualpa] had no doubt that he would do it because [Pizarro] believed that he was expecting him in order to make peace and an alliance. And with such cunning, they could enter the square in an orderly fashion and surround the lodgings and attack them all at once and capture and kill them.[5] In order to do this they should arm themselves secretly to prevent them from knowing their scheme, and each one should do whatever his captain or commander ordered him.

While Atahualpa was speaking, thousands of them put on breast plates of knotted palm fronds so strong that the lance and the sword
fol. 51v find them hard, and they wore a woolen shirt to conceal their weapons. And others, thus disguised, carried slings and bags of stones, others metal clubs with long and sharp points, others ayllus, and all wore their clothes so artfully that no one who would see them would realize that they were armed. There were also other squadrons behind these who were to enter first into battle, furnished with other arms. The lord's litter was open and uncovered and opulently and beautifully adorned, and ahead of it went those designated to clean the road so that not a piece of grass or stone could be seen. The orejones and natives of Cuzco went next to the litter, dressed in a livery as the king's attendants.[6] The guard went between them, and the litter had to be carried by chiefs, men who came from the highest lineages or were lords of many vassals. Twelve thousand armed men went in their squadrons, as has been said, ahead of everybody as the center; then went another five thousand Indians with the ayllus, instructed to capture the horses with them. The rest of the people—which they say would have been a total of seventy[7] thousand warriors with more than thirty thousand service [Indians], not counting the women—all went, placing themselves in the order that was commanded.

The Christians saw the movement. They knew that soon they would be surrounded by those who were advancing against them. Pizarro encouraged them once again, dispelling their fear of the multitude that was with Atahualpa, to whom he sent one of the Indians who was there to tell him that he begged him to come quickly because he was expecting him to dine. Atahualpa asked this messenger about the state of the Christians. He assured him that they were fearful, news that made him more presumptuous. And, in keeping with his design and aims, he sent one chieftain to tell Pizarro that he would have already come to see him, but he could not convince his people because they had such great fear of the horses and dogs, and this fear became deeper seeing them at closer range. Therefore, he begged him—if he wished to meet him—to order that the horses and dogs be firmly tied and that the Christians should all hide, some in one place and others in another, so that none would appear while they conversed together, and thus his people would lose the great fear they felt. And because his people were accustomed to carry arms, [Pizarro] should not be alarmed if some have them when he comes. When this Indian reached the Christians and the governor heard the message, he understood the snare that Atahualpa had devised. He then called for his brothers and great leaders in his camp to seek advice about what they should do. They all reassured themselves. They said that the Holy Spirit had inspired Atahualpa to send such a message because through it they learned his plan, and they could prepare themselves; stationed inside the houses, they would attack the Indians in such a way that they would soon be defeated. Certainly, if what Atahualpa directed were not done, it would be impossible for our men, being in the field, to defend themselves from the many against them. *fol. 52*

There were only two gates on the plaza; the wall was a little more than an *estado* and a half.[8] In the meantime, Atahualpa was approaching with his people in formation, and when he arrived very close to where the Christians were, he commanded his camp to be set up, placing his large and opulent tent in the center. When the Christians saw this, they became concerned because there was only a little daylight left, and they believed that the Indians wanted to attack them at nightfall. Pizarro, who was the most apprehensive about this, said that he would be gratified if one of the Christians would dare to deliver his message to Atahualpa. One, called Hernando de Aldana,[9] heard this and replied that he would go to Atahualpa and tell him whatever he commanded. Pizarro was pleased and ordered him to tell Atahualpa that because it was already late, he begged him to hurry and come to where he was expecting him so that they could arrange what was suitable for the benefit of all. Aldana then left. He understood a little of the Indian language because he had tried to learn it. Pizarro ordered that everyone should be prepared—the horses saddled, and the reins and lances in their hands.

Aldana went until he reached Atahualpa's tent. He found him sitting at its entrance, attended by many lords and captains. He explained the message he had brought. [Atahualpa] did not answer him, but rose up angrily, and assailing the Christian, he wanted to take his sword. But he held it so tightly that he could not. Some of the chieftains who were there rose up, intending to kill him and to take his sword. Atahualpa, who had received an affront because he could not *fol. 52v* take it from him, ordered them to release him. He told him with a benevolent expression that he should return and tell Pizarro that he would leave soon to please him and that they would see each other. Aldana, who was apprehensive, paid his respects and quickly returned to where Pizarro was. He related to him what had happened and that Atahualpa carried a large quantity of gold and silver cups and vessels, and that it seemed to him that he had evil intentions and was full of arrogance.

Notes

1 Thirty. The estimates of the number in the Inca camp vary.

2 who were with him

3 which was convenient that it

4 alone

5 without letting any escape

6 For the attendants Cieza uses the word *continuos,* who were the royal guards in Spain. In this passage the chronicler consistently applies European terminology and concepts ("livery," "lords of vassals") to the Andean world.

7 fifty

8 As a vertical measure, the estado was approximately 1.67 meters, the height of an average man at the time; thus, the wall must have been approximately 2.59 meters high. According to the Peruvian archaeologist Federico Kauffmann Doig (*Manual de arqueología peruana* [Lima: Iberia, 1983], p. 711), the walled plaza, tending to appear triangular, was about four hundred by two hundred meters wide.

9 Hernando de Aldana was born around 1481 in Valencia de Alcántara (Extremadura). He was recruited by Pizarro in Spain in 1529. After Cajamarca, he became a town councillor in Cuzco. Although a staunch Pizarrist, he maintained good relations with Diego de Almagro. During the Gonzalo Pizarro rebellion he was jailed, then executed in Cuzco by Francisco de Carvajal, who hated the Aldanas. Busto calls Hernando the "first Quechuist in Peru," *Diccionario,* 1:48; see also Lockhart, *Men of Cajamarca,* pp. 212–14.

XLV

About how Atahualpa entered the plaza where the Christians were, and how he was seized and many of his people were killed and wounded

Don Francisco Pizarro had ordered that General Hernando Pizarro and the captains Soto, Mena, and Belalcázar and the Spaniards on horseback ready for battle should be prepared to charge at the enemy because Atahualpa had sent word that they should be hidden and even the horses tied up. They put some small guns in a high place designated for watching games or making sacrifices, so that Pedro de Candia could discharge them when a certain signal, agreed upon by all of them, was given. At that [signal], the horsemen and footmen were to boldly charge, and about only fifteen shield bearers would stay with the governor. They would prudently allow some squadrons and Atahualpa to enter the plaza, but then they would take the two gates, and if [the Indians] wanted war, they would lance and capture those that they could. But they also discussed that if Atahualpa came in peace, they would uphold it.

[Atahualpa] began to depart from where he had halted; in a short time all the tents were raised, and the people kept the order and arrangement of their squadrons, many with hidden arms, as has been written. They carried large drums, many trumpets, and their banners were raised; it certainly was a marvelous sight to see such an army mobilized for so few. Every so often an Indian came to survey *fol. 53* the condition of the Spaniards. Each one would return joyfully, [saying] that they all hid out of fear in the houses, and only their captain with very few men were visible. When Atahualpa heard this, his pride grew further, and he seemed fiercer than he later appeared. Most of his men urged him to go or give them permission to go and tie up the Christians, who did not emerge, already fearful because they saw their strength. When [Atahualpa] arrived within a crossbow shot of the lodgings, some Indians went ahead, surveying more carefully how our men were. They saw what they had heard: not a horse or a Christian other than the governor with those few could be seen.

15. Friar Valverde, Francisco Pizarro, and Atahualpa at Cajamarca. Felipe Guaman Poma de Ayala, *El primer nueva corónica y buen gobierno,* 3 vols., ed. Rolena Adorno and John V. Murra (Mexico City: Siglo Veintiuno, 1980), f. 384. Courtesy of Siglo Veintiuno Editores.

They talked about [the Christians] as if they already were prisoners in their power.

They began to enter the plaza. When the squadrons reached the center of it,[1] they formed a very large circle. Atahualpa entered after many of his captains and their people had done so. He passed all of them before his litter was set down. Because he was in the middle of the people, he stood up on top of the platform. He spoke loudly that they should be brave, that they should take care that no Christian escape them, or any horse, and that they should know that [the Christians] were hiding in fear. He reminded them how they had always vanquished many people and nations, serving under his and his father's banners. He assured them that if because of their sins the Christians should prevail against them, it would be the end of their pleasures and religious beliefs because they would do with them what they had heard had been done with those of Coaque and Puná. He took one banner in his hand and vigorously waved it.

When Pizarro saw that Atahualpa had halted in the plaza, he ordered Friar Vicente de Valverde,[2] a Dominican, to go to Atahualpa and prod him to come because it was already so late that the sun was about to set and to admonish him to put down the weapons and come in peace. The friar took along Felipillo so that his cause would be understood by Atahualpa. When he reached him, he told him what has been said and that he was a priest of God who preached His law *fol. 53v* and strove whenever possible for peace rather than war because that pleased God very much. While he was saying this, he held his breviary in his hands. Atahualpa listened to this as something of a mockery. Through the interpreter he understood everything well. He asked Friar Valverde for his breviary. He placed it in his hands, somewhat disconcerted from finding himself among such people. Atahualpa looked at it and looked at it again, and he leafed through it once or twice. Annoyed with so many pages, he flung it into the air without knowing what it was because to have understood it, they should have told him in another way, but the friars never preach around here, except where there is no danger or raised lances. And looking at Friar Vicente and Felipillo, [Atahualpa] said to tell Pizarro that he would not move from the place where he was until they return and restitute to him all the gold, silver, stones, cloth, Indian men and women, and everything else that they had stolen. With this answer, having collected the breviary, the skirts of his habit flying high, [the friar] rushed back to Pizarro, telling him that this tyrant Atahualpa was like a wounded dog and that they should attack him.

When the friar left,[3] according to what they tell us now, in order to provoke his people's anger Atahualpa told them that the Christians—in contempt of him and after having raped so many women and killed so many men and pillaged whatever they could without shame or fear—were asking for peace with the intention to gain supremacy. They let out loud cries and sounded their instruments. The rest of the squadrons had arrived, but they did not enter the plaza because it was so full; they remained next to it on another plain. When Pizarro learned what had happened to Friar Vicente with Atahualpa, and realizing that there was no time to spare, he raised a towel, the signal to move against the Indians. Candia fired the shots, a novelty for them[4] and frightening, but even more so were the horses and the horsemen who loudly shouting "Santiago, Santiago!" came charging out of the lodgings against the enemies, who were stunned and did not make use of the artifices they had planned. They did not fight; rather, they looked where they could flee. The horsemen entered among them, quickly defeating them. Many were killed and wounded.

With the footmen, who fought with buckler and sword, the gov-
fol. 54 ernor pushed toward the litter where there was a group of lords. They gave some slashes that would sever the hand or arm of those who held the litter, who then with great courage would hold it with the other, wishing to protect their Inca from death or prison. A foot soldier, Miguel Estete,[5] native of Santo Domingo de la Calzada, arrived—the first one to lay a hand on Atahualpa in order to seize him. Then Alonso de Mesa arrived. Pizarro, shouting that they should not kill [Atahualpa], came next to the litter. Because there were so many Indians, they hurt each other more; the horses fell between them everywhere, and they had neither the spirit nor the inclination to fight; they were found wanting that day, or God wished to blind them. They wanted to leave the plaza, but could not because so many filled it. They did a deed never seen or heard: in one furious throng they went for one part of the bulwark that surrounded the plaza, and because the wall was wide, they forced it with such vehemence that they broke it and made way to flee.

They wailed loudly. They were shocked by what they were seeing.

They asked each other if it was real or if they were dreaming. And the Inca, where was he? More than two thousand Indians died, and many were wounded. [The Spaniards] went out of the plaza in pursuit to where Atahualpa's camp was. A heavy rain came, which was sufficient relief for the Indians. The Lord Atahualpa was taken by the governor to the lodging, and he ordered that he should be given full honors and good treatment. Some of the Christians shouted to the Indians to come and see Atahualpa because they would find him alive and well and without any wounds—a joyous news for all of them. Thus, more than five thousand Indians without weapons were collected that night; the others dispersed throughout the district of Cajamarca, proclaiming the great misfortune that befell them and shedding many tears for the capture of the lord whom they loved so much.

All the Christians came together and assembled, and Pizarro ordered that they should fire a shot so they could hear what he wanted.[6] There were great spoils of gold and silver vessels, cups of thousands of shapes, cloth of great value, and other jewels of gold and precious stones. Many principal ladies of royal lineage or of caciques of the kingdom became captives—some very lovely and beautiful, with long hair, dressed according to their fashion, which is of an elegant style. *fol. 54v* They also held many mamaconas, who are the virgins in the temples. The loot that these 160 men could have had was so great that if they had learned about it without killing Atahualpa and had asked him for more gold and silver,[7] although what he gave was a lot, there would not have been in the world anyone who could equal them. None of the Spaniards had been in danger. They all believed it was a miracle that God allowed it to transpire as it did, and therefore they gave Him many thanks for it. This defeat and capture of Atahualpa took place in the province of Cajamarca, in the jurisdiction of what is today the city of Trujillo, on Friday, the day of the Holy Cross of May[8] of the year of the Lord fifteen hundred and thirty-three[9] years.

Notes

1 the great plaza

2 Valverde was born in Oropesa, studied at the University of Salamanca, and professed there as a Dominican in 1524. He was one of six Dominicans

authorized to go to Peru in the 1529 agreement; only Valverde reached the highlands. He went to Spain in 1534, taking important documents with him. Nominated bishop of Cuzco in 1535, he returned with other friars to Lima in 1538. In 1541 he left to meet Vaca de Castro but never reached his destination because he was captured and killed by the Indians of Puná. See Lockhart, *Men of Cajamarca*, pp. 201–207.

3 returned

4 the Indians

5 Estete is less known than his namesake, the chronicler. He was a resident encomendero of Jauja, then Lima, before settling in Huamanga in 1539, where he often served on the city council. Estete saved Atahualpa's fringe, and in 1557, as Sairi Tupac left his stronghold to make peace with the invaders, Estete presented it to him as a demonstration of goodwill. See Lockhart, *Men of Cajamarca*, pp. 320–22.

6 he ordered that they should thus do it

7 as much as he had given

8 May 3, the day that St. Gregory of Tours established as the date when St. Helena found the true cross in 326. Cieza's date is wrong. Atahualpa was captured on Saturday, 16 November 1532.

9 two. Obviously Cieza was unsure of the exact date and in the end chose the incorrect year.

XLVI

About how in the morning of the following day the Spaniards went to survey the countryside, and how the news of Atahualpa's capture spread throughout the entire realm

It seems that by capturing Atahualpa the Spaniards were certain to avoid war. Knowing this, they took great care to guard him. Pizarro allowed him to have his wives and household servants because some of them had joined him. He appeared well, feigning more joy than sadness. He reassured those of his people that he saw, telling them that it was customary in war to vanquish and to be vanquished.

Then when it was daytime, on Saturday, Pizarro ordered that horsemen should ride into the countryside until they reached Atahualpa's royal residence. They did that. They found great treasures of superb pieces, many very heavy, all of pure gold and fine silver; the cloth was squandered—had it been kept, it would have been worth more than one million, and not just a little more, but much more. They saw the large pile of weapons that [the Indians] had left. They collected what they could, and with that they returned to their quarters. They did not bother the Indians because they did not take up arms either. They were overwhelmed, weeping about their misfortune. Our men admonished them to go and see Atahualpa and learn what he was commanding; many went. With the interpreters, Pizarro consoled them, assuring them that he would not wage war if they did not start it first; such argument greatly reassured them. *fol. 55*

The news that his brother had been imprisoned reached Atahualpa. He laughed when he learned of it, saying that he was laughing at the diversity of the world because on the same day he was both the vanquished and the victor. He asked to speak to Pizarro, who then came, consoling him with soothing words. [Pizarro] told him that he should not be distressed or stop eating; indeed, he was a great lord, and he should act accordingly. He promised to treat him as such and indicated that if any of his wives or relatives were in the power of some Christian, [Atahualpa] should let him know because he would order that they be given to him. Atahualpa was encouraged by what Pizarro said and more confident in really wanting to fully understand the Spaniards' intention. And that is what he wanted to ask their captain and no one else, saying that he would be pleased if they told him who they were, from what land they had come, and if they had a god and a king. Pizarro replied that they were Christians, natives of Spain, a large province, and that they believed in and worshiped God Almighty, Jesus Christ, Creator, Maker of heaven, earth, and sea, and everything that exists therein. And that if he became Christian, receiving baptismal water, he would enjoy the glory and vision of God; if not, he would be condemned, as all are who die without the light of the faith. He further told him that they were vassals of Emperor Don Carlos, a great lord. Atahualpa marveled at what he heard. After that he did not discuss any more of this or any other thing with Pizarro, except to commit to him his life, person, children, and wives.

When [Atahualpa] was captured, many Indians fled to different parts of the realm, as has been said. They took along great treasures stolen from the camps. Zope-Zopahua, Rumiñavi, and others returned to Quito, looting much of the treasure from the temples and royal palaces. It is rumored that they hid more than three thousand *cargas* of gold and silver that is still lost today. They were usurping.[1] Therefore, with the power or support that they had, many became lords of what was not theirs, killing the natives. The virgins of the temples left and went about as harlots. Finally, the good laws of the Incas were no longer observed. Their entire government was lost. They had no fear because there was no one to punish them; their dignity was gone, and that which had risen so much fell with the entry of the Spaniards. And because it is relevant, I will relate what one native
fol. 55v lady, who said it in my presence, remarked to Friar Domingo de Santo Tomás,[2] who was asking her certain things about the Incas. She said: "Father, you must know that God became tired of tolerating the great sins of the Indians of this land, and He sent the Incas to punish them; they did not last very long either, and by their fault God also tired of tolerating them, and you came and took their land in which you are; and God will also tire of tolerating you, and others will come who will replace you, as you deserve." This Indian lady said this one Sun-

day morning; therefore, you can see that they understand that God punishes kingdoms for their sins.

Returning to the subject, the Indians make great exclamations when they relate the evils that happened in all the provinces while Atahualpa was imprisoned. They did not dare to rise up in arms against the Christians because [Atahualpa] had ordered that they should not do it, nor could they conceive of anything other than to obey him. When the news spread that he was imprisoned, it caused great wonder. They were astonished at how powerful 160 men were to do it. Many rejoiced; others wept, sighing from the sorrow they felt. Chalcuchima[3] was the captain who showed the most resentment. He complained about his gods[4] because they had allowed such a thing. He relegated the guarding of Huascar to the appropriate captains and went to the Jauja Valley to calm an uprising of the Huancas, where he did considerable harm.

When the news of Atahualpa's capture reached Cuzco, the Hanan-Cuzcos rejoiced.[5] They took such an event for a miracle. They believed that God Almighty, whom they call Ticsi Viracocha,[6] sent his children from heaven to liberate Huascar and to restore him on the throne from which he had been ousted. They ordered that the temples should remain as they were and the virgins stay in them until they learned the will of those whom they called "Viracocha," a name they gave them, according to what they say, because they were believed to be Ticsi Viracocha's children. Others say they are called that because they came by sea like foam. I have written more about it earlier.[7] They waited to see what the Christians would do with Atahualpa. It was never thought that they would kill him, nor did Atahualpa suspect it. And with that, I will relate at this point the departure from Panama of Marshal Don Diego de Almagro with the succor.

Notes

1 many

2 Santo Tomás was born in Seville and professed as a Dominican in 1520. He traveled to Peru in 1540 and held posts in various Dominican establishments there. He was interested in native languages and compiled a Quechua dic-

tionary and grammar that was published in Valladolid in 1560. He was one of the founders of the University of San Marcos in Lima in 1551. In 1563 he was named bishop of Charcas and died seven years later. See editor Rodolfo Cerrón-Palomino's introduction to Domingo de Santo Tomás, *Grammática o arte de la lengua general de los indios de los reynos del Perú* (Madrid: Ediciones de Cultura Hispánica, 1994), pp. iii–vi.

3 Chalcuchima controlled some thirty-five thousand men at Jauja at this time and represented a formidable threat to the Spaniards; see John Hemming, *The Conquest of the Incas* (London: Sphere Books, 1972), pp. 29, 65–70.

4 the fortune

5 Like many parts of the realm, Cuzco was divided into upper *(hanan)* and lower *(hurin)* halves (similar although distinct from moieties). The upper half supported Huascar. For an introduction, see R. Tom Zuidema, *Inca Civilization in Cuzco* (Austin: University of Texas Press, 1990), pp. 14–22.

6 Cieza learned from native informants in Cuzco that in times before the Incas the universe was engulfed in darkness. From the south a tall and light-skinned man came, creating the mountains and valleys and the springs. He was called Ticsi Viracocha, and he marched northward, teaching people to live peacefully. See MacCormack, *Religion in the Andes,* pp. 99–107.

7 *Part Two,* chapter 5.

XLVII

About how Almagro set out on ships from Panama to Peru to aid Pizarro and what happened to him

When Pizarro left Panama, his partner Almagro had remained in order to contrive with his usual diligence to recruit people and horses to follow in pursuit of Pizarro. And although he was ill, he accomplished it so that he assembled 153 Spaniards and fifty horses, equipped with the arms that each one had and could have. And he built a large ship with two top-sails so that in this one and those of Hernán Ponce, which had returned with the gold from Coaque, the people could travel. Thus, beginning the journey, he left Panama, accompanied by the pilot, Bartolomé Ruiz, who deserved a better reward than they had given him for all that he did. *fol. 56*

They sailed several days until they arrived at the Bay of San Mateo, where while they were anchored a ship came into port, bringing some Spaniards from the province of Nicaragua. Their captain was Francisco de Godoy.[1] Almagro let them know that he was Francisco Pizarro's partner and was on his way to succor him; therefore, they should all unite in order to go together, submitting to him. Godoy did not want to relinquish command nor enter under such circumstances where Pizarro was. Rodrigo Orgoños,[2] Juan de Barrios,[3] and others were with him, and they advised him not to disobey the marshal [Almagro]. Thus, everything was done as he ordered, and when they met, they spoke to each other with great courtesy and politeness. They had as pilot of this ship one Juan Fernández. They decided that the ships, with whatever belonged to them, would sail along the edge of the coast, and some would go by land until they had notice of Pizarro. With this arrangement they arrived at Pasado.

The Indians reported that the Christians were several days march ahead. It was distrusted because the messengers were not very astute. Because they did not find the news satisfactory, they ordered one of the ships to go ahead, and when they got the information they were seeking and knew exactly where the Christians were, they should not go any further, but turn around to notify them. The ship sailed for several days. They say that it stopped in a place on the point of Santa

Elena, and when the other ships arrived, they learned the scanty news that they had for them. They suspected sad cases of dead or captive Christians. Almagro and his men were coming by land, where they *fol. 56v* suffered great hardship, going[4] through dangerous river beds and marshes that they encountered; furthermore, they lacked provisions and were in want of food. The weary Spaniards were as tormented and full of anxiety as you can imagine, which was the reason that more than thirty of them died, and even Almagro himself was very ill. And when they learned that the ship had not found any reliable news or fresh trace of the Christians, they were overcome by grief and sadness. They did not stop, nor did they abandon their fate.

Another ship that went to find out about the Christians did not stop until it arrived at Tumbez, where the Indians appeared when they saw it. They went to it in more than eight hundred balsas, which caused some fear among the Christians, who believed that they were coming to surround the ship and attack them. Soon it dissipated because the Indians lovingly received them, gave them food, and told them that the Christians were in Tangarará, which was nearby. Those traveling on the ship were overjoyed with this news. Those who were needed disembarked in their land, and they rejoiced when they saw so many herds of sheep in the fields.

They soon learned in San Miguel that a ship was in Tumbez. The lieutenent, Navarro, immediately ordered four or five horsemen to go and see who they were and from where they had come. These came to talk with those others that I said had disembarked, from whom they learned that Almagro was coming with people and horses to succor Pizarro. They also learned the news of Atahualpa being captive in Cajamarca, where a great treasure had been found. With this news, the ship returned to inform Almagro, who reached it before it arrived at Puerto Viejo. When Almagro and his men heard such good news, they were overjoyed. They could not wait to be in such a fine land. Before this news had arrived, they were determined to return to Panama, according to the opinion of some, or to settle in Puerto Viejo. Some of those who are alive today say that Almagro intended to head north and occupy the [region] of Quito and petition the king for its governance instead of providing Pizarro with assistance. Others contradict it, saying that he never contemplated such a thing; yet, they strangely persist in this. These are people's opinions, and most of the time they are uncertain. Besides, those who live in these parts are clever and cunning, and they look for a thousand ways to create enmity between those who command, so that, being needed, they can do what they have done and will do as long as the instigators of such plots remain unpunished.

The marshal brought as his secretary one whom they called Rodrigo Pérez, who they say wrote to the governor any way he could, warning him that Almagro had a ruinous design against him and planned to become lord of the best part of the land and other similar things, believing he would thus gain Pizarro's favor. And [Pizarro] was perturbed by such news and called his brothers as well as some others whom he held as his closest friends and discussed it with them. With their advice, he ordered Pedro Sancho[5] and Diego de Agüero to go and meet Almagro with letters for him; feigning ignorance, they would inform him about how they had imprisoned Atahualpa, from whom they expected great treasures, and that he should come quickly because they would all get portions of it. Furthermore, joyful and gracious letters were written to the most important men who were coming with Almagro, to seek their friendship so that they would learn the marshal's intentions and then inform [Pizarro] with the utmost speed. *fol. 57*

Almagro came toward the city of San Miguel, where they also say other plotters were not lacking who secretly warned him to beware of Pizarro and be on his guard because he wanted to kill him and take the people he was bringing. The partners' spirits were troubled by these things. Almagro found out about the roguishness of his secretary[6] and how he had written something that had never entered his mind. He ordered him taken to the ships where they tortured him, and [Almagro] learned of the wickedness. Therefore, Almagro ordered him to confess, and they hanged him on the lateen yard of the ship. This done, Almagro continued until Tumbez, where he met Pedro Sancho and Diego de Agüero. They wrote to Pizarro that Almagro did not have the designs he was believed to have, but rather a great desire to see [Pizarro] and to bring him succor. From Tumbez, Almagro went to the city of San Miguel, where he had some indisposition; he was swiftly cured.

Notes

1 Godoy was from Cáceres and related to Hernando de Aldana. See Lockhart, *Men of Cajamarca,* p. 213.

2 Born in Oropesa, Orgoños had been active in the Italian campaigns. He was a friend of Bishop Valverde and related by marriage. He received an Indian encomienda at Pachacamac. See Lockhart, *Spanish Peru,* p. 140, and *Men of Cajamarca,* pp. 256–57. For Orgoños's correspondence with his family in Spain, see Porras Barrenechea, *Cartas del Perú,* pp. 131–33, 146, 164–68.

3 Born around 1505, Barrios was in the Indies before 1525 and became a vecino of León, Nicaragua. He was very active in Peru. In 1537 he received the encomienda of Hanan Ica and in 1541 was elected alcalde of Lima. See Busto, *Diccionario,* 1:219–20.

4 another ship went; they know what they wish

5 Pizarro's secretary, probably from Medina de Rioseco. After Francisco de Jerez returned to Spain in 1533, Pedro Sancho became Pizarro's first secretary and prepared a chronicle of events in Peru (to July 1534). He went back to Spain a rich man in 1536 and settled in Toledo. His wealth dissipated, and he returned to the Indies. He formed an uneasy alliance with Pedro de Valdivia and reached Chile. Following an accusation of treason, he was executed on Valdivia's orders. See Lockhart, *Men of Cajamarca,* pp. 276–83.

6 Rodrigo Pérez.

XLVIII

About how Atahualpa promised the Spaniards a great treasure as his ransom, and about the death of King Huascar

Because gold and silver has played such a part in making the Spaniards come over to these parts, little is needed to know our greed and the great longing that we have for money. And being imprisoned, Atahualpa found no better means for gaining freedom than to promise the great treasures that he had and that his captains had taken in *fol. 57v* the war of Cuzco. He told Pizarro that he would give as his ransom ten thousand ingots of gold and so many silver vessels that it would be enough to fill a large house[1] that was there, and as long as they would set him free without causing him any more trouble or injury, he would deposit into it, aside from the ingots, a quantity of gold pieces and jewelry. They thought such a great promise insane because it seemed to them impossible to fulfill. But he kept insisting, declaring that if they kept the agreement, he would fulfill the promise without cunning or cheating.

So much was told about Cuzco and Pachacamac, about Quito, Vilcas, and other places[2] where there were temples of the Sun that, on the other hand, some Christians thought that Atahualpa could give what he promised and much more. Pizarro talked to him about it and found him firm in his word. [Atahualpa] was invigorated in captivity with hope of liberty. It became known that a great captain was coming, again with many Christians and horses; they were talking about Almagro and those who were coming with him. Because Atahualpa wished so much to be free, and believing that he could command as he did before the Spaniards came to the land, he insisted that he would give the said gold and silver so that they would let him go. And Pizarro promised it through the interpreters. He gave his word and the assurance that Atahualpa asked for to leave him as free as he was before he captured him if [Atahualpa] would give as much gold and silver for his ransom as he said. Happy with this decision and the agreement that he so desired, Atahualpa then dispatched to all parts, to the capitals of the provinces as well as to the city of Cuzco, that he had promised a room full of gold for his liberty and that they should collect what was necessary to comply and bring it to Cajamarca. Furthermore, he ordered that they should not contemplate war or aggravate the Christians; instead, they should serve them and obey them as they would him, and supply them with provisions and anything else that they might ask for and need. And so that the treasure could be accumulated in the shortest possible time, because it would be such a large quantity, Atahualpa spoke to Pizarro, saying that he should order two or three Christians to go to Cuzco so that they could bring the treasure from the Temple of Coricancha.[3] They would go in litters carried by Indians on their shoulders, who would protect them *fol. 58* and bring them back without being bothered or harmed. Pizarro was pleased with that, and he immediately ordered that three Christians named Pedro de Moguer,[4] Zárate,[5] and Martín Bueno[6] should go with the Indians to Cuzco to bring the treasure of the temple. They started the journey, carried in litters by the Indians, who were many.

Quizquiz had entered into Cuzco, where he committed great cruelties to Huascar's party, which were the Hanan-Cuzcos. He killed thirty brothers of Huascar, sons of Huayna Capac and of different mothers; he stole great treasures, so much that he took more than four hundred cargas of gold and silver metal. In the meantime, they were approaching Cajamarca with the captive King Huascar. He had learned that Atahualpa was in the power of the Spaniards, and so that they would set him free, he had promised to give them a house filled with gold and silver. [Huascar] made great exclamations, asking great and powerful God for justice against the traitor, his brother, because he had caused him so much harm and disgrace. He said further that if [Atahualpa] had promised one house of gold, he would give two to the Christians, people sent by God's hand because although there were so few of them, they had the power to capture such a great usurper as was his enemy, who would not have been able to give what he had promised if he had not taken it from him [Huascar], the true lord of it all. Those who were in charge of him agreed to be loyal to Atahualpa and traitors to him. They were not startled by such strange news. They decided to send a messenger to let [Atahualpa] know how close they were and that they would do what he ordered because Huascar was exhibiting a great desire to be in the power of the Christians, [Atahualpa's] enemies. When this messenger arrived, he spoke extensively with Atahualpa about these things. Because he was so prudent and clever, it seemed to him inadvisable that his brother should live or appear before the Christians because they would esteem him more for being the legitimate lord. But he did not dare to order him killed for fear of Pizarro, who had asked about him many times. And in order to find out if his death would cause [Pizarro] grief or if he would compel him to bring him alive, he pretended to be full of emotion and grief, so that Pizarro learned of it and came to console him, asking him why he was so dismayed. Atahualpa, pretending to be even more so, told him that he should know that at the time he came to Cajamarca with the Christians there had been a war fought between his brother Huascar and him. And after having fought many battles with each other, he stayed in Cajamarca and committed the business of the war to his captains, who had captured Huascar, whom they were to bring to where he was without harming him, but coming with him they had killed him on the way, *fol. 58v* according to the news he heard, which was the reason for his great distress. Believing that he was telling the truth, Pizarro consoled him, telling him he should not grieve because war brings with it similar reverses, and necessarily some in it have to die, and others be captured and vanquished. Atahualpa did not wish to hear more than he already learned because if Pizarro had said, "Bring me Huascar alive, without hurting him, because these reports are lies," they would have come with him to Cajamarca. But because he said what Atahualpa had hoped for, he ordered the same messenger to return with full speed to meet those who were bringing Huascar and to tell them that without further consideration they should kill him and dispose of him where not a trace of him would appear.

They were already close to Huamachuco, in what they call Andamarca. It was soon whispered that Huascar was going to die; he found out about it and became frightened and terrified. He argued with pitiful words that they should not do it, making them great promises, but to no avail because God allowed it to happen for the reason only He knows. [Huascar] complained about Atahualpa, condemning his cruelty, because although he was the sovereign lord and true Inca, he had brought him to such a state. He said that God and the Christians would avenge him. They drowned him in the Andamarca River, and they cast him into it without giving him a burial, a deplorable thing for these people, who consider those who drowned or burned in the fire as damned. They value having magnificent tombs where their bones can rest and allowing the placement of their treasures and women inside so that they can serve them where the soul goes—their blindness. Some who were of Huascar's family killed themselves in order to accompany him. The Indians who are alive today relate great things about him: his kindness, how he was merciful, generous, not given to usurpation or theft, but in all a friend of truth and justice, preferring all the good things to the bad. Regardless of all this, he died so wretchedly, as has been said. And the one who ordered him killed lived only a short time, as we shall see, the Christians being as cruel with him as he had been with Huascar, who was the last king of the Incas. And there were eleven of them, and the Indians say that they ruled more than four hundred years in Peru.[7]

Notes

1 Sources are relatively consistent on the dimensions of the room. Jerez suggests 22 by 17 feet; Mena, 25 by 15; Hernando Pizarro, 30–35 by 17–18; and Ruiz de Arce, 20 by 15. Gold was to be stacked to a height of one and one-half estados, a little more than eight feet. The ransom stipulated one room of gold and two of silver. See Hemming, *Conquest,* pp. 48, 550.

2 parts

3 The great Temple of the Sun, later taken by the Dominicans as their monastery.

4 From Moguer, Pedro began his career as a grommet and ended as an infantryman. He eventually settled in Cuzco and received an encomienda in Canas. He was killed by his Indians at the beginning of the 1536 uprising. See Busto, *Hueste perulera,* pp. 267–71; and Lockhart, *Men of Cajamarca,* pp. 403–404.

5 Juan de Zárate, was born in Orduña. He was a notary and accountant and wrote two reports about the Cuzco experience; both are apparently lost. He planned to settle in Cuzco, but returned to Spain in 1535. See Lockhart, *Men of Cajamarca,* pp. 285–86.

6 Bueno, a sailor from Moguer, came to Peru from Nicaragua with Belalcázar. He continued with Pizarro to Jauja, then to Cuzco, but then returned to Moguer in Spain. See Lockhart, *Men of Cajamarca,* pp. 401–402.

7 The chronology and the number of dynasties is a matter of much dispute. For an introduction to the subject see Richard W. Keatinge, ed., *Peruvian Prehistory* (Cambridge: Cambridge University Press, 1988); Gary Urton, *The History of a Myth: Pacariqtambo and the Origin of the Inkas* (Austin: University of Texas Press, 1990); and Geoffrey W. Conrad and Arthur A. Demarest, *Religion and Empire: The Dynamics of Aztec and Inca Expansionism* (Cambridge: Cambridge University Press, 1984).

XLIX

How the three Christians who went to Cuzco arrived in that city and what happened to them; and how by Pizarro's order his brother Hernando Pizarro left Cajamarca to get the treasure of the Temple of Pachacamac

fol. 59 In the previous chapters I related how Martín Bueno and the other two Christians left the province of Cajamarca to bring the gold and silver from the Temple of Coricancha. They worked their way in the direction of Cuzco. The Indians served them wherever they went; they regarded them so highly that they came close to worshiping them as gods. They believed that some deity was enclosed within them. The Christians were amazed to see such great reason in the Indians, the vast amounts of provisions of all kinds that they had, and the extent of their highways and how clean and filled with lodgings they were.

The news that they were coming and why reached Cuzco. The city was ruled by Atahualpa's followers. At that point they did not know Huascar was dead, and he too had many secret defenders and servants because no one dared to name him in public. But they were so pleased when they learned that the Christians were coming to their city that they raised great clamor, praising God because he had remembered them in such a calamitous time. They expected to be revenged on Atahualpa and his followers by the hand of the Christians. They ordered the virgins of their lineage, who were in the temple and were called mamaconas, to gather and with their dignity and authority serve those who were coming because they believed [the Christians] to be children of God. When [the Christians] arrived in Cuzco, they gave them a grand and solemn reception in their manner, lodging them as honorably as was possible for them and prostrating themselves on the ground, bowing their heads. These three [Spaniards] were of little intelligence; they failed to prudently preserve their *fol. 59v* status so that their departure would be as honored as their entry. Instead, perceiving such novelty as a curiosity, they laughed and hence revealed themselves unworthy of such high honor. They were aston-

16. Cuzco. Pedro de Cieza de León's *Primera Parte* (Seville, 1553), p. 107v. Courtesy of the Jay I. Kislak Foundation, Miami Lakes, Florida.

ished to see the wealth of the solemn Temple of the Sun and the beauty of the many ladies who were in it.

Those whom Atahualpa had empowered informed the governors and rulers of the city and the high priest, Villac Umu,[1] how the great[2] Lord Atahualpa, in order to free himself from the shackles of prison, had negotiated with the captain of the Christians to give as his ransom a house filled with gold and silver, with which those who had him in their power would be content. Therefore, in the name of the high and powerful Sun, the Sea, and the Earth, and all the other gods, they begged them and admonished them to give what was needed of those metals to fulfill his promise. Indeed, there was enough to take much more than that without removing anything from the service of the Incas, their fathers, or their tombs, but only from the temple and what had belonged to Huascar.[3] The news of his death also reached Cuzco at this time. Those who loved him lamented such a sad event, but seeing that strange people were in their land, they did not attempt anything new in the business of the Christians. Instead, they attempted to remove a good stockpile from Cuzco. It is common knowledge that more than one thousand *quintales* of gold in known pieces was taken from there, much of what Manco Inca later had, and the rest is lost in the entrails of the earth. And there was so much gold in Cuzco, and silver, that many individuals buried large sums, and they took to Cajamarca what you will hear about, and Quizquiz stole what I have also said. And even with all this, Pizarro found more to distribute, which he distributed in Cajamarca—grandeur never seen or heard or known by people in any previous century.

In the meantime, the Christians succeeded in collecting gold only from the temple, where there was more of this metal, in my opin-
fol. 60 ion, than in any other that existed in the world. Many buildings of the temple had their walls covered with sheets of gold; they began to peel them off, pulling the band that girded them. And with what had not been hidden [by the Indians] they began to create loads of many very heavy gold and silver vessels, ornaments, beads, and other unusual things. The sacred mamaconas served the three Christians with great reverence and obeisance. They did not appreciate it, and it is well known that, feeling secure because of Atahualpa's imprisonment, they chose the most beautiful of these women of the temple, and they lay with them as if they were their concubines, and disparaging what [the Indians] held high, they corrupted them without any shame or fear of God. Because the Indian orejones are so wise, they realized immediately that the Christians were neither saints nor children of God as they had titled them, but worse than devils. After that, they abhorred their lechery and greed, and wept that such people might rule their land. They believed that many more would come in ships, that they would take their wives and daughters because the three already mentioned, being alone, dared to free their passions as they had done. They discussed killing them, but they did not dare to do it because of Atahualpa's command. Instead, they hastened their departure from Cuzco, making something like panniers to carry the treasure to Cajamarca, where the gold and silver was beginning to accumulate.

It was already known for certain that Almagro and his people were approaching and that he had executed his secretary, Rodrigo Pérez, which pleased Pizarro, who exclaimed: "Praised be the Lord that evil men are unable to make Almagro and me part!" There were great reports that there was a large treasure in the Temple of Pachacamac, which was in the Yungas, four leagues outside the City of the Kings,[4] as I have written in my *Part One.*[5] Don Francisco Pizarro decided to send his brother, General Hernando Pizarro, and several Spaniards to go and get it. He consulted with Atahualpa, who was content that so much would be put into the house to be filled for his ransom. And he sent messengers ordering that wherever Hernando Pizarro and those who went with him passed through, [the Indians] should serve them and supply them with provisions and guides without vexing or assail- *fol. 60v* ing them. After this was arranged, Hernando Pizarro departed, along with his brothers, Juan Pizarro and Gonzalo Pizarro, who were very involved in that conquest, and other Spaniards whom the governor had sent.

Atahualpa's captain-general was in Jauja, where he caused ample harm to the Huancas, but he did not want to lead any uprising until he saw what his lord ordered him. And because [Atahualpa] thought he would be free by means of the large ransom that he had promised, and wishing to see Chalcuchima, he sent an order to Jauja that he should come immediately to Cajamarca. Even though Atahualpa was imprisoned and [Chalcuchima] was celebrated for being such a great captain, he entered barefoot to talk to him, carrying a weight, and he displayed such humility,[6] as if Atahualpa were totally free in Cuzco and he were a humble man. And pausing in this for now, I will discuss how Don Diego de Almagro entered Cajamarca.

Notes

1 His name literally means the "soothsayer who speaks." Related to Huayna Capac, he was in charge of the ceremonies of the cult. He was a major leader of the rebellion that broke out against the Spanish in 1536. In October 1539 he surrendered to Pedro de los Ríos in Condesuyu; Francisco Pizarro ordered him burned alive. See Hemming, *Conquest*, pp. 128, 133, 143–44, 177–79, 187–201, 236–54.

2 and powerful

3 Cieza hints at the nature of Inca Cuzco. Within the various sectors of the urban complex were temple compounds, each dedicated to the service and veneration of one of the earlier royal *panacas*, or lineages. Large retinues were associated with each panaca, and support for their activities was provided by assignments of people and resources in various parts of the realm. See Conrad and Demarest, *Religion and Empire.*

4 At the time of the events narrated in this chapter, Lima had not yet been founded. It would be established early in 1535.

5 In *Part One,* chapter 72, Cieza writes that "no other could equal that of Pachacamac."

6 In *Part Two,* chapter 13, Cieza relates that anyone entering the presence of the Inca would remove his sandals and place a weight on his shoulders. Large or small, it was a sign of reverence or respect for the ruler. Those of status would do this once each time they returned after an absence.

L

About how Almagro and his people entered Cajamarca, where he was well received by those who were there, and about what happened to Hernando Pizarro during the journey to Pachacamac

The officials of the king, the ones who are encharged with collecting his fifth and who guard everything pertaining to his royal personage, had remained in Tangarará. When they learned about Atahualpa's capture and that he had promised such a large treasure as his ransom, they left the plains and ascended into the highlands to join the governor. They should not have done this because it is common knowledge among those from here that all the time that Pizarro and the 160 were alone, there was harmony and love among all of them, but when the officials and Almagro's people arrived, they had quarrels with each other as well as their jealousies, which never ceased.

Almagro also wished to finally meet with his partner, and so he marched each day on the way to Cajamarca, being very well provisioned by the villages that he passed through because due to the lord's imprisonment, all was safe. Almagro did not send a single Christian on a raid, and taking great care, ordered that they refrain from doing any harm. And so they went until they were close to Caja- *fol. 61*
marca. Pizarro and the Spaniards who were with him came out to welcome him, and they showed great joy in seeing each other. Atahualpa learned that Almagro, the captain who was coming, was equal to Pizarro in command and other things; he wished to see him to gain his favor. When they entered Cajamarca, they settled into their lodgings, and the Indians provided what was needed.

After the Spaniards discovered it, the beautiful province of Cajamarca did not have what it used to have. Nor is it any use to discuss the ravages that we commit in these lands during conquest or war because many times it befell me to see in some parts where we were countryside covered with so many cultivated fields, houses, and orchards that the eyes could see nothing else. And in truth, in less than one month it seemed that all the pestilence of the world had assailed it. How much worse it would be where [Spaniards] remained more than seven months!

Some suggest that although Almagro and Pizarro conversed amicably, they were suspicious of each other and harbored some secret rancor of enmity, a surge of ambition caused by finally being in such a magnificent land and expecting to possess so many treasures. Perhaps it could be the opposite of this because only God knows the designs and is able to pry into the thoughts of men. The governor named as alcalde mayor an hidalgo from among the conquistadors, called Juan de Porras,[1] who tried disputes among the Spaniards, severely punishing those who sinned by swearing and being involved in gambling. And a few days later he named Captain Hernando de Soto as his lieutenant.

Almagro visited Atahualpa, speaking to him kindly and proffering to be his good friend, which comforted the prisoner. The Spaniards relate great things about this Atahualpa—that he had already learned how to play chess and understood some of our language. He asked admirable questions and made intelligent and sometimes witty remarks. Nevertheless, he wished to see the treasure collected because when Almagro arrived, it was beginning to be brought in, and ten or twelve cargas of gold were in Cajamarca. In just a few days the gold and silver from Cuzco arrived, brought by the three Christians, who
fol. 61v related great things about that city; they praised its buildings and the many riches that were there. Pizarro and his men were astonished when these huge and well-worked pieces arrived; they were put in an assigned place with a guard of Spaniards so that none of it would be stolen or appropriated. Atahualpa was always careful to send chiefs and *mandones*[2] to bring the gold and silver from the places and regions that he had ordered, and it was entering Cajamarca on most days.

As Hernando Pizarro and those who went with him marched toward Pachacamac,[3] the news of it went to that valley, where, according to what the natives say, they had learned how the three Christians who went to Cuzco had violated the temple, corrupted the virgins, and treated the sacred objects with inhumanity and little reverence. The priests and chieftains of the valley extensively discussed that event. They affirm that they decided they would not witness with their eyes such great ruin and enormous sin as the destruction of such an old and venerable temple as theirs. Indeed, there was more than enough to collect for Atahualpa's ransom in other parts without taking what they were coming for. Then they ordered the virgin mamaconas to leave the Temple of the Sun from where—as well as from the Temple of Pachacamac—they say they removed more than four hundred cargas of gold. They hid it in secret places, and it has not appeared to this day, nor will it appear, except by chance, because all those who knew about it and hid it, as well as those who had ordered it, are dead. Although they had taken away as much as this, they left some adornments and quantity of gold in the temple, and it is rumored that much more is buried.

Hernando Pizarro traveled until he descended to the plains, and he was the first Christian captain who was in those parts. The Indians served him a great deal, and he ordered that they should be treated well. After they arrived at Pachacamac, they defiled the wicked temple where the devil had been worshiped and revered so many times. They collected—they have assured me—ninety thousand castellanos, without counting what was stolen, which you may faithfully believe was not a little. After staying a few days in Pachacamac, Hernando Pizarro returned to Cajamarca. He intended to travel through the beautiful Jauja Valley, to which Chalcuchima had returned, and to take him to his brother [Francisco Pizarro]. And returning on the road that led *fol. 62*
to Jauja, he proceeded until he arrived in that valley,[4] and he was delighted to see it so well populated even though it had been laid to waste.

Chalcuchima knew that Hernando Pizarro was the brother of the one who held Atahualpa captive, and because [Hernando Pizarro] was coming with the intention to know him and speak to him, he decided to surrender to him without any apprehension. And thus, after Hernando Pizarro sent him an invitation with mild and loving words to come and see him, he then did it, accompanied by some chieftains and captains. Hernando Pizarro received him well, promising always to look after his person in accordance with his rank and the high office that he held. He replied that he had come full of joyous confidence that he would meet with him so easily. They say that this Captain Chalcuchima was a robust man, with wide shoulders, and he was highly respected and considered valiant among the Indians. He displayed a fierce face and had a short and very thick neck. Hernando

Pizarro spoke to the legitimate lords of the valley, confirming the friendship of the Spaniards and assuring them that they would be well treated and favored by them. They replied that they would not take up arms against [the Spaniards].

Following this, Hernando Pizarro left Jauja and after several days arrived in Cajamarca,[5] where he learned that the Marshal Don Diego de Almagro was there. [Hernando Pizarro] was angry at [Almagro] for what had been believed about him, which was talked about before he had left for Pachacamac. And they say that it annoyed him when he learned that [Almagro] and his brother were in such agreement and that the Indians believed [Almagro] was [his brother's] equal and had as great an authority. When Pizarro learned that he was approaching Cajamarca, he went together with Almagro and many Spaniards to receive him. When they came together, they spoke with each other, and although Hernando Pizarro saw Almagro and knew him and had spoken to him, he rode past him without paying him any attention. Pizarro asked him to speak to the marshal, who was there. He did not return, nor did he comply with what the governor told him, which angered Almagro, who saw clearly demonstrated the loathing the Pizarros felt for him. Pizarro spoke to his brother, reproaching him for the lack of courtesy he had shown Almagro, his partner. He assured him that everything that had been said was wickedness, and *fol. 62v* that [Almagro] had hanged Rodrigo Pérez for it, and that he would like for them to go to [Almagro's] quarters right away to see him. Hernando Pizarro had to comply with the governor's will, and they went to Almagro, and they spoke to each other and begged each other's pardon for the previous incivility, and in public they reached agreement. Then, Hernando Pizarro went to where Atahualpa was imprisoned and talked to him, and Atahualpa was pleased to see him. Chalcuchima had already visited him and reported what had been happening. Pizarro, who knew how useful it was to honor a man as important as this captain, spoke to him when he saw him, promising that he would always be well treated.

Notes

1 See chapter 32.
2 The mandones were second-rank administrators. The Spanish term comes from the verb *mandar,* to rule or to order.
3 They set out on Sunday 5 January 1533, with some fourteen horsemen, nine footmen, and a number of Indian transporters. Miguel Estete, the veedor, left the best account of the expedition; other important Spaniards included Rodrigo de Chaves, Lucas Martínez Vegaso, Luis Maza, Juan Pizarro de Orellana, Juan de Rojas Solís, and Diego de Trujillo. The high priest of Pachacamac and four orejones assigned by Atahualpa also went. Their route took them through Huamachuco, Corongo, Huaylas, Caras, Yungay, Huaraz, Recuay, Paramonga, Barranca, and Huaura. They entered Pachacamac on 1 February. See Busto, *Historia general,* pp. 82–87.
4 They returned on the coast to Huaura, then climbed to Cajatambo, Bombón, then Tarma, and entered Jauja on 16 March.
5 Monday, 14 April 1533.

LI

About how keeping the promise he had made to the Spaniards, Atahualpa filled the house with treasure, and how those who came with Almagro claimed shares like those who were there first

Because it took days to collect the treasure being gathered by Atahualpa's order, so much had come that there was enough to fulfill the promise to the Spaniards. The Indians brought it in loads, putting it where they were shown, and there was no key or any other security than what Pizarro had ordered. I heard it said that a large quantity of gold was stolen and that the ones whose hands reached the deepest were the captains. There were also many emeralds and stones of great value. Atahualpa said that they should set him free because he had fulfilled their agreement.

There was a dispute among the Spaniards; those who came with Almagro claimed a share in what had been collected. They maintained that they came at a crucial and vital time, arriving when the treasure began to be collected, and with their horses they acted as guards, engaged in what they had been ordered. Those who were with Pizarro argued that they were the true conquistadors, that they had suffered more hardships and destitution before arriving in Cajamarca; because there were so few of them, they had exposed themselves to such great danger and captured Atahualpa, and it was their due and nobody else's to claim what he had given for his ransom. And if [the *fol. 63* others] kept watch and formed a guard, they were forced to do it to protect themselves. There were great disputes and debates among them about this, which stopped everything, and it was resolved that before the distribution was made among those with Pizarro, one hundred thousand ducats would be removed to distribute among those with Almagro. With that, they were somewhat appeased. It was decided that the rest should be divided, and according to what is said, Almagro told Pizarro that first—not counting the fifth—they should offer the emperor a rich donation and divide the rest according to the quality of each person. To this Pizarro replied, faithful to his companions, that not everyone was to have [a share]; rather, it should be in keeping with how much they had done. After they removed first the jewel from the bench and others of great weight, the distribution was arranged in this manner:

A decree made in Cajamarca, copied to the letter from the original:

In the town of Cajamarca of these kingdoms of New Castile, on the seventeenth day of the month of June, year of the birth of Our Saviour Jesus Christ fifteen hundred and thirty-three, the very magnificent lord commander Francisco Pizarro, adelantado, lieutenant, captain-general, and governor for His Majesty in these kingdoms, in the presence of me, Pedro Sancho, deputy of the general notary in them for the señor secretary Juan de Sámano,[1] said: Because of the capture and defeat of the cacique Atahualpa and his army, there was some gold in this said town, and later the said cacique Atahualpa promised and ordered the Spanish Christians who were present in his capture a certain quantity of gold. This quantity he indicated by saying that it would be a full hut and ten thousand small ingots and a lot of silver that he had and possessed and that his captains in his name had seized in the war and the capture of Cuzco and in the conquest of this land, for many reasons that he declared, as it is contained in greater detail in the decree that had been made about it, which was passed before a notary. And of that the said cacique had given and brought and had ordered to give and bring a part of. It is fitting to make a division and distribution of gold and silver as well as pearls and emerald stones that he had given, and of its value, among the individuals who were present in the capture of the said cacique, who won and took the said gold and silver, to whom the said cacique had ordered and promised it and had given and delivered it, so that each person would have and possess that which should pertain to him. And so that in a short time his lordship and the Spaniards *fol. 63v* could leave and depart from this town to go and settle and pacify the land ahead, and for many other reasons that are not expressed here, the said lord governor therefore said: His Majesty, by his royal provisions he gave him for the governance of these kingdoms and their administration, orders him that all the profits and fruits and other things that there were and would be gained in the land he should give and distribute among the individuals who would have gained it as conquerors, according to and as it would seem to him and as each one might deserve according to his deeds and personage. Taking into account all the aforesaid and other things that are true and should be considered in making a distribution, and to give to each one the silver that the said cacique had given and that they had and will have and that each should be given as His Majesty orders, he wishes to indicate and name before me, the said notary, the silver that each person is to have and to take, according to what our Lord God would give him to understand, using his conscience. And in order to be able to do it better he asked for help from God our Lord and invoked divine assistance.[2]

Notes

1 Secretary of the Council of the Indies.

2 Pizarro's decree was issued within the competencies conferred on him under the 1529 agreement with the Crown.

LII

About how the great treasure that had been collected in Cajamarca by the order of the great lord Atahualpa was divided among the Spaniards and the names of all the Christians who were present at his capture

My principal aim has been to give a careful and full account of all events here to those of today as well as those who will follow, and I have ignored neither a municipal book or an archive where I believed that I could find a genuine page to aid me. The record of the shares that was made in Cajamarca came into my hands in this City of the Kings; it was and is among the registers of the secretary, Jerónimo de Aliaga.[1] Because I named the thirteen who had discovered the coast, I decided to put down here the names of all the 160 who were present in the capture of Atahualpa, who are what we call here the first conquistadors. I could well indicate what share each one received, but I do not want to because of some considerations I have pondered. But I will state what all of them took together, without there being one *real* more or less. And this I will do in order to always satisfy the reader with the truth because I do not possess any ornateness or eloquence —nor do I want it—and it is unnecessary for this type of narrative.

Returning to the subject, those who were present in Cajamarca are *fol. 64* the following:[2]

Horsemen

The Governor Don Francisco Pizarro; Hernando Pizarro; Hernando de Soto; Juan Pizarro; Pedro de Candia; Gonzalo Pizarro; Juan Cortés; Sebastián de Belalcázar; Cristóbal de Mena; Ruy Hernández Briceño; Juan de Salcedo; Miguel Estete; Francisco de Jerez; Gonzalo de Pineda; Alonso de Medina; Alonso Briceño; Juan Pizarro de Orellana; Luis Maza; Jerónimo de Aliaga; Gonzalo Pérez; Pedro Barrantes; Rodrigo Núñez; Pedro de Anadel; Francisco Malaver; Diego Maldonado; Rodrigo de Chaves; Diego de Ojuelos; Ginés de Carranza;[3] Juan de Quincoces; Alonso de Morales; Lope Vélez; Juan de Barbarán; Pedro de Aguirre; Pedro de León; Diego Mejía; Martín

Alonso; Juan de Rojas; Pedro Cataño; Pedro Ortiz; Juan de Morgovejo;[4] Hernando de Toro; Diego de Agüero; Alonso Pérez; Hernando Beltrán; Pedro Barrera; Baena;[5] Francisco López; Sebastián de Torres; Juan Ruiz; Francisco de Fuentes; Gonzalo del Castillo; Nicolás de Azpeitia; Diego de Molina; Alonso Peto; Miguel Ruiz;[6] Juan de Salinas, horseshoer;[7] Juan de Salinas de la Hoz; Cristóbal Gallego; Rodrigo de Cantillana; Gabriel Félix; Hernán Sánchez; Pedro de Páramo.

These were the horsemen, and they divided among them according to their deeds because some had endured more than others; 24,230 marks of silver were divided among them.

Footmen

Those who had entered and were without horses are the following: Juan de Porras; Gregorio de Sotelo; García de Paredes; Pedro Sancho; Juan de Valdevieso; Gonzalo Maldonado; Pedro Navarro; Juan Ronquillo; Antonio de Vergara; Alonso de la Carrera; Alonso Romero; Melchor Verdugo; Martín Bueno; Juan Pérez de Tudela; Iñigo Tabuyo; Nuño González; Juan de Herrera; Francisco Dávalos; Hernando de Aldana; Martín de Marquina; Antonio de Herrera; Sandoval;[8] Miguel Estete;[9] Juan Borrallo;[10] Pedro de Moguer; Francisco Peces;[11] Melchor Palomino; Pedro de Alconchel;[12] Juan de Segovia; Crisóstomo de Hontiveros; Hernando Muñoz;[13] Alonso de Mesa; Juan Pérez de Osma;[14] Diego de Trujillo;[15] Palomino, cooper;[16] Alonso Jiménez; Pedro de Torres; Alonso de Toro; Diego Escudero; Diego
fol. 64v López; Francisco Gallego; Bonilla;[17] Francisco de Almendras; Escalante;[18] Andrés Jiménez; Juan Jiménez; García Martín; Alonso Ruiz; Lucas Martínez;[19] Gómez González; Alburquerque;[20] Francisco de Vargas;[21] Diego Gavilán; Contreras;[22] Herrera,[23] musketeer; Martín de Florencia;[24] Antonio de Oviedo; Jorge Griego;[25] Pedro de San Millán; Pedro Catalán; Pedro Román; Francisco de la Torre; Francisco Gorducho; Juan Pérez de Zamora; Diego de Narváez; Gabriel de Olivares; Juan García de Santa Olalla; Juan García, musketeer; Pedro de Mendoza; Juan Pérez; Francisco Martín; Bartolomé Sánchez, sailor; Martín Pizarro;[26] Hernando de Montalbo; Pedro Pinelo; Lázaro Sánchez; Miguel Cornejo; Francisco González; Francisco Muñiz;[27] Zárate;[28] Hernando de Sosa; Cristóbal de Sosa; Juan de Niza; Francisco de Solares; Hernando del Tiemblo; Juan Sánchez; Sancho de Villegas; Pedro de Ulloa; Juan Chico; Robles, tailor;[29] Pedro de Salinas de la Hoz; Antón García; Juan Delgado; Pedro de Valencia; Alonso

Sánchez de Talavera; Miguel Sánchez; Juan García, crier;[30] Lozano;[31] García López; Juan Martínez; Estéban García; Juan de Beranga;[32] Juan de Salvatierra; Pedro Calderón.

These were the footmen, and fifteen thousand marks of silver and ounces were distributed among them, each one taking according to his deeds and not all equally. When the silver was divided, the governor wanted to do the same with the gold, and he ordered that a decree be issued for it, which, copied to the letter from the original, says:

Decree for Division of Gold

Following the aforesaid, in the town of Cajamarca on the sixteenth day of the month of July of the said year fifteen hundred and thirty-three, the said Lord Governor Francisco Pizarro, before me the said notary, said: That of the gold that has been obtained until today, the said day, and that Atahualpa has given, all this is melted and numbered and that the fifth for His Majesty is taken from all of it, as well as the rights of the assayer, founder, marker, and the expenses that the company has made. Of the rest that is left he would like to make a division among the individuals who were present in gaining it and having it as His Majesty commands, mindful of what his lordship had said in the decree that was made in the division of silver to give each one what each one should have of the said gold as His Majesty commands. He wants *fol. 65* to indicate and name before me, the said notary, the weights of gold that each person is to have and take according to what God Our Lord would give him to understand, mindful of his conscience and what His Majesty commands.

This done, when the founding was carried out and according to the account, they learned what the mound that had to be divided amounted to. After removing the rights and costs of it and what the company owed and the bench[33] and some jewels of great weight, not counting what had been stolen, which was a lot, and without the one hundred thousand ducats removed for Almagro's people, the rest was divided among the governor and his companions. [Pizarro] took the shares of governor and captain-general, and the captains and notable people and the rest according to their deeds. I have already said that I could put down what each one took and was entitled to because I had [this information] in my possession. But, for the reasons I have said, I did not want to deal with it individually, but I state and relate as certain that 1,326,539 pesos was divided among them. And 262,259 pesos went as the fifth of the gold to the emperor. And they assigned ridiculous weight on this gold; much that was fourteen carats they called seven, and another of twenty, they called ten; and the silver accordingly. This blindness was the reason that many merchants greatly enriched themselves from trading in only gold and silver. And I further state as certain that if the Spaniards had not killed Atahualpa so quickly and had wanted to collect gold and silver and precious stones, this was a tenth of what could have been collected because the treasures of the Incas from Cuzco, Vilcas, Chile, Charcas, Quito, Tomebamba, and Caranqui were still viable, but nothing came of that except what they removed from Coricancha. And the huacas were full of treasures, as I will relate, and they were not few, but many and very notable. This appeared clear because the Indians kept bringing the gold, but when they learned of Atahualpa's death, they hid some of it, and some of it they themselves took, and some of it they left where they were when they heard of the death of their lord, and the Spaniards found it.

The treasure was divided so quickly, according to what I learned, that it caused envy among the Spaniards because those of Alma-
fol. 65v gro grumbled—why were they there, they wanted to do more than search for food; and other things that happened between them were enough that the distribution, which was large, was made. And the ransom of Atahualpa was one that would be given by such a great lord, who—whether or not he had usurped it—ruled the richest region and the most replete with metals that in my opinion exists in the world. I have heard many times great theologians debate and discuss whether what the king and the Spaniards took was rightfully obtained and not unscrupulous because they killed [Atahualpa] with so little justice after first divesting him of his property. It is not a subject for me to treat; those who got [the shares] should be asked. And you should know that if I had been entitled to a share, I would have done the same.

They say that each one of these shares amounted to 4,120 pesos of gold and 180 marks of pure silver for the footmen. To some they gave one share, to others three-quarters, and there were some who took half a share; consequently, some of the horsemen took two shares and others one and a half, according to their service and quality.[34]

But because they had so much money among so few, there was great gambling. Things were sold at very excessive prices. Many of them were well provided by important and beautiful ladies and had them as concubines, a great sin, which those who commanded should have avoided because the primary reason why the Indians loathed them so much was that they saw how they disparaged them and how they used their wives and daughters without any shame. God has punished our men, and most of these leaders have died miserably in wretched deaths, a frightening thought to serve as a warning. And for that [purpose] writing should serve, so we can delight in reading about the events and mend our ways by the examples, because all else are profanities and novels composed to please rather than to tell the truth.

Notes

1 Aliaga was at Cajamarca when the distribution took place. See also chapter 34.

2 As noted earlier, James Lockhart's *Men of Cajamarca* is an indispensable guide to the 160 men listed by Cieza. The author diligently traces the recipients of Atahualpa's treasure, actually 168 men, and provides a biographical sketch of each one of them. In modernizing names we have used Lockhart's spelling.

3 Cieza used the wrong name, Gómez de Carranza, as Lockhart and Busto point out. He was probably born in Granada in 1510, was with Pedrarias in Nicaragua, and traveled to Peru with Soto. He was with Soto on horse during the first encounter with Atahualpa. He returned to Spain around 1534, settling in Granada, where he became a member of the city council. See Lockhart, *Men of Cajamarca,* pp. 216–17; and Busto, *Diccionario,* 1:341–42.

4 Juan Morgovejo de Quiñones was born in Mayorga. He was in Nicaragua by 1528 and came to Peru with Belalcázar. He was killed in the Indian uprising of 1536. According to Lockhart, he always spelled his name "Morgovejo," rather than the more familiar current "Mogrovejo." Moreover, there is a town named Morgovejo in Spain; *Men of Cajamarca,* pp. 230–32.

5 Francisco de Baena was born around 1505. He spent about five years in Nicaragua and was a town councillor of León. He was also with Soto at the first meeting with the Inca and went with Hernando Pizarro to Pachacamac. He returned to Spain in July 1533 and probably settled in Madrid. See Busto, *Diccionario,* 1:188; and Lockhart, *Men of Cajamarca,* pp. 315–16.

6 Ruiz was a Mulatto from Seville. Little is known about him. He was killed during an Indian attack at Vilcaconga in November 1533 (see chapter 62). He left a son, Miguel, whose mother was likely a Nicaraguan Indian servant. His widow in Seville was still attempting to get control of the estate in 1550. See Lockhart, *Men of Cajamarca,* pp. 421–23.

7 Juan de Salinas, *herrador* (horseshoer), was also a veterinarian who cared for the horses during the expedition. He was listed by his trade in order to separate him from Juan de Salinas de la Hoz. See Lockhart, *Men of Cajamarca,* pp. 393–95.

8 Sandoval's exact identity is unclear, but it might be Rodrigo de Sandoval, who was in Coaque in April 1531 and could have been on the following expedition. See Lockhart, *Men of Cajamarca,* pp. 445–46.

9 See chapter 45.

10 Cieza calls him "Bonallo."

11 Cieza incorrectly uses "Pérez." Peces was from Sonseca, near Toledo, and was recruited by the Pizarros in 1529. He held an encomienda and was on the Cuzco city council in 1534. He shifted to the Almagro side in 1535 and was made alcalde, but was executed by royal officials after their victory at Chupas in 1542. Lockhart, *Men of Cajamarca,* pp. 334–36.

12 Pedro de Alconchel, an illiterate Extremaduran trumpeter, received a full share of gold and silver. This distinction may reflect the crucial role assigned to trumpeters: to stun and frighten the enemy with the powerful blast of their instruments. Alconchel was a native of a village called La Garganta, literally "the throat." There were two trumpeters at Cajamarca; the other one was Juan de Segovia. Lockhart, *Men of Cajamarca,* pp. 370–72; 395–96.

13 Not "Martínez" as Cieza wrote. See Lockhart, *Men of Cajamarca,* p. 440.

14 Lockhart (*Men of Cajamarca,* pp. 441–42) prefers the alternate spelling "Juan Pérez de Oma."

15 Cieza wrote "Alonso." Diego was born in Trujillo and was recruited in 1529. He left Peru in 1534, escorting Pedro de Alvarado to Guatemala, and then went to Spain. He returned to Peru in 1546, acquired a small encomienda, married, and secured a Cuzco council seat by 1559. Viceroy Francisco de Toledo heard of him in 1571, and suggested he dictate his memoirs. Diego died in 1576; see Lockhart, *Men of Cajamarca,* pp. 362–65.

16 Probably Alonso Palomino, a relative of Melchor Palomino, another footman at Cajamarca. In October of 1544, on the eve of Gonzalo Pizarro's occupation of Lima, Palomino left for Spain because he was ill and died shortly after his return. See Lockhart, *Men of Cajamarca,* pp. 390–91.

17 Lockhart (*Men of Cajamarca,* pp. 428–29) identifies him as either Francisco de Bonilla or Francisco Díaz de Bonilla from Bonilla de la Sierra, a village near Avila.

18 Juan de Escalante was born about 1492 in Escalante and was a carpenter who served in Nicaragua and Panama. He probably marched to Quito with Almagro. He received an Indian grant in Jauja, but quickly settled in Lima in 1535. Although he was granted an encomienda in the Ica Valley, Pizarro later forced him to release it to Nicolás de Ribera. See Lockhart, *Men of Cajamarca,* pp. 375–76; and Busto, *Hueste perulera,* pp. 223–24.

19 Martínez was born in Trujillo around 1511 and was recruited by Pizarro in 1529. He was a colorful character, whose career ranged from merchant to encomendero, from conquistador to rebel. He was one of the founders of Arequipa, where he also held and lost encomiendas. He died in 1567, just a few days after he married a daughter of Nicolás de Ribera. See Lockhart, *Men of Cajamarca,* pp. 300–305; and Efraín Trelles Arestegui, *Lucas Martínez Vegazo: Funcionamiento de una encomienda peruana inicial* (Lima: Pontificia Universidad Católica del Perú, 1982).

20 Alonso de Alburquerque.

21 Cieza uses "Baragas."

22 Pedro López de Contreras was listed in other sources as Contreras *difunto,* or deceased, because he was the only Spaniard who had died, cause unknown, before the distribution of Atahualpa's ransom. He nevertheless received a share, though only a partial one. He left no testament, and much of the money was absorbed by those administering his property, and one wonders if Mari Vázquez, his wife in Spain, ever received anything. Lockhart, *Men of Cajamarca,* p. 430.

23 Rodrigo de Herrera.

24 Of Italian and perhaps *converso* descent, Florencia was from Barbastro in Aragon and was an expert crossbowman. He always remained loyal to the crown and was well rewarded for it with a coat of arms and an encomienda in the Cuzco district. He was executed by the rebels during the Gonzalo Pizarro revolt in 1544. See Lockhart, *Men of Cajamarca,* pp. 377–79; and Busto, *Hueste perulera,* pp. 139–43.

25 Griego was born about 1504 and was of Greek origin. He may have been with Candia in Panama. He was a resident and encomendero in Jauja, then moved to Lima. By 1544 he had returned to Spain and settled in Seville's maritime district of Triana. See Lockhart, *Men of Cajamarca,* pp. 414–15.

26 It seems doubtful that Martín is a relative of the other Pizarros. Born about 1510, he was recruited in Trujillo in 1529. He became a vecino of Lima and received the small encomienda of Huamantanga. He died in 1557. See Lockhart, *Men of Cajamarca,* pp. 417–20.

27 Lockhart (*Men of Cajamarca,* pp. 388–89) identifies this man as Francisco Martínez, a tailor.

28 Juan de Zárate, see chapter 48.

29 Possibly Francisco de Robles, who was with another tailor, Francisco Martínez, in Jauja on 1 March 1534. See Lockhart, *Men of Cajamarca*, pp. 392–93.

30 Juan García was known both as *pregonero,* crier, and *gaitero,* piper, and in keeping with Spanish custom for those holding these positions, was either Black or Mulatto. In Cajamarca he was the one who weighed most of the gold and silver. See Lockhart, *Men of Cajamarca*, pp. 380–84.

31 Lockhart (*Men of Cajamarca*, pp. 436–37) proposes several identifications of this footman. Part of the difficulty lies in his insignificant role in Cajamarca and elsewhere during these years.

32 Lockhart (*Men of Cajamarca*, pp. 291–92) identifies Cieza's Juan de Vergara as Juan de Beranga. The fact that he appears also as "Berando," "Verenga," or "Verarga" causes much confusion, as Busto (*Diccionario*, 1:240–41) points out. He died, perhaps in Cuzco, in 1536.

33 An opulent seat, or "throne" made of gold.

34 as I have discussed at other times

LIII

How after the treasure was divided, Pizarro decided that his brother Hernando Pizarro should go with the news to the emperor

After what history has related occurred in the province of Cajamarca, *fol. 66* and Atahualpa realized that [the Spaniards] had divided the treasure but did not want to set him free, he was dejected. He did not show it because he had considerable trust in the word that Pizarro had given him and because he had fulfilled so generously what he had promised. Some of his knights and captains secretly asked permission to rise up against the Christians and attack them, but he did not accede to such talk; rather, he commanded the usual, which was that they should serve and obey them.

There were many yanaconas who served the Christians and who secured ample riches and fine clothing that no one but the Incas, or orejones and caciques, were allowed to wear. These scoundrels, along with the interpreters, circulated a thousand false reports, wishing that the Spaniards would kill Atahualpa so that they could go on with their impudence. And a great rumor was spreading in Cajamarca through these Indians that large squadrons of warriors were coming against the Christians to kill them and to attempt to set Atahualpa free. There was no one who could have carried it out, but it was generally affirmed to be the truth and that Chalcuchima was attempting it. It was a grossly false accusation because he neither attempted it nor ordered it.

Pizarro ordered that those who guarded Atahualpa should watch him very carefully and that the same should be done in the camp by the night watch and patrols. Atahualpa tried to rid [the Spaniards'] minds of such ideas, stating that peace or war were dependent on him. They did not believe him. Pizarro became angry at the innocent Chalcuchima, and on the advice of some, he decided to order him burned. They affirm that if it were not for Hernando Pizarro, who impeded it, they would have killed him cruelly with fire. The poor captain defended himself, swearing that he did not incite through envoys or in discourse any uprising or mobilization of people. They were reassured by what he said.

Pizarro believed that it would be important to the service of the emperor to send him information and report about the great land that he had discovered and about the large treasure they had encountered and hoped to find in the future because with such joyous tidings, His Majesty would be served. After he conferred with the leaders who were with him, he decided that his brother, Hernando Pizarro, should go to Spain and announce it, and that he should take with him a portion of these great treasures it pleased God to present them.

Hernando Pizarro accepted the command and made ready. The *fol. 66v* governor sent His Majesty a request to grant him an expansion of his governance and other things. The marshal also wrote to the emperor, informing him how much he had served him, and he petitioned for a grant to name him his governor and adelantado of the land beyond that which was governed by Don Francisco Pizarro. He gave Hernando Pizarro sufficient power to negotiate it, and promised him more than twenty thousand ducats for the endeavor of soliciting it. The royal officials sent the emperor the share he was entitled to from his fifth and the jewel from the bench. Hernando Pizarro removed from this kingdom a quantity of his gold and that of his brothers. Captain Salcedo[1] and Captain Cristóbal de Mena[2] and others asked permission to depart for Spain. One of them had his gold and silver carried by rams, and one ram ran off loaded with gold, which he never found, nor did it reappear. They were taking forty thousand castellanos, and sixty and thirty and twenty and more and less. They all took their leave of the governor.

Atahualpa was distressed by Hernando Pizarro's departure. Some maintain that [Atahualpa] would not have died if he had stayed and that he would have attempted to save his life. But if it pleased God that he should die, neither Hernando Pizarro nor anyone else had the power to prevent it. Some horsemen accompanied [Pizarro] from Cajamarca to the city of San Miguel. All those who were to go to Spain embarked for Tierra Firme, where [the people] were astonished when they saw so much gold and silver, and they easily sold it and became wealthy. One smith of Panama became mysteriously rich just from dividing bars of silver and gold. Wherever they heard the great news, they knew to take merchandise to Peru.

And because it is expedient to return to finish [the business] of Cajamarca and relate the death of Atahualpa, I will not deal with this other than to say that because Almagro was uncertain of Hernando Pizarro's friendship, he secretly told Cristóbal de Mena that should he notice [Hernando Pizarro] failing to act correctly and honorably, then he should inform the gentlemen of the Royal Council of the Indies of the entire truth so that they would know and understand it. And he gave [Mena] power, with only a few realizing it and knowing about it.

Notes

1 See chapter 2.

2 See chapter 32.

LIV

About how false news came that warriors were advancing against the Spaniards, and about how Pizarro, breaking the word and the contract that he made with Atahualpa, put him to death with great cruelty and little justice

fol. 67 After Hernando Pizarro left for Spain, as has been related in the past chapter, Atahualpa's death came to pass, which was the most ignoble act the Spaniards have ever done in all this empire of the Indies, and as such it is condemned and viewed as a great sin. Enough principal men were against him, and God permitted his life to be taken and that Pizarro would venture to give such sentence. This death came about as I will relate [according] to the inquiry that I have made about it and without adding or deleting anything.

Atahualpa had as wives and concubines many principal Indian ladies, natives of the kingdom's provinces, most of them extremely beautiful and some very white and of exquisite figures. Felipillo, interpreter and wicked traitor, had fallen in love with one of them, so much so that he was desperate to have her. While the lord was alive, he did not find courage—by entreaty, threat, or promise—to gain her, but it seemed to him that if [Atahualpa] were to die, he would ask Pizarro for her or he would take her and she would be his. The camp was full of thieves, whom we call yanaconas—the name of a perpetual servant—so having such a design, [Felipillo] had some conversations with them and other local Indians whom he understood because he was an interpreter and who were on bad terms with Atahualpa: they should spread the fictitious news that Indian warriors were coming from all parts, assembled on Atahualpa's orders to attack the Spaniards. And they should affirm it, even if they were asked about it in the presence of Atahualpa himself because he [Felipillo] was the interpreter and whatever he might interject would be believed.

Deceived by Felipillo's assertions and vows, the Spaniards began to whisper among themselves that the entire force of Cuzco and Quito was coming against them. Pizarro regretted this news. Apprehensive

17. The execution of Atahualpa. Felipe Guaman Poma de Ayala, *El primer nueva corónica y buen gobierno,* 3 vols., ed. Rolena Adorno and John V. Murra (Mexico City: Siglo Veintiuno, 1980), f. 390. Courtesy of Siglo Veintiuno Editores.

about finding himself in a bind, he went to speak to Atahualpa. He told him that there was no reason to be as conniving in his dealings with the Christians as they were telling him he was in procuring, with deceit and treacherous cunning, warriors to descend on them to kill them, even after he [Pizarro] had honored him and treated his person as the great lord that he was. Atahualpa did not stir. He listened to Pizarro's reasoning and responded with few words, though very serious and resentful, saying that he was shocked that he could be so impudent and that the Incas never lied, nor did they ever cease to tell
fol. 67v the truth. Moreover, while he was in their power and their prisoner, his fear of being killed by them should assure them not to believe such a thing. He swore it and gave him his royal word that this was a lie and a great fabrication invented by someone who wished him ill. And that ever since they had seized him, he never tried to do anything other than to give orders that they should be served and provided for. They should understand that in the entire realm not a man was stirring or taking up arms. The men always fulfilled what he commanded; moreover, not even the leaves on trees moved without his consent. When he said that, Pizarro departed, believing that he was telling the truth in everything.

They say that a certain Indian, I do not know why, went to church, and Pizarro and Atahualpa ordered his removal, which angered Friar Vicente de Valverde so that he said loudly enough that some could hear, looking toward the part where Atahualpa was: "I promise that if I could, I would have you burned"—the words of a soldier not of a priest.

The notices that warriors were advancing against them did not cease coming to Cajamarca. Because it was in his hands, Felipillo was saying one thing to the Christians and another to the Indians, informing according to his will. He affirmed to Pizarro that the Indians were undoubtedly saying the truth and that if he killed Atahualpa, then everything would cease. With all this, the Spaniards felt anxious, and the prisoner Atahualpa exclaimed that this was not true and that he had been deceived by them because after making them rich, they were seeking his death. The Spaniards, with the exception of a few, did not wish his death; rather, they were soliciting his life. But because of what they were hearing, some were stating that he should die; others were saying that he should be sent to Spain to the emperor.

They watched him and the camp very carefully. Chalcuchima was seized and put in a place where he could not speak to [Atahualpa]. In the meantime, Felipillo was proclaiming that the Indian warriors were already approaching and were near. They say—indeed, they all affirm it—that some or all of the royal officials were shouting to Pizarro that he should kill Atahualpa then and there without delay because it was in the interest of the pacification of the land, and doing otherwise would be a disservice to the king. Meanwhile, another false notice arrived that the warriors were no more than four leagues from *fol. 68* Cajamarca. Following this news, some argued that Atahualpa should die; they believed that if they killed him, neither would a man confront another, nor would a lance be raised. Others shouted loudly that it was an evil deed. The officials, especially Riquelme,[1] insisted that he should be executed right away without waiting any longer.

Poor Atahualpa was upset by what they told him was happening. He knew from his Indians that it was all a lie and that no troops were assembled to come and attack. He was distraught because Hernando Pizarro had gone, and he feared that the Spaniards, after having robbed and deceived him, wanted to kill him. He tried to reassure them, but he was not believed because the traitor Felipillo was his enemy. The governor resolved to put him to death. First, it was ordered that Hernando de Soto and several horsemen should go out in the direction of where the warriors were affirmed to be, to see if [the rumor] were true. If so, then Atahualpa would be put to death, but if not, then he would be saved without being harmed or injured.

Soto, Lope Vélez,[2] and others left, ready to determine if the news was accurate, yet with great hopes that it would turn out to be a lie so that Atahualpa would not die. I have learned and know from some that Almagro was in favor of Atahualpa's death—advising the governor, as did others, that he should do it—and from others, especially the *beneficiado* Morales,[3] a cleric, who was there and buried Atahualpa, that this did not happen, nor did Almagro advocate it; rather, he said that he spoke to Pizarro, asking him: "Why do you want to kill this Indian?" And he replied: "This you ask? Do you want them to attack and kill us?" At that, Almagro said, weeping for Atahualpa, his death weighing heavily upon him: "Oh, if only he never knew you!"

Following these things, Felipillo again warned that people were coming from many directions, and there was such a commotion about this that without waiting for Soto to return, a suit was brought against [Atahualpa]. The witnesses were Indians, and the interpreter intimidating them was Felipillo: Look at Atahualpa's life, how it went! He had no defender, and neither was he believed, nor was more done than to review the charges, which they say[4] were taken to Friar Vicente so that he could examine them. He said that [they were] sufficient to execute him and that he would authorize it, signing his name. They say also that Riquelme was very anxious and could not wait to see him dead. Because of the suit against him, the governor sentenced [Atahualpa] to be burned.

fol. 68v When Atahualpa learned of the cruel sentence, he lamented to God Almighty how those who had seized him had failed to keep their word. He could not find a way to escape. If he believed that he could do it with more gold, he would have given them another house, even four more. He said many pitiful things: that those who were listening to him should have mercy because of his youth; he asked why they were killing him, even though he had given them so much and not caused them any harm or injury. He complained about Pizarro, and with reason.

At about seven[5] in the evening they removed him from where he was held. They took him to where the execution would take place; Friar Vicente, Juan de Porras, Captain Salcedo, and some others went with him. On the way he kept repeating: "Why are they killing me? Why am I being killed? What have I done, and my children and my wives?" and other similar words. Friar Vicente was admonishing him to become a Christian and abandon his beliefs. [Atahualpa] asked to be baptized, and the friar did it. And then they strangled him, and to fulfill the sentence they burned some of his hair with pieces of straw, which was another foolishness. Some of the Indians say that before they killed him, Atahualpa exclaimed that they should await him in Quito, that they would see him again in the form of a snake. These must be their sayings.[6]

The grief of the wives and women servants was so great that their cries seemed to tear the clouds asunder. Many wanted to kill themselves and be buried in the tomb with him, but they were not allowed to. They placed the fringe in the tomb. Morales, the priest, removed it and took it to Spain.[7] When the women saw that they could not inter themselves with their lord, they withdrew and hanged themselves from their own hair and with rope. Pizarro was notified of this, and had he not rectified it, most of the women would have hanged and killed themselves. The cleric interred Atahualpa, giving him an ecclesiastical burial with all pomp possible, and some wore hats as a sign of mourning. A prayer to God: if he asked for baptism from the heart, he too would be in His glory, which would be another delight and rich thing to send to Peru. And those who killed him in such an evil way, pardon them, because all of them are there. And in Atahualpa's case one could quote the proverb: "You kill, and you will be killed; and those who will kill you, will be killed." Thus, those who are blamed for his death died disastrous deaths: Pizarro was stabbed; Almagro was garroted; Friar Vicente was killed by the Indians in Puná; Riquelme died suddenly; and Pedro Sancho, the notary, was put to a cruel death in Chile by a garrote and a rope.

Notes

1 Treasurer Alonso Riquelme was probably from Seville. By the royal orders of 24 May 1529 he would have been placed in charge of the venture if both Pizarro and Almagro had died. He was largely independent, representing the fiscal interests of the Crown, and was therefore never liked by the Pizarros. He died in Lima late in 1546 or early 1547, leaving massive debts to the Royal Treasury. See Cook, "Libros de cargo," pp. 43–50.

2 Lope Vélez de Guevara was born in Palos around 1505. He had been active in Honduras in the mid-1520s. He went on to Nicaragua, became a close associate of Soto, and probably came with him to Peru. He returned to Spain in 1535. See Lockhart, *Men of Cajamarca,* pp. 367–68.

3 Francisco de Morales.

4 some today

5 nine. Saturday, 26 July 1533.

6 Quickly, myths evolved centering on the return of Atahualpa. Within a half century plays were enacted depicting the events, and later his reappearance was seen as ushering in a new age. See MacCormack, *Religion in the Andes,* p. 415; Manuel Burga, *Nacimiento de una utopía: Muerte y resurrección de los Incas* (Lima: Instituto de Apoyo Agrario, 1988), pp. 69–84, 389–400; and Pease, *Los últimos Incas,* pp. 122–31, 147–67.

7 Miguel Estete took Atahualpa's fringe when he was seized; see chapter 45, note 5. Morales took the fringe that Atahualpa was wearing at the time of his execution. The fringe was not like the European crown; it was simply a headdress only the Inca could wear—part of his "uniform." Franklin Pease, personal communication, 27 September 1997. See also Lockhart, *Men of Cajamarca,* p. 321.

LV

About what else happened in Cajamarca after Atahualpa died, and how Soto returned without seeing or encountering any warriors

Men here are so swift in relating what is happening that notice of anything is spread from one to another in a short time. They themselves affirm as very certain how quickly it spread in all directions that Atahualpa had been killed by the Christians. They never believed this could happen because, they said, they had stayed safe and calm in their lands without ever having offended the Spaniards, and that although they had captured Atahualpa, they would release him for the ransom. But when the end became known, many wept profusely for the deceased, calling fortunate the past Incas who had died without knowledge of such cruel, bloodthirsty, and vicious people. Their rage deepened as they thought the matter over again and again. They decided to form an alliance against them, to wage war on them, which they had not waged because Atahualpa had always ordered them to serve and provision them. Many loads of gold and silver for these very Christians were coming from several places; wherever the news reached them they stopped, and most of them took [the treasure], whereas others left it. Many men and women killed themselves, trusting that they would go to serve his soul in the high heavens where they believe the Incas go. They say that they disinterred the body from that site and placed it in an opulent tomb in Cuzco. The Christians could never find where they had buried him although they had attempted it in order to remove the treasure that was deposited with him. *fol. 69*

With some, Quizquiz went toward Quito;[1] and in all places powerful men appropriated property and dominions that were not theirs, and all of Peru was in disarray because many who had feuded with Atahualpa rejoiced at his death. The Spaniards, conquistadors who were with Pizarro and others, some of whom had come with Almagro, deplored the death of this lord, and many wept, sighing and saying that they would have been glad never to have seen him or his

gold because they were so grief stricken by his death. And the sorrow of all in general increased when Soto returned to Cajamarca, after he
fol. 69v had gone to where they said the troops were but did not find more than some Indians coming to serve the Christians. And, after learning what had happened, [Soto] and those who had gone with him were anguished, cursing themselves for not having arrived sooner. They faulted the governor for not having waited until they had returned to report what they had been ordered.

Following this, instead of esteeming those ladies of the royal lineage of the Incas, daughters of Huayna Capac, who was such a powerful and famous prince, and marrying them in order to gain the favor of the natives through such union, Pizarro and the leaders who were with him, took them as concubines. This misconduct began with the governor himself. Thus, these people were disparaged to such a degree that today we hold them so low, as you who are here can see.

They say that after what this chronicle has related had occurred, Pizarro asked the principal orejones there who among them would be worthy of the fringe and the rank of the Inca because he wanted to grant it to the one who had the right to possess it. They considered it frivolous to be crowned king[2] unless it were in the city of Cuzco. The realm should have devolved on the oldest of Huascar's sons, but they had killed almost all of them so that few remained alive. Many of Huayna Capac's [lineage] claimed the realm, but because those who were in Cajamarca were followers of Atahualpa, they told Pizarro to name as Inca one of his sons called Tupac Huallpa.[3] Pizarro was satisfied, and the native lords together, in the manner of their ancestors, hailed [Tupac Huallpa] as a new king, killing as a sacrifice a lamb of one color without spots, and some of them wore feather diadems to honor him. Pizarro was planning to leave Cajamarca shortly, and he named Captain Sebastián de Belalcázar as his deputy of the city of San Miguel in the plains. He ordered him to depart to maintain justice in that city.

Because at this time the Adelantado Don Pedro de Alvarado, governor of Guatemala, decided to come to Peru, I want to relate the reason for it, according to what I learned from some of that land
fol. 70 who came with him. And the story goes that in Nicaragua Belalcázar and the pilot, Juan Fernández, had made a certain partnership, and in

Cajamarca they had an argument about the interest gained from each share; and when the pilot, Juan Fernández, returned to Nicaragua, he went to the Adelantado Alvarado, to whom he described the marvels of Peru and how large the land was, where they said great things about the treasures of Quito, in addition to those of Cuzco. [Juan Fernández] advised him that because he had license for discovery from the emperor, he should go with his fleet to those places. This one said so much to the adelantado that because of his talk and the lofty rumors already floating about Peru, Alvarado decided to take people and horses from his governance to occupy what he could of the land outside the boundaries designated for Don Francisco Pizarro. And then it became known that they wanted to make this expedition.

When the Licentiate Castañeda, a judge of Nicaragua,[4] learned that Alvarado was determined to go with the armada's contingent, he wished to win Pizarro's friendship and favor, so he secretly took testimony from witnesses who knew the enterprise and sent it to Peru to be placed in [Pizarro's] hands. He entrusted a knight, who later became an important man in this kingdom and a vecino of Cuzco, named Gabriel de Rojas,[5] to take it. And, wishing to do it, he set out on a ship from Nicaragua.

Notes

1 Cuzco

2 Another example of using European concepts for Andean customs.

3 Cieza wrote "Toparpa." He made a mistake. Tupac Huallpa was the son of Huayna Capac, not of Atahualpa. The Spanish hoped to secure the goodwill of the Huascar faction in Cuzco as they began the southward march; Hemming, *Conquest*, p. 86.

4 Licentiate Francisco de Castañeda left Spain in 1527. In 1530 he was in company with Soto and Ponce to construct two ships to take to Peru, but Pedrarias refused authorization to sail. When Pedrarias died in 1531, Castañeda became governor, continuing to 1535. Although he had attacked the abuse of Nicaraguan Indians, especially the slave trade, he was thoroughly involved in it and controlled export license to Peru. When charges were lodged against him, he fled to Peru, taking many slaves to sell, but was brought to justice and imprisoned in 1540. See William L. Sherman, *Forced*

Native Labor in Sixteenth-Century Central America (Lincoln: University of Nebraska Press, 1979), pp. 10, 54–57, 70, 98–99, 108, 382–83, 387; and Lockhart, *Men of Cajamarca*, pp. 82, 124, 193, 225, 244.

5 Born in Cuéllar, Rojas came to the Indies around 1514 and was involved in the conquest of Nicaragua. When he came to Peru, he joined Almagro and was imprisoned by the Pizarrists after the Battle of Salinas (1538), but was soon freed. During the Gonzalo Pizarro uprising he switched sides several times, but ultimately defended the royal cause. He died in Cuzco in 1548. See Mendiburu, *Diccionario*, 9:466–71; and Alexandra Parma Cook and Noble David Cook, *Good Faith and Truthful Ignorance: A Case of Transatlantic Bigamy* (Durham, N.C.: Duke University Press, 1991), pp. 94, 181.

LVI

About how Pizarro left Cajamarca for the city of Cuzco and what happened to him until he arrived in the Jauja Valley

Pizarro had been given great notices about the city of Cuzco. He was eager to set out in order to populate it with Christians and pacify all the provinces along the way. He had stayed in Cajamarca more than seven months, and that beautiful and plentiful province was in such a state that [the Spaniards] were saddened to see how they were leaving it, remembering how flawless they had found it.

Captain Chalcuchima was imprisoned—apprehensive, because of his authority, not to incite some people to start a war against the Spaniards. Pizarro believed that with Atahualpa dead everything was secure and there was nothing to fear. He ordered him released, admonishing him to value the friendship of the Christians and being in their favor. The Spaniards, ready to depart, ordered the natives of the district to come and carry their hoard on their shoulders. So many came that there were plenty and even some extra. The new Inca set out in a litter, and Chalcuchima did the same; they went together *fol. 70v* with the Christians.

They went until they reached the province of Huamachuco, which is well populated by a pure and wise people. They found them peaceful, without any sign of uprising, and they were well received and served by them. Pizarro stayed four days in Huamachuco.[1] He ordered his men not to harm the natives. He spoke with the lords of the province, praising their good intention to have peace and alliance with the Spaniards. He asked them to take him beyond Huamachuco. The Spaniards went on the royal highway of the Incas until they arrived [in] Andamarca, without coming across resistance in any village because all the Indians that they encountered were peaceful and completely unarmed. But there was news that ahead, in the region of Tarma and Bombón, there was a throng of people planning to attack them in retaliation for Atahualpa's death and to prevent them from seizing power in the land as they had been proclaiming.

Pizarro ordered that one of Huayna Capac's sons and another chief, accompanied by some Indians, should go and find out what was going on. And some relate that after they left, the son of Huayna Capac[2] was killed near Bombón by the captains and warriors there, who called him traitor to his land and kin because he was serving such cruel, evil, and deceitful people as were the Spaniards. The other one who went with him was able to escape and return to Pizarro, whom he warned of what was occurring. Because the great captain Chalcuchima's status and authority in the kingdom were so great, it was enough to learn that there were troops in order to believe that they were taking up arms for him, thus giving rise to another false accusation, as [with] Atahualpa. Among the Indians themselves there were some who were so evil and mendacious that they confirmed it to Pizarro, who ordered [Chalcuchima] seized and placed in custody. He proceeded on his journey through that land—which, although it is a level country, it is very rough, with high mountains that seem to reach the clouds and descend again infinitely into profound valleys. Although this is true, the royal highway of the Incas, who were so powerful, is also so well made and built through slopes and sections that one almost does not feel the height of the mountains.

The Spaniards went through some snow-covered passes, which made them quite anxious. Near them were captains and orejones of Huayna Capac's lineage who were determined to attack our men in a
fol. 71 place that they found most appropriate. They had warning of it, and they were on the alert so that they would not be taken by surprise.

When the Indians, who I have said intended to attack the Spaniards, were close to them, they did not appear as fierce as they had at first. Presumptuous of being valiant, well satiated from filling their stomachs with chicha, and berating the Spaniards, they saw themselves as victors, judging them as vanquished. They blamed the capture of Atahualpa and the great defeat at Cajamarca on everyone going into the enclosure and plaza formed by the lodgings, where the horses and Christians could easily do what they did. But now when they came within sight of their beards and saw that they carried swords and lances and that the horses were fatter and fiercer than when they had entered Cajamarca,[3] they were afraid, and with everyone's consent they agreed to retreat toward Jauja, saying that it would be more prudent to fight the Spaniards in that valley than there.

In the meantime, Pizarro and his people marched in good order, with Almagro and a few horsemen always in the vanguard. They arrived at what they call Tarma. Further on, by Bombón, five or six leagues toward the south, in a comfortable place, Pizarro decided to leave the baggage they were carrying with a necessary guard, because it was a great nuisance to march like that.[4] In the *tambos* of Chocamarca they encountered some quantity of gold that had been left by those who were carrying it to Cajamarca in the previous days. While Pizarro and his men were in the principal lodging of Tarma, news arrived with great urgency that the enemy was coming against them in many squadrons, which was false. It was sent by the natives so that the encampment would be lifted from their villages, and the Spaniards would leave. But because Pizarro and his captains were unaware of this, they had a conference about what they should do. They decided to leave where they were and position themselves in an open field to await those who might come. And all of them quickly departed, leaving behind the tents and stocks, not taking anything other than weapons and horses. They all positioned themselves in a cold, open plain, believing that the Indians would attack them that night. There were no huts, except for one in which Pizarro and Friar Vicente fit. The night was frightening, with so much rain and so cold, that *fol. 71v* they thought they would perish because they had no other cover than the bellies of the horses and the irons of the lances. When daytime came, they recovered from the hard night that they had gone through and proceeded on their way, nearing the beautiful Jauja Valley.

In Tarma they encountered several pieces of pure gold. But at that time they sought neither silver nor gold nor anything other than to become masters and to trample on the land and rule over the city of Cuzco and populate it with Christians. Almagro, as I have said, always led the advance. In Yanamarca they saw more than four thousand dead men from the time past when Huascar and Atahualpa had their wars. With the accord of the leaders who were with him, Pizarro decided that Almagro, Juan Pizarro, and Hernando de Soto should go ahead with some shield bearers to Jauja and survey what was there.[5]

The name of the captain-general of the warriors who I related were assembled against the Christians was Incurabayo.[6] They had already arrived in the Jauja Valley. And because Almagro and the rest who were with him were rushing, they went until they were within sight of the valley. They saw it so beautiful and well populated that they were astonished. Diego de Agüero, Pedro de Candia, and Quincoces arrived[7] first and reconnoitered. The Indian warriors retreated to the western part of the valley, and crossing the river, they made great clamor, insulting our men with foul words. They also asked why [the Spaniards] were in their land against their will, that they should return to theirs, satisfied with the harm they had already done and with having killed Atahualpa after they had stolen such great treasure from him with such artifice and cunning. Almagro, consulting with Juan Pizarro and Hernando de Soto, decided to set upon the Indians. He thought it was important to punish them in such a way that, being chastised in the contest, they themselves would ask for peace. And thus, having commended themselves to God, our Lord, all of them together launched out at the Indians. They crossed the raging river with difficulties because, aside from being large, it was rising from the melting snow that had entered it, and [the Indians] had destroyed the bridge so that they could not cross easily.

Some of the Indians became frightened when they saw their enemies heading toward them, saying that they should flee their wrath and the fury of the horses; others who viewed it with more spirit *fol. 72* insisted that they should take a stand against them and await them and attempt to kill them. In the meantime, the Christians were coming very close to them, so without discussing what to do, they formed a squadron and quickly retreated. Hernando de Soto and some horsemen realized how and where the Indians would leave, being—as I say—in a squadron, and he positioned himself in front of them in such a way that several of them could not avoid being lanced. Juan Pizarro and others went along the river and Almagro on the same path that the Indians were taking, and by attacking them, they forced them to separate into two parts, distraught to see the horses upon them. And as they tore the lances from their bodies, making way for the souls to leave, they separated: some took the highlands that lie to the north of the valley, and the others moved toward the west along the same river, anguished and frightened to see what fierce enemies they had. The Spaniards assailed both groups so vigorously that blood from the dead bodies flowed in all directions. And weary of killing,[8] they retreated and returned to the flat valley where they found the governor who had already arrived with the rest of the Spaniards. And he saw how they had ignited many of the lodgings where many precious and very valuable things burned. Using great care as he had ordered, some storehouses, where more than one hundred thousand fanegas of maize had remained, as well as other houses with more than five hundred cargas of fine and stitched cloth, were repaired.

In the Temple of the Sun and other places of this valley some quantity of gold and silver was found, as well as mamaconas, who are the virgins of the temple. And if Atahualpa's captains had not stolen what there had been in this valley, great spoils would have been found because it is one of the marvels of Peru. At that time, the valley was very populated and beautiful. Through our sins, wars have never been lacking in this kingdom, and the natives have been so molested and abused that most of the people are gone from it, which is a great shame because it happened in such a short time.

It will be expedient to leave Pizarro in this valley, where he founded a city, in order to return to speak of Belalcázar and what he did in San Miguel; indeed, for the clarity of the narrative, no less can be allowed. Then I will quickly return to the principal subject.

Notes

1 Busto (*Historia general*, p. 97) argues they were there on 17 August 1533.

2 Huaritico. See Hemming, *Conquest*, p. 92.

3 The rest at Cajamarca helped the horses to recuperate and become acclimated to the high elevations. There was ample pasture in the marshy grasslands; the corn in the Inca storehouses proved ideal for the horses; and *quinua*, a high-elevation Andean cereal, was highly nutritious.

4 Cieza wrote in the margin of the manuscript: "Note: I have to indicate in *Part One* how this road goes, to give more impact."

5 The Spanish remained there from 12 to 27 October 1533. See Hemming, *Conquest*, pp. 95–96.

6 Incurabayo was one of Atahualpa's principal leaders and, following Chalcuchima's death, was the major opponent of the Spanish. See Hemming, *Conquest*, p. 561.

7 always went

8 the Spaniards of fighting

LVII

About how Sebastián de Belalcázar arrived in the city of San Miguel and how, desirous to explore Quito, he negotiated with the cabildo to request him to go against the warriors who were said to be coming against them

fol. 72v Don Francisco Pizarro had named Captain Sebastián de Belalcázar as his lieutenant of the city of San Miguel, as had been related in its place. After he left that province, he went until he reached the city, where, by virtue of the provision that he carried, he was admitted[1] to the office. Because Hernando Pizarro had reported in Panama what they had discovered and about the great riches of the land, anyone who could tried to set sail to where so much gold had been found. And because San Miguel was settled on the coast, many of those that I mention landed with horses and arms in that city. This stirred up Belalcázar to attempt to claim Quito, where it was affirmed that there were houses filled with gold and that there was such quantity of this metal that Cajamarca and Cuzco had nothing compared to it.

At this time, Gabriel de Rojas had also arrived, coming with the testimony that the Licentiate Castañeda took regarding the expedition to Peru planned by Adelantado Don Pedro de Alvarado. Diego Palomino[2] and others left San Miguel to accompany him so that he could arrive safely where Pizarro was. Belalcázar had influence in the cabildo where the councilmen and the justice of the city gathered. He wished that they themselves would request him to go to the highlands to defend the province from Indian warriors. Furthermore, news had spread throughout the plains that the highlanders, angered by Atahualpa's death, were forming a league in order to attack the Spanish vecinos and inhabitants of the new city. Belalcázar even said that it would serve Pizarro as well as all of them to go and occupy Quito, a place of distinction and renown, and that because it had a reputation of such wealth, Don Pedro de Alvarado was on his way to explore it. To many, Belalcázar's reasons seemed good, and because he kept manipulating [the issue], and because some councilmen in the cabildo were his friends, they resolved that the city should request him to go and defeat the Indians who were said to be coming in war against them. And other things occurred so that Belalcázar was pleased, and he wrote letters to the governor to excuse himself for leaving the city without his authorization, saying that the cabildo had requested him to do it, but that he would try to return soon. And then, spending the money he took from Cajamarca, he began to trade in horses and recruit people.

He and all of them believed that they would find in Quito much more to divide than in Cajamarca, so 140 Spaniards, footmen and horsemen, gathered for the expedition. One Miguel Muñoz, an acquaintance or relative of Belalcázar himself, went as standard bearer, Francisco Pacheco and Juan Gutiérrez as captains, and Falcón de la Cerda as camp master. They left the city and went to Corobamba, a province in the highlands, where they all united and were well housed by the Indians and supplied with provisions, without giving them any payment for it. But this custom has been common in all the Indies. *fol. 73*

[The Indians] learned in Quito that the Christians were coming to occupy the provinces and rob the treasure. Everyone from those regions was distressed when they learned of Atahualpa's death because they loved him very much, and they marveled how [the Spaniards]—being so few—could defeat so many and capture such a powerful prince. Rumiñavi, Zope-Zopahua, and others took command of the republic.[3] The robbery that they say Otavalo committed in Caranqui also happened, as I have written in *Part One,* to which I am referring because to write one thing many times in a narrative is tedious.[4] To the last person they all decided to defend the land, not consenting that the Spaniards become masters of it. They made great supplications and solemn sacrifices to their gods, communicating with the demon through the oracles about the end of the war, how it would be. They had learned as a certainty that greed for gold and no other reason was bringing [the Spaniards] against them. They were so hungry for it that they were never satiated. And to prevent them from seeing such pleasure or possessing what was not theirs or what was owed them for any reason of natural law, it is commonly known among many that Rumiñavi and other chiefs and priests took more than six hundred cargas of gold that they had collected from the sacred temples of the Sun and that at the time was in the palaces of the Incas. They took it to a lake, according to what some say, and threw it into its deepest part. And according to what others say, they buried it in great crags among heaps of snow, and they killed those who carried it on their backs so that they would not reveal it, a great cruelty. And although they themselves later died in torture, strangely they did not *fol. 73v* want to reveal what they knew, but wanted to die believing that they would be going to live forever with the Incas, their sovereign lords. Others suggest that there was no treasure, or only a little; because the head of the empire was Cuzco, it was there where these metals had been taken and deposited. But although it is said and I relate the opinions, I truly believe and hold that the missing treasure of Quito is great because the depository of Huayna Capac and his treasury remained there, and because Atahualpa thought that it would be a second Cuzco, he left his there also. Later, those who had revolted collected [the treasures] of Tomebamba, Latacunga, Caranqui, and other important places where there were temples and palaces, but not one piece went to Cajamarca or to this day has appeared.

Those who were mitimaes and held command in these regions did what the others had done: each one occupied what he could. They knew that there was no Inca to ask them for an account and that the Spaniards, who were the ones whom they already feared,[5] understood little about the quipus; after they formed an alliance of all to wage war on them, they began to prepare those weapons that they use. As captain-general they chose Rumiñavi, which means "eye of stone," because they call stone *rumi* and eye *ñavi*. He encouraged them all he could, proclaiming that the Spaniards were very cruel, lecherous, and destroyers of fields and villages.

Belalcázar had already left Corobamba and endured great hardship of hunger and cold with his people when he marched through desolate places until he arrived in Zoropalta. They had news that the province of the Cañari[6] was near, where they would find many provisions. Because they were a little more than four leagues from Tomebamba, which is the capital of that land, Belalcázar and thirty horsemen went ahead, while the rest of the people remained in Pacheco's charge.

Notes

1 received
2 From the Jaén area in Spain, Palomino was first in Nicaragua, then at Tumbez. He remained at San Miguel in 1532. Settling in Peru's north, he led an expedition into the interior in 1548 to conquer the Bracamoros. In 1549 he founded the Peruvian city of Jaén. See Lockhart, *Men of Cajamarca*, pp. 339–41, 391; and Newson, *Life and Death*, p. 92.
3 Cieza uses the word "republic" in the sense of the body politic.
4 *Part One*, chapter 39. According to Cieza, both the Caranqui and Otavalo Indians had been devastated by Inca expansion. Huayna Capac had ordered the execution of all adult males; after that disaster the peoples of the area were called the *guamaraconas* (Huambracunas), or "boys." But the Caranqui remained wealthier; the cacique held both their own and Inca treasure in royal storehouses. Therefore, the Otavaleños concocted a scheme to despoil their neighbors. They placed their largest llamas on the ridges above the valley of the Caranqui, mounted by women and children disguised as Spanish soldiers. A group of Otavaleños entered the Caranqui territory, shouting that they had been attacked and were fleeing for their lives. The Caranqui saw the foreign troops on the hilltops and joined in the flight. After they left, a contingent of the Otavaleños ransacked the storehouses, taking all that they could with them.
5 who were feared in all parts
6 The Cañari ethnic group in southeastern Ecuador was famous for its brave warriors. Some fifteen thousand of their fighters had been moved, as mitimaes, to Cuzco, where because of their loyalty they became personal guards of the Inca elite. After Huayna Capac's death they supported Huascar and were persecuted by Atahualpa's followers. They joined the Spaniards in defense of Cuzco during the native uprising of 1536–37. As a reward, the Spanish granted them permanent exemption from tribute payment and the forced labor draft, the *mita*. See Noble David Cook, *Demographic Collapse: Indian Peru, 1520–1620* (Cambridge: Cambridge University Press, 1981), pp. 82–83.

LVIII

About how Belalcázar defeated a captain they had sent against him, and the natives were delighted to see the Christians when they arrived in Tomebamba, and they formed a friendship with them, and about how the captains of Quito went out to wage war against them

fol. 74 Rumiñavi and Zope-Zopahua, who was the governor of Quito, decided that a captain of the Inca lineage named Chiaquitinta[1] should go and station himself with a garrison near Zoropalta[2] in order to assail the Christians, their enemies, before they could penetrate into the land of the Cañari. He offered to carry out some great deed. He took with him a little more than one thousand warriors. After he halted near Zoropalta, he wished for the Spaniards to arrive because he and those who accompanied him believed that it would not be a great exploit to defeat and kill them all.

Belalcázar, who had gone ahead of his people with thirty horsemen, as has been said, arrived within sight of the warriors, who were so astonished to see the horses and that they were already upon them that they began to flee full of fear and fright. The Spaniards pursued them, capturing some men and women; among them, one lady was seized who had been a wife of Huayna Capac. These people defeated, Belalcázar stayed in that place eight days, during which time the camp arrived, and they all united.

The Cañari knew that the Spaniards were coming against those of Quito, which gratified and elated them because Atahualpa and the others who had stayed in his name had destroyed and pillaged most and the best of their property. Belalcázar was informed that in that land they awaited the Spaniards with peace and love. He then sent messengers, encouraging their resolve, praising their virtue and that of their ancestors. They were delighted with this message. Furthermore, with more than three hundred armed men to aid them, the Cañari and the chiefs of this land went to meet Belalcázar. All of them wept bitterly, and they were pleased to see the Spaniards, imploring their help against their cruel enemies, declaring that God, having taken pity on them, placed such power on their side that what they did sufficed for [the Cañari] to be avenged on those who without reason or justice had robbed and killed most of them. Belalcázar received them well; he promised them friendship and to take revenge against their enemies. This peace was firm. It was not broken, nor did it falter, even though the Spaniards at various times and in incidents that took place were a nuisance to these Cañari and mistreated them and did to them what they usually do to all the rest. [The Cañari] willingly served them, without duplicity, carrying on their shoulders the loads of baggage until they reached their province, where during the whole time that they spent there they were well cared for and sufficiently provisioned with what they needed. *fol. 74v*

Belalcázar and those who went with him carefully observed the dwellings that they found in Tomebamba[3]—how many and how opulent they were, how well designed, and the building of the delicately placed stones, and in all of them a cavity made for sitting. They realized that the Indians had told the truth regarding the great treasures that had been stolen from the temple and the palaces because they saw evidence of where they had been.[4] They saw great herds of sheep and lambs. They all believed that it would be expedient to march quickly toward Quito because there they planned to stuff their pockets with the many treasures that were said to be in Quito.

Then it became known how the Spaniards entered the Cañari region, and how they formed a friendship with each other after having defeated the captain that they had sent [from Quito]. The chiefs and mandones, along with the priests of the temples, again conferred with each other. They considered new suggestions about how best to prevent the Christians from prevailing against them because it was clear that if they defeated them, they would forever remain in servitude and captivity of foreign and such cruel[5] people, as they knew from experience. And they talked about other things regarding this, encouraging each other for the defense of their land and their own preservation in tranquil peace, thus to be able to enjoy their festivals and religion as their ancestors did. To appease the Sun—their supreme god and the great god creator of things, whom they called Ticsi Viracocha—and their other gods, so that having pity and mercy on them they would grant them victory against the Christians, they made great sacrifices according to their custom. They killed many animals, whose blood they sprinkled on the altars where there were channels to make the offering. And according to the advice of those who spoke with the demon and to the opinion of all the priests, it was decided that the captains and mandones would set forth with all the warriors to confront their enemies the Christians. They felt confident that they would defeat and kill them.

The captains ordered the scattered people to unite so that they could set out and defend against the penetration of the Spaniards into their land. More than fifty thousand warriors assembled, all with their weapons and equipment pertaining to war. And in good order,
fol. 75 carrying necessary provisions, they left Quito, marching on the royal highway until they reached Teocajas,[6] where, following their agreement, they decided to wait for the Christians because they knew they were already very close to them. Spies who knew the land well left to get information about what [the Christians] were doing and how far they had come.

In the meantime, Belalcázar, who was a brave captain for these conquests, arrived in the good order and accord that he fostered in his people and entered the principal tambos of Teocajas, where our men took up lodging. Rui Díaz[7] and ten horsemen under his command left to reconnoiter the countryside. The Indian warriors were informed by the spies about the departure of these ten Christians. They rejoiced, believing that they would easily kill them at the bottom of a high and wide hill to which the road they were taking led. Thus, Zope-Zopahua, governor of Quito, with his people and Rumiñavi with his prepared themselves. The ten Spaniards had descended the mountain and arrived on a plain where a river flowed, when an Indian shouted: "You see them here! What are you waiting for?" They attacked them with a hellish cry, and for [each] Christian there were a thousand Indians. It pleased God to protect them by harming the others because many were killed with lances, and the Spaniards conducted themselves with great courage. One of them, seeing the difficulty and danger they were in, returned to the tambo in spite of the Indians, where he reported to Belalcázar how they were surrounded by the force of all the Indians. Then, the footmen and the horsemen with their arms went out, while some remained to guard the camp.

The Spaniards united with those nine who had gone with Rui Díaz, and the captains of the Indians came out in all directions, and the battle among all of them was fought indeed. [The Indians] encouraged each other, pointing out how few the Spaniards were and that if their sins allowed [the Spaniards] to vanquish them, they would become masters of their ancient land and of them also, and they would treat them harshly. The Christians also reckoned that it was advisable to fight vigorously because they had no less than their lives at stake. The horsemen rode into the squadrons. The field was full of the dead who had fallen, and the Indians fought as steadily as can be told be- *fol. 75v* cause although they realized their ruin and the great advantage that the Spaniards had over them, even though they were so few, they continued fighting without abandoning the battle, until He who can do anything—who is God—came between by sending the darkness of night, which was the reason that they parted from each other, neither vanquished nor victors. The Indians killed two horses and wounded several Christians. One of the horses belonged to Albarrán and the other to Girón, which upset all of them because these horses are the strength of the war and of those who waged it against these Indians. According to what I learned, more than four hundred of the Indians died, and a larger number was wounded.

After Belalcázar collected his people, he returned to the tambos. The Indians told them that they should not think it would be the same as in Cajamarca, that here [the Indians] would kill all of them. And when it was nighttime, they united, sending the wounded to be cured, while the rest ate and made walls and fortifications to be secure from the Spaniards, who had also attended the wounded and were resting, along with their horses, from their earlier exertion. It has been said that the Indians cut off the head and legs of one of the dead horses and sent them as a gift to the lords of the region because they rated having been able to kill it higher than avoiding the loss of those among them who had died.

Belalcázar and his men deliberated about what they should do to be able to go to Quito safely because they learned from some who were passing through that there were many Indian warriors and that they had built fortifications along the highway they would be taking. They decided to take another one that would lead to Chimu and Purúas. It was very difficult not knowing the land because they were entering it for the first time. The horsemen left, and the footmen carried the baggage. They set fire to the tambos when they were leaving; some say it was to be able to leave unseen by the enemy in the obscurity of the smoke, and others relate that it was to burn the two horses that the Indians killed so that they could not cut off their heads and legs. And others also relate that it was so [the Indians] would not presume that they were able to kill horses because some of them believed them to be immortal. I do not believe this nor did I hear anything like this from them.

fol. 76 They marched the entire night through some hills, very anxious because they were uncertain if they were on the right track. Wanting to gain their friendship, one Indian from that land who had been in Cajamarca warned that Rumiñavi and Zope-Zopahua and other captains were positioned with a great throng of people on the royal highway, waiting to attack them, but for the love of them he would guide them on a safe road and would take them away from the dangerous place. The captain thanked him, telling him to do it and to have complete faith in the Spaniards, that they would pay him well for it. And with this Indian in the lead they marched. He knew the land so well that he took them through some small valleys until they came out by a river below the warriors, who had already realized what had happened and the route the Christians were taking. This made them very anxious and dismayed, and feeling unsafe where they were, they abandoned that field, leaving only a few Indians to act as if all of them were there. Belalcázar urged [his people] to cross the river, believing that they would be safer on the other side, and with the haste and speed that men have in these parts, it was then done very quickly.

Notes

1 Cieza spells his name "Chuquitinto."

2 Probably the fortress of Paquishapa; its ruins are close to modern Saraguro. See Hemming, *Conquest*, pp. 155, 568.

3 Now Cuenca (Ecuador), Tomebamba was the principal administrative center for the region. Cieza (*Part One*, chapter 44) describes its residences as "among the finest and richest in all Peru, and the buildings the largest and most important."

4 and they removed it

5 bad

6 Located in the high paramo above the tree line, it was an area of ichu grass, swamps, mist, and rain. The battle was fought on 3 May 1534. See Hemming, *Conquest,* pp. 156–58.

7 Díaz came to Peru with Almagro. After the Quito expedition, he was one of those surveying for the foundation of Lima. During the native rebellion Almagro sent Díaz to negotiate with Manco Inca, but Manco imprisoned and tortured him. He later escaped. A leader of Almagro's horse at the Battle of Salinas in 1538, he was captured and killed by a Pizarrist. See Mendiburu, *Diccionario,* 4:372–74; and Hemming, *Conquest,* pp. 156–59, 226–32.

LIX

About what else happened to the Spaniards and the Indians until they reached the tableland of Riobamba, where [the Indians] had dug many pits so that the horses would fall into them

The Indians and captains who had been in Teocajas thought in every way, means, and manner of how they could kill the Spaniards because there were so few of them, and they were so many. On the one hand, they considered how expedient it would be to defy any danger in order to expel them from the land so that they would not become its masters. On the other hand, they believed that [the Spaniards] were accompanied by some deity or that divine force battled for them because although they were so few, they were able to do such deeds. [The Indians] feared them and their horses, and they did not dare to ridicule them as in Teocajas. But, after considering it well and dis-
fol. 76v cussing it, they decided to dig a large number of pits near Riobamba, deepened in such a way that they would be wide enough to harm them and their horses, but they could be lightly covered with grass so that they could not see them. These pits remain today—I saw them along most of the way when I passed through that part. They believed that the Spaniards, provoked by them to do battle, would proceed until they fell with their horses into the pits, and thus they tried to incite them into combat in that area.

The Spaniards marched on their way. The Indians came out at them with clamor. When Belalcázar saw that the Indians were assembling and shouting at them so much, he collected his companions and ordered thirty horsemen to stay in the rearguard to face the Indians until those who went in the vanguard would have gained a small hill ahead of them. Thus, the ones stayed while the others went. The cries of the Indians increased when they saw them thin out so much, so that the thirty horsemen asked the captain to send reinforcements because the Indians were coming to attack them. Belalcázar replied in a loud voice that if thirty horsemen were unable to defend themselves against the Indians, then they should bury themselves alive. And because Zope-Zopagua and Rumiñavi had mobilized the region, so many people had assembled that Belalcázar exclaimed, "Good God, where did so many people come from? The earth is springing up Indians!" And they gave such terrible cries in order to frighten them; and they do succeed with those who recently come from Spain, until they understand this custom and leave them barking without paying any attention to it. The Spaniards were on the said hill; they as well as their horses were very tired, and they decided to descend to a flat plain that was near a lake.

Because there were many of the Christians, the Indians decided to proceed with their plan to attack them in three or four places, believing that they would frighten them by surrounding them. Therefore, one of their captains positioned himself on a hill above the Spaniards, and with a throng of people another one occupied another [hill] that was on one side, and the rest took the slope of the mountain ridge that was near the lake. Rumiñavi and Zope-Zopahua moved about in opulent litters rousing and encouraging all the people, and they went to position themselves with other chiefs at the top of the Riobamba hill, so that they had the few Christians and horses surrounded on all sides. They were waiting for the Spaniards to attack them, and then in the place where the pits were they would kill them all. And to infuri- *fol. 77* ate them, they lashed out at them, yelling so much that no other thing was heard except their voices. And because there were among the Spaniards some recent arrivals from Spain—whom we call *chapetones* here—they feared what they heard because for them it was a novelty.

The Spaniards did not lack maize where they were, which was a great relief for them. The grace of God our Lord inspired one of the Indians, who came and on his own will told them[1] what was happening regarding the pits and that there were so many that they encompassed a large area. They valued greatly such useful warning, giving many thanks to God, and after deliberating they decided to abandon the road leading to Riobamba, where the pits were filled with sharp-pointed stakes and cleverly covered above with straw from the fields, and to march over the rugged ridges of some hills, where in spite of certain difficulties and hardship for the horses, they were able to avoid the pits.[2]

When the Indians realized this new development, they yelled like madmen, asking where the warning to their enemies came from because it was clear that they abandoned that route because they suspected danger. They were furious with each other and lamented their fortune. They were beginning to believe that [the Spaniards] had some special favor from God in order to succeed with their plans. Some suggested that it would be a healthy remedy to offer them peace, but the usurpers Rumiñavi and others disagreed, saying that it would be better to die than to see themselves and their wives and daughters living in the power of such wicked people.

In the meantime, our men, little by little, had arrived in the tambos of Riobamba, situated in a lovely and beautiful tableland, and they stationed themselves there. Belalcázar went out with thirty horsemen for a skirmish with the Indians, but because they had become terrified of the horses, and the wretched people do not have defensive weapons that would protect them from the swords and the lances, or offensive ones other than their darts and slings and ayllus, they quickly began to flee without daring to wait for them.

They found some depositories full of maize, from which place Belalcázar returned to the camp, leaving five[3] horsemen to watch out *fol. 77v* in case the Indians descended from the heights to which they had climbed. These were Vasco de Guevara,[4] Rui Díaz, Hernán Sánchez Morillo,[5] Varela, and Domingo de la Presa. When the Indians saw that only five Christians had dared to remain to face them, and considering this a great outrage and affront, they sent three or four men to engage them in combat. [The Spaniards] charged to lance them, and [the Indians] led them into the middle of a squadron of twelve[6] thousand warriors, and they no more than five. But they were so capable that after killing and wounding some, they forced them to retreat and were able to safely return to Riobamba, where they reported to the captain what had happened to them. And he ordered that all the horsemen go out, as well as the swordsmen and shield bearers and the crossbowmen, in order to attack the enemy, who, when they saw their determination, lost their courage, and lacking any spirit they retreated in great silence. The powerful and preeminent of them were still carried on the shoulders of their men, and they went on until they reached the river that passes through Ambato—which I believe is the name of the river itself. There they ordered that ditches and pits be made to once again tempt their fortune against the Spaniards, who, lodged in the large palaces of Riobamba, were well served for twelve days by the Cañari, their friends.

Afterwards they left there in good order. Belalcázar sent messengers to the Indians to come and enjoy peace by putting down arms and promising not to wage any war on them. But they could not convince the captains. And when [the Spaniards] arrived at the aforesaid river, [the Indians] defended the crossing for a little more than half an hour. The horsemen tried to cross any way they could to gain the hill held by the Indians, who soon fled. At this time, as in the past, when the Spaniards saw them fleeing, they pursued them, and treating them harshly, they killed so many of those whom they caught up with that it was a great pity to see them because they followed them until Latacunga, where there were large lodgings, and from them they removed a considerable treasure. The warriors who remained[7] made many[8] pits in the manner of those of Riobamba.

No horse or Christian fell, which was lucky because the one [group] of Indians and the others were fleeing together—those who were moving through that area as well as those whom the Spaniards were chasing—and [the Spaniards] cut open many of their backs with lances, nailing their hearts with the sharp irons. The pursuit lasted until they[9] arrived at a wild river full of large rocks that a volcano had *fol. 78*
spewed out.

Notes

1 the Spaniards

2 where they had devised the trap and laid the snare

3 four

4 Probably from New Castile, he was in León, Nicaragua in 1529; see Lockhart, *Men of Cajamarca*, pp. 423–24.

5 Sánchez Morillo settled in the region and was nominated councillor of Quito in 1536. See Lockhart, *Men of Cajamarca*, pp. 352–53.

6 more than

7 united

8 large

9 the Spaniards

LX

How a volcano or a mouth of fire erupted near Quito and what happened to the Christians and the Indians

In the past there was among these people a fallacious belief held as true, which was if sacrifices were made to a certain oracle in the province, a demon would answer. We believe that in all the Indies there is among the natives this custom of consulting with the demon, and it is also known that not all speak or have this privilege, but only those whom they hold as the holiest. Priests are chosen for it, and I truly believe that they often faked deliriums in order to be credible with their people, assuring that the very demon was within their body. Indeed, a story on this subject is disseminated that one of them said they should know that when a volcano or mouth of fire near Latacunga erupted, foreign people from a faraway land would come to wage war on them, and they would be so powerful that they would become their masters. The demon cannot tell what is to come because it is clear that the movements of the times are enclosed in God's wisdom, and no creature, even if he were an angel, can affirm against His will what is to happen. But because the demon is so sly, at times he says things according to what he sees is happening and hits the mark, although he speaks of soothsaying. And because he saw that the Spaniards were preparing to come to this kingdom, and he knew that the volcano was ready to erupt, he believed that he could use the correlation of the eruption of the volcano so that they would honor him with sacrifices and blindly follow his deceit. That people did come who would lord over them in their land gave his affirmation more credibility. And so it happened that when the Spaniards were in Riobamba, this volcano or mouth of fire erupted, making great noise, expelling so many rocks from within that it is an indescribable wonder. The fire that it had within destroyed many Indian houses, killed many men and women, and it threw into the air so many ashes as dense as smoke that one
fol. 78v could not see while these ashes floated, and the amount that I said was all over. So much fell that those who did not know believed that from the heavens it was raining ashes, which fell more than twenty

days, and those who were coming with the Adelantado Don Pedro de Alvarado saw it, as I will later tell.

Because this volcano erupted, the Indians had great faith in what the oracle had predicted. Then they understood that they should negotiate peace with the Spaniards. Rumiñavi and Zope-Zopahua and the other captains hampered them. Belalcázar reached Panzaleo and even further in the direction of Quito, and many Indians were killed and wounded, which distressed him, and with the agreement of his men he decided to send them a messenger of peace. He called a local Indian and placed a cross in his hands, a sign that we use in war with them in order to call them to peace and to know that the one carrying such insignia can safely go and return. He ordered him to go to Rumiñavi and the others and to ask them on his behalf why they enjoyed seeing each other die and being as restless as they were. They should put down their weapons and establish peace among all with honest conditions, something that would please him very much. No harm would come to them from him as long as above all they swore obedience to the Emperor Don Carlos, and if they wanted, they could become Christians. And they would all be friends and partners because [the Spaniards] wanted nothing more from them than that and to have the treasure of Quito to divide, as happened in Cajamarca.

The messenger arrived where the squadrons of Indians were, and when Rumiñavi heard the message, he became furious. Looking at those who were with him, he exclaimed: "Look at the ruses with which they want to deceive us and with what words they want to convince us, so they can take away from us the treasure they think is in Quito in order to later kill us and take our wives and daughters to keep as concubines! Who saw in Cajamarca how the other cruel bearded ones cajoled Atahualpa, with what cunning they took most of the treasure from the Temple of Coricancha, what ways they sought to kill him then, falsely accusing him with such affrontery. God forbid we should trust these people who neither told the truth nor will tell it; let us rather die by their hands and their horses so that they do not oppress and force us to willingly follow their excesses and fulfill their pretentions."

They all praised his counsel, calling him *hatund apo*,[1] which means *fol. 79*
great lord. Angry that the messenger was so bold, they cruelly killed

him although he was not to blame. It was later learned from those whom they caught up with and captured what Rumiñavi had said and that they killed this messenger, as has been said.

The Spaniards were in the village of Panzaleo, and because the Indians were aware of their enormous greed for gold, one of them said that their horses, or twice as many, would be unable to carry the amount that there was in Quito, as if he did not know that those who placed it in safety had already reached it and hidden it. And because it is already time to return to talk about Pizarro, let us leave the story dealing with this issue until the time comes.

Note

1 *Hatun apu.*

LXI

About how Governor Don Francisco Pizarro founded a city in the Jauja Valley, which is the one that was later moved to the Lima Valley, and about the death of the Inca and other things that happened

Pizarro, as was said before, entered Jauja with his men. He tried to bring the Huancas and Yauyos to his side, but he was unable to accomplish it at that time.

Almagro and Hernando de Soto left with some horsemen in search of the Indian warriors, who were joined by many from the districts to defend their lands from the Spaniards. They declared that if the Spaniards had prevailed against them, it was because the Indians were complying with the command given by Atahualpa, who always ordered that they should serve them and not fight against them even though there were as few of them in Cajamarca as there were before Almagro arrived, and although the Indians knew how badly they fared in combat, they encouraged themselves, believing that it would please God to defend them without allowing the immense harm that was coming their way. They made great sacrifices. They have the Sun as their sovereign god, but during greatest adversity, they ask favor of the great god of the heavens, maker of everything created, whom—as I have said many times—they call Ticsi Viracocha. They saw how the Spaniards settled in the valley; they were anxious that they not burn and destroy everything. They were retreating on the royal highway that leads to Cuzco without thinking that they[1] might follow them, *fol. 79v* but when they least expected it, they heard the snorting of the horses, which frightened them, although there were many of them. They did not know what to do; instead, fearing [the horses], they broke their ranks trying to escape alive.

The Spaniards cruelly killed them so that in many places one could see nothing but the profusion of blood streaming from their wounds. And thus they continued their pursuit, in which they pillaged a great deal, capturing many and very beautiful ladies and other Indian women and natives of various provinces of the kingdom, among whom were known to be two or three daughters of King Huayna Capac. With this loot they returned, considering the killings that they had inflicted upon the unarmed and timid Indians as a great deed.

The Huancas and Yauyos and other lords began to come peacefully to Jauja, excusing themselves before Pizarro for not having come sooner, declaring that it was not in their hands. He received them all very well, making sure that they were not mistreated or robbed. He admonished them to be faithful to the Spaniards. He gave them to understand that he was coming by the mandate of the emperor to populate those lands with Christians and to reveal to them our faith[2] so that hearing the word of the holy gospel they would become Christians, and he told them other things about this subject. They replied that what they saw was enough to make them certain. Most of these lords are alive, and they describe these things as fully as if they had happened yesterday.[3]

When Pizarro saw that they had some friends and that the Jauja Valley was large, and that in addition to being so populated, it was in the center of that region, he decided with the agreement of those who were with him to establish there a new settlement of Spaniards. And thus a city was founded here, which is the City of the Kings itself, and that is the reason why in *Part One* I did not deal with this foundation: because it did not remain. They stayed here more than twenty days, amusing themselves with jousting. They did not participate in elegant attire, but they looked as extravagant as they wanted to with the gold they wore. They realized what favor God had granted them in giving them grace and courage to discover such a great land filled with such wealth.

From this valley Pizarro sent certain Spaniards to survey the coast of Pachacamac, to see if it would be appropriate to make another settlement in the Yungas with the people who were arriving every-
fol. 80 day on ships. At the same time he ordered Captain Hernando de Soto to set out with sixty horsemen in the direction of the city of Cuzco, without going too quickly because after settling some things that were needed in the new city, he would depart to join him. Soto and those who were to go with him then left.

Incurabayo and the other captains had made their drywalls and fortification in order to attack the Spaniards. Soto learned about it;[4]

he alerted Pizarro to leave right away. The new Inca who had been crowned in Cajamarca became ill in this valley and died.[5] It distressed Pizarro because he had given indications of a sound friendship. He commanded the treasurer Riquelme to stay as his deputy and justice, with the necessary people. He left Jauja with the rest.[6] The Indians were in Vilcas, a principal and very important place in this kingdom, as I related in *Part One*,[7] to which I refer. There were beautiful buildings and a temple with great wealth. They burned the most important of them and removed the sacred women and the treasures so that the Spaniards could not take advantage of them. Two royal highways, if not three, lead from this [place] that they call Vilcas. The Indians occupied all of them, and because they were on a high summit, they hurled shots at the Spaniards, who were already approaching. They had become so afraid of the horses that they had lost all courage. When they did not see them, they acted fiercely, and they believed that they could fight a thousand Spaniards, but when they heard their neighing[8] and [saw] their shape, they trembled in fear, and they neither fought nor did anything other than flee. That is what happened to them that day, and many were killed and wounded in the struggle and pursuit by the Spaniards. They did not injure or kill any Christians or horses. Soto rested that night from the exertion.

Pizarro was coming. He arrived in Vilcas[9] at the end of three days, and there he found letters from Soto about what had happened to him. The Indians reproached themselves; they were shocked that they lacked the courage they had in times of the Incas; after all, they had won so many battles. Thinking about the horses unsettled them; on the one hand, they feared them; on the other, they were upset that foreign people, who were so different from them, should lord over them. This convinced them they would rather die than to see it. They decided to wait at the Apurímac River to see if someday a mishap would befall their enemies. *fol. 80v*

Soto went on to Curapampa and the Abancay River. I have heard one thing said: that in these pursuits they found the bridges of the rivers Abancay and Apurímac destroyed and that they crossed them on the horses, but that afterward it was never seen that one could wade through them on a horse, especially the Apurímac, although I have been also told that they crossed them over bridges, but narrow ones.[10] The Indians who were in Apurímac, deliberating again, agreed not to wait there but to proceed to Limatambo. Soto learned of it, and he went on until he and the horsemen who were with him found themselves on the other side of the river, by wading or [crossing] over a bridge. Most of them[11] believed that it would be appropriate to await the arrival of the governor and the rest of the people. Soto said that it was not the time to stop, but to march in pursuit of victory because it had pleased God to grant it to them. When he said that, they departed. They left that place, marching on the royal highway of Chinchasuyu[12] through where the [Indian] troops were.

Notes

1 the Spaniards

2 so that to them the religious

3 Cieza was collecting information from native informants only fifteen years after the event.

4 had a warning of it

5 Tupac Huallpa.

6 he and the marshal

7 Chapter 89. Cieza's description of the great Temple of the Sun—the sacrificial altars, the stone oratories, the vast storehouses of cloth, food, and military supplies—is based on accounts of eyewitnesses who saw Vilcas before it fell into a state of ruin.

8 the snorting of the horses

9 he joined Soto

10 and that they crossed with difficulties. Andean peoples crossed deep gorges by constructing suspension bridges, whose strong cables were woven from a variety of fibers.

11 to all

12 The western sector of Tawantinsuyu, the Inca land of the four quarters. See Franklin Pease G.Y., "Notas sobre Wiraqocha y sus itinerarios," *Histórica* 10 (1986): 230.

LXII

About how the Indians waited to battle the Christians in the highlands of Vilcaconga, and how when Soto arrived, they fought each other, and what happened until Almagro and several horsemen came to their rescue

The Indians were unwilling to stop in any of the places that they passed because they believed that they would be safer in the highlands of Vilcaconga, which are in that region, slightly more than seven leagues from Cuzco. They considered it an effective place to wage war against the Spaniards and very difficult for the horses because it has a somewhat long climb. They dug some pits and drove in stakes with sharp points. They supplied themselves with provisions, calling on their neighbors and kin, assuring them that no more than sixty Spaniards were coming against all of them. They should not lose such an opportunity, but give thanks to God for granting it to them, and they should risk everything in order to kill them.

Soto and his companions were steadily following them, wishing to engage them before a larger force could assemble. When they reached the beginning of the highlands of Vilcaconga, they prodded the horses slightly and moved ahead. The Indians saw them; they counted them many times, rejoicing because there were so few of them. They were scattered in all parts of the highlands, threatening to kill them; they all carried their slings, darts, clubs, ayllus, and other weapons. Soto told his men not to fear the multitude of enemies before them because in other places there were fewer of them than they were, and they had defeated a larger force of Indians. The Christians commended themselves to God, and tightly grasping their lances they went to receive the blows of the Indians, disparaging them.

According to their custom the Indians had sworn by the Sun and the Earth to die or to kill those Christians, who although so few dared to seek them. And thus the battle began between them in which more than eight hundred Indians died, according to the count that some give, and slightly fewer were wounded. With their incessant shots the

Indians mortally wounded five Spaniards, and they later died. Their names were Hernández, Toro,[1] Miguel Ruiz, Marquina,[2] and Francisco Martín Soitino.[3] They also killed one horse and one mare.

Soto and Pedro Ortiz[4] were first to arrive at the hill; they were lancing the Indians. Some of the horses could not finish the climb because the two that died were in the way. Juan Ronquillo[5] and Malaver[6] dismounted. One put himself on one side and the other on the other side, and they made it possible for the rest to pass. The Indians made a great deal of clamor and cries; they were eager to kill all the Christians, but many lost their lives without having this satisfaction. Both sides were so tired that they could not move.

The Indians withdrew near a spring[7] on the same slope where Soto and the Christians stationed themselves. They took an arroyo that was an arquebus shot away from the Indians, where they thought they would be safer. When they united, they realized that not counting the five Christians whom the Indians had killed, eleven more and fourteen horses had also been wounded. They bandaged their wounds as well as they could. They had no other food than what was left by chance in some of the knapsacks that they carried. They implored God to send them help because they were few and were facing many enemies. The Indians did not know about the wounded, but they had *fol. 81v* counted very well that there were five killed and two horses. They let it be known throughout the land so that they would be encouraged to kill those [Christians] who remained. Soto, heedful to avoid more disgrace, ordered that all should be on war alert so that they would not be taken by surprize.

Pizarro was coming. He regretted that Soto had not waited for him. Almagro wanted to go ahead with thirty horsemen in order to join [Soto], and he went more than twelve leagues that day on the highway, which is entirely in the highlands. In Limatambo he learned from two tired Indians he found there that the Christians and the Indians were in the highlands of Vilcaconga. He went quickly and arrived at the beginning of the ascent when it was already night. In order that Soto and those who were with him could hear him, he ordered that a trumpet be played while they climbed up to the highlands. Those who were at the top did not hear anything then, but when it played again, the trumpet was heard, which made them very happy. Soto carried another trumpet with which they replied; some say that it was a shell horn of the Indians.[8] In the meantime, Almagro's march was not disturbed by the night, and he arrived within sight of the Indians and Christians. When they all united, they rejoiced, though later Almagro was distressed when he learned of the death of the five Spaniards. When morning came, Almagro ordered that several healthy men should go along with the wounded ones so that they suffered no more harm. When the Indians[9] detected the reinforcement that had come to the Spaniards, at a time when they themselves were awaiting a larger troop to kill those that they had there, they were notably upset, and lamenting they all took flight. Almagro and Soto went in pursuit, killing and wounding them. They captured some, and when they deemed it enough, they stopped and determined to wait for the governor, who marched so quickly that they all joined together that day. And indeed, now that they are with each other, it will be convenient that the chronicle ceases to talk about them in order to deal with the departure of the Adelantado Don Pedro de Alvarado from Guatemala because otherwise we would lose the order, and what is to be related would not be easily understood.

Notes

1 Hernando de Toro and his brother Alonso (see chapter 36) were recruited in Trujillo and went to the Indies in 1530. Hernando was Hernando Pizarro's personal attendant. He left an estate of twelve thousand pesos, mostly his Cajamarca share, which his heirs fought over in the courts for years. See Lockhart, *Men of Cajamarca*, pp. 360–61.

2 Gaspar Marquina, or Gárate, was born about 1508 in Elgoibar, near San Sebastián. He was Pedrarias's page in Nicaragua in the 1520s and probably came to Peru with Soto, where he became Gonzalo Pizarro's page. See Lockhart, *Men of Cajamarca*, pp. 330–31, and especially Gaspar's letters to his father, pp. 457–63.

3 He was born around 1505 in Alburquerque. He went to the Indies in 1527 and soon met a childhood friend, Juan Ruiz de Arce. He was recruited in Panama and became very ill in Coaque in 1531. See Lockhart, *Men of Cajamarca*, pp. 438–39.

4 He was probably from Ampuero and was at Cajamarca, but disappears from the record after Jauja in June 1534; Lockhart, *Men of Cajamarca*, pp. 233–34.

5 Ronquillo became an encomendero and city official of Cuzco, but disappears from the record after 1535. See Lockhart, *Men of Cajamarca*, p. 443.

6 Francisco Malaver came with Belalcázar in 1531. He is mostly known for his gambling, fighting, and drinking, for which he was fined. He left Peru in 1534 with one of the largest treasures of the peruleros: more than thirty thousand pesos of gold. See Lockhart, *Men of Cajamarca*, p. 329.

7 In the left margin of the manuscript Cieza wrote: "si era fuente o fuerte" (if it was a spring or a fort).

8 The pututo.

9 believed that

LXIII

About how the Adelantado Don Pedro de Alvarado, governor of Guatemala, left the port of La Posesión[1] in order to come with a great fleet to this kingdom

I have so much to write regarding the civil wars and the quarrels some Spaniards had with others that I would like to swiftly get through what I am relating. But considering that if it is not done in a way that can be understood, my work will be in vain, and I want to convey it to satisfy the readers. I will not dwell on any subject, nor will I relate more than the event.

I say therefore that the Adelantado Don Pedro de Alvarado was one of the most famous captains in this new world of the Indies.[2] His Majesty made him governor of the province of Guatemala, with the license—according to what I heard—to explore by sea because a pilot named Ortiz Jiménez, knowledgeable in navigation, put into his head that he would take him to the Tarsis Islands.[3] Others say to China, where there would be great riches.[4] He prepared ships, supplied them with victuals, and tried to recruit men and horses to go out in pursuit of his enterprise. But it happened that he found out from a ship that took port in that land how Peru had been discovered and Francisco Pizarro was named governor of a certain part of it and that he had found great treasures and had news of greater wealth ahead. Alvarado, advised by his favorites, decided to stop his expedition and to send a ship on the South Sea to the coast of Peru in order to get information about what was there and what the land was like. He ordered a knight from Cáceres, named García Holguín, to go, and he came to this coast. He encountered strong currents and such contrary winds that he could not pass beyond Puerto Viejo. There he learned that Pizarro had just a short time earlier left the coast for the highlands. García Holguín returned with this news, telling the adelantado that the land of Peru was vast and plentiful and could be easily explored.

Alvarado came to the port of La Posesión. Licentiate Castañeda sent Gabriel de Rojas with a testimony on the adelantado's plan. [Alvarado] had also been informed by the pilot, Juan Fernández, who *fol. 82v* used to be Captain Belalcázar's partner, about the great wealth that was said to be in Quito. Given that the reports about Peru were so remarkable, he decided to explore in person what he could and what would not be occupied by Pizarro or his people. He took from Guatemala and Nicaragua the most magnificent fleet that was ever put together in the Indies—according to what many have confirmed to me—in which went approximately 500 men and 327 horses, many weapons and other equipment necessary for war and conquests. And had there been more ships, he would have taken another 200 Spaniards and horses. Among those who were going were his brother Gómez de Alvarado, Diego de Alvarado, Alonso de Alvarado, who later became marshal, Garcilaso de la Vega,[5] Don Juan Enríquez de Guzmán,[6] Luis de Moscoso, Licentiate Caldera,[7] Gómez de Alvarado de Zafra, Alonso de Alvarado de Palomas, Vítores de Alvarado, Captain Benavides,[8] Pedro de Añasco,[9] Antón Ruiz de Guevara, Francisco de Morales, Juan de Saavedra, Francisco Calderón,[10] Juan de Herrada,[11] Miguel de la Serna, Francisco García de Tovar, Juan de Ampudia,[12] Pedro de Puelles, Gómez de Estacio, Sancho de la Carrera,[13] Antonio Picado, García Holguín, Pedro de Villareal, and the father Friar Marcos.[14] Many more knights came, and very presumptuous; I did not know their names, but these I put down because all of them or most of them distinguished themselves in either doing good deeds or in committing great evil in the times of the tyrannies.[15] They chose the pilot, Juan Fernández, as captain of the galleon, which was a beautiful ship. They left who had [blank] embarked from the port of La Posesión [blank] of the month [blank] of the year fifteen hundred and thirty [blank] years.

After sailing more than thirty days, they came to reconnoiter the Cape of San Francisco.[16] Although they had told the adelantado so much about the riches of Quito, he did not claim it but proceeded to explore beyond Chincha, where he knew Pizarro's governance reached. There are so many currents along this coast, as those who have sailed there know, that they impeded the navigation, which did not go as Alvarado would have liked. Following along the coast, as he wanted, they arrived at the Bay of Caráquez,[17] where all went ashore, as well as the horses, of whom many had died at sea. In this place the adelantado spoke to the people with the words that the governors here use to mislead in order to carry out their deeds. He said that he had plenty for himself and he was governor of Guatemala, but so that all could become rich and have repartimientos, he wanted to take *fol. 83* on the present endeavor. Therefore, realizing how much they were indebted to him, they should be faithful and good friends to him. Because it was expedient to put the field regiment in order, he decided to choose captains and other necessary officers. Thus, he then named Diego de Alvarado as his campmaster, and as captains of the cavalry, Gómez de Alvarado, his brother, and Luis de Moscoso. He chose Don Juan Enríquez de Guzmán[18] as captain of the infantry; Benavides of the arquebuses; and Mateo Lascano of the crossbowmen. He encharged Francisco Calderón to be the general standard bearer and ordered Rodrigo de Chaves to be the captain of the guard. And he named as chief justice of the camp Licentiate Caldera and Juan de Saavedra as the high constable. All these offices were given and announced with the agreement of the Licentiate Caldera and the highest leaders. Alvarado decided that the ships would go to Puerto Viejo[19] and that the people should march on land with the horses and the service people, many men and women whom they took from Guatemala and Nicaragua, and many of whom died either because of the sea or from the great hardship they suffered on land. One of the notable harms and cruelties that the Spaniards have done in these Indies was to take from their lands the poor Indians and their wives, who were peaceful, in order to bring them along into lands that they intended to discover and plunder.

After he made this provision, the adelantado and some attendants who accompanied him went to Manta, where the ships were. He planned, as already told, to explore the land beyond Chincha, where the boundaries of Pizarro's governance ended. He ordered the pilot, Juan Fernández, to sail along the coast with the galleon, carrying as much as those who were to march on land could spare, until he was outside the limits of Pizarro's governance. He carried a special notice to place in all the ports where he would land—signs to indicate that it had been discovered—and he would take possession in the name of the king of Castile and his [Alvarado's]. When the rest of the ships arrived, [Alvarado] sent to Nicaragua and Panama so they could bring more people. He then returned to his camp with great news of the many riches that were in Quito, which he heard from an Indian who said that he had seen them with his own eyes.

Notes

1 Named "Possession" because it was "taken" in the king's name by Gil González Dávila in the early 1520s. It was probably situated between the Gulf of Papagayo and the Gulf of Fonseca, on the western coast of Nicaragua near modern Corinto.

2 Pedro de Alvarado y Mesía was born around 1485 in Badajoz and came to the Indies in 1510. He participated in Juan de Grijalva's reconnaissance of Mexico's coast and was a major figure in Hernán Cortés's conquest of Mexico. In 1523 he led the Spanish expedition to Guatemala, El Salvador, and Honduras and became Guatemala's governor. He left for Quito in 1534. When he came back to Guatemala, he faced legal charges and had to go to Spain to defend himself. Vindicated and with a renewed appointment as governor of Guatemala, he returned in 1539. The following year he mounted a large expedition to the Spice Islands, but was diverted to Mexico to help put down a revolt in Nueva Galicia. He was killed there in 1541, crushed by his horse during a skirmish. See Adrián Recinos, *Pedro de Alvarado, conquistador de México y Guatemala,* 2d ed. (Mexico City: CENALTEX, 1986).

3 Ophir, or Tarsis, thought to be the island where the gold of Solomon's Temple was to be found. There were many theories as to its location. According to Las Casas, Columbus at one time believed it was Hispaniola. See Brading, *First America,* pp. 14, 314–42; and Bartolomé de Las Casas, *Historia de las Indias,* 3 vols. (Mexico City: Fondo de Cultura Económica, 1951), 2:331.

4 Cantú's edition of *Part Three* says "La Chira," which is an island in the upper part of the Gulf of Nicoya. It was a center for the lucrative export of slaves to Panama and Peru. See Radell, "Indian Slave Trade," p. 73. On the other hand, Saenz de Santa María's edition of Cieza's chronicle (*Obras completas,* 1:305) says "La China," which makes sense in the context of the reference to Tarsis Islands and the expectation of "great riches."

5 Father of the famous mestizo chronicler.

6 In the manuscript Cieza vacillated between Juan and Alonso, but kept Alonso. He made a mistake. This is Don Juan Enríquez de Guzmán, who is later killed; see chapter 66. Don Alonso Enríquez de Guzmán came to Peru from Spain with Hernando Pizarro in 1535-36; see chapter 86.

7 Hernando de Caldera was born in Seville and served in Hispaniola and New Spain. He returned to Spain with Hernando de Soto. See Busto, *Diccionario,* 1:301.

8 Rodrigo de Benavides served with Alvarado in Guatemala. Later he was sent by Diego de Almagro to Lima to collect supplies to reinforce the Chilean expedition. See Busto, *Diccionario,* 1:239.

9 There were at least two Pedro de Añascos, cousins. One fought with Belalcázar and was in Quito, Popayán, and Cali. On an expedition to conquer the Valley of Ayunga he was captured by natives, put into a makeshift jail, and slowly cut to pieces and fed to his captors for several days. The other Añasco did not come to Peru until 1536. See Busto, *Diccionario,* 1:142–44.

10 Calderón was involved in the conquest of Guatemala with Alvarado. After the expedition along the Ecuadorian coast, he returned to Guatemala, one of the few to do so. He went back to Peru with Pedro de la Gasca and fought with the royalists at Jaquijahuana, but Viceroy Marqués de Cañete ordered him to return to Guatemala to his wife and family. He died in Santiago de Guatemala in 1560. See Busto, *Diccionario,* 1:302–3; and Wendy Kramer, *Encomienda Politics in Early Colonial Guatemala, 1524–1544: Dividing the Spoils* (Boulder: Westview Press, 1994), pp. 114, 132, 135.

11 Cieza uses "Juan de Rada" sometimes and at others "Juan de Herrada"; Herrada is correct. For a biographical sketch, see chapter 97.

12 From Jerez de la Frontera, Ampudia was with Belalcázar at San Miguel and at Quito. He was also involved in the conquest of Popayán and Bogotá. He later died in an Indian skirmish in the Popayán district; see Busto, *Diccionario,* 1:129–30.

13 Carrera was born in Toro, went to Mexico in 1530, and went with Alvarado to Guatemala. After he came to Peru, he joined Belalcázar's conquest of Quito. He received two encomiendas in the Quito district and became Quito's constable in 1544 and councilman in 1545. He fought against the rebels with Viceroy Blasco Núñez Vela at Añaquito. After the defeat, he hid from the Pizarrists in the Dominican monastery in Quito, but was discovered and garroted. See Busto, *Diccionario,* 1:343–44.

14 Friar Marcos de Niza was the leader of the first Franciscans in Peru. He was in León, Nicaragua, in 1531, awaiting transportation to Peru and probably went there with other members of the order. In 1534 Pizarro set aside land for their monastery in Cuzco. It seems Niza may have gone back to Nicaragua and was at this time returning to Peru with Pedro de Alvarado, whose chaplain he was. Niza left the Andes in 1536 for work in Guatemala and New Spain. See Tibesar, *Franciscan Beginnings,* pp. 10–18.

15 Cieza refers here to the civil wars.

16 On the Ecuadorian coast, just south of the Bay of San Mateo.

17 About 150 kilometers south of the Cape of San Francisco; Manta is at the south of the bay.

18 Cieza again mistakenly wrote "Alonso."

19 The original site was closer to the sea than the modern city, which is now about thirty kilometers inland from the port of Manta; see Newson, *Life and Death,* pp. 248–49.

LXIV

About what the Spaniards whom Pizarro sent from Jauja to the coast of the South Sea were doing

fol. 83v In the previous chapters I have related how while in Jauja Don Francisco Pizarro had sent certain Spaniards to the plains to survey the seacoast in order to establish a city with the people who were arriving on ships. They left for Pachacamac and went along the coast toward the northern part, through all the valleys and rivers, taking possession for the emperor and Pizarro in his name, which was attested by a notary who went with them.[1] And they placed crosses, a sign well-known by the Christians in these parts and with much reason. They proceeded in this way until the Huarmey Valley,[2] from where they returned to Pachacamac. Gabriel de Rojas and those who were coming with him from San Miguel arrived where the Christians were and were given guides to take them to Pizarro.

They say that in the meantime Quizquiz and the other captains, wishing to lay waste to all the provinces so that the Christians would not find them intact, ordered one of the captains to go with some Cañari and Chachapoyas Indians and orejones to join those of Ica and to cause those of Chincha as much harm as he could.[3] And some say that this [captain], Ucache, killed the principal lord of Ica[4] and acquired that lordship by usurping it. Others relate that no, the rule rightfully belonged to him. Whichever it might be, I am informed that those of Chincha sent messengers to the Christians who were in Pachacamac, imploring their aid against those enemies, begging them to come to their valley to support them. They replied that they would gladly do it, and then five or six horsemen went to Chincha, where they were well received by the natives, and they rejoiced in seeing such a lovely and beautiful valley. They praised God as they contemplated its coolness and such delightful groves. It was then more populated than it is now. Three or four thousand Indians of Chincha went out against the enemies coming with Ucache, who would have been about the same [number]. At the crack of dawn they came face to face where they fought the battle. It did not last long because when those of Ica saw the horses, they turned around and began to flee. The Spaniards took a small cross and placed it into the hands of one Indian, commanding him to give it to Ucache as a sign of friendship and to tell him on their behalf that he should come to see them without any hesi- *fol. 84* tation. They say that Ucache consulted with the elders of the valley, and learning that undoubtedly the Spaniards were to become masters of the realm because the Incas were already dead and their power broken, he decided to conclude peace with those who had offered it to him, and he sent the word with some chiefs. And before too many days went by, Ucache himself peacefully took—according to what they told me—certain cups and gold jewels as gifts. They took possession of all those places for the emperor as they had done earlier.

Notes

1 named

2 Huarmey is on the coast in Casma, approximately 160 kilometers north of Lima.

3 Earlier Inca expansion into Chincha is examined by María Rostworowski de Diez Canseco, *Historia del Tahuantinsuyu* (Lima: Instituto de Estudios Peruanos, 1988), pp. 100–104.

4 The Ica Valley is about 160 kilometers south of Lima; Chincha is roughly halfway between Lima and Ica.

LXV

About how Adelantado Don Pedro de Alvarado decided to go to Quito and about some notable things that happened to him

It is impossible for me to pursue one subject to the end because all the events that I am relating were occurring simultaneously. So that the readers can understand and are not confused—and as you see, the work is up to me—I move forward, and by turning the pages they will find what they wish.

I described how Adelantado Don Pedro de Alvarado came with his people to this kingdom and named the captains, and how he learned from one Indian whom he captured that there were great treasures in Quito, and how his only intention had been to pass beyond Chincha. But so many leaders in his camp maintained and affirmed that he should go to Quito—that he had to go through with it because they thought that what had been divided in Cajamarca was nothing compared with what they believed they would find in Quito, and then they would certainly return rich to Spain. But another fate befell them as I will be relating.

The Indian who had declared to have seen the treasure and to have been in Quito promised to lead them on a safe route to the city. Alvarado thanked him and promised him a substantial payment for it. As best as they could, they set out on the road and those wretched native men of Guatemala carried most of their loads so that this expedition cost them dearly, and a prayer to God does not redeem the souls of the Christians who were responsible.

fol. 84v In two days' journey they arrived in a thicket where they felt a need for water because there was no spring or stream or anything other than what they found in some gourds in the houses, which was very brackish. They proceeded ahead as best as they could until the province of Jipijapa,[1] and from there went to another village that they called Del Oro because of how much [gold] they found there. The natives had no warning of their coming, which was why [the Spaniards] took them by surprise. When they saw the horses among their houses, they lost the strength and spirit to offer resistance. Those who could escape saw themselves as very lucky, and thus, many men with their wives and children left the village. Others were captured by our men and their village robbed and plundered, and they found there infinite riches of fine gold in lovely jewels and silver. Many did not appreciate it or make much of it, except for some who took several pots and other vessels for their service. There were also many emeralds, so precious that if they had saved them all and sold them, they would have been worth a great treasure. But ignorant of their value, and judging them to be glass, as if the Indians had some furnaces for it, they underrated them. I was told that a silversmith knew that they were precious stones and that he surreptitiously filled a knapsack with as many as he could in order to return with them to Spain. He did not see himself in such glory because in the later snow and cold he froze along with his bag of emeralds.

They found more in this village, according to what some told me: some armor with which four men armed themselves, made of gold plates and nailed with nails of the same; the gauntlets were wide,[2] something like four inches,[3] and somewhat long; and gold armor for heads, like helmets, of the same metal covered with emeralds. They must have been so precious that in Milan more than four hundred could be outfitted with their worth. All the gold was collected, and they carried it as best as they could, although all this seemed little to them, nothing in comparison with what they would find waiting to fill their pockets in Quito. Further ahead was a village that they named Las Golondrinas because of the many [swallows] they found there. When they arrived there, the guide who was to take them to Quito saw an opportunity and fled while they were delighting their *fol. 85* eyes. The adelantado was furious, and they were all thrown into disarray because they did not know the land or which were the right roads. Because it seemed expedient, he ordered Captain Luis de Moscoso to explore and find out what would be advisable for them to do. He left with several Spaniards in the easterly direction and discovered a village called Bani, from where he left and discovered another village called Chonana,[4] where there were many provisions and some natives were captured. The adelantado was informed about it; he moved with his camp and arrived in this land. Some honorable gentlemen alive today, from among those who had entered into this kingdom with

Adelantado Don Pedro de Alvarado, reported to me that the Indians whom they had brought from Guatemala ate countless native people of these villages, which fall in the district of Puerto Viejo, and afterward most of them froze in the cold and starved to death—as will be told. And thus in some parts these people are diminishing in great misfortunes, punished by God for their detestable sins because it is evident that in this part of Puerto Viejo there are many who practice sodomy and those who came from Guatemala have the custom of eating one another—sins so enormous that they deserved to suffer what they suffered; indeed, God permitted it.

Returning to the subject. Because Alvarado was already involved in the journey to Quito and because he had no guides, he believed that it would be dishonorable to take an unfamiliar and unknown road with so many people. Instead, several captains were to go and explore one part and another and report what they found[5] so that according to what they saw, the safest could be ordered. Therefore, he commanded his brother, Gómez de Alvarado, to explore toward the north with thirty horsemen and some footmen. And he also ordered Captain Benavides to explore at the same time in the easterly direction. And this Captain Benavides and those who went with him discovered the river and the village called Daule.[6] Gómez de Alvarado discovered the village of Yagual,[7] where he found certain lions,[8] and further ahead he reached the territory of Niza. The Indians of all these lands fled; others became prisoners in power of the Spaniards. Some of them took up arms against Gómez de Alvarado, and they did not fare well because most of them were wounded and killed, and the others fled from such foolishness. Those who had been captured said they knew the road to Quito and that they would take them there on this highway and that they would be there shortly.

fol. 85v Gómez de Alvarado summoned six horsemen and ordered them to go to inform the adelantado that it would be expedient to come with the camp to that territory. And news arrived that the Indians had killed one Spaniard and wounded another, who had gone off to furtively rob the Indians, who when they realized that there were not more of them, killed the one, whose name was Juan Luz. They immediately rode to punish the Indians, who were without fault, in my opinion. Indeed, they did not sin in killing those who were killing and robbing so many of them in their own lands and houses. But they hid in safety, so [the Spaniards] did not encounter anyone. They found the Christian dead, his head cut off. [Gómez de Alvarado] then decided not to send any horsemen, but to go himself with those who were there to report to the adelantado, and that is what he did. He told him that the Indians were saying that where he had explored was the safest way to Quito and that it would be advantageous to take it. Benavides also arrived, having discovered Rio Grande and other villages where it was said that they could also go to Quito very well the other way.

In spite of what the captives brought by Captain Alvarado were declaring, the adelantado decided that they would take the way Benavides had discovered, and immediately the departure was ordered. They went until they reached the Daule River, where they lost the road because the Indians use the river itself for their trafficking.

Notes

1 Located approximately twenty kilometers east of the Ecuadorian coast and forty kilometers south of Manta and Puerto Viejo; see Newson, *Life and Death*, pp. 248, 253.

2 small

3 Cieza used the word *dedo* (finger), which is about one inch.

4 A major settlement of Huancavilcas. See Newson, *Life and Death*, p. 72.

5 might see

6 Twenty-five kilometers north of Guayaquil, on the edge of Daule River. See Newson, *Life and Death*, p. 248.

7 Yagual had a tributary population of about one thousand in Pizarro times; in 1574 only 110 remained. See Newson, *Life and Death*, pp. 250–51.

8 Pumas.

LXVI

About how the adelantado ordered people to go out and find a road, and about how they encountered many marshes and rivers, and how several Spaniards died, among them Captain Don Juan Enríquez de Guzmán

When the adelantado chose not to take the road discovered by Gómez de Alvarado, but the way Captain Benavides went, and after they reached the Daule River[1] and still could not find any [road], he ordered squads of Spaniards to go out in all directions to see where the highway to Quito was. Don Juan Enríquez left with some from his company to explore wherever fortune would lead him. After he had gone almost ten leagues, he reached a large place where he found *fol. 86* abundant provisions of maize and roots[2] and fish. There were so many marshes and bogs everywhere, and because it was winter, they were to suffer great hardship. He then sent a message to the adelantado, who was delighted when he learned that there were provisions, and he ordered that they should join Don Juan. With all the hardship that they suffered and the poor food that they ate, many Spaniards became ill and too weary. And when Alvarado saw one of these ailing men move with such anguish, he placed him on his horse with his own hands, which was the reason that several others who went on horseback, wanting to imitate him, gave a ride on their horses to those who were ill. They arrived as best as they could at the place where Don Juan Enríquez de Guzmán was waiting for them. And the adelantado and his people stayed there several days, eating the provisions that the natives had for the sustenance of their lives. The Spaniards continued to fall ill. They did not have a reliable way that would take them to Quito, which was what they wished. Time went by, which weighed heavily upon the adelantado, and with the agreement of the leaders it was decided that they should go out all over that region to see if they could find a way. The sickness remained among the Spaniards. It was a fever like *modorra*.[3] Among the ill was one called Pedro de Alcalá, and when his fever became worse, he got up from where he was lying, took out a sword, and went out shouting, "Who speaks evil of me?" He went toward a stable and with one thrust killed his horse, and before they could prevent it, with two more he killed other good horses—at a time when in Peru a horse was worth three and four thousand castellanos. They seized him as he was about to wound a Black, and they put him in chains.

At this time those who had gone searching for a road returned without having come across any because of the many rivers and lakes that they encountered. This dismayed everyone, thrust in such poor land neither seen nor known by any of them. Captain Don Juan Enríquez de Guzmán, of whom they relate that he was a very noble and honored knight, said to the adelantado that in order to serve him he wanted to go and find a way somewhere. The adelantado was *fol. 86v* grateful to him. Luis de Moscoso left with him, along with several able Spaniards, and he went not knowing where. They passed many raging rivers and swampy lakes until, while going through a thick forest full of large shrubbery and thickets, they discovered a village, where they killed several natives who stood up to defend their lands and property. The rest fled, terrified at seeing the horses. They found the type of food that the Indians usually eat in this land that they discovered; and as lords of the land they took up lodging there as if it were theirs, while the true lords fled for fear of being killed by them and their horses.

Don Juan and Captain Luis de Moscoso sent messengers to the adelantado, who then with the whole camp came as quickly as he could to where the captains were. He stayed there several days, and some of the Spaniards who were sick died there, among them this Captain Don Juan Enríquez de Guzmán, who died of an affliction that he had. These Spaniards died in great misery, without any comfort or anything other than the hardship of marching, and for mattresses the bare ground,[4] and for cover the sky. They had neither raisins nor pippins[5] to smell, only some yucca roots and maize. *We are describing our existence*[6] so that in Spain they can understand the great hardships those of us involved in exploration suffer in these Indies, and that they should consider themselves lucky if without coming here they are able to go through the course of this short life with some honesty.

The adelantado asked the Indians who had been captured in that land to tell him where the highway to Quito was and to tell him why they had so few roads. They replied they did not know and other answers that the Indians usually give.

Notes

1 The Daule River begins almost due west of Quito and empties into the Pacific at modern Guayaquil.

2 Could be potatoes or yucca.

3 It may have been influenza or epidemic meningitis or another disease. Licentiate Luis Ponce de León, who came to Mexico around 1526, died from modorra. His physician described the course of the disease: high fever, lethargy, delirium, coma, and within a week death. See Francisco López de Gómara, *Cortés: The Life of the Conqueror by His Secretary* [1552], trans. Lesley Byrd Simpson (Berkeley: University of California Press, 1964), p. 382.

4 beds

5 A variety of apple.

6 This italicized statement was written in the margin of the manuscript in a different handwriting.

LXVII

About the things that further happened to the adelantado, and about the great hardships and needs that his people suffered

The adelantado regretted not having taken the other road that his brother Captain Gómez de Alvarado had discovered because the Indians had insisted they would take him that way to Quito. *fol. 87* And although by his command they went out in many directions to search for a road, none was found, which further increased his grief. There was in his camp a diligent and very capable man named Francisco García de Tovar, who later became captain in Popayán, and I knew him well. [The adelantado] summoned him and insistently exhorted him to go with forty Spaniards and try to find some road in the northerly direction where they could come out of the land they were in. He instructed him that even if he had to slash with a machete and an ax, he should go for several days because inevitably he would come upon a wide and royal highway that Juan Fernández, the pilot, assured him extended through the highlands of Peru.

Tovar and forty men set out, taking a compass[1] in order not to become lost in the highlands, and with great hardship they went into those unexplored and unknown forests, slashing with machetes[2] in order to penetrate through the great thickness of the undergrowth. During the nights they slept in whatever place they found themselves in; he who fit into a dry place to rest his body or had some branches to put underneath was considered lucky, and they used their bucklers as pillows. They ate the scraps that they carried in the knapsacks. In this manner they went on until they arrived at a large river. Although it was as wild as it appeared, it contained some turf growing within the water itself, and there was so much of it and so entangled that no bridge was needed to cross it. Tovar and his companions crossed the river with no other aim than to discover a settlement and a road to Quito. And after these forty were quite tired, it pleased God that a little further ahead of this large river they discovered a village of twenty houses well stocked with provisions. Although the Indians

were upset by their arrival and the harm that would befall them with their visit, they were unable to escape, which was the reason that some were seized as guides. They ate whatever they found there and left with the news that they would find a settlement, but they did not believe that the Indians were telling the truth. And so that hunger would not make an appearance in the adelantado's camp because of their tardiness, they proceeded on their way, still to the north. After they had gone on for two days[3] and during the nights slept in the forests, the next day, already late, they arrived in a village with a large
fol. 87v population and with many cultivated fields, maize, and some roots. They believed it would be safe to inform the adelantado that he and all his people should come with celerity to where they awaited him. And thus those necessary returned with the news. They sent some venison to him, which they had found in the houses of the Indians, because only a few or none of them ate meat anymore, and the Spaniards were dying from disease and illnesses.

When [Alvarado] learned that Tovar had discovered that village, he departed from where he was. And while the adelantado marched, the volcano that erupted near Quito—which I told about earlier—had[4] scattered[5] everywhere so much ash or earth in the air that it seemed the clouds were expelling it from within, and all who were unaware of it believed that because of something supernatural, earth and ash were raining from the sky. And so much of it fell where the adelantado passed that he was astounded, and it did not cease to fall for several days.[6]

Because there was not a continuous or wide enough road for the horses, they went on with much hardship, and most days the Indians whom they had taken wailing from Guatemala were dying; indeed, they had brought them from their lands and environment to die so miserably. And falling and rising, they arrived at the aforesaid river. There they found themselves in greater disarray; although there was a bridge over those turfs and bogs for the men to cross, it was unsuitable for the horses because they were heavy and those roots were joined and woven so that they ensnared all the horses even if they were strong. Furthermore, there was no uncovered place to hazard it because [the river] was full of those plants. They did not know what means to use to escape such fate, but necessity teaches men great things, and more in these parts than in any other in the whole world. Thus, as a good captain, Alvarado ordered them to cut some trees, similar to fig trees, which they call *aurumas* because they are somewhat hollow inside, and they brought so many that they made a bridge strongly tied to the turfs with reeds (I have explained what they are in *Part One*). It was so long that it extended three hundred feet and in width a little more than twenty. And when they finished it, while arguing whether or not the horses could cross easily, one of them, in order to break the impasse, burst forth and reached the bridge with full speed, crossed it, and then returned to where he had left from. They were thrilled by it, and the horses crossed without any danger. And they went to the village where Francisco García de Tovar *fol. 88* was. The adelantado then ordered the captains to go out in squads in all directions to explore. And they discovered another place called Chongos, where they seized some local Indians, who related that a four-day march from there was a village called Noa.

Near this land of Chongos there is such a large river that horses can cross only in balsas. And when the adelantado was informed about it, he departed with some, leaving the camp in charge of Licentiate Caldera, his chief justice, whom he ordered to follow him after an interval, being very careful with the sick. And after he ordered this, he set out with those he chose and went until he reached a river where some natives had assembled[7] to wage war on them because they wanted to take their lands against their will and without their consent. They had positioned themselves on the other side of the river, making great clamor and launching many shots against the adelantado and his men. The ensign, Francisco Calderón, who carried the standard, rode at full speed into the river and crossed it with considerable exertion, emerging where the Indians were. Some of the knights who were with Alvarado did the same and laboriously crossed the river.

The Indians were upset when they saw how swiftly they were crossing, and with the shots that they were launching they wounded Juan de Herrada and his horse. Because our men were close to them, they lost their courage and began to flee, frightened to see the horses and their speed; they had already heard great things about them. Proceeding on their way, the adelantado went until he reached the village, where he awaited the Licentiate Caldera, who with great hardship and want arrived to join him. And when they were all together, after they had their conference, it was decided that Diego de Alvarado would go with several horsemen and footmen to explore to the north, through a forest extending toward some nearby highlands. Further, the adelantado, with those that he deemed necessary, would follow, and Licentiate Caldera would remain with the rest of the camp in order to follow them in the best order that he could.

Diego de Alvarado took eighty Spaniards, split between the horsemen and the footmen, and they went into the forest, so somber and frightening that the thickness of the trees almost kept out the sun-
fol. 88v light with their branches. And they went an entire day without seeing level ground, which was the reason that they and their horses slept in the forest, suffering hardships. Although there were great ravines and streams of water on both sides of them, they found none where they were, and they felt thirsty, and the horses, who were very tired, more so. If they tried to descend into the ravines, it would cause a delay and great exertion, even more so because they were not on a road but in a forest filled with thistles and brambles. They went another day with the same hardship and through the same terrain until they arrived at a great plantation of the thick canes whose nature I have related in *Part One,* to which I refer. Their anguish doubled and their thirst grew because they did not find water where there were conditions to have it, although one usually finds springs in cane plantations. Night was quickly approaching, which made the inhospitable forest even darker. Unwillingly, they had to stop there. They could not move or the horses walk from thirst. Almighty God provides for people who deserve it in a thousand ways and means. And thus a Black, while cutting the cane that I say exists there to make some shelter, found in the internode of one of them more than one half arroba of water, so clear and tasty, that it could not be better because when it rains, it enters through the openings that the canes have in the knots, and the internodes fill up. And thus the Black joyfully announced the good news, which was such that everyone rejoiced. And although it was late, they cut the cane with machetes and swords, where they found so much water that they all—including the horses—drank, and even if there were many more of them, there would have been some left over; they spent that night talking about the water. And when it was daytime they set out, always in the northerly direction, and they went through the forest until almost sunset when they reached the flat land of the campaign, which made them overjoyed, and they thanked God for it.

And in the fields they saw some herds of sheep, which increased their joy, and they discovered a village that I believe is called Ajo, where there was a lot of salt for trade between the natives. All the Indians were warned about the coming of the Spaniards, news that greatly amazed them because they thought they were crazy to suffer such hardships in order to search for gold. They did not dare to wait for *fol. 89* them; instead they fled.

Diego de Alvarado and those who arrived with him rested from the hardship and hunger, eating those good rams that they found there, which are extraordinary and more flavorful than the excellent ones of Spain. He decided to send notice to the adelantado, as well as some meat and salt. He ordered Melchor de Valdés to return with six footmen and to take twenty-five sheep and salt. They then began the journey, but when the Indians saw that they were so few, they wanted to kill them. They did not distinguish themselves, nor did they carry out their design; instead, some of those who were bolder and came to where the swords could reach them died.

In the meantime, the adelantado, on his way and the Licentiate Caldera on his, kept going with great hardship and weariness, and they felt such currish hunger that they would even eat a horse that might have died or lizards, mice, snakes, and anything that they could put into their mouths even if it were these repugnant things. And the hunger was so great that everyday Spaniards, Indians, and Blacks were dying, which was very distressing. And during this scarcity, the general standard bearer, Francisco Calderón,[8] had a female greyhound that he highly prized, and realizing that he could never provide more benefit than what her meat would give at that time, he ordered her to be killed for food and made a banquet with most of her for the knights his friends. Luis de Moscoso was unwell from something he ate, and wanting to purge, he did it with a kidney of this greyhound, esteeming it more than if it were a fat hen. I am not shocked by these things because I have had my share of destitution, but it will be good for it to be known and understood in Spain that this is the way that money is earned around here.

Licentiate Caldera suffered extreme hardship in order to go on with the sick he was bringing. And I leave off relating plenty of remarkable things that happened in order to quickly conclude this subject. Valdés[9] reached the adelantado with the sheep, and he was glad to

see them, as can be imagined. He distributed among the sick what was possible and ordered part of it sent to those who were going with Licentiate Caldera because at this time the camp was divided into three parts: one with Diego de Alvarado, another with the adelantado, and another with Caldera. But when they all learned that Diego de Alvarado had found flat land of the campaign, they were so invigorated that the past hardships seemed insignificant to them, and they gave many thanks to God our Lord because in such calamitous times He works with the greatest mercy for His creatures. And thus, those who were going with the adelantado as well as those who had
fol. 89v stayed with Caldera could not wait to set foot in such land because with their hardships and starvation they did not pine as much after the gold of Quito as they did in the beginning. And because at this time Francisco Pizarro had already entered the city of Cuzco, and it is essential to write about it in order not to lose the sequence that we follow, which is necessary so that the events are written linked with each other as they were happening, and because I have justified myself in this, I stop and will deal with the said subject.

Notes

1 Cieza wrote the word *reloj,* or clock, but must be referring to a compass.

2 According to Covarrubias, the single-bladed short sword comes from the Greek word *machaera;* the case may also be made for a Caribbean origin—the Taino hardwood *macana* that was used to slash away dense undergrowth. See Sauer, *Early Spanish Main,* p. 52.

3 nights

4 so much fell

5 expelled

6 Mt. Cotopaxi is located about halfway between Quito and Ambato. It is the world's tallest active volcano at 19,347 feet. There are about twenty active volcanoes in the district, all cone-shaped and potentially explosive. The highest is Mt. Chimborazo at 20,561 feet; see Hemming, *Conquest,* p. 161.

7 with the will to

8 See chapter 63.

9 Melchor de Valdés.

LXVIII

About how Pizarro marched on the way to Cuzco, ordering that Atahualpa's captain-general, Chalcuchima, be burned in the valley of Jaquijahuana, and about other notable things that happened

I have related earlier how Pizarro arrived with his people to join Almagro and Soto in the highlands of Vilcaconga. From there he set out with all of them the next day, yearning to quickly enter the city of Cuzco, where he believed they would find great treasures because it had been the head of the Inca Empire and their mummy bundles and other marvels were there.[1] He was bringing imprisoned and under security Chalcuchima, a famous captain among the Indians who came from a great lineage. They say of him—if they are not inventing it—that when he saw that Pizarro had divided his camp before joining Soto, he rejoiced, believing that the Indians could kill both groups. And he secretly sent a messenger to Captain Quizquiz, encouraging him to be brave and attempt to kill their enemies the Christians—whom they called Viracocha, as they refer to them to this day—by joining the other captains from Cuzco who were combating them. And that Quizquiz, with the greatest force that he could, came at the time when the Spaniards had defeated the others and were descending from the highlands of Vilcaconga. Pizarro was warned about what Chalcuchima was up to, and he became angry at his prisoner because he was trying to gain his freedom with the support of his kin and countrymen. He then ordered them to watch him more carefully. Some horsemen descended against the people that Quizquiz was bringing so that he could not join the other captains whom [the Spaniards] had defeated earlier. They failed because the men here are swift, and Captain Incurabayo encouraged them to quickly join him. Proceeding ahead, Pizarro arrived in the valley of Jaquijahuana, where he was again informed by some Indian, who must have been drunk, that Chalcuchima was assembling those troops to kill them *fol. 90*
and to free him from captivity. Pizarro learned these things while he

was in the valley of Jaquijahuana, and without wanting to hear his excuses, he ordered this Captain Chalcuchima burned. He perished wretchedly, having such a dreadful death. And for them even more so because they believe that if the bodies are consumed by fire, so are the souls. Chalcuchima had a great reputation among the Indians, and Atahualpa did not do any great deed without him, yet he without Atahualpa did many. And it was believed among the Indians themselves that if he had been present in Cajamarca when the Spaniards entered there, they would not have succeeded with their enterprise so easily.[2]

There were in this valley of Jaquijahuana sumptuous dwellings and many storehouses. The Indians had not destroyed them because they had no strength for it when they were defeated by the Spaniards, nor could they descend on the highway that led to them, although they did take a large quantity of treasure in silver and gold. But there was still found a large amount of these metals and many cargas of that very fine wool cloth that was so prized by those from here, and they took more than two hundred ladies—those who observed religion, most of them young girls and very beautiful and elegantly dressed according to their manner. Pizarro ordered some Spaniards to remain on guard with all these spoils, and with the captains and the rest of the people he marched, nearing Cuzco. At that time this valley was so populated and cultivated that one could give thanks to our highest God just to contemplate its beauty, and the fields, made with such exquisite skill, are worth seeing for their singularity. I have already written about it in *Part One*.[3]

In the meantime, the captains of the Indians realized that they had been unable to defeat the Spaniards and that they would enter Cuzco without any resistance in order to master such a famous city, where they themselves had experienced many pleasures and delights and that the Incas had embellished with such grand buildings and wealth never seen or heard before. Also, that without lifting a finger their enemies would go and take it for themselves, without being justified or having a cause or good reason. Deploring these things and pondering them, they made their sacrifices and new supplications to their gods, and they resolutely agreed to await them in a narrow place of that valley, attached to the most easterly mountains, in order to kill all of them. And they would remain in the field as a sign that they
fol. 90v died defending their fatherlands from such people. The Christians

were warned about these things by the runaways. It was decided that Almagro, Hernando de Soto, Juan Pizarro, and all the available horsemen would go ahead in order to defeat them and that Pizarro and the rest of the people would follow them. Carrying it out, they marched until they came upon the Indians, with whom they had a skirmish, killing some of them with the lances.

Manco Inca Yupanqui, son of Huayna Capac, to whom some say his father's realm rightfully belonged, had left Cuzco and taken with him some orejones in order to join his relatives. But when he saw how badly it had gone for them, he realized that the Spaniards would come to rule the entire kingdom, and it seemed to him a sound idea to ally himself with them. Accompanied by one of his knights,[4] he went to Pizarro. When Pizarro learned of it, he was delighted. He treated him well and commanded that they should honor him as the son of as powerful a king as was Huayna Capac. When the captains and his kin learned of it, they were considerably distressed. They became so desperate they decided that because they could not prevail against the Spaniards, they would go to the city and set fire to its buildings and royal houses and take away the great treasures so that those whom they considered great enemies could not have them. Then they carried it out, and from among them one who had a graceful figure appeared before Pizarro and warned him of the deed that the Indians were intending. When he learned of this, he consulted with the captains and other leaders, and it was decided that Juan Pizarro and Hernando de Soto, with most of the horsemen, would ride at full speed to enter into Cuzco and prevent the Indians from destroying the city as they planned. And although they rode rapidly, the Indians had entered first and had stolen a great deal of treasure. They plundered the temple, taking with them the sacred maidens who had remained there, and they set fires in some places. Because the Spaniards were late, albeit only slightly, the destruction that [the Indians] did in Cuzco was great and considerable. Because they knew [the Spaniards] were coming on their heels, they left the city, taking all the young people, men and women, so that only a few remained who were either old, weary, or useless for war. But when Hernando de Soto and Juan Pizarro entered the city, they remedied what they could so that the fire ceased, and it was not long before Pizarro arrived, with the rest of the people, in the city itself.[5]

Notes

1 The bodies of the ancestors, especially the founders of lineages, were venerated and were believed to hold special powers. When the Inca ruler died, the body was prepared, annointed, and wrapped with strips of cloth, then cared for by a group of people who watched over the mummy bundle and saw to its needs. For a description see *Part Two*, chapter 11.

2 He was burned 13 November 1533. Valverde attempted a last minute conversion, but Chalcuchima refused. As the flames engulfed him, he shouted out to Viracocha, an idol, Huanacauri, and especially Quizquiz to seek revenge. See Hemming, *Conquest*, p. 110.

3 In *Part One*, chapter 91 Cieza describes the Andean terraced fields: "They were made in the order of wide walls or terraces, with one jutting out from the edge of the next, and having enough space between the retaining wall of one and its neighbor for them to plant their crops of maize and other plants. And they were constructed in this manner, attached to the mountainsides."

4 Cieza uses the word *caballero*, a knight, which in the case of the horseless Incas was quite inappropriate. This is another example of European terminology incorrectly used in the Andean context.

5 They entered Cuzco on Saturday, 15 November 1533; Hemming, *Conquest*, p. 117.

LXIX

About how the Spaniards entered the ancient city of Cuzco, where they found great treasures and precious things

In the month of October of the year of the Lord fifteen hundred and thirty-four[1] the Spaniards entered the city of Cuzco, head of the great empire of the Incas, where their court was as well as the solemn Temple of the Sun and their greatest marvels. *fol. 91*

It was founded—according to the opinion of the most knowledgeable of the orejones—by Manco Capac, from whose time to Huascar's eleven princes reigned, so that these lords did not rule this great kingdom for a long time. When they won and subjugated it, the people had lived in independent villages; they used little reason and scarcely cared for public order; when they lost it, there existed such laws and government as the readers have seen in their history. The Spaniards entered the city, as has been related, after the Indians in order to prevent them from destroying it. Pizarro and Almagro, with the rest of the people, arrived shortly, and when they entered, they scattered throughout its streets and hills. They saw two large houses with human [trophy] skin, which were the Chancas, killed there in the time of Viracocha Inca. According to the law of ancient times it was not allowed to remove gold or silver that had entered Cuzco, and not counting the kings, the heads of the orejones and many other lords and noble men resided there. Although treasure for Atahualpa's ransom was taken to Cajamarca, and Quizquiz robbed what has already been related, and even though the Indians thought of destroying it and took a great deal, it did not seem to make a dent in how much remained. It was a marvelous thing and worthy of contemplating because no loot equaled this one, nor in all the Indies was there found such wealth. Neither a Christian nor a pagan prince has or possesses such a wealthy region as the one where this famous city is founded. The high priest abandoned the temple, where [the Spaniards] plundered the garden of gold[2] and the sheep and shepherds of this metal along with so much silver that it is unbelievable and precious stones, which, if they were collected, would be worth a city.

Indeed, when the Spaniards entered and opened the doors of the *fol. 91v*

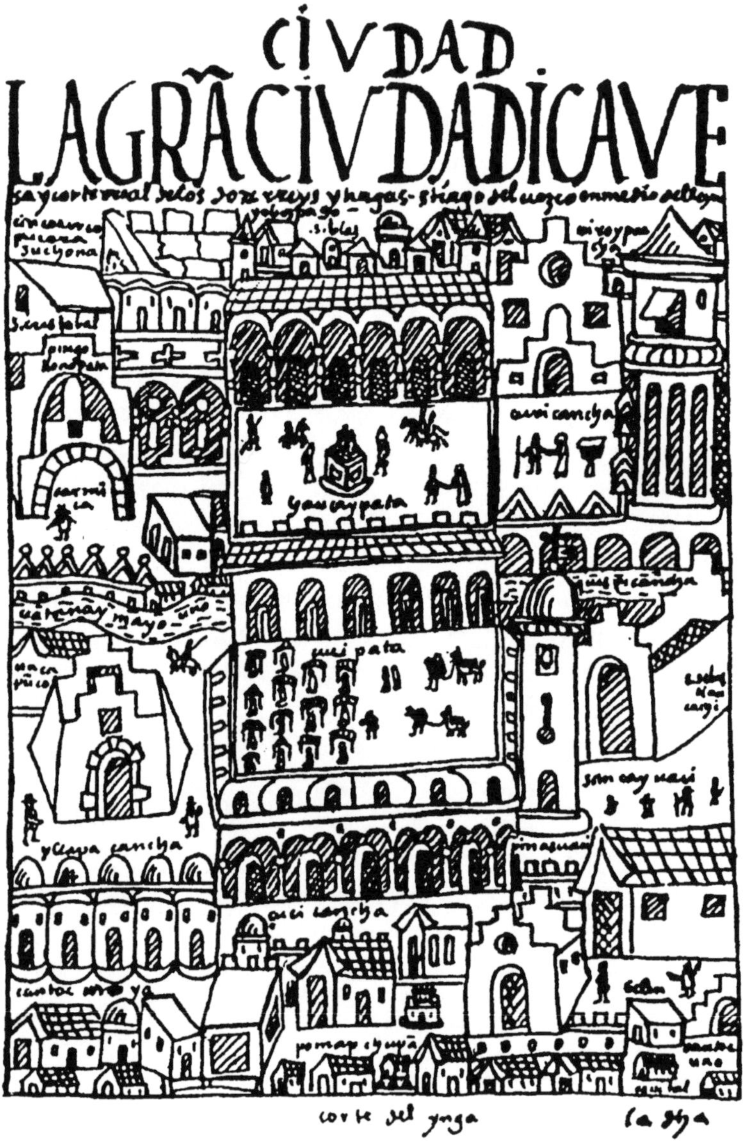

18. Guaman Poma de Ayala's Cuzco. Felipe Guaman Poma de Ayala, *El primer nueva corónica y buen gobierno,* 3 vols., ed. Rolena Adorno and John V. Murra (Mexico City: Siglo Veintiuno, 1980), f. 1051. Courtesy of Siglo Veintiuno Editores.

houses, in some they found heaps of very heavy and splendid gold pieces, in others large silver vessels. It irritated them to see so much gold. Many left it, scoffing at it, not wanting to take more than some delicate and fine little jewels for their Indian women.[3] Others found beads, feathers, gold ingots, and silver in bullion; indeed, the city was full of treasures. In the fortress, the royal house of the Sun, they found unseen and unheard of grandeur because the kings had deposits there of all the things that can be imagined and thought about. Plenty was stolen by the yanaconas, and some Spaniards did the same.

Pizarro ordered that all the gold and silver should be collected in a principal house of the city, and thus it was done. The fine cloth that could have been collected at that time, had it been preserved, would have been worth more than three million. Because the governor had ordered and solicited it, a great heap of silver and gold was collected, and after robbing what can be safely believed, 480[4] shares were made and distributed among the Spaniards. Some say that each share was 4,000 pesos;[5] others say 2,700 marks of silver. There was an abundance of precious stones.[6] Most of them were kept by those who found them wherever they went around the city. When they attacked villages, they found large amounts of silver. They brought some to the mound and left a great deal because they did not appreciate it. Pizarro believed that it would be beneficial to deal with what was paramount in the service of God. Thus, after he entered the city of Cuzco, he cleansed it of the filth of the idols, and he assigned the site for a church, a decent place to say mass and where the gospel could be preached so that the name of Jesus Christ could be praised. Furthermore, crosses were placed along the roads, which was a great terror for the demons because they were taking away the dominion they held in that city, God having allowed that the residents had been so subjugated by them. And this done, [Pizarro] told a notary to attest how he was taking possession of that city as the head of the entire kingdom of Peru in the name of the Emperor Charles, fifth of this name, king of Spain, and had witnesses to it and was naming alcaldes and councilmen. The city of Cuzco was rebuilt by him, which I have related in *Part One,* where I direct the reader.

Incurabayo and Quizquiz were still accompanied by many people, *fol. 92* residents of Cuzco as well as mitimaes. Their sorrow increased when they saw that the Spaniards had seized their city. They wept over

their destiny; they complained about their gods; they sighed for the Incas; and they cursed the birth of Huascar and Atahualpa; because of their feuds and vain disputes the Spaniards had gained such a great land. There were among them the Huambracuna,[7] who are of the lineage and ancestry of those who I related in *Part Two* were living in the villages of Caranqui, Otavalo, Cayambe, and others that fall in the province of Quito. King Huayna Capac, because of some offense, killed so many that a large lake where they threw them turned the color of blood, and from then on until today and forevermore that lake is called "Yaguarcocha," which means sea of blood. The children of these became very courageous and in the wars were granted privileges, and many were with these captains of Cuzco.[8] Because he was clever, Quizquiz intended to win their favor so that if they were unable to prevail against the Spaniards, he would go with them to Quito, where he believed he had a reputation. Taking them aside, he reminded them of the fertility of their land and how joyful it was, and that because fortune had been so favorable to the Christians, they had gained the greater part of Chinchasuyu; therefore, it would be a good idea for them to return there[9] to live in the fields that their fathers cultivated and be buried in the ancient tombs of their elders. And if they swore to him by the sovereign Sun and the sacred Earth that they would have him as captain and would be faithful, that he would take them to their lands and would die for what might concern the least one of them. They say that after the Huambracuna thought it over, they replied that they were content to do what he was advising them. Therefore, it would be best to first tempt fortune and again wage war on the Christians, and if they fared as the first ones did, they would
fol. 92v then set out for their fatherlands and take him as captain. Incurabayo, the orejones, and the other captains sent word to various parts of the provinces that they should come and join them to wage war on the Spaniards, who had already become masters of the city of Cuzco. And they quickly began to make weapons and to prepare to go against them, making great sacrifices to their gods.

And leaving this subject, I will again talk about what was happening in the equatorial provinces.

Notes

1 November of 1533.

2 Coricancha, the Temple of the Sun, contained many precious objects even after its exterior had been stripped for Atahualpa's ransom. Gold and silver life-size models of men, women, llamas, and maize filled the garden. In the center of the temple was a large gold disk of the sun, and replicas of the moon, the stars, and a representation of Illapa, the thunder. See Hemming, *Conquest*, pp. 132–34.

3 concubines

4 two

5 and one hundred

6 Part of Cuzco's treasure was assayed on 14 March 1534. The royal fifth consisted of a large quantity of gold ingots and "four llamas of gold, and eleven gold women." See Cook, "Libros de cargo," p. 79.

7 Newson, *Life and Death*, p. 124; Cieza uses "Guamaraconas" or "Guamaconas." See also chapter 57, n. 4.

8 The Inca massacre at Yaguarcocha cost the lives of thousands—accounts offer ranges from twenty to fifty thousand—of the Caranqui and Cayambe. Young survivors became bodyguards of the Inca at Cuzco; see Newson, *Life and Death*, pp. 123–24.

9 to their lands

LXX

About how Rumiñavi abandoned the city of Quito, first killing many principal women so that they could not be enjoyed by the Christians, who were very upset when they entered in it and did not see the treasure they sought, and what else happened

Earlier I wrote[1] about what happened to Captain Sebastián de Belalcázar until he arrived in the village of Panzaleo,[2] where an Indian whom they had seized told them that there was so much gold and silver in Quito that their horses could not carry a twentieth part of it. Therefore, the Spaniards became quite arrogant, believing that each one of them already had more than ten of those of Cajamarca. Although the Indian warriors were defeated, they continued to bear up against the Spaniards, and near Quito in a somewhat rugged ravine they fortified themselves within the dry walls that were there. From there they discharged so many shots that they detained them for a while. But [the Spaniards] climbed up next to them in order to capture the stronghold, and in spite of [the Indians'] efforts they killed many of them. And [the Indians] quickly went to the city of Quito, shouting loudly to those who were in it to abandon it without delay and go into the highlands. And they did this with great agitation because it seemed to them that the horses were on top of them. There were many principal ladies of the temples, those who had been the wives of Huayna Capac and Atahualpa and of other chiefs who had died in
fol. 93 the wars. Rumiñavi spoke to them cunningly, telling them that they already saw that the Spaniards were about to enter the city and that those of them who wanted to leave with him should start the journey. The rest of them would have to look after themselves because once those enemies entered, they were so evil and lecherous that they would take all of them to dishonor them as they had done to many others whom they took with them. When he said that, those who wanted to left without further delay; the others, who were more than

three hundred, said that they did not want to leave Quito, but would stay and await whatever fate had in store for them. Rumiñavi, furious and calling them *pampayrunas,*[3] ordered all of them killed, none to remain, and according to what I have been told, some of them were extremely beautiful and genteel women. When they killed them, they cast them into deep pits that were nearby.

After this, all those who were following the captains of their nation left the city, taking with them as much as they could remove from there. When they saw that the Christians, their enemies, were already approaching, and feeling anguished by it, they set fire to some of the lodgings and important houses. Belalcázar came so close to the city that he entered while these things were taking place. Some Indians launched shots, but because the warriors had already left, [the Spaniards] found little resistance, and many of the yanaconas came to join them to serve them, and the women who could did the same. They went through the city elated to be there.[4] They looked for the treasure, believing that they would find houses filled with it. But because it had been already placed into safety, they did not find or come across any, which was the reason that their joy turned into sadness, and they were shocked that what they believed to be so certain had been a joke. They surveyed the city and searched, but they did not encounter any joy. Belalcázar earnestly asked the Indians whom they met where the treasure of Quito was. They answered as if astonished, that they knew no more than that Rumiñavi had taken it and that not one of those who carried the loads away was alive because it is rumored that he killed all of them to prevent them from revealing where so much wealth had been placed. Although many were asked, none had a different explanation. The Spaniards became dejected and full of melancholy because in order to come on this expedition they had spent and suffered a great deal. They felt enormous hatred for Rumiñavi, about whom news arrived in the city that he was entrenched a little more than three leagues from there. *fol. 93v*

When Belalcázar learned this, he ordered Pacheco to go out one night with forty Spaniards with sword and buckler and try to seize him and bring him into his power. Rumiñavi had so many spies placed all over that they could not go anywhere without his being informed of it. And thus it happened that when Pacheco and those already named left to look for him, a message about it quickly went to [Ru-

miñavi], and when he learned it, he rapidly went with his [people] through some mountains to a village called Zinubo, where he halted. They learned in Quito about Rumiñavi's move. Belalcázar ordered anew that Rui Díaz[5] should go against him with seventy Spanish footmen. There were some among the yanaconas who were betraying everything that the Spaniards considered and decided. And when Rui Díaz was ordered to leave with so many Spaniards, and Pacheco the same, they reported that those who remained were few and mostly sick, news that all the natives thought joyful. And more than fifteen thousand warriors quickly joined the lord of Latacunga, whose name was Tucomango, and the lord of Chillo, whom they called Quingalumba,[6] with the goal to assail the city of Quito and kill the Spaniards who had remained in it. And they carried it out and arrived there on the second night watch. The Cañari, allies of the Christians, had learned about this manoeuver. Quito has a moat for fortification that the Inca kings had ordered constructed in the time of their reign. Outside it were patrols and sentinels who could hear the clamor made by the Indians coming in war, and they immediately warned Belalcázar, who ordered the horsemen to go out to the plaza, as well as the armed footmen, in order to confront the enemy coming against them. Because of the commotion that they heard, [the Indians] learned that they detected them, and opening their mouths, they shouted many threats, as is always their custom.[7] The Cañari, hating all of them because of the harm that they had caused them when they were with Atahualpa, attacked them, confident of the Spaniards' support, and they had their battle. Although it was night, they saw each other by the illumination coming from the many houses of the city burned by the enemy because they stood on the other side of the moat. The combat between them lasted until daybreak, when those who had
fol. 94 come against the city retreated. The horsemen went out after them. They caught up with them and killed and wounded so many that [the Indians] were so chastised that they thought it best never to repeat a similar trick.

Rui Díaz and the Spaniards who went with him proceeded until they entered into the rainforest of Yumbo. Rumiñavi learned about it and, not feeling safe in that land, retreated. Although the Christians could not have his person, they did have a great booty that they took from his depository—of fine cloth and other opulent ornaments and several gold and silver cups and vessels, as well as many very beautiful women—and they returned to Quito to report to the captain. Because they did not find the treasure that they had expected, they became restless, and they[8] persistently pressed the Indians to divulge if they knew where it had been hidden. Some of them stated that a large part of the treasure was buried in Cayambe, and believing that this information was accurate, Belalcázar himself left with all the people who were in Quito because those who had left to explore had not yet arrived. And when they reached a village called Quinche,[9] which is next to Purataco,[10] they say that after finding many women and boys because the men were away with the captains, he ordered that they should all be killed, although they were guilty of nothing, which was a great cruelty. Another Cañari Indian, who had been captured in an expedition by Vasco de Guevara, also claimed that he knew where some large vessels of gold and silver were. Belalcázar, greedy to get it, ordered the footmen to go with the provisions on the royal highway toward Cayambe; some horsemen went with them for protection. And he, with the rest of the people, took another road. Having gone a good distance, they arrived where the Cañari said there would be what they were looking for, and digging in the earth, they found ten vessels of pure silver and two of gold of standard weight and five of clay unusually enameled, with metal between the clay and soldered with the greatest perfection. This was found within a mound rising in the marsh where they dug to remove it. And then Belalcázar returned to meet his people, and they all went to Cayambe, where they saw fields full of herds of large and beautiful rams and sheep. They did not find any treasure, nor did they proceed ahead because Miguel Muñoz, Belalcázar's standard bearer, came with a message that Almagro was staying in Quito. And we would do well to relate how he came and *fol. 94v* for what reason.

Notes

1 I related before

2 An Ecuadorian village equidistant between Latacunga and Ambato; see Newson, *Life and Death,* p. 204.

3 Rumiñavi called them prostitutes. "Pampa" in Quechua means open

place, or plaza; "runa" is man or woman. Domingo de Santo Tomás (1560) defines the term as "women given (in the physical sense) to men." Cieza spells it "panpayronas."

4 They entered about 22 June 1534; see Hemming, *Conquest,* p. 159.

5 See chapter 58.

6 Cieza spells it "Quinbalinbo"; Hemming, *Conquest,* p. 159.

7 The line "that they detected them, and opening their mouths, they shouted" was left out of the Peruvian edition of *Part Three.* To complete the text we have used Francesca Cantú, *Pedro de Cieza de León e il "Descubrimiento y conquista del Peru"* (Rome: Instituto Storico Italiano, 1979), p. 344.

8 Belalcázar

9 The Inca had established a garrison there, made up in part of mitimae from the Cuzco area. It is located on the Guayllabamba River; Newson, *Life and Death,* pp. 33, 131, 157–58.

10 Cieza spells it "Puritaco." It is near Quinche; see Newson, *Life and Death,* map on p. 158.

LXXI

About what happened in the city of Cuzco, and about how Almagro and Hernando de Soto went out against the Indians, and Gabriel de Rojas arrived

Captain Quizquiz and the Huambracuna had discussed a return to Quito, but with the agreement of the priests of the temples and the elder orejones it was decided to once again wage war against the Christians, who in spite of all of them carried on in Cuzco as they pleased. After they collected many Indians of the districts, armed with their weapons, they converged on the city, making loud cries to frighten the Christians. Almagro ordered fifty horsemen and footmen to prepare, and with them and with Soto he set out to fight the Indians, who fled although there were so many that it is shameful to say it. They retreated toward the bridge of the Apurímac, where the Christians caught up with them, and killed and wounded many of them. Because it was late, our men slept there, and in the morning they set out in pursuit of the Indians, whom they trailed[1] all the way to Vilcas, a place where there were large and splendid buildings, as I have related in *Part One.*[2] Quizquiz and his followers went swiftly until they reached the Jauja Valley, where he intended to kill the Christians who were there with the treasurer, Riquelme, and to destroy the new city.

Gabriel de Rojas had arrived and with him the news that Adelantado Don Pedro de Alvarado had disembarked in Puerto Viejo with many horses and Spaniards, and the pilot Juan Fernández was exploring in a galleon along the coast. Riquelme learned from the Indians that Almagro was in Vilcas. He sent him warning of this news with a Black and some Indians. When he learned of it, in order to be entirely certain, he commanded two Spaniards, called Juan Núñez de Santa Marta and Alonso Prieto,[3] to go to Jauja and immediately return with the information to where he was awaiting them.

In the meantime, Quizquiz had seized more than sixty yanaconas *fol. 95* of the Spaniards. The treasurer went out with the horsemen and footmen he could assemble and with many of the yanaconas. He fought with the Indians, who wounded him and his horse. Unable to prevail against the Spaniards, and after he killed the yanaconas and Indian women they had,[4] Quizquiz went with the Huambracuna back to Quito, without having accomplished anything that he had intended. He had been praised for being a very brave and wise captain and of good judgment. The very Huambracuna who went with him killed him near Quito in the village of Tiacambe.[5]

The two Spaniards whom Don Diego de Almagro had sent from Vilcas arrived in Jauja and went back with what they had learned. Indeed, as soon as Almagro knew that Alvarado's expedition in the kingdom was certain, and fearing that he might occupy his northerly provinces, where it was believed there were large and wealthy lands, he decided to go to San Miguel as quickly as he could to consider there what would be best. He believed that the business was so important that it could not be delayed by informing his partner and waiting for his orders. With the utmost speed, he sent with couriers a report about everything that was happening, and he ordered Captain Hernando de Soto to stay for a few days in those lodgings of Vilcas and hold that frontier against Captain Incurabayo because they already knew that Quizquiz had been totally defeated. After he made this provision, he set out for the city of Jauja, where he spoke with Gabriel de Rojas. He ordered him to go immediately to Cuzco and report to Francisco Pizarro about [Alvarado's] coming, and he departed[6] [for] Pachacamac. Alonso de Morales,[7] Juan Alonso de Badajoz, Juan Cerico, Juan García de Palos,[8] Francisco López,[9] and a footman named Juan Vaca went with him. And he went on until he arrived in that valley,[10] where Juan Alonso de Badajoz remained. And with the rest he continued at a forced march on the royal highway of the plains, hoping to have the news that he had been expecting for days, that his ships had come from Panama. He arrived with this wish in the beautiful valley of Jayanca,[11] where he met some Spaniards who had recently come. He learned from them how Adelantado Don Pedro de Alvarado, after disembarking on the coast of Puerto Viejo, *fol. 95v* headed inland on the way to Quito, while sending Juan Fernández, his pilot and galleon captain, to explore the coast ahead in the east.

Almagro became very angry at Juan Fernández because he found out that he was largely responsible for Alvarado leaving his governance to come to Peru. He wrote to Nicolás de Ribera and the others who were staying[12] at Pachacamac that should [Fernández] land and they could get their hands on him, they should right then and without further delay hang him. And he proceeded on his way until he entered the city of San Miguel. There he learned that Belalcázar had left without the governor's orders, which upset him and he reviled him terribly. There were those who were disgruntled with Belalcázar and who, in order to make [Almagro] even more inflamed against him, declared that he was a rebel and was intending to join Alvarado. The marshal believed it was inadvisable to halt for long, that instead he should go swiftly, before Alvarado could set out for Quito, and take for himself the people that Belalcázar had. And with a larger company than the one with which he had come, he left the city. He went and arrived in Quito while Belalcázar was looking for the treasure that they said was in Cayambe and that the Cañari Indian showed him. [Almagro] then ordered his standard bearer, Miguel Muñoz, to go and summon [Belalcázar] and all the people. And with that I will return to discuss Don Pedro de Alvarado.

Notes

1 following

2 Chapter 89.

3 Prieto, originally from Palos, often used the alternative "Peto." He came to Peru with Belalcázar from Nicaragua, but left in 1534. He returned to Spain in 1535 with his substantial share of gold and silver. See Lockhart, *Men of Cajamarca*, pp. 406–407.

4 taken

5 The slow retreat, coupled with the arrival of fresh Spanish forces, left Quizquiz in an untenable position. He and his men could still defeat isolated groups of foreigners, but they could not win major battles against the Spanish cavalry. Ultimately, his warriors wanted to sue for peace and return home. He refused. Huaypalcon attacked him, and others joined in with battle axes and clubs and killed him. See Hemming, *Conquest*, p. 166.

6 and from where he then left for

7 Also known as Alonso López del Moral, he was born about 1503 in Moral de Calatrava. He left for Peru with the Pizarros in 1530 and served as retainer of Juan and Gonzalo Pizarro. He stayed in San Miguel, where he had an en-

comienda, and later went to Cuzco. He decided to return to Spain in late 1534. See Lockhart, *Men of Cajamarca*, pp. 333–34.

8 He was probably from Palos and also called himself Juan García de Calzadilla. See Lockhart, *Men of Cajamarca*, p. 434n.

9 A barber from Cádiz. He was in Nicaragua by 1525 and shared an encomienda with Alonso Lozano. In 1531 he joined the Panama expedition. He remained in Jauja while the major group continued to Cuzco. He returned to Spain in 1535 with a substantial fortune. See Lockhart, *Men of Cajamarca*, pp. 387–88.

10 at Pachacamac

11 Cieza spells it "Jayanque."

12 on the coast

LXXII

How Adelantado Alvarado arrived in the village discovered by Diego de Alvarado, who had left to explore and came upon some snow-covered mountain passes, and about the hardship that the Spaniards suffered

When the adelantado learned about the village that Diego de Alvarado had discovered, he and those who were with him went quickly, eager to be enveloped by the many sheep that were there. Licentiate Caldera followed with great hardship caused by the sick they were bringing, of whom some died almost everyday. After Diego de Alvarado sent notice to the adelantado about what he had discovered, he decided with the agreement of those who were with him to proceed ahead and explore what they could. And that is what they did, taking their slaves and yanaconas. After they went along a road, they reached *fol. 96* some large mountains as covered by snow as others usually are by forests. The south wind blew so strongly that it was an even greater evil because the cold was extreme. It was impossible to cross in another place, even though they wanted to attempt it by going the long way around. They feared the mountains, but[1] forced by the necessity to learn what lay ahead, they plunged into that snow. This great perseverance speaks of the courage of the Spaniards because they suffered so many hardships in these Indies. It horrifies one to describe them—that they would go into this snow without knowing when or where they would end up or without any other information than whatever the natives gave them. Indeed, when they entered the snow-covered passes, huge[2] snowflakes were falling from the clouds, which bothered them so much that they did not dare to[3] raise their eyes to see the sky because the snow would burn their eyelashes. The Indians whom they brought could not move their feet. They took on the horses those whom they could, and because they did not carry great baggage and traveled lightly, they squeezed through as much as they could with such difficulties that they thought they would all be dead. After they had gone more than six leagues, it pleased God that they did cross the peaks, although it was already late; and coming out of so much snow, they arrived in a somewhat large village where they found many sheep and other provisions. Then a report of all these things was sent to the adelantado, advising him how and in what way he should cross the snow and how afterwards all would find provisions to eat.

The adelantado was coming, as has been said, ahead of Licentiate Caldera, who was coming with most of the people and baggage,[4] and he arrived at the village of Ajo, which Diego de Alvarado had left. The Spaniards never ceased to die. They auctioned their goods, and many of the buyers wanted to pay immediately in pure gold. They did not want to be burdened with such work, but instead they wanted to use promissory notes to pay on demand. Licentiate Caldera went with great hardship because of the reasons that I have already written about at other times. They all knew about the snow that lay ahead. Because they never ceased to forge ahead, they reached the snow; they feared what they had to cross. They went into it, and many more[5] fell than when Diego de Alvarado had passed through. All the Indians who were with them—natives of the province of Guatemala and some of Nicaragua, and others that they had captured in the kingdom—have very delicate constitutions and are weak, although to *fol. 96v* their detriment and our benefit we always judge otherwise. And being in such difficulties they despaired because the falling snow burned their eyes, and many lost their fingers and feet when they walked, and others froze to death with their expressions fixed. It was very cold. The south wind did not cease to blow. The Spaniards, those on foot as well as those on horse, were as you can imagine, but because they have great constitutions and such marvelous courage, they strove to go on. In the meantime, night fell with great darkness, which was another extreme torment. They had no other comfort than to commend themselves to God—neither shelter nor fire, nor anywhere or anything with which to make it. They put up some tents as well as they could to somewhat cover themselves. Many groaned and all chattered their teeth. Several Blacks and many Indian men and women froze to death.

The adelantado was so weary from the bitter cold that he thought it would have been better if he had never left his governance. And it would have been beneficial, especially for his soul, because it would have prevented the death of the many Indians who died because they were taken from their surroundings and homeland. They longed so much for the daylight that it seemed as if it would never come. But when dawn signaled what they had wished for, without further discussion or debate, like those who flee from the plague or are escaping a great storm, which is what they were in, they left the provisions that they had brought, and not wanting to go ahead, they returned to where they had started, the village they left behind. Licentiate Caldera also arrived there with the misfortune and hardship he endured because of the sick. Furthermore, when they arrived at a ravine, they found some small grapes, which look like blueberries,[6] about whose characteristics I believe I have written in *Part One*. And because they were hungry, without knowing what they were eating, most of them stuffed themselves and not long afterwards they violently fell unconscious to the ground, heaving and wriggling so that they seemed to be dying. And they remained like that until this indisposition passed and the fruit stopped its virulent course.

Following these things that the chronicle has related, the adelantado conferred with Licentiate Caldera and the other leaders who were present. It was decided that so they would not be completely lost, it would be expedient to cross the mountains in any way they could because they knew that where Diego de Alvarado was there was such good land and so many herds of sheep as they had heard about. Licentiate Caldera had issued many public proclamations that *fol. 97*
anyone who wanted gold that they were carrying from the loads taken on the coast could have it, but he would be obligated to pay the fifth with that. They derided him and his proclamations. There was one Spaniard who, when his Black joyfully brought him a carga of those gold jewels, struck him with it, exclaiming: "In such a time you bring me gold to eat? What food do you bring? I do not want gold!" And before crossing the mountains, the adelantado himself ordered it to be proclaimed that whoever wanted gold could freely take it without being obligated to do more than to pay the king his fifth, but they did not consider it better. They had to carry stones for grinding wheat and other things,[7] which was the reason that all that gold was lost, left behind in those places—and everyone after all had been looking for

nothing else but that to enrich themselves. No proclamation given by Licentiate Caldera was enough for anyone to take along either a little or a lot of it.

Notes

1 which they saw

2 and thick

3 could not

4 Cieza noted in the margin: "that of the thirst has to come here."

5 snow

6 The word Cieza uses is *mortiño,* which is a type of blueberry in Ecuador.

7 The Spanish had introduced wheat into the uplands of Central America, and it grew reasonably well. It is amazing that they carried cumbersome supplies rather than living off the land. Spanish preference for wheat bread is well known; see Sherman, *Forced Native Labor,* p. 240.

LXXIII

How Adelantado Alvarado went with great hardship through the snow, where some Spaniards and many Indian men and women and Blacks died, unable to escape the cold, wind, and snow, which was enough to kill them

Knowing what he had seen in the snow, the adelantado was distressed that the people could not stop dying in those snowdrifts. He longed as if for salvation to be in the territory that Diego de Alvarado had discovered. Hiding this anguish, he tried to animate the Spaniards, speaking encouragingly to them so that they would have the fortitude to go on. He knew that they would rather confront an enemy who had an advantage over them in battle than to fight against the elements. They commended themselves to Almighty God, and setting out on the way, they marched, talking about the snow, until they came to about one-half league from it, and they stationed themselves there. The next day, as best they could, they climbed the mountains without seeing the sun or the sky or anything other than snow. The day was so dismal and full of torment that even if I exaggerate a great deal, I cannot come close in describing what the horsemen endured. Those who rode the horses went frozen without energy, and they suffered much more than those who went on foot and were warmed with the exertion of walking. The unfortunate Indian men and women who went with them cried out about dying so miserably, lamenting their misfortune and calling out with dreadful voices to their elders. The wind was so strong that it penetrated through them and caused them to *fol. 97v* lose all feeling. They had no cloaks, and the cold was so terrible that they fell down deprived of all strength, and expiring, they released their souls from their bodies. There were many who out of exhaustion leaned against some rocks and ledges that were in the snow, and as soon as they rested, they froze to death and expired in such a way that they looked like scarecrows. The Spaniards who had the strength and walked without stopping were lucky; they escaped, as did those who rode horses without taking the reins or turning back their heads.

Many Blacks also froze to death, and although the Spaniards have a better constitution than any nation in the world, some of them began to die, without having any other graves than the snow.

They did not get through all[1] of it that day because as when one who is to die is given the sentence, he delays with all his forces as long as he can until that hour comes, so these were saying, "We will stay another day.[2] With luck the weather will calm." But they all had one fate, and theirs was the same as the others. They were leaving their weapons, their clothes, and everything they had in that snow, and they did not want or attempt anything other than to escape with their lives. They did not protect one another or bend down to raise one who had fallen, even if it were a son or a brother. The assayer, Pedro Gómez, and his horse froze to death, along with the many emeralds that he had collected. Guzmán and his wife and two young daughters whom he brought froze to death, which is painful to relate because of their cries and the tears that they shed in the short time that life sustained them. Another Spaniard who was in the camp, very robust, was riding on a mare[3] and began to alight in order to tighten a loose girth, but before he put his feet on the ground, he and she[4] perished. Fifteen Spaniards and six Spanish women died in these snows, and many Blacks and more than three thousand Indian men and women of those who had gone.[5] They seemed dead without color or vigor, yellow[6] and so emaciated that it was pitiful to see them. Many of the Indians who did not die escaped maimed, some without fingers and others without feet and some completely blind.

The natives were informed of this misfortune. Some bands came to kill them and to steal all that they left. They killed one Spaniard and injured another, who was a blacksmith, in the eye. After suffering the hardship that has been related and much more, the adelantado and those who escaped arrived in the village of Pasa. There
fol. 98 they realized that from the time they had left the coast, eighty-five Spaniards, many horses, and so many Indians had died that it is painful to say. The captaincies became undone with this calamity. They tried as well as they could to recuperate in that land, and cure those who were ill. A review was ordered to see who remained and what weapons they had salvaged. And after they regained strength, they left and went to a village called Quizapincha, from where in one day's journey they reached the great and royal highway of the Incas. And

when they had marched between the villages of Ambato and Muliambato,[7] they found hoofprints of horses and traces of Spaniards, which distressed them, and the adelantado decided that they should go with some horsemen to find the camp of Diego de Alvarado.

Notes

1 the snow

2 one more day

3 on his horse

4 and the horse

5 Cieza provides a tantalizing glimpse of the social composition of this group and, by implication, of others like it. Thousands of Indian men and women, many of them taken as slaves in Nicaragua, participated in the Andean venture, and many died. Furthermore, Spanish women went on some of the expeditions, but few were recorded. See Luis Martín, *Daughters of the Conquistadores: Women of the Viceroyalty of Peru* (Albuquerque: University of New Mexico Press, 1983), pp. 12–16; Lockhart, *Spanish Peru,* pp. 150–52; and Radell, "Indian Slave Trade," pp. 67–76.

6 The word *amarillo* (yellow) was used to describe those who were seriously ill or near death; we might say pale or ashen.

7 Muliambato is roughly thirty kilometers north of Ambato and twenty kilometers south of Latacunga in central Ecuador; see Newson, *Life and Death,* p. 204.

LXXIV

How Captain Belalcázar returned with his people to Quito, from where Almagro departed, and how certain scouts that [Almagro] sent were seized by Diego de Alvarado

When Sebastián de Belalcázar learned that Almagro was in Quito and had summoned him, he returned with those who were with him. When Almagro saw him, he reprimanded him for having left San Miguel without the governor's order. He took for himself all the people, treating Belalcázar as a prisoner, and some of his friends also. [Belalcázar] justified himself, declaring that it was the wish to serve that had motivated him to do what he did and not what his rivals had stated. Don Diego de Almagro extolled the riches of Cuzco, the great provinces of its territories, and the many cities that would be founded, where everyone would have wealthy repartimientos. He won them over with all this talk. He decided to leave that land to return to where he came from and to find out where Adelantado Alvarado had gone. Belalcázar and all the Spaniards left Quito with him, a little more than 180 between the horsemen and the footmen.

The Indians had killed three Christians who were coming in pursuit of Almagro, which was the reason why they very proudly went on the highway until they reached a fairly large river, where they shouted at those who were coming with Almagro. More than eighty Cañari, friends of the Christians, drowned. The horsemen rode into the river; those who were weighted down returned to the shore, but ten or twelve reached the other side. They sufficed to kill many Indi-
fol. 98v ans and cause the others to flee without daring to wait. And they tried to make a bridge for all those who were with Almagro to cross over. They captured many Indians and caciques in that pursuit, one of whom declared that many Christians and horses had crossed the snowy mountains and that they were near them. They at once realized that these were none other than those who were with the adelantado. Almagro believed that it would be a good idea to send out scouts to find out how they had come and how far they had gone. He ordered Diego Pacheco, Lope de Idiáquez, Cristóbal de Ayala,[1] Lope

Ortiz Aguilera,[2] and Román Morales to do it and to inform him with all speed.

In the meantime, the adelantado had sent Diego de Alvarado and some horsemen to reconnoiter, while he marched with the rest of the people on the royal highway until he arrived at Panzaleo. There he learned that for fear of the Christians, he who had been governor of Quito, named Zope-Zopahua, had fortified himself in a stronghold in the land that they call Sicchos, which lies behind on the lefthand side.[3] The adelantado believed that it would be very important to seize such a powerful lord. He ordered several horsemen, arquebusiers, and crossbowmen to prepare to go with him to besiege the place in order to capture him.[4] Diego de Alvarado had returned with those who had gone with him, and the rest of the camp was placed in his charge. When the adelantado arrived in Sicchos, he felt that he had brought too few people. He sent an order to the camp that some more should come. Diego de Alvarado himself wanted to go with those he chose, but before they had gone an entire league, they encountered Almagro's scouts. When he saw them, he commanded that they should surround them so that none could return to give a warning. Because [the scouts] were so few, they did not resist; instead, they gave up their weapons as they were ordered to do. Diego de Alvarado spoke with great polish, and he learned from them that Almagro was in Riobamba with his people. He ordered Juan de Herrada to quickly report these things to the adelantado, who as soon as he heard it, abandoned the siege against Zope-Zopahua and returned to meet Diego de Alvarado. And when he saw the messengers, he spoke to them courteously, telling them that he did not come to cause offense or to provoke war, but to discover new lands whereby the emperor would be served, and other things. To this, Almagro's [scouts] replied that no other thing had been presumed of his lordship, especially because it would be evident to him that that land fell within the boundaries of Don Francisco Pizarro. The adelantado gave them some ornaments *fol. 99* and jewels from those that had been saved from the snow.

Notes

1 He came to Peru with Alvarado and was one of the town officials named by Almagro when Quito was founded; see Javier Ortiz de la Tabla Ducasse,

Los encomenderos de Quito, 1534–1660: Origen y evolución de una elite colonial (Seville: Escuela de Estudios Hispano-americanos, 1993), p. 122; and Busto, *Diccionario,* 1:177.

2 Also named by Almagro as one of the town officials of Quito at its foundation in 1534; see Ortiz de la Tabla, *Encomenderos de Quito,* p. 122.

3 Sicchos is about forty kilometers northwest of Latacunga, over the mountains at the head of another valley; Newson, *Life and Death,* p. 204.

4 that lord

LXXV

How Almagro learned that his scouts were captured, and how he founded a city in Riobamba, and they went to enjoin the adelantado, and what else happened between them

Indeed, when Almagro's scouts were detained by Diego de Alvarado, as has been told, it was not long before [Almagro] found out from the service Indians who had gone with them. He was distressed and became very upset. But when that agitation passed, he said with great spirit that he would defend the land from those who came there without a provision or command of the emperor. In the meantime, having obtained sufficient information from the scouts, the adelantado allowed them to return freely, and he wrote gracious letters to the marshal to take with them. He stated that because he had a commission from the emperor to discover new lands, regardless that he had in his charge the government of the province of Guatemala, he had spent a large sum of gold for ships and war supplies belonging to the fleet with the intention of exploring what he could in this South Sea, in the eastern part, which would fall outside the boundaries of the governance that had been designated for Don Francisco Pizarro. He did not intend to offend or to cause dissension or any scandals, and he would come to Riobamba, where they could discuss honest conditions that would be to the advantage of everyone. The scouts arrived with these letters, and they told the marshal about the benevolence of the adelantado and how he had honored them and treated them in a friendly manner. Afterwards, having conferred about it, Almagro decided to found a city in Riobamba,[1] which is within the dominion of Quito, and taking possession, he established the foundation in the name of the emperor, and he asked to have it witnessed. He then chose the mayor and councillors. He summoned Captain Rui Díaz, Diego de Agüero,[2] and Father Bartolomé de Segovia, a cleric, and ordered them to go as ambassadors to the adelantado to congratulate him on his behalf for his coming and to assure him that he was much distressed by the *fol. 99v* great hardships and dangers that his lordship had suffered in the snow and since his departure from Guatemala. Furthermore, he believed that having always served the emperor, [the adelantado] would not do anything other than what he had written to him because it was clear to him that his partner Don Francisco Pizarro was governor of the greater part of that kingdom. Also, for days [Almagro] had been waiting for the king to send him the title of governor of what lay ahead.[3]

The adelantado was staying in the village of Mulahaló,[4] and he ordered that the rest of the people who had remained in Panzaleo should come there; leaving that place, he kept coming closer to the marshal. He met the messengers. He received them very well; after they spoke to him cautiously, they affirmed, in order to win the goodwill of those who were with him, that there were great treasures to divide in Cuzco and that it was nothing compared to how much there was in the undisturbed temples and Indian huacas. In addition, the large provinces that are in that kingdom, as they have heard, were to be divided among those who would settle there. It was a great enterprize, which would be advantageous for them to consider. They realized that the time was right for such an opportunity, and they could enjoy it without exploring snow and bad ventures. Those hearing such talk became quite excited; they already wished to be in Cuzco. After the adelantado discussed it, he ordered messengers to be called, and he sent them to tell the marshal to send him messengers when he approached Riobamba. And when they left camp, he marched until they set up [camp] in Mocha,[5] which is more or less five leagues from Riobamba. From there they engaged in some communications; Alvarado sent Martín de Estete[6] to ask Almagro to provide him with some interpreters and to safeguard his way for going ahead to explore what was not in Pizarro's governance. Almagro replied with protractions and excuses that he could not, nor could it be allowed that, in order to explore, such a sizeable army should pass through what had been won, and that he was unable to furnish provisions for so many people. Almagro answered this to the adelantado, but he never ceased giving great hopes to those who were coming on [the adelantado's] behalf, wishing that they would come over to him, knowing that greed—which is what subjects the Spanish nation to great evil—would move them to want to follow him. And as all here deal with cunning, there
fol. 100 was no absence of those who came on behalf of the adelantado and

who contrived for Felipillo, the interpreter, to run away one day and cross over to their camp, where he was well received. He reported how many Spaniards were with Almagro and that around where they were, there were many deep pits that fortified that place. But if he wanted, he could arrange it for the local Indians to assemble and all of them to set fires everywhere so that, fearing the blaze, [those with Almagro] would come out from there.

With the adelantado there was one whom they called Antonio [Picado], who later, as we will relate, was Pizarro's secretary and shared much with him.[7] When he heard such great things about Cuzco, confident of his ability because he immediately believed he would be what he became, and even though he was in Alvarado's service and named as his retainer, he went to Riobamba as surreptitiously as he could and appeared before Almagro, offering himself into his service. Almagro received him well. He learned of the adelantado's designs and what the traitor Felipillo had told him. Because Picado had disappeared, and they learned that he had gone to Riobamba to Almagro, the adelantado became furious, threatening to kill him if he caught him. He ordered all the horsemen and footmen to arm themselves and go out to a clear field that was nearby. He commanded that of all the Spaniards four hundred should go out, and the others should stay to guard the camp. He ordered that forty horsemen should go next to the royal standard and that Diego de Alvarado should take the vanguard with thirty horsemen. Gómez de Alvarado, with thirty, was to go personally with him. Mateo Lascano went as captain of sixty arquebusiers and crossbowmen. The guard was in the charge of Rodrigo de Chaves;[8] Rodrigo de Benavides[9] was captain of the rest of the men. The adelantado declared that in order for them to deliver Picado to him, he would have to defeat the marshal. They marched in perfect order until they reached Riobamba, where the adelantado sent an attendant to tell Diego de Alvarado to halt without fighting a skirmish or quarreling with the opponents. Neither Almagro nor those who were with him were unaware of all this, and even though they were so few, as has been related, they were prepared with full determination for anything that might occur.

The adelantado sent word that [Almagro] should hand Picado over *fol. 100v* to him because although he was his retainer, he had treated him very badly. Almagro replied that Picado was free to come and go, and he

could not force him to do anything. And having given this answer, he ordered Cristóbal de Ayala, the alcalde of the new city, and Domingo de la Presa, a notary, to go and enjoin the adelantado on God's and the emperor's behalf not to cause any turmoil or suppress royal justice or enter the city they had settled. Rather, he should return to his governance of Guatemala and leave the one that the king had granted to Francisco Pizarro. They were to reproach him for the harm and the deaths and the destruction of the natives that had grown from it, and ask him for testimony. The adelantado replied, without acknowledging [Almagro's] protestations, that he was the governor and captain-general of His Majesty and that he had a commission to explore on sea and land, and that he had entered Peru to explore what had not been given in governance. And if they had settled in Riobamba, he would not injure or cause them harm other than to buy with his money what they might need. The alcalde and the notary replied that regardless of the answer he had given, he was being required to withdraw one league back toward Mocha to set up his camp, from where they could negotiate with each other what would be best. The adelantado did not wish to do disservice to the king, and he ordered Licentiate Caldera,[10] his chief justice, to return with those who had come and to talk with the marshal on his behalf regarding what would suit all of them. And he ordered Luis de Moscoso to do the same and that they should both go together to negotiate it with great prudence and discretion. Not all the Spaniards in either camp were of the same belief or desired the issues to be resolved because some delighted in war and others in peace, and each one wished what he thought would be most advantageous for him. They ate and lived off the poor Indians without rule or reason. When Luis de Moscoso and Licentiate Caldera arrived where Almagro was, they spoke to him for a good while about those things. He always replied that all of that [land] was the governance of his partner Pizarro and that the adelantado should re-
fol. 101 turn to his own governance. And following these and other things, Luis de Moscoso and Licentiate Caldera returned to where they had left the adelantado. Both sides had agreed that the adelantado would stay in some ancient lodgings next to Riobamba, and from there to conclude what would be decided.

Notes

1 15 August 1534; Newson, *Life and Death*, p. 203.

2 See chapter 33.

3 what is left over

4 At the upper end of the Cutuchi River, twenty kilometers north of Latacunga; Newson, *Life and Death*, pp. 138, 208.

5 Mocha is about thirty kilometers north of Riobamba, at a much higher elevation, on the flank of Mt. Chimborazo; Newson, *Life and Death*, p. 204.

6 A notary and secretary who worked under Pedrarias in Panama and Nicaragua. Estete ultimately settled in Trujillo; see Lockhart, *Men of Cajamarca*, p. 265.

7 Picado eventually settled in Lima, where he became one of its first councilmen. He received a substantial encomienda in the Jauja district. He hated the Almagrists, and they him. The day Francisco Pizarro was assassinated, the Almagrists sacked Picado's house. He had hidden in the residence of the treasurer Riquelme, but they found him and executed him. Mendiburu, *Diccionario*, 9:4–6.

8 Chaves was from Extremadura. He remained with Pizarro after Alvarado left Peru. He overheard a dispute between his cousin Nuño de Chaves and a Montenegro regarding a greyhound. In anger Rodrigo stabbed Montenegro and cut off his head. As punishment, Pizarro exiled the cousins to the fledgling city of Lima, thus depriving them of greater opportunities elsewhere. See Busto, *Diccionario*, 1:425–26.

9 Cieza wrote incorrectly Jorge.

10 See chapter 63.

LXXVI

About how Adelantado Don Pedro de Alvarado and Marshal Don Diego de Almagro met, and about the agreement made between them, guided and steered by Licentiate Caldera and other judicious men who came with the adelantado

Following the things that have been described, and after the adelantado took up lodging in the said place, an alcalde of the city of Riobamba went there with Caldera and Moscoso. The marshal always spoke to those who were with him so that if the adelantado tried anything, they would be informed and in good spirits, and he assured them that if things reached such a pass, he had the word of many of [the adelantado's] men that they would cross over to him. It was clear that all of them were willing to die for whatever he commanded. And the adelantado had several thoughts. On the one hand, he believed that it would be disgraceful for him, who was with so many and such important people, to show any regard for Almagro. Instead, he should proceed in spite of him and do what would benefit them. On the other hand, he considered that he was in another's governance, and whatever might happen would be a disservice to the emperor. He also thought that he had spent a large sum of gold pesos in ships and expenses for the fleet and that those who had come with him did the same. Furthermore, if he wanted to go back to the sea to embark on the ships and explore the coast ahead, it would be an interminable task because the ships had returned to the ports of Nicaragua and Tierra Firme. Even if they were on the coast, by returning through the snow they would all end up dying and being lost. Indeed, to march along the highlands until they left the limits of Pizarro's governance seemed to him another and greater hardship, and they would not let him do it.

There were great discussions and meetings about this subject *fol. 101v* among his men. Some insisted on one thing, others on another. On the one hand, those who were younger and hot-blooded, advised him not to wait for an accord with Almagro, that they should descend

on him and seize him and those who were with him, and that he should settle this land by himself and discover the treasure of Quito. On the other hand, countering this, others encouraged him that in spite of Almagro and Pizarro he should go on land, eating whatever he might find without doing any harm until he left Pizarro's governance, which ended in Chincha; from there on he could populate and conquer. But there were many judicious and good men among them, and very honored, and they condemned these statements, telling him that he should not allow any turmoil or any disservice to His Majesty in the new city and in his camp. They spent that night suspicious of each other, being very cautious and without being shrouded by sleepiness, which would impede their watchfulness. But when daytime came, accompanied by several knights, all armed with hidden weapons, the adelantado went to the city of Riobamba to meet with the marshal. When they met, they embraced, and the adelantado delivered a rather long speech. He said that it was well-known in all the kingdoms of the Indies what services he had done for the emperor and with how much loyalty. And although His Majesty had rewarded him for it with the repartimientos that he had given him and the grant that he should govern in his name such a great kingdom as that of Guatemala, it did not seem honest to him or to fulfill his sense of honor to remain idle, but that he should be occupied in new endeavors so that his reputation would grow. And in order to achieve his goal he had secured a new provision from His Majesty to explore by sea. He had decided to go to the discovery of the Tarsis Islands, but he had abandoned it when he learned that there was such a great and rich land in this South Sea, where he expected to discover with his people what lay beyond Pizarro's governance. But events had taken a very different course from what he had hoped. Because God had permitted that he find the land already settled and taken possession of in the name of the Crown of Castile, he was placing himself under [Almagro's] jurisdiction because he did not want or intend to cause disservice to God our Lord or to His Majesty. Almagro replied to the adelantado. He said that no other thing had been presumed about *fol. 102*
him than that he always would do what would be of service to God and the king. And while they were engaged in these discussions, Belalcázar, Vasco de Guevara, Diego de Agüero, Pacheco,[1] Girón, and others who were in Riobamba arrived to kiss [the adelantado's] hands.

He received them very well, treating them with great courtesy, and at the same time those who had come with the adelantado bowed to the marshal, talking to the knights who were with him. Antonio Picado appeared before the adelantado, who pardoned him without showing any displeasure. Felipillo was returned to Almagro, who also did not reprimand or punish him for what he had done.

When the adelantado returned to his camp, there were many discussions and considerations about what would be expedient for them to do. Nothing was concluded, and therefore I will not deal with it, other than in an outline of the business. Licentiate Hernando de Caldera and other judicious men from among those knights who were there took part in it, and it was decided that the adelantado would leave the people and ships in Peru and return to his governance, and [Pizarro and Almagro] would pay the large expenses he had incurred for the fleet. Many were upset about this decision, others rejoiced; they believed that it was better to remain in such a land, and so plentiful, than to return and explore again. They came and went from Riobamba to the camp, and from the camp to Riobamba, until the final conclusion, which was that they would give the adelantado one hundred thousand or one hundred twenty thousand castellanos as recompense for the large amount he had spent on the fleet—to be paid to him where Pizarro was—and the adelantado had to hand over the ships and people without having command or any power over them. With the most loving words possible, the adelantado gave his people to understand that he had made that pact in order not to be of disservice to the king and so that they could remain in such a prosperous land, begging them to regard him well and to go and speak to the marshal. When it became clearly understood, some were distressed, asking whether they were Blacks that they had been sold for money. Diego de Alvarado angrily flung his arms, exclaiming: "What a great disgrace this has been for the Alvarados!"[2] The adelantado tried to appease him, saying, in addition to what he had said, that he would meet with Francisco Pizarro and would make sure that they would be given food and as much respect as they deserved, and that *fol. 102v* they should go and speak to the marshal. Vítores de Alvarado replied: "And I will go see him to get to know him and to have him as lord, but not in fulfillment of your lordship's command."

These and other things happened in Alvarado's camp, but because it was already concluded and sworn, the most principal men went to speak to [Almagro] and to become acquainted with him. And he received them very well, giving great hope that shortly they all would[3] be rich and prosperous in Peru. Then Alvarado and Almagro sent messengers to Don Francisco Pizarro about these events, and we will tell what he did after rebuilding the city of Cuzco.

Notes

1 Perhaps Francisco Pacheco; see chapter 57.

2 Called "El Bueno," he was Pedro de Alvarado's uncle and had participated in the settlement of Guatemala. As did many who went with Almagro to Chile, he later fought with him at the Battle of Salinas. He was captured by the Pizarrists, but was well treated. He became the executor of Almagro's will. He later escaped to Panama, then went to Spain to give account of events in Peru, especially the negative role of Hernando Pizarro. Within days he was dead, some say by poison. His testimony was one of the reasons for Hernando's long imprisonment in La Mota. Busto, *Diccionario,* 1:102–3.

3 will be

LXXVII

About how Soto and Gabriel de Rojas arrived in Cuzco, and how Pizarro left that city and the things that he did until he descended to the plains after abandoning the city of Jauja

After Pizarro divided the great treasure that had been collected in Cuzco,[1] he determined to send messengers to the natives of that region, granting them friendship and favor of the Spaniards, and asking them not to wage any more war or to cause upheavals; indeed, they had always fared badly with them. Hernando de Soto arrived from Vilcas, where he had remained when Almagro departed, as did Gabriel de Rojas, from whom Pizarro had just learned about Don Pedro de Alvarado. He believed it would be useful to descend to the coast, and he did. He took as many Spaniards from the city as he could and named some as vecinos [of Cuzco], which neither would they have become nor would they have the repartimientos that they had if the people whom I say were the most important had remained. He left Juan Pizarro[2] there as lieutenant. Before leaving, he first discussed with the orejones and leaders of the Indians that because of the end and death of Huascar and Atahualpa, the Inca succession went to Manco Inca, son of Huayna Capac, and that they should receive him as such because the emperor would be served by it; indeed, he greatly desired that they should be well treated and not have possession of their dominions wrested from them. They replied that they were content, and according to the ancient custom, Manco was received as Inca, and he took the fringe.[3]

fol. 103 Following this, Pizarro left for Jauja. Because he knew his partner Almagro's route from his letters, he sent him from there powers and provisions to both issue and revoke as he himself would have. He ordered Diego de Agüero,[4] Pedro Román,[5] and Jerónimo Suárez to ride as fast as they could until they reached him. And they were so adroit that they reached him before he had entered San Miguel, and from there they went with him to Quito.

And without tarrying in Jauja, Pizarro left with hopes to establish a Christian town on the coast. He went until he reached the Pachacamac Valley, where there were traces of the large treasure that had been in the temple and that the Indians had hidden, but none appeared. That is how secret some things of these people are. Pizarro ordered six horsemen to go from the Pachacamac Valley along the coast until they could find a proper site for settlement, which would have the necessary components and a safe port of entry for ships that would come and go. These men went looking along the entire coast. Nowhere did they find anything better or a more secure port than that which they call Sangallán.[6] It is between the lovely valleys of Chincha and Nazca, and they call it Cajamarca by another name.

Pizarro learned of it and wanted to go see it and then to found a city. The Indians, who were upset by it, spread false news that the Spaniards who had remained in Jauja were in great difficulty because the highland Indians had them surrounded. So that no harm would come to those who were vecinos of Jauja, Pizarro decided to return to help that city. He ordered the treasurer Riquelme to go to Sangallán and settle a Christian town in that valley. That is what he did; naming alcaldes and councillors, and marking a gallows and a pillar, he took possession of those lands in the name of the emperor. And while this was happening, the governor arrived in Jauja. He found that all were well and quite calm. He took down testimony from the royal officials and other people that it would be expedient to abandon that city and move it to the coastal plains. Those who had Indians in the Yungas were pleased and praised such a plan; those who had them in the highlands, opposed it; everyone looking out only for his own interest. But Pizarro, who strove to do what would serve God and king best, disregarded what either side was saying and ordered them to abandon [the city]. He made a solemn promise that the partition that had been made would stand until they arrived at a better site, where they would again make a settlement of the same city that they were moving.

Almagro's messenger, Diego de Agüero, and those of the adelantado, Moscoso and others, came from Riobamba. When [Pizarro] *fol. 103v*
learned what had happened, he rejoiced and treated the messengers of the adelantado with great honors; not counting the jewels and ornaments that he gave them, he promised to favor them in the land. The pilot, Juan Fernández, was exploring along the coast, and he learned what had been agreed between the adelantado and the marshal. He left the galleon in charge of those who were with him and

came to fall at Pizarro's feet. He received him very well and promised to give him Indians in repartimiento because he was merciful and the civil wars had not arrived yet, which was what made the hearts of the men here as hard as steel. The galleon had arrived at the port of Sangallán. Pizarro sent an order there that it should stop and that possession should be taken of it in his name. Because Don Francisco Pizarro had decided to populate the city that was in the flatlands of Jauja, he sent an order to the treasurer Riquelme that he should not proceed with the new settlement he had made in Sangallán. And now that he need not fear the adelantado anymore, he wanted to settle in the valleys neighboring Pachacamac because the district was both in the highlands and the plains. Thus, when those who were in Sangallán saw the governor's command, they came to Pachacamac, where Pizarro had already arrived with a great desire to find the convenient and necessary site to establish the city.[7]

Notes

1 The treasure was assayed and the royal fifth registered in mid-March 1534; see Cook, "Libros de cargo," pp. 78–80.

2 Juan Pizarro, Francisco's half-brother, was born illegitimate, but was recognized by his father. He often represented Francisco in local administration of Cuzco. He was killed during the uprising of Manco Inca. See Lockhart, *Men of Cajamarca*, pp. 168–75.

3 Manco Inca was treated reasonably well until Francisco Pizarro and the main forces left for the coast. With Juan and Gonzalo Pizarro in charge of Cuzco, the Inca's position quickly worsened, especially when Gonzalo demanded for himself Manco's sister-wife Cura Ocllo. See Hemming, *Conquest*, pp. 178–86.

4 See chapter 33.

5 Román received an encomienda in Cuzco and defended the city during the native uprising. His dislike of Hernando Pizarro led him to join Diego de Almagro when he returned from Chile. He died at the Battle of Salinas. See Lockhart, *Men of Cajamarca*, pp. 420–21.

6 Near or at modern Pisco. The site was abandoned within months, but some later referred to it as Old Lima. A large island, just off the Paracas Peninsula, retains the name Sangallán. See Juan Bromley, *La fundación de la*

Ciudad de los Reyes (Lima: Excelsior, 1935), pp. 31–32; and Stiglich, *Diccionario geográfico*, p. 959.

7 The Lurín and Rímac valleys provided nearer and easier access to the central highlands and especially the city of Jauja; hence, foundation of a coastal capital at Sangallán was aborted.

LXXVIII

How Pizarro was falsely informed that Almagro had agreed to divest him of his governance and life, and how after some notable things occurred, they arrived at Pachacamac, and what else happened until the City of the Kings was founded

I understand that Don Francisco Pizarro was delighted his partner Don Diego de Almagro had succeeded so well in Quito, so Morgovejo de Quiñones[1]—either inventing it himself or gathering it from others who were upset that there should be peace between the two partners—warned him that he should beware and look out for himself because the adelantado and Almagro had come to an agreement to divest him of the governance and even his life, and that the two of them
fol. 104 had made a partnership. Pizarro was disturbed by such talk, although he did not entirely believe it. And what happened was that before the adelantado and the marshal had concluded an agreement in the way that has been said, they say that Alvarado tried to form a partnership with Pizarro and Almagro in which he would not receive any money, but would leave the ships and people with certain stipulations that he asked for, and that for it to hold firm, Almagro would marry his son to [Alvarado's] daughter. It did not come about, nor was it necessary to write about it, other than to enlighten the reader about all this. Almagro was not involved in any of this, replying that so many partners could not have peace, but in this miserable land because of our sins evil men were never lacking, and they had already put him on a bad footing with the other wretched one [Pizarro] so that through their wickedness there inevitably would be what in the end there was.

Alvarado and Almagro were on the way to Jauja, where they thought they would find Pizarro. The marshal believed that because Belalcázar had succeeded in the past, it would be just to leave him the command of lieutenant-captain of that land. Further, because the city of Riobamba was not in a good district, it should be abandoned and established in Quito. Thus, many of those who had come from Guatemala stayed and remained with Belalcázar, and he founded a city in

Quito, about whose foundation I have copiously written in *Part One.*[2] The natives of these villages were worn out from so much service, the [supplying of] food, and the indiscriminate destruction caused by so many groups of Spaniards in their lands. And although they had so many fine and beautiful herds, as we all saw, which fully covered some areas of the fields, there are now so few that there are almost none because Belalcázar imposed little order. So that one could satiate himself with brains, he killed five or six sheep, and so that they could make him pastry with the marrows, another killed just as many. In truth, I have heard some of those who did this boast as if they had done some great deed, and those unfortunates who raised them perished from cold because they lacked wool to make cloth. If I were to say what I know about this and other things, we would never finish the narrative. What concerns God and my soul is to warn those who explore among and deal with these Indians that they should reform and know that just as everything they have taken was and is from the sweat of blood, so we have seen in our days that the worst of the perpetrators have been meted out Almighty God's notable punishments.[3]

The adelantado and the marshal, and the many who were with them, went from Riobamba until they arrived in San Miguel. There *fol. 104v* Almagro ordered Pacheco to go to Puerto Viejo and found a village in the best district so that the Indians would not be mistreated by those who were coming on the ships. I have written about the events regarding this settlement and what happened in the book of foundations; whoever wants to can see it there.[4] A full account of Almagro's largesse during this expedition would be endless because he showed such generosity and liberality that his fame flew in all directions. But he made these grants inflated by vainglory because he did not want to give anything privately. In public and where there were many people, he enjoyed their supplications, and neither did he turn away, nor did they see him dejected. This was mainly the reason why most of the knights who had arrived with the adelantado came to love [Almagro] and became as devoted to him as they were.

From San Miguel they went to the Chimu Valley, stopping first in the Chicama Valley to punish the Indians because they had killed certain Christians who had landed there in a ship. They say that Almagro thought it would be good to found a city in Chimu. He traced its boundaries and ordered Martín de Estete[5] to stay with some Spaniards in that valley.[6] They departed from there, and when they reached Pachacamac, they found Pizarro waiting for them. When he learned that they were approaching, he came out to receive them with many horsemen. When they met, Pizarro and the adelantado and the marshal embraced, and the governor warmly received all the knights who came with them. They went to take up quarters in the lodgings of Pachacamac, where they enjoyed and delighted in being with each other. Almagro and Pizarro discussed everything so that it became clear that what had been said was a lie. The next day they all heard mass together, and shortly after that, in the presence of some captains who were there, the adelantado addressed Pizarro and told him he knew well that because of the information Gabriel de Rojas had brought, [Pizarro] had been aware many days earlier of his coming to this region, and that he was on the way to discover other lands by sea, and that after leaving his governance, he planned to explore the part in the east that had not been discovered. But they had had so many notices of Quito that they had decided to go directly to where they said there were so many treasures because they did not think that they would find any of [Pizarro's] captains there. And after they *fol. 105* had suffered so many hardships and losses of property, they had come to where they found Don Diego de Almagro already settled. In order not to do disservice to the king or to have any dispute with them, he had resolved to come to the agreement that was made. And so that he could depart completely satisfied, it was only necessary that [Pizarro] would give him his word to accept into his company the many important knights who had accompanied him and to honor and favor them because many had left their Indians and estates and spent all they had to come with him. Pizarro joyfully replied, promising to treat them as his own brothers and that shortly each one of them would have repartimientos; they would go in conquests to take them for themselves and to give them to others.

Following this, they ate, and then they went to see the Temple of Pachacamac, so renowned in those plains. There was still a great number of those gold nails driven into the wall to hold the many large [gold] plates that were originally there. They say that a pilot named Quintero asked the governor for the grant of those nails that appeared on the walls, and as a joke, he granted it to him. And he took an abundant quantity of gold in them because they were long and round, and more than four thousand marks of silver.

Before either the adelantado or the marshal arrived, Don Francisco Pizarro had sent Hernando de Soto to Cuzco as his lieutenant. He ordered him to collect the money to pay the one hundred twenty thousand castellanos, even if it were necessary to take it from the dead. And as he wished to send Alvarado quickly on his way, the money was collected and paid to him, giving him many jewels and very valuable stones. Because several of the conquistadors who were with Pizarro had become very wealthy, and they saw a good opportunity to leave the kingdom, they asked the governor permission. They went with the adelantado to the coast, embarked, and left Peru.[7]

Following what the chronicle has related, Don Francisco Pizarro was eager to find a good site to establish the city that had been in Jauja. They had surveyed the Lima Valley several times. After they saw it again, and because they all thought it was a good place, with one of the best ports of the coast, they decided to found the city there. Therefore, Pizarro ordered Juan Tello[8] to distribute the plots in the order that they were designated in the plan. And they say that Juan Tello, who was knowledgeable in this, remarked that this land would be another Italy and in trade a second Venice because with such a *fol. 105v*
quantity of gold and silver it was impossible for it to be otherwise. After the town was laid out, Pizarro returned to Pachacamac, where he and Almagro had time to discuss private matters regarding their property and brotherhood, and wishing to have the greatest accord, they formed a new partnership with firm guarantees and oaths. After this happened, these two partners were totally at peace[9] and full of affection because God had not yet begun to punish them. Pizarro told Almagro to go to Cuzco with the provisions he had ordered drawn, to engage in whatever he believed was convenient regarding the[10] city. And, if he wanted to, because he had such great equipment for it, he should go to explore what they call Chiriguano,[11] which is in the eastern part. Or, he should choose a person to send and the necessary cost be split between the two of them. Almagro set out with most of those who had come from Guatemala. All of them were striving to win his favor because in truth, although Pizarro had the title of governor, which he was, Almagro revoked and named and commanded

according to his will. When he left, Pizarro remained engaged in the foundation of the new City of the Kings, which took place in the year fifteen hundred and thirty-four.[12]

And because this subject is described in *Part One,*[13] I will go on, leaving at this point the events that had happened in Peru from its discovery until the present time, and I will deal with the arrival in Spain of Hernando Pizarro in order to return to the principal subject. I will be in all as brief as I have promised, saying only what occurred, to the letter, and without including any falsehood.

Notes

1 See chapter 52.

2 Chapter 40.

3 Throughout his work, Cieza shows concern for the protection of the Amerindian and preservation of natural resources. It seems he was not alone. The first town council of Lima, worried that the vecinos were depleting the trees in the valley (especially the fruit trees of the natives) because they needed wood for building houses, ordered the residents to stop, and those with land were required to replant. See Bertram T. Lee and Juan Bromley, eds., *Libros de cabildos de Lima,* 23 vols. (Lima, 1935–), 1:18, 57.

4 *Part One,* chapter 51. According to Cieza's dating, Captain Francisco Pacheco laid out Puerto Viejo from the existing Indian village of Piquaza on 12 March 1535.

5 Cieza incorrectly wrote Miguel.

6 Almagro thus set in motion in December 1534 the settlement that became Trujillo, but it was Francisco Pizarro who finally established the city around 3 February 1535.

7 This is another early group of peruleros, or rich returnees.

8 Captain Juan Tello de Sotomayor was from Seville. With Nicolás de Ribera the Elder, he became the first alcalde of Lima. Although he supported Almagro at the Battle of Salinas, Pizarro sent him (1539) to found the city of León de Huánuco. During the civil wars he remained loyal to the Crown. After 1561 he held the encomienda of Chinchaycocha, previously held by the treasurer Riquelme. See Mendiburu, *Diccionario,* 10:288–90; and José de la Puente Brunke, *Encomienda y encomenderos en el Perú* (Seville: Diputación Provincial, 1992), p. 397.

9 agreement

10 new

11 The Chiriguano, a Tupi-speaking people, lived in the eastern lowlands of today's Bolivia. They were fierce warriors and resisted both Inca and Spanish penetration. See Steward and Faron, *Native Peoples,* pp. 114, 289.

12 The City of the Kings, or Lima, was actually founded on 18 January 1535.

13 Chapter 71.

LXXIX

About how Hernando Pizarro arrived in Spain, where great news about Peru was spreading because of how much wealth was coming from there, and what Hernando Pizarro did[1] at court

After Hernando Pizarro and those who went with him arrived at Tierra Firme, carrying so much silver and gold that the ships were ballasted with these metals, he left from Nombre de Dios and several
fol. 106 days later arrived in Spain. He entered Seville with all the treasure.[2]
This news excited all of Spain because it rang throughout that the House of Trade was filled with golden vessels and jars and other praiseworthy pieces, and of great weight. There was talk of nothing but Peru, and many were stirring to go there. A courier was sent immediately to the emperor regarding these matters. He learned the news in Calatayud, near Zaragoza, in the kingdom of Aragon because he had gone to have the Cortes in Monzón. The news about Peru had reached His Majesty before then, via Nicaragua, but now substantially more was known. He ordered Hernando Pizarro to come to Toledo, where His Majesty saw many of those large and opulent pieces that they brought him as his fifth. He inquired about the matters of that land, its nature and characteristics, and how its inhabitants and natives lived, if [the Christians] were impressing upon them the faith and many other things. Hernando Pizarro answered all this with great judgment and prudence. [His Majesty] ordered the steward to lodge him in the city, saying that he had been well served by his brother, Francisco Pizarro, and by Almagro, and that he would always grant them favors.

They say that while at court Hernando Pizarro tried in any way he could to destroy Almagro's reputation, concealing his services. But when Cristóbal de Mena arrived, he reported the opposite of that, giving Almagro's letters to the emperor and the gentlemen of the Council. But they still relate that Hernando Pizarro persisted in his design, wishing that they would not give any governance to Almagro. But because the emperor is a most Christian prince, and in those times it was believed that the Indies were well governed by governors, he granted Almagro the government of two hundred leagues of the coast beyond what Pizarro governed because he had exerted himself so much in order that Peru be discovered. Hernando Pizarro was informed of His Majesty's decision. It is well known that in order to secure what Almagro had promised if he brought him the governance, [Hernando Pizarro] immediately presented the petition, describing the services that the said Don Diego de Almagro had performed. And the provision was dispatched, with Cristóbal de Mena[3] and Juan de Sosa[4] continually providing good reports about Almagro. They carried Almagro's power, which would not revoke that of Hernando Pizarro, but if he did not want to make use of it, then they in [Almagro's] name would ask for the grants.

A new grant was bestowed on Francisco Pizarro, increasing his governance another seventy leagues along the coast following the meridian so that Almagro's governance, which was named the prov- *fol. 106v*
ince[5] of New Toledo, would be counted from there. The emperor settled with Hernando Pizarro in Almagro's name the terms that are usually settled on other governors. The officials of the Royal Treasury of this province were named: Turuegano as inspector; Manuel de Espinar as treasurer; Juan de Guzmán as accountant; and Almagro was given the title of adelantado.

Because so many things were told about Peru, and Spain had become so excited with the treasures that had come, in order to travel there many sold their property, with which they could have lived as their fathers had done, and they died most miserably in Nombre de Dios and at sea and in the wars that came later, so that only a few have returned of the many who went. Eager for gold and silver, officials left their occupations, and many their wives. Not without reason is it said that greed is the root of all evil. Because many left behind their young and beautiful wives, I remember hearing a song when I was in Cordova while still a boy, which said, among other things: "Those of you who might be going to Peru, beware of horns."[6]

Notes

1 happened to

2 Hernando left Cajamarca on 12 June 1533 and reached Seville on 9 January 1534; Hemming, *Conquest*, pp. 72–73, 88–89.

3 See chapter 32. Mena reached Seville just before Hernando Pizarro, on 5 December 1533; Hemming, *Conquest*, p. 88.

4 Sosa, a priest, was born in Seville and came to the Indies in 1528. His activities are unclear until he appears in San Miguel in 1532 as a vicar. He received a share at Cajamarca, even though he was in San Miguel during Atahualpa's capture. After he came to Spain, he wanted to return to the Indies to head an expedition. As a priest, he could not do it openly, but he was the moving force behind the failed expedition to Veragua in 1536. Sosa then went to Peru again. He supported Gonzalo Pizarro's rebellion, for which he was punished by the bishop of Cuzco, who suspended him from priesthood for two years and exiled him. Sosa went back to Spain. Lockhart, *Men of Cajamarca*, pp. 465–68.

5 the governance.

6 That is, beware of being cuckolded.

LXXX

About how His Majesty granted Hernando Pizarro the Order of Santiago, and how he departed from court and embarked for the Indies

Following the things that have been related, and while Captain Hernando Pizarro was still at the court of the emperor, His Majesty bestowed on him the knighthood of Santiago[1] and other grants, and he prepared to return to Peru. He had a large household and retinue, as one who deserved it and had brought so much. He negotiated with the emperor that he would procure in the kingdom of Peru a donation, not counting the fifth, of a large subsidy to aid in the[2] wars and the necessities of His Majesty. The court had moved to Valladolid, from where Hernando Pizarro departed for his homeland in the city of Trujillo in Extremadura, carrying very advantageous letters that the emperor gave him for his brother, Don Francisco Pizarro, and the Adelantado Don Diego de Almagro. Many knights enlisted with Hernando Pizarro, all the very youngest, to come with him to these parts. Some had incomes and pastureland, others estates *fol. 107* and good positions. They all gathered in Seville, where they were equipped with what they needed for the journey. Among those who came from Spain to this kingdom with Hernando Pizarro were Illán Suárez de Carvajal,[3] who was coming as the king's agent; Licentiate Benito Suárez de Carvajal, his brother; Baltazar de Gaete and Melchor de Cervantes, a brother of Baltazar de Gaete;[4] Pedro de Hinojosa; Gonzalo de Tapia; Juan Bravo; Gonzalo de Olmos; Captain Don Pedro Portocarrero; Juan Ortiz de Zárate; Pedro Suárez; Diego de Silva; Francisco de Chaves; and others whose names I cannot remember.[5] They embarked at the port of Sanlúcar de Barrameda. They navigated at sea, and from the Golfo de las Yeguas they sailed with such a great storm that they thought they would perish, and they ended up at the port of Gibraltar. There they embarked again and went through another storm and were forced to land once more somewhere, but I am not certain of the place. After they had endured many dangers at sea, they arrived at the port of Nombre de Dios. Many people had come there from all over to travel to Peru, which was the reason why when Hernando Pizarro arrived, there was as great a food shortage as has ever been seen here. They were becoming ill from hunger in that land, and they were dying because more always die in those towns than in other parts due to the extreme sultriness and heat there. They gave a silk jacket for a hen—and for other lesser items, velvet coats, breeches, and doublets as splendid as can be imagined. Those who were there as well as those who came with Hernando Pizarro died from illnesses.

Here Hernando Pizarro learned what had happened in Peru after he had left and about the expedition of Adelantado Don Pedro de Alvarado and about the agreement that he made with the governor, his brother. He yearned to be in that land. He left Panama as quickly as he could, and they sailed until they arrived in the land of Peru. Hernando Pizarro ordered Gonzalo de Olmos to remain in Puerto Viejo.[6] Governor Francisco Pizarro sent him a provision that made him lieutenant and captain of those provinces, regardless that Francisco Pacheco had made the foundation when Almagro ordered him to go there from San Miguel.

Hernando Pizarro marched on land with some of the knights who were coming with him, longing to be in the City of the Kings. And because many great events occurred in the kingdom before Hernando Pizarro arrived there, we will leave him in order to extensively describe them.[7]

Notes

1 The Order of Santiago, founded in the twelfth century, is perhaps the most famous of the Spanish military orders that include Calatrava and Alcántara.

2 great

3 In 1544 Illán Suárez de Carvajal was stabbed to death in Lima by the enraged Viceroy Blasco Núñez Vela in the upheaval leading up to the Gonzalo Pizarro revolt. Cieza describes the event in *Part Four: Quito,* chapter 58.

4 In the margin of the manuscript it is noted: "learn the Christian names."

5 Many of those who went to Peru with Hernando Pizarro played important roles in the coming civil wars.

6 With the Indian uprising Olmos was called to the defense of Lima, and he took with him some men and about seventy horses; Hemming, *Conquest*, p. 209.
7 Cieza wrote in the margin: "This chapter about Hernando Pizarro has to go where there is another sign like this O" (see the end of chapter 87). Regardless of this directive we have left the chapter in its original place. The change would have created confusion in the chronology of events.

LXXXI

How Almagro set out from Pachacamac for Cuzco, from where Pizarro left a few days later to found Trujillo in the Chimu Valley

fol. 107v I have related in the previous chapters that it was decided that Don Diego de Almagro would go from Pachacamac to Cuzco to do what has been told in its place. Most of the people he was bringing went through the highlands. With those that he chose, he himself went through the plains, pleased to see the buildings that were in most of the valleys. A few days after he had departed, Francisco Pizarro left to found a city in the Chimu Valley. While going through the Huaura Valley,[1] he encountered a knight named Téllez de Guzmán,[2] who was coming from the island of Hispaniola. He was sent by the president and the justices of the Chancellery Court, which resides in the city of Santo Domingo, with provisions they issued when they learned that Adelantado Alvarado was coming to Peru with his people and a fleet so that there would not be any upheaval or dispute between him and Pizarro and Almagro. They ordered that Alvarado should immediately leave the boundaries of Pizarro's governance or face grave penalties, a provision seen as very proper. To thank [Téllez de Guzmán] for his coming, Pizarro offered him hope of a handsome reward. He also met in the same valley Captain Ochoa de Ribas, who came from New Spain. He commanded him to go to the City of the Kings, where he promised him an Indian repartimiento.

Pizarro then arrived in the Chimu Valley and made the foundation of the city that they called Trujillo.[3] I have written about this foundation in the part quoted by me in other sections of this chronicle. He designated Estete, whom Almagro had left there with the vecinos chosen to remain with repartimientos, as his lieutenant and captain.[4] And while Don Francisco Pizarro was engaged in this foundation, a young man called Cazalla arrived, proclaiming that Almagro was governor of Chincha and beyond, and that he had the decrees to show it. But he brought only a simple copy, which had not been attested by a notary, of the agreement that the emperor ordered to be made with

Hernando Pizarro. Immediately, there was commotion among those who heard it; some were pleased, others distressed, and without waiting to hear more, Diego de Agüero[5] left in great haste to give such news to Almagro, expecting rich rewards for taking it to him.

Almagro was marching through the plains until he began ascending into the highlands, eager to be in Cuzco. Diego de Agüero reached him by the Abancay bridge,[6] where he joyfully told him why he had come and congratulated him, calling him the best and richest adelantado and captain-general in Peru. Almagro thanked him for coming. [Agüero] proclaimed that he was pleased that no one would enter the land that [Almagro] and his partner had won with such hardship. Moreover, he would now be as much a governor as Pizarro and more; *fol. 108* indeed, he commanded what he wanted. They affirm that [Agüero's] reward for all this hypocrisy was worth more than seven thousand castellanos.

When Almagro arrived in Cuzco, Soto, who was lieutenant, Juan Pizarro, Gonzalo Pizarro, and all the vecinos and honorable men of the city came out to receive him. In the meantime, Pizarro was staying in the new city of Trujillo. Because there were many public and secret discussions regarding what was said about Almagro being governor of Chincha and beyond, Antonio Picado, Licentiate Caldera, and others advised [Pizarro] to order that these provisions be shown to him. He should examine them and look out for himself and his honor because if it were true that Almagro governed from Chincha and beyond, it would be better to give it all to him than to come out short and be ruined. Having heard these things, he summoned that young man Cazalla to show him the decrees that he claimed he was bringing for Don Diego de Almagro. He showed what he was carrying, which was the simple copy of the agreement. Pizarro returned it to him without any reaction. But [Cazalla], who had been cast by the demon to kindle the cruel fire that followed, departed, saying that he did not want to show Pizarro everything that he was carrying. And this is what he wrote to Cuzco to Don Diego de Almagro, who became so inflated with pride when he learned this news that regardless that he possessed such extensive provisions and powers from the governor, sufficient to govern the city of Cuzco, he refused to use them because he believed that it would be demeaning for him to hold an inferior office in a land where he regarded himself as superior. He waited for days for the emperor's decrees so that he would be by virtue of them governor of Chincha and beyond, as has been said. His friends, who were many and very important, inflated his head with pride. They held the Pizarros so low already that even mangroves seemed too good for them to govern. They tried to win Almagro's favor in every way, and from then on there were two factions: one bound to the Pizarros and another to the Almagros. It was the root of all the evil that the demon tried to plant there, God permitting it because of the great sins of men.

On the other hand, those who were friends of Don Francisco Pizarro in Trujillo, where he was, were admonishing him to suspend forthwith and expeditiously the extensive and ample power he had given Don Diego de Almagro and revoke it so that he could not use it. If [Almagro] were in command of Cuzco and some decrees came to him, even if they were insufficient, he would then secure for himself possession of the best and most important of the kingdom, although it was [Pizarro] who had won it and suffered such hardships and risk *fol. 108v* to his life. They suggested this and other things to Governor Pizarro. And as much friendship and brotherhood of many years as existed between him and Almagro, self-interest severed these, greed clouded his mind, and ambition to rule and distribute acted against what would have been more lasting if they were in poverty and want, not having come upon such a wealthy land as the two of them did—so uneducated that they did not know the letters of the alphabet as such—but there was only envy, deceit, and other unjust ways. And to his advantage, Almagro decided not to use the provisions and powers that Pizarro had so that no harm came to him when they advised [Pizarro] to revoke and annul them.

Notes

1 On the coast a little more than one hundred kilometers north of Lima; the meeting probably took place where the modern city of Huacho is located.

2 Antonio Téllez de Guzmán. Cieza wrote Tello de Guzmán, though in later chapters he corrected himself.

3 February 1535.

4 Also called Martín de Astete. He was a notary as well as a secretary to

Pedrarias. He had first settled in Panama, then Nicaragua, and finally Trujillo. He was dead before 1539 because by then Francisco de Chaves was married to Estete's widow, María de Escobar. Porras Barrenechea, *Cartas del Perú*, pp. 300–301.

5 See chapter 33.

6 An Inca suspension bridge.

LXXXII

About how Don Francisco Pizarro sent Verdugo to Cuzco with powers for his brother Juan Pizarro to have the lieutenancy of the city, and about the discussions that took place there, and what else happened

When Governor Pizarro made this decision, he immediately wrote letters to his brother Juan Pizarro, a respected man who, according to what they say, was the flower of all these Pizarros. He informed him about what has been announced regarding a governance coming for Almagro. And although he lacked official notice, it would be of service to the king and his honor that Don Diego de Almagro did not have command of Cuzco or did anything other than recruit people for the exploration of Chiriguano. Therefore, in virtue of the new provision and power that he was sending him, [Juan Pizarro] should take office as his lieutenant of that city and be in charge of it until he otherwise decreed. He wrote to the city council what was necessary regarding the business. And he wrote to the marshal—with pretense and deceit in order to keep him from knowing the reason for that step—that he should not be alarmed because he was doing it for certain just reasons and principally because he believed that [Almagro] would be more involved in the business of the expedition to Chiriguano than in what concerned Cuzco. Melchor Verdugo[1] departed with the dispatch of all this. Pizarro ordered him to ride swiftly until he reached Cuzco. The news Cazalla was proclaiming with his unofficial decrees had already arrived there, but nobody saw what it was except that [people] believed they were looking at the royal seal and the authentic decrees so that Almagro could forthwith, as governor, act as he pleased.

Verdugo sped on his way. Juan Pizarro understood well what his brother had commanded. He had the vecinos on his side, but not all of them: Almagro had the rest and all those who planned to go
fol. 109 to Chiriguano, who were many. There were long discussions among all of them regarding what would be best to do, which some said and others thought. Soto was lieutenant; he was leaning somewhat

toward Almagro's side because of self-interest, and he was waiting to see the decrees. The acceptance of either one or the other was not dealt with. Juan Pizarro and Gonzalo Pizarro were most resentful of Almagro because they disliked him, and they demonstrated it on this occasion. Almagro's friends coaxed him, telling him to look out for himself; the king had made him lord, so he should truly be one, and he should immediately send for those decrees that were coming and take possession of what the king had designated as his governance. Vasco de Guevara and several horsemen left Cuzco in order to meet that young man who was bringing [the decrees]. It spread throughout the city that Vasco de Guevara had left. The Pizarros proclaimed that [the Almagrists] were going to kill the governor, and they wanted to go out in order to stop Vasco de Guevara. They spoke with Soto, who was lieutenant, because in the dispatch that Verdugo had brought, the governor ordered that if Almagro did not use the office then [Soto] should stay on [as lieutenant], but if Almagro did have it, then neither one of them but Juan Pizarro, his brother, should have it. Soto replied to those who spoke with him that they should not be alarmed because Vasco de Guevara was not going for the reason that they thought. Juan Pizarro was proud, and he was envious that Almagro would be governor of what [the Pizarros] said that they had won and conquered. He recruited people, enlisting friends of his brother and reassuring them of his friendship. He exaggerated the harm that Almagro was causing him by wanting to take away the governance from him, and that [Almagro] was going to have him killed and other things. Those who were pleased to hear such things joined him.

Hernando de Soto learned about it. He became angry at [the Pizarros] for stirring up trouble in this way. He went to their lodgings, and with moderation and exquisite courtesy he admonished them to calm down and not give way to any evil. They answered Hernando with arrogance and contempt, saying that he was Almagro's friend and that he was clearly demonstrating his affection for him. Soto held his staff[2] in his hand, and they their weapons without ceasing to speak angrily so that, furious, he left them and went to Almagro's lodgings. He requested assistance from him because although he was the chief justice in that city, they had denigrated and even threatened him. When Almagro heard that, he said it was just an imprudence of youth, but he ordered many knights who were his allies to assist the king's justice with all their forces. With that reinforcement, Soto returned to enjoin Juan Pizarro to stay in his house and not leave the city because they say that he wanted to go after Vasco de Guevara. But yielding even less to Soto than before, he replied with more rudeness and pride, appearing resolved to achieve what he wanted. One *fol. 109v* word led to another, and they came to arms, with Soto invoking assistance for justice and the other the friendship of his brother. They went out to the plaza, boiling with anger, thrusting lances at each other, and certainly if it had lasted, the evil would have increased. But fearing that Almagro might come out to assist Soto, Juan Pizarro and Gonzalo Pizarro with their defenders did not go on, nor did Soto himself allow it in order to prevent turmoil, although he still felt offended by those who had been so insolent. They again enjoined Juan Pizarro and his brother and others not to leave their lodgings, which [Soto] ordered to become their prisons, and he barricaded the marshal in his. All of them were so frenzied and full of envy of each other that it was a wonder they did not all kill each other. It has been affirmed that these were the first passions in this land between the Almagros and the Pizarros or brought about on their behalf.

Notes

1 Verdugo was born around 1514 in Avila and came to Panama around 1529. He was one of the youngest recipients of shares at Cajamarca. He settled in Trujillo with a large encomienda, and Pizarro made him permanent councilman. During the civil wars, he led a group of royalists from Trujillo to Nicaragua, then the Caribbean, where they sacked Nombre de Dios—then held by Pizarrists. Verdugo died in Trujillo in 1567. See Lockhart, *Men of Cajamarca,* pp. 250–55; and Busto, *Hueste perulera,* pp. 63–138.

2 A symbol of his office as chief justice.

LXXXIII

About how Don Francisco Pizarro returned to the City of the Kings, then left to go to the city of Cuzco when he learned of the things that were happening there

Pizarro yearned for his brother to come back from Spain. He spent the time that he was in Trujillo populating that city and trying to bring the local Indians to peace. He sent a provision that made him captain and lieutenant-general to Belalcázar, who was in Quito, and to Puerto Viejo and other parts he sent appropriate orders. He returned to the City of the Kings, where he was well received. He wished to have news from Cuzco. Francisco Martín de Alcántara arrived from Panama, where he had gone, and he brought with him Don Diego, Almagro's son.[1] One Andrés Enamorado had left Cuzco at the time of the strife that has already been written about, in order to inform Pizarro about it. When he arrived in the City of the Kings, he exaggerated the reason for his coming and stated that [Pizarro's] brothers were in great danger because Soto and Almagro had such dispute with them that they were lancing each other. Pizarro was distressed by this news. He complained about Almagro without knowing the truth and declared to those who were listening that it was because of him that the turmoil had erupted. He summoned some of his friends to go quickly to Cuzco. He took with him Licentiate Caldera and Antonio Picado, his secretary. He left Ochoa de Ribas as lieutenant in *fol. 110* the City of the Kings.

In the previous chapter I also told how Vasco de Guevara had left Cuzco on Almagro's orders to get the decrees that I had said were coming in the power of that young man who was bringing them. After having gone more than twenty leagues, [Guevara][2] came upon him and took him to Don Diego de Almagro, who was furious when he saw no more than an unofficial paper because it had been proclaimed everywhere that the decrees of governor were already on their way to him. But he continued telling his friends that the real ones could not be far behind; after all, that one was copied from it word for word. Juan Pizarro and his brother's followers were happy, ridiculing Almagro because he had believed so easily what others told him. And they said that they believed that Hernando was the bird who would bring what benefitted the governor because he knew and understood it.

Also, after Don Francisco Pizarro departed[3] from the City of the Kings, he marched on the way to Cuzco, where, when Almagro had learned that Andrés Enamorado had left, he ordered Luis de Moscoso to go out and meet [Pizzaro][4] and tell him what had happened in that city, truthfully without any additions. But before he arrived, [Pizarro] had already learned the news from a friar, which calmed some of his agitation. When he arrived in what they call Huaytara, he met Moscoso and the others who came, and he received them well. Regarding what they told him, he said he was pleased that most of what Andrés Enamorado had said turned out to be a lie. At the site of the lodgings of Vilcas he received a letter written by a great friend of Juan Pizarro named Pedro Alonso Carrasco,[5] vecino of the city. They say that in one of its sections he told [Pizarro] that unless he arrived in Cuzco quickly, he would not find his brothers and friends alive. This letter caused some uneasiness, and he told Moscoso and the friar that they had not told him the truth. They replied with some anger that it was rather those who had written the letter. It was decided that Luis de Moscoso himself and Antonio Picado would go ahead to the city and collect true testimony about the situation. And when they arrived, they learned that there was no more than what Moscoso had related and that the other were designs of restless men wishing for discord between the two partners in order to augment their own repartimientos. Pizarro learned what I say from his secretary, Picado, and from Moscoso. He proceeded on the way, and in Abancay he found two of his retainers, named Alonso de Mesa[6] and Pedro Pizarro.[7] They said that they had written letters about what Almagro had done in Cuzco, *fol. 110v* and if necessary, they would confirm it. Pizarro did not pay attention to any more talk; instead, he marched until he reached the valley of Jaquijahuana. There, going a little further, he found[8] Luis de Moscoso and Picado, who were waiting for him because the information they had given him was by letters. He also found here Diego Gavilán,[9] who had gone to Cuzco before all this to find out how things were going with all of them and with the others who had come.

The governor went on until he reached the city,[10] without permitting it to be known that he was so close.[11] This was the reason why they did not come out to receive him—except for Toro,[12] Juan Ronquillo,[13] and Cermeño[14] who learned of it. He alighted in the church to say a prayer. Almagro learned of his arrival. He went to where[15] he was when he alighted, and they embraced, shedding plenty of tears. If they had been wandering through mangroves and were not in Cuzco, I would declare that they stemmed from affection and love. They say that Pizarro told him: "You forced me to come on these roads, dying without a bed or a tent, or food other than cooked maize. Where was your judgment that without regarding what is at stake, you were the cause of picking quarrels with my brothers, whom I had commanded to respect you as they would me?" And Almagro answered that he did not need to come with such haste because he had sent him a report about what had happened. And regarding the rest, it was time he learned the truth of all of it and that his brothers had treated him badly because they could not conceal that it bothered and irritated them that the king made him governor.

After these and other discussions, Captain Hernando de Soto and many Guatemalan knights and vecinos arrived[16] to kiss [Pizarro's] hands, and all were well received by him. And when he settled into his lodgings, he strongly reprimanded his brothers for what they had done. They excused themselves, saying that Almagro already acted as if he were governor of Cuzco and was planning to divide the provinces among his friends and not among those who had toiled for it, and that they did what was fitting for his honor and service.

Manco Inca Yupanqui, who had rightfully become Inca, joyfully came to see and embrace Pizarro, who was pleased with him, as with the other lords and chiefs who came to see him. Téllez de Guzmán had brought the decree that I have mentioned earlier, dispatched from the Royal Chancellery. And when he learned what had happened in Cuzco, he came with the intention to enjoin the governor and the marshal with it so that there would not be any turmoil. And thus he carried it out, declaring it and taking it in testimony. Licentiate Caldera had come with the governor, and he always provided good advice and means to prevent discord or disservice to the emperor. He *fol. 111*
spoke secretly with Pizarro, telling him to accommodate Almagro because he could see how generally beloved he was and knew that the flower of the knights who had come with Alvarado were on [Alma-

gro's] side, and he told him other things. Pizarro knew that he was giving him good counsel and decided to act on it. He had named as his lieutenant-general and chief justice this Licentiate Caldera, who also spoke with Almagro. He told him he should look at the burden he was to Don Francisco Pizarro and that it was hardly worth it to become enemies because he would be as much a governor as the other and more; indeed, he was governing, and in all the towns there were even councilmen named by him, and he spent money as if it were only his. Caldera said other things so that after he and Doctor Loaysa[17] intervened, they reconciled and created friendship among all of them, and in public they were very friendly and in secret as God knows.

Notes

1 Known as Almagro the Younger, he was born in Panama in 1522. His mother, Ana Martínez, was a Panamanian Indian. Although very young, he participated in many actions, including the march to Chile. After his father's execution in 1538, he wanted to be named governor of New Toledo, as stipulated in both the Crown grant and his father's will. A group of malcontents quickly formed around him. They assassinated Francisco Pizarro in June 1541 and proclaimed the younger Almagro, who was not directly involved, governor. Royalist forces under Cristóbal Vaca de Castro defeated the Almagrists at the Battle of Chupas, near Huamanga, on 16 September 1542. Almagro the Younger was captured and executed in Cuzco, then buried alongside his father in the Mercedarian church. Busto, *Diccionario,* 1:59–61.

2 he reached him

3 left

4 the governor

5 Carrasco was born in Zorita around 1509, came to Peru with Pizarro in 1530, and remained in San Miguel. He was in Cuzco when it became a Spanish city and went with Soto in pursuit of Quizquiz. He fought in the siege of Cuzco and was one of the horsemen to attack the fortress of Sacsahuaman. He held an encomienda in Cuzco and died in 1571; see Busto, *Diccionario,* 1:78–80.

6 Mesa was born in Toledo about 1515 and was recruited by Pizarro in 1529. After Cajamarca, he settled in Cuzco. He remained loyal to the Crown during the civil wars and by 1552 was an alcalde and one of the richest men in Cuzco. He had numerous mestizo children by various women in his house-

hold, but finally married Doña Catalina Huaco Ocllo. See Lockhart, *Men of Cajamarca*, pp. 227–30.

7 Pedro was born in Toledo about 1515. He was a page and a relative of Francisco Pizarro. Although he remained at San Miguel, he entered Cuzco with Pizarro and received a share of treasure. He defended Cuzco during the native siege. After Francisco's assassination, he was captured by the Almagrists, but escaped and fought with Vaca de Castro at Chupas. Pedro supported Gonzalo Pizarro, but in the end joined Pedro de la Gasca's royal force. Gasca let him retain part of his encomiendas, and he settled in Arequipa. Viceroy Toledo asked Pedro to write down his recollections. He completed the "Relación del descubrimiento y conquista de los Reinos del Perú" in 1571, but it was not published until 1844. Pedro Pizarro died in 1587. See Raúl Porras Barrenechea, *Los cronistas del Perú (1528–1650) y otros ensayos*, ed. Franklin Pease G. Y. (Lima: Banco de Crédito del Perú, 1986), pp. 134–45; and Guillermo Lohmann Villena, ed., *Relación del descubrimiento y conquista del Perú* (Lima: Pontificia Universidad Católica del Perú, 1978).

8 met

9 Born in Guadalcanal, Gavilán came to Peru with Soto and received a share at Cajamarca. He was involved in mercantile activities in Lima. In 1539 he was forced to move to Huamanga where his encomienda was located and became active in economic and political affairs in the city. By 1550 he was also married. He died around 1569; see Lockhart, *Men of Cajamarca*, pp. 296–97.

10 in Cuzco

11 the city

12 Alonso de Toro; see chapter 36.

13 See chapter 62.

14 Pedro Cermeño was born in Sanlúcar de Barrameda and came to Peru in 1530. He defended Cuzco during the native uprising in 1536 and was later very active in the rebellion of Gonzalo Pizarro. He probably died at the Battle of Añaquito in 1546. See Busto, *Diccionario*, 1:381–82.

15 to the church

16 came

17 Diego de Loaysa.

LXXXIV

About how the governors reached a new accord, making a solemn oath to proceed with the partnership

After the events that have been related occurred in the city of Cuzco, Pizarro and Almagro thought that because they had reached a new accord and enjoyed peace and affection, they should share the host, the holy body of God, between the two and make an oath presided by a vested priest with strong bonds and guarantees that they would never break it. And when it was decided, it was done at once. And because it is a notable thing—this oath and that God fulfilled it as they asked Him, with great harm and destruction of those who swore to it—I will put it here to the letter, without removing or adding a single one. Copied from the original, it says:

> We, Don Francisco Pizarro, adelantado, captain-general, governor by His Majesty of these kingdoms of New Castile, and Don Diego de Almagro, likewise governor by His Majesty of the province of [New] Toledo, say that because of the intimate friendship and partnership that has remained between us with so much affection, and God Our Lord wishing it thus, it was motive and cause that the emperor and king, our lord, has received notable services with the conquest, subjugation, and settlement of these provinces and lands, attracting such a mass of infidels to the conversion and knowledge of our Holy Catholic Faith, and His Sacred Majesty trusting that during our friendship and partnership his royal patrimony will increase. Thus, for having this purpose, as well as for past services, His Catholic Majesty was gracious to grant me, the said Don Francisco Pizarro, the governance of these new kingdoms and
> *fol. 111v* to me, the said Don Diego de Almagro, the governance of the province of [New] Toledo. From these grants that we have received by his royal munificence, a new obligation results, that our lives and patrimonies, and of those who will follow us in his royal service, will perpetually be spent and consumed. And so that this will have a more certain and a better effect and His Majesty's confidence in us does not fail, and renouncing the law that applies regarding such oaths, we promise and swear in the presence of God our Lord, in whose worship we are, to

keep and fulfill duly and completely without deception or any other understanding what is expressed and contained in the following chapters. And we supplicate to His infinite goodness that whichever one of us should act contrary to what is here agreed, He should permit with the full rigor of justice the perdition of his soul, a ruinous death and end of his life, and the destruction and loss of his soul and reputation, honor and estate, because as a breaker of his oath, which we give to each other, and not fearing His presence, he should receive such just vengeance from Him. And we, each one of us, swear and promise the following:

First, that our friendship and partnership is to be conserved and maintained from here on with the same love and willingness that has existed between us until the present day, not changing or breaking it for any self-interest, greed, or ambition of whatever honors or offices, but that it will be shared between us in a brotherly way and that we will be partners in all the benefits that God Our Lord might wish to grant us.

Moreover, we say, under the weight of the oath and promise we are making, that neither one of us will slander or attempt anything that can result in or cause harm and injury to the honor, life, and estate of the other, or be the cause of it directly or indirectly, he himself or through another person, tacitly or by causing it expressly or permitting it; instead, he will procure every good and honor and will strive to arrive at it and acquire it and avoid all the losses and harm that could arise by not informing the other party.

Morever, we swear to maintain, keep, and fulfill what is agreed between us, to which we refer, and neither one of us will act in any way, cause, or manner in the contrary or will break it, or will endeavor, protest, or make any reclamation, and that if he makes any, he would withdraw and desist from it and renounce it according to the said oath.

Likewise, we swear that together, both of us—and not one without the other— will inform and write to His Majesty regarding the issues *fol. 112*
that according to our judgment are most expedient for his royal service, supplicating him and informing him about everything with which his Catholic conscience most can be relieved and these provinces and kingdoms most and best can be conserved and governed. And that there will not be a private report by either of us, fraudulently and deceitfully made and with the intent to harm and injure the other by acquiring for himself, delaying service to our Lord God and to His Majesty and

breaking our friendship and partnership. And likewise he will not permit it to be made, said, or communicated by another person, he will neither permit it nor consent to it, but everything will be done openly between both so that His Majesty might better understand the zeal we have to serve him because he has shown so much trust in our friendship and partnership.

Item, we swear that all the profits and interests that might accrue to us — those that I, Don Francisco Pizarro, might have and acquire in this governance through whatever means and reasons, as well as the others that I, Don Diego de Almagro, might have in the conquest and discovery that I make in the name and by the command of His Majesty — we will openly bring them without distinction to be reckoned in the manner that the partnership we have made in this case remains, with no fraud, cunning, or any deceit in it. And the expenses that both of us or either one of us might have should be moderate and discreet, according to the need that might arise, avoiding the excessive and superfluous, and aiding and providing as necessary. All of which, according to the said rules, it is therefore our will to keep and fulfill according to the oath that we have made, and placing God our Lord as judge and His glorious mother, Saint Mary, with all the saints as witnesses.

And so that what we thus swear and promise is well-known to all, we sign it with our names — being present as witnesses Licentiate Hernando de Caldera, by the lord governor general deputy of the governor in these kingdoms, and Francisco Pineda, chaplain of his lordship, and Antonio Picado, his secretary, and Antonio Téllez de Guzmán, and Doctor Diego de Loaysa. The said oath was made in the city of Cuzco, in the house of the said Lord Governor Don Diego de Almagro, and present saying mass, Father Bartolomé de Segovia, cleric. And after saying the Lord's Prayer, the said governors placed their right hands on the consecrated hand, on the twelfth of June of fifteen hundred and thirty-five years: Francisco Pizarro, Adelantado Don Diego de Almagro, Licentiate Caldera, Antonio Téllez de Guzmán, and I, Antonio Picado, *fol. 112v* clerk of His Majesty and his public notary in all his kingdoms and dominions, was present to see the said oath made by the said governors in one with the said witnesses, and I wrote it according to what passed before me, and therefore I made here this our sign to this in testimony of truth. Antonio Picado, notary of His Majesty.

This that you have seen was the oath made in Cuzco. Consider it carefully and note what they asked for because you will find it fulfilled during the course of this work—to such a degree that it is shocking and something to fear to make such an oath because with it they tempt God Almighty,[1] who does not permit condemnation of their souls as they had also asked for.

To all this I have to say that when the Indians saw the great power of the Spaniards—knowing from experience that they did not fare well in taking arms against them and being vexed by the many who had died in the past wars—they had settled and negotiated peace, but with a mix of pretense and a wish to see them divided and in such a way that they could avenge the great harm they had received. And having this design and knowing [the Spaniards'] great greed[2] and their excessive avarice, they proclaimed great things about Chiriguano, affirming that there was so much gold and silver, that of Cuzco was nothing in comparison. The Spaniards believed it and planned to stuff their pockets in that land. Captains Rodrigo Orgoños[3] and Hernando de Soto strove to go as generals in the discovery. Each one proclaimed that Almagro had promised him the expedition because he did not plan to go personally, but to send the people and to wait to receive the decrees that he already knew Hernando Pizarro was bringing him.

Because the Indians, who wanted to see them gone from Cuzco, were saying such great things, and because of the dispute between those captains, which was so serious that they nearly challenged each other, [Almagro] decided, in order to keep them from fighting, to go himself,[4] and that is what he announced. Soto was upset, but he neither let it be known nor wanted to go with him. [Almagro] promised Orgoños to make him his general.

Notes

1 and He comes to allow

2 of the Spaniards

3 For his early career, see chapter 47. He became a steadfast Almagro supporter and leader of his forces. Orgoños fought bravely at the Battle of Salinas, but was wounded, captured, and executed by the Pizarrists. See Hemming, *Conquest*, pp. 228–33, 579n.

4 Almagro

LXXXV

About how Almagro spent a large sum of gold and silver on those who were to go, and how he departed from Cuzco

When it was proclaimed and those who were in Cuzco learned that Almagro was going personally on the expedition, they were over-*fol. 113* joyed. And they say that in order that they could equip themselves with horses, arms, and other things necessary for an expedition, he ordered more than 180 cargas of silver and gold removed from his lodgings. He distributed more than twenty to all of them, and those that he wanted made promissory notes to repay it with what they would get in the land that they were going to. He decided to send his secretary, Juan de Espinosa, to Spain; Pizarro was content with that. And when he distributed the gold and silver, he told [Pizarro] that he should order one hundred thousand castellanos from his purse be given to negotiate certain issues of marriages he was discussing with the cardinal of Sigüenza and to purchase rents for his son. Pizarro replied that he was satisfied, and thus Juan de Herrada, Almagro's majordomo, and Juan Alonso de Badajoz, his steward, and the secretary, Juan de Espinosa, left Cuzco to go to the City of the Kings, where the governor wrote to Pedro de Villareal, his steward, to give the said amount. And this done, Adelantado Don Diego de Almagro hurried the departure.

There was among Huayna Capac's sons one whom they called Paullu.[1] Almagro wanted to take him and Villac Umu, their high priest,[2] with him so that the Indians would serve and fear them. And they also say that after [Paullu and Villac Umu] first made a pact with Manco Inca to rebel against the Christians, they would try to kill them when they were in the provinces of Collasuyu or another suitable region. And that [Manco Inca] would mobilize the villages of Condesuyu, Antisuyu, and Chinchasuyu in order to kill those who were remaining in Cuzco and in the other parts of his great realm.[3]

For the expenses of the expedition, there was a founding of metals in Cuzco, which was very large because there was so much gold and silver in the city that soon they took it for granted. They say that while Almagro was in the foundry, one Juan de Lepe asked him for

19. Lake Titicaca. Pedro de Cieza de León's *Primera Parte* (Seville, 1553), p. 117v. Courtesy of the Jay I. Kislak Foundation, Miami Lakes, Florida.

one of the many rings that were in a huge load, saying that he wanted it for his daughter, and that he generously replied that he should take as many as he could grasp with his hands. And knowing that [Lepe] was married, he ordered 400 pesos be given to him so that he could return with it to his wife. They also told me that when one Bartolomé Pérez, who had been warden of the Santo Domingo jail, gave him a leather shield,[4] he ordered that 400 pesos and one silver vessel that weighed 40 marks, with handles of two lion mouths made of gold that weighed[5] 340 pesos, be given to him for it. And before that, they told me that Montenegro presented him with the first cat seen in this land and that he ordered 600 pesos of gold to be given to him. They relate many other of his generous acts, which were always made in

public because he enjoyed such boasting and vainglory, something
fol. 113v that Pizarro never did. Everything that he gave, even though it was more than is being affirmed about Almagro, he gave secretly so that his attendants neither knew about it nor pursued it.

And when Almagro was ready to leave Cuzco, he ordered Captain Rui Díaz[6] and Captain Benavides[7] to go to the City of the Kings to recruit followers. And he left his general, Rodrigo Orgoños, in Cuzco in order to march and join him later with those who came for the expedition and in case there were more in Cuzco after he had left. And because already many were eager to be out of the city, he ordered Captain Juan de Saavedra to set out and march as far as the land of Collao, and halt there and await him and those who were not going then. Most of them went well provided with beautiful Indian women and yanaconas for their service, so that it is distressing to consider how dearly these discoveries cost and how many natives of Peru died in them, when their lives were more important than what [the Spaniards] were attempting to discover. Although I also say, that without abundant service or the many horses that we explored with in the North Sea,[8] in no way, form, or manner could any expedition have been undertaken. And even with this good fortune, there were burials of Spaniards. Indeed, what they have endured is astonishing and amazing, and men have never before experienced such or were as courageous.

Paullu, the Inca, set out with his retinue and wives to go on the expedition, and Villac Umu did the same, having made the pact with Manco Inca, which has been written about. When Juan de Saavedra left Cuzco, the natives from the villages that they passed through served them and provisioned them very well, giving them all they needed and carrying their baggage on their backs from one place to another. And because men-at-arms can never be restrained, many of the soldiers exploited the Indians, taking from them by force whatever they wanted. Because it was in the beginnings, [the Indians] did not learn how to denounce it, nor did they do more than be patient.[9]

Before Almagro departed from Cuzco, he told Pizarro that he was aware his brothers were upset because the king had made him governor. From this, he deduced that they would try to create discord between them, blinded by the envy they felt. Therefore, he believed that [Pizarro] should send them to Spain and give them from their estates whatever amount of money they wanted because he would be satisfied and take this chance in order to always have peace. Pizarro replied that he should not believe such a thing about his brothers because they all loved him and felt paternal affection for him and other things that concluded the discussion. And after all the people had already left *fol. 114* Cuzco, Almagro did the same, accompanied by the governor and his brothers and many of the vecinos of the city who, in order to honor him, wanted to go part of the way with him. After he said farewell to all of them, he did not stop until Mohina,[10] where he halted for five days, sufficient time for all of them to join together. From there he set out, well served by the Indians who were coming from all parts to the great highway to see him and provision him with whatever was needed. The Indians were so good to the Spaniards, which was the reason that five of them went ahead in one direction and three in another, without waiting for the captains. In the Canches, Canas, and Collas[11] Almagro encountered many remarkable buildings of the Incas, which pleased him very much. And marching daily, he joined Captain Juan de Saavedra.

Bringing large and very opulent gifts, the chiefs of the province of Paria[12] came to see him. He joyfully received them, honoring them with courteous words. He asked them to relate to him clearly and openly what there was in the land of Chile because in Cuzco he had been informed that so much gold and silver was there that the houses were covered with it. They dashed his hopes, stating that those were unfounded sayings and that there was no such grandeur in Chile; rather, they promptly took the gold they were paying as tribute to the Incas, in small ingots or pure in grains, and delivered it to their treasurers or chief majordomos. Furthermore, they said that the roads were very difficult—in parts dry without water, in others filled with snowdrifts and other oddities that he would see if he proceeded with the expedition. The statements of these lords were very bothersome and vexing to the adelantado as well as to those who were with him. To refute and contradict it they said that [the lords] were tricksters and liars, and that they were doing it so that our people would stay away from their lands. And thus, without asking them more, [Almagro] ordered that it would be best if they accompanied them for a few days and that afterward they could return to their lands.

It was decided that until they reached Tupiza,[13] the Spaniards and horses would go out in bands because there was not much water, and thus it was done. The three Christians who went ahead, enjoying the gifts of the Indians, had already arrived in Tupiza; they were followed by the other five. Wherever the Spaniards passed through, the natives came to despise them; they saw them as harsh and false people who commit great sins. They secretly proclaimed that they were their capital enemies and that they were in their lands without justice or reason, *fol. 114v* taking from them their women and property. But because they traveled with so many horses, crossbows, and swords, they did not show this enmity openly. Wherever the five Christians went, they grabbed spoils. [The Indians] were planning to kill them and make a solemn sacrifice to their gods with them, and they informed each other about carrying out this deed. And when they were in the province of Jujuy,[14] they attacked them and killed three. And the two were so brave that when they fled from their midst, swiftly escaping death, they ended up among other Indians who, fearing the adelantado who was near, did not kill them. Instead, they advised them to go to Tupiza, where they joined the Christians, who received them grimly because they had gone ahead without orders.

Notes

1 Paullu was a half-brother of Manco Inca and just a few months younger. He at first supported Manco's role as puppet ruler. See Hemming, *Conquest*, pp. 174, 283.

2 See chapter 49.

3 Thus, the four sections (not provinces as Cieza calls them) of the Inca realm, or Tawantinsuyu, would rise against the invaders.

4 *Adarga*, an oval or heart-shaped leather shield.

5 thirty

6 See chapter 58.

7 See chapter 63.

8 The Atlantic Ocean.

9 Here, Cieza makes a reference to the subsequent laws passed to protect the Amerindians, who quickly learned to use the Spanish courts to protest abuses. See Steve Stern, *Peru's Indian Peoples and the Challenge of Spanish Conquest: Huamanga to 1640* (Madison: University of Wisconsin Press, 1982).

10 In the province of Quispicanche; see Noble David Cook, ed., *Tasa de la visita general de Francisco de Toledo* (Lima: San Marcos, 1975), pp. xxxix, 131–32.

11 Still within the district of Cuzco.

12 On the north shore of the salt Lake Poopó.

13 In southern Bolivia, about one hundred kilometers north of the modern border of Argentina.

14 In modern Argentina, some forty kilometers north of Salta. From Tupiza to Jujuy the Spaniards were on the edge of the Chiriguano frontier. From here they changed direction, taking an almost due west course and beginning a trek across high Andean passes.

LXXXVI

About how Pizarro left Cuzco to return to the City of the Kings

When the adelantado left for the Chiriguano expedition the governor decided to return to the City of the Kings to be in the center of the realm and engage in what most benefitted the service of God and the emperor, and the conversion and good treatment of the natives. He distributed some provinces among individuals whom he chose, giving them letters of appointment or encomiendas. I believe his brother Juan Pizarro remained as lieutenant; he exhorted him to treat the Indians well. He said farewell to all, as well as to Manco Inca and the most important lords who were in Cuzco. When he left, he traveled until he arrived near the City of the Kings, where the councilmen and vecinos joyfully came out to receive him, and among them two brothers, Don Alonso Enríquez[1] and Don Luis,[2] quite duplicitous and deceitful.

He found in the city the bishop of Tierra Firme, Don Friar Tomás de Berlanga,[3] who had come with the king's commission to divide the limits of the governances between [Pizarro] and Almagro. At this time, Pizarro made some particular secret and public grants: he ordered that Don Luis be given two thousand pesos of silver, valued at such a small price that in Spain they were worth more than five; and to his brother, Don Alonso, he gave another two thousand and consented that he draw lots at very excessive prices for some jewels that he had. They did not appreciate it and let everyone know, and Pizarro believed them to be inconstant and false. A friar from La
fol. 115 Trinidad asked him for alms to marry some sisters, and he ordered his steward, Pedro de Villareal, to give him one thousand pesos. They say that he gave plenty of money to Licentiate Caldera, Doctor Loaysa, and Téllez de Guzmán.

The Indians of all the regions, from the plains as well as from the highlands, served them well. There were few friars and no bishop, which was the reason there was little progress in what was most important—the conversion of these peoples. And if there were any friars, they were just as avaricious as the seculars, surreptitiously trying to stuff their purses. The Spaniards who were in the land in those days were served a great deal. [The Indians] carried them in litters or hammocks. Pizarro prohibited trade with unmarked gold or silver so that the king would not lose his fifth. Alonso de Alvarado came from Trujillo to the City of the Kings; he was well received by Pizarro, and because there were great reports about the Chachapoyas and the other lands that lie much more to the east, he gave him a commission to undertake that conquest, naming him as his captain. With that, he returned to the new city of Trujillo.

Notes

1 Don Alonso Enríquez de Guzmán, an illegitimate son of a family closely related to the kings of Spain, was the prototype of the picaro. Born in Seville in 1501, he was constantly in trouble with authorities—dueling, drinking, and gambling. He fought in Italy and Ibiza, and served at court. He came to Peru with Hernando Pizarro, but shifted to Almagro on his return from Chile. He was in charge of the city of Cuzco during the Battle of Salinas and paid five thousand pesos to Hernando Pizarro to avoid execution. In 1538 the king ordered his imprisonment, and he was sent to Spain. Powerful friends intervened, and he was ultimately absolved. He went on to fight in Germany and continued to be active at court until his death around 1549. He wrote an account of his deeds; approximately one-fourth of the *Libro de la vida y hechos de don Alonso Enríquez de Guzmán el caballero noble desbaratado* deals with events in the Indies. See Porras Barrenechea, *Los cronistas,* pp. 153–56.

2 Don Luis Enríquez de Guzmán came to Peru with his brother and several servants; they arrived in Lima in August 1535. See Porras Barrenechea, *Los cronistas,* p. 155.

3 Bishop Berlanga arrived in Lima in July 1535 and returned to Panama the following February. See Hemming, *Conquest,* p. 572n.

LXXXVII

About how Belalcázar moved the city of Riobamba to Quito, and about what happened in that land

Before I deal with the matters of Adelantado Almagro, it seems to me useful to write something about what was happening in the northern regions. And I will do that briefly from here on so that it is no more than a digression because if I were to write minutely about the events that happened, the perils and the expeditions and discoveries that were made, this history would never be finished.

Almagro left Belalcázar in charge, and many of those who had come from Guatemala and Tierra Firme remained with him. Within a few days Pizarro confirmed the power, sending him the provisions with one Tapia. [Belalcázar] believed that the city was not prospering in Riobamba. Under an official decree that he issued, he moved it to Quito, naming it San Francisco de Quito.[1] The choice of this foundation had been made by Almagro, about which I have written in *Part One*,[2] the reason that I will not reiterate it here.

They went out in various expeditions to get their hands on the lords who had rebelled. They attacked ridgetops and secured many drywalls. They entered among the flock of sheep in such disarray that with their disorder they reduced the great multitude of them to nothing. Juan de Ampudia, native of Jerez,[3] went out one day on Be-
fol. 115v lalcázar's orders. He learned where Zope-Zopahua was, and he sent messengers to him from among his relatives, admonishing him not to die in defeat, or allow the Spaniards to capture him in battle, but instead to come on his own in friendship. He replied that he wished to do that, but he feared their cruelty because they rarely kept their word. Ampudia answered that it would not be like that, nor would any harm or injury come to him. Zope-Zopahua feared that they would press him for the gold of Quito because it was clear that the Christians sought or strove for no other thing than that and silver. But he could not be safe anywhere because the natives themselves were already traitors to each other. They did not maintain either friendship or kinship, nor did they want more than to be sustained with the support of our people. He could not decide what he should do. Am-

pudia learned the exact place where he was. Three or four horsemen went at night, who sufficed to bring him, some say by force; others relate that he came to them freely. Quingalumba and other captains of the Incas came out peacefully, and with that [Ampudia] returned to Quito, bringing plenty of livestock[4] for provisions.

Rumiñavi was roving around in order to flee from the Christians. They had ousted him from many strongholds and ridgetops, and he strove to incite revolt by using his authority. It was useless because all the natives were weary and exhausted from great hardships, and those who had escaped the wars wanted to live peacefully and in tranquility. It was not long before someone informed Belalcázar where [Rumiñavi] was. Certain horsemen went out with the guide. They went through such roundabout places that they came upon him, and with him there were a little more than thirty men and many women with loads of his baggage. And when they unexpectedly attacked, some fled, and the lord, dejected, hid in a small hut. The guide learned of it and informed a Christian named Valle, who seized him, but he did not change his expression or lose his seriousness.[5]

With these captures ended the upheavals of war, which always would have existed if he had not been seized.

Afterwards, Belalcázar treated them with such cruelty, subjecting them to great tortures because they would not tell him about the gold that they had removed from Quito. They were so immutable in keeping the secret that they deprived him of the ecstasy that he expected. And although they had no other fault, he had them executed, allowing it to be harsh and very inhumane.[6]

At this time Captain Tapia[7] left the area of Chinto by Belalcázar's *fol. 116* order to explore the northern region. Thirty horsemen and thirty footmen went with him. He went through Cotocallao, Aguayla, and Charanzaque, and he crossed to Carangue, Coangue, Mira, Tuza, Guaca, and other villages, exploring until he reached the Angasmayo River, from where he returned to Quito, remembering the names of the villages that he had discovered.[8] In Tuza the Indians attacked him, but it was neither fierce nor dangerous. In Latacunga a Spaniard named Luis Daza seized an Indian, who it became at once known was a foreigner. They asked him which was his native land. He replied that he came from a large province named Cundinamarca,[9] subject to a very powerful lord who in past years was engaged in great wars and battles with a nation that they called the Chicas,[10] so brave that they put the aforementioned lord in great difficulty and created the need to seek support. He had sent him and others to Atahualpa because he was such a great lord—to beg him for aid to fight against those enemies. But because of the war with his brother Huascar, he did not send what he promised he would do when that conflict ended, and he ordered him and another one to stay in his camps until they could return with what they wished. And, doing that they went until they reached Cajamarca, where of all his companions he alone had escaped and had come with Rumiñavi to that region. They asked him many questions about his land. He told them such things and so positively that unbelievably according to him everything abounded in gold, and the rivers carried a great quantity of this metal. The things that this Indian said, although they turned out to be untrue, spread the search in all directions for what they call El Dorado, which has cost many of our people so dearly. Belalcázar ordered Pedro de Añasco[11] to go with forty horsemen and as many footmen with that Indian, who said that his land was ten or twelve days march away, and those who were to go were chosen. When they heard what he said, they looked for hoes, crowbars, and some pickaxes to get the gold that they believed to be in the rivers.

They went through Guayllabamba and marched among the villages of the Quillacingas. They went through fearful dense forests and found nothing of what they expected. After a few days, Captain Juan de Ampudia with a number of Spaniards left Quito on orders of
fol. 116v Belalcázar himself to follow Añasco, carrying license to explore. And he went until he joined the said Captain Añasco and took the people under his charge.

Belalcázar left to settle Guayaquil, trying to make peace with those of that coast, and in the place that seemed appropriate he founded a town where he left one of the alcaldes as captain. The Christians were so vexing to the Indians, pressuring them for gold and beautiful women, that they rose up and killed most of them. Those who escaped went with great risk to Quito where Captain Juan Díaz Hidalgo was lieutenant.[13] Afterwards they suffered some perils in that province until Captain Zaera populated it by Pizarro's commission, as I have written in *Part One.*[13]

Notes

1 Founded on 6 December 1534.

2 Chapter 40.

3 Jerez de la Frontera. On Ampudia see chapter 63.

4 Camelidae.

5 In a service report of 1555, Miguel de la Chica claims he was the one who captured Rumiñavi. Riding ahead of the main party led by Alonso del Valle, he wrote that he "emerged through a short cut that led to a lake. When I reached the lake, the lord Rumiñavi was beside a hillock, leaning against a tree. I recognized him by the insignia he was wearing. I closed with him and after struggling for a very long time, I captured him." See Hemming, *Conquest*, pp. 167–68, 569–70n.

6 Both Rumiñavi and Zope-Zopahua were burned on the square of Quito. Hemming, *Conquest*, pp. 167–68; see also chapter 90.

7 Diego de Tapia. The expeditionary force left Quito in February 1535. See Hemming, *Conquest*, p. 168; and Newson, *Life and Death*, p. 174.

8 Most of the villages mentioned are located in the Otavalo district of northern highland Ecuador. See Newson, *Life and Death*, p. 158.

9 Cundinamarca, or roughly the district of present Bogota, Colombia.

10 Probably the Chibchas, as is clear from the text that follows.

11 See chapter 63.

12 Juan Díaz Hidalgo later became a town councilman and received land grants in the Quito basin. See Newson, *Life and Death*, pp. 174, 181.

13 In the margin is written "Here should enter the chapter about Hernando Pizarro which has this sign O" (see chapter 80).

LXXXVIII

About how wanting to make a founding in the City of the Kings, they waited until Hernando Pizarro arrived, and how the bishop of Tierra Firme and others who were rich left from the port

They relate that at this time an enormous treasure had been collected in the City of the Kings. Because there was plenty in the provinces and the native lords did not have an assessment of what they were to contribute, [the Spaniards] tried to squeeze them so that they were left with nothing but the skin on their backs. The governor had ordered a founding so that the royal fifth would not diminish. Hernando Pizarro learned this news and was rushing in order to be present. He wrote to his brother and sent it with a courier to delay the founding until they came. It was done, and with the knights who were accompanying him, Hernando arrived near the city, and they were very well received by the governor as well as by all the vecinos and most of the Spaniards who were in the city. Before then, Friar Miguel de Orenes,[1] commander of Our Lady of Mercy, had arrived, and after he asked for a site, he founded the present monastery of this order. And the bishop of Tierra Firme was negotiating with the city council to retrace the city in a way that the plaza would lie more in the center because if the church were to be large, it would not have enough space.

fol. 117 It was neither concluded, nor could it be finished. And considering that this province is so rich and the greatest treasures ever seen in the world were found here, those who first entered it took little care in adorning the temples, which should have been established in gold and silver and have such services and ornaments that would be renowned everywhere. For an example they only needed to look at the Indians, who as idolaters had theirs[2] so opulent and filled with vessels of gold, silver, and precious stones as those who saw them know, and they worshipped nothing other than their gods and demons. Yet taking the sacrament and preaching the gospel was being done in houses of straw. And, if anything was done in this city, it was later when Don

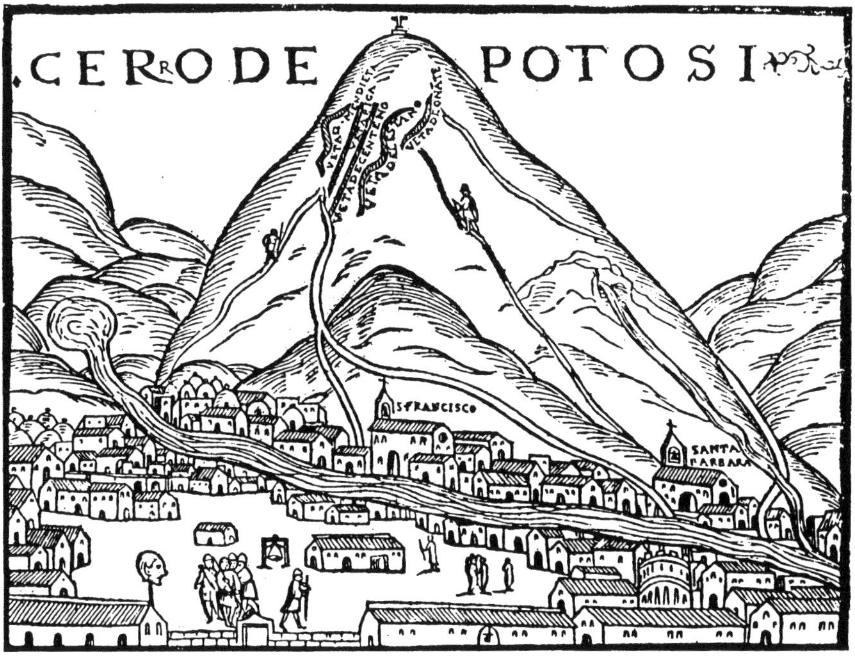

20. Potosí. Pedro de Cieza de León's *Primera Parte* (Seville, 1553), p. 122v. Courtesy of the Jay I. Kislak Foundation, Miami Lakes, Florida.

Jerónimo de Loaysa was bishop.[3] The Indians carefully observe this, and they see that what[4] is done is the opposite of everything that [the Christians] preach to them when they deal with their conversion. And perhaps for this and other things that I will set down later, God Almighty has permitted the punishments that he meted out with his arm of justice, which when fully considered is enough to be frightening. I note this because so many towers and rooftop terraces are built for the residences of those who inhabit them that it would be right for them to remember that everything they possess was given to them by God and that it would be beneficial to embellish His temples and to act in such a manner that the Indians do not say what they have said about it.

After spending several days in the City of the Kings, the bishop of Tierra Firme decided to return to his bishopric. But first he announced that the men of that land were very cunning and false; he observed that when they were apart they slandered and maligned each other, and when together they exceedingly flattered each other and with great pretense. There were some who because they were quite wealthy asked the governor for permission to go to Spain. Among them were Captain Hernando de Soto, Téllez de Guzmán,[5] Don Luis,[6] Doctor Loaysa,[7] and after he gave most of them a large amount of gold and silver, Pizarro ordered that they all be provided with what they needed. He wanted to make a certain donation of these metals to the bishop, but he did not want to receive or take it, except for one box of silver spoons that could have been worth a little more than two marks. Pizarro begged him that although he did not wish to receive anything from him, he should take on his behalf six hundred castellanos for the hospital of Panama and four hundred *fol. 117v* for that of Nicaragua. [Pizarro] and most of the vecinos accompanied him as far as the sea.

Juan de Herrada and Benavides were in the city recruiting people. They—that is, Juan de Herrada—were to take with them Almagro's son.[8] Pizarro hurried their departure so that they could reach the adelantado before he would be too far inland. Returning to deal with Hernando Pizarro, the governor was delighted when he came, and they privately spoke about what he had done in Spain and how His Majesty had received him and how he could not avoid bringing the governance to Don Diego de Almagro, but for [Francisco Pizarro] the emperor had added seventy leagues of the coast beyond the two hundred that he had in governance, which consequently included Cuzco and the best of the provinces.

Alonso de Alvarado left Trujillo on the way to Chachapoyas—accompanied by Alonso de Chávez, Francisco de Fuentes,[9] Juan Sánchez,[10] Agustín Díaz, Juan Pérez Casas, Diego Díaz, and others, who altogether were thirteen. They arrived at Cochabamba,[11] where they were well received by the natives, who came from the entire region to see them. Alvarado did not allow any harm or aggravation done to them. He told the caciques and lords that he came because he had reports about them and of what lay ahead, and to let them know that he would shortly return with many Christians and would inform all of them of our sacred religion, because to be saved they should not worship the Sun or stone statues, but God Almighty, universal Creator of heaven, earth, the sea, and everything else. The Indians were astonished to hear these things. They heard them eagerly and said that they would be pleased to be Christians and to receive baptismal water. They and their wives gathered in the plaza, and they did a dance arranged according to their custom. They came adorned with pieces of gold and silver, and they made a mound with all of it and gave it to Alvarado. Seeing such goodwill, he told the Spaniards who came with him to remain in that land until he returned with more people to settle and divide it. They were pleased about it. After he spoke extensively with the lords, took information from them about the land ahead, and encouraged their friendship with the Spaniards, he returned to Trujillo. From there he did not halt until he reached the sea in order to inform the governor, who was very content that he would settle a city of Christians in that district. He agreed that [Alvarado] could keep the gold and silver they had given him to aid the expedition.

This Alonso de Alvarado is a native of Burgos, of genteel presence and great authority, and he was very distinguished in this kingdom because he took part in all the important enterprises, always in the *fol. 118* service of the emperor. And in the time ahead, after the war of Chupas had ended, he granted him the title of marshal and the knighthood of Santiago, as the story will say.[12] Because he had great hope of making a vast fortune in the province of Chachapoyas, he said farewell to Pizarro and went to Trujillo, where he tried to get people and horses to return there.

Notes

1 Orenes was present at the foundation of San Miguel, and some suggest the city was named after him. The Mercedarians were the first order to establish a monastery in Lima slightly before the Dominicans, in 1535. See Fernando Armas Medina, *Cristianización del Perú (1532–1600)* (Seville: Escuela de Estudios Hispano-americanos, 1953), pp. 29–31; and Robert D. Wood, *"Teach Them Good Customs": Colonial Indian Education and Acculturation in the Andes* (Culver City, Calif.: Labyrinthos, 1986).

2 their temples

3 Jerónimo de Loaysa professed as a Dominican in Cordova and continued his studies in Valladolid. His brother was archbishop of Seville, president of the Council of the Indies, and confessor of Charles V. Jerónimo worked in the missions in Cartagena de Indias, then returned to Spain. In 1537 he be-

came bishop of Cartegena. Later, Charles V named him bishop of Lima, and he reached his post in 1543. In January 1545 Pope Paul III raised the see to metropolitan and made Loaysa its first archbishop. He died in 1575. See Mendiburu, *Diccionario,* 7:38–66; and Armas Medina, *Cristianización del Perú,* pp. 212–13.

4 everything

5 Antonio Téllez de Guzmán.

6 Don Luis Enríquez de Guzmán.

7 Diego de Loaysa.

8 Juan de Herrada became his guardian after Diego de Almagro was executed.

9 See chapter 32.

10 This could be the "obscure" Juan Sánchez who was at Cajamarca, but the name is too common; see Lockhart, *Men of Cajamarca,* p. 444.

11 Stiglich mentions thirty-five places named Cochabamba. The likely spot may be in the district of Chota, or it could have been Levanto, near modern Chachapoyas. Stiglich, *Diccionario geográfico,* pp. 252–53.

12 Alonso de Alvarado, born in 1508 in Secadura de Trasmiera, was Pedro de Alvarado's nephew. Unlike most who came from Guatemala, he became a Pizarrist. After Pizarro's assassination he joined Vaca de Castro and fought at the Battle of Chupas (1542). He then returned to Spain. He settled in Burgos, married, and received various rewards, including the title of marshal of Peru. In 1546 he accompanied Pedro de la Gasca to Peru as camp master. After the Battle of Jaquijahuana (1548), he sentenced Gonzalo Pizarro and other rebels to death. Gasca generously rewarded him, though he lost his encomienda of Chachapoyas. In 1553 he went to La Plata and Potosí as captain-general and chief justice to put down the rebellion of Sebastián de Castilla. In 1554, he met Francisco Hernández Girón's rebel forces at Chuquinga, but was defeated. Following a deep depression, he died in Lima in 1555. Busto, *Diccionario,* 1:93–101.

LXXXIX

About how Alonso de Alvarado left Trujillo to settle a city in Chachapoyas

Alonso de Alvarado stayed in Trujillo only a few days, then left with the horsemen and footmen he was able to collect for the settlement and conquest that he was planning. He went without stopping until he arrived in Cochabamba, where he had left the Christians, as I said in the previous chapter. He ordered that all who had joined him should come out in public because he wanted to see how the footmen were armed. They appeared with bucklers and swords or crossbows, short coats, and strong padding, useful for the war here, and the horsemen with their lances and morions[1] and other armor made of cotton. He placed one Luis Valera in charge of the crossbowmen. When the Indians saw him return with so many people, and knowing that above all the Spaniards are oppressive, most of them were distressed that what he had said turned out to be true. He reassured them as much as he could and left Cochabamba for the east, where later the town was settled as we will tell.

He learned how the inhabitants of faraway and distant regions had become upset with those who were from the lands he was in because they had supported [the Spaniards]. And these from the east implored him to give them some support to go out against their enemies, who came to plunder their fields and plots, and who were natives of a land they called Longuita[2] and Jumbilla.[3] Alvarado was pleased to do it and ordered Ruy Barba de Coronado[4] to go with some Spaniards to aid the Indians, their allies, who had already gathered, placed in readiness with their arms. They went until they arrived at a stronghold named Quita, where they stayed for a few days. Those coming in war *fol. 118v* learned of their presence in the fort; they attacked them. The Christians came out with the horses, which frightened them so much that they fled. Our men pursued them until they were caught in great difficulties. Because it was summer, the grass was dry and very tall, and [the Indians] set fire to it and surrounded them. It was windy. The fire was so dreadful that they thought they would perish. They could not extinguish it or escape it. The enemies laughed that with this help they planned to kill them. Ruy Barba and another one named Pedro Ruiz went out with their horses on a summit, but not so easily because the horse of Pedro Ruiz rolled down in full view of the Indians and Christians. Ruy Barba commended himself to God and attacked them[5] with full force. Then came his [Indian] friends, who shot many darts and arrows at [their enemies] and pressed them so much that they made them run away. The fire had been already taken care of so that those who were in it came out without danger.

Alvarado learned of this incident; he departed with those who had remained with him until they entered in the district of Longuita, where he tried to negotiate peace with the natives, admonishing them to conclude it with him. Realizing that they would benefit by it, they accepted. After he secured that land, he left to another province named Charrasmal, which is to the east, and he took many of his allies to help him. When he arrived there, he set up camp on a plain of the tableland, near another region named Gomorá. Bellicose people lived there, regarded among [the Indians] as very brave. They not only refused to conclude peace with the Spaniards, but even ridiculed those who had done it. Arrogantly boasting and demonstrating great fierceness, they believed that the horses and Christians were already in their power. The captain, not wishing to spill blood, sent messengers to them to come and see him, promising not to harm any of them. His endeavor failed, which was the reason why he immediately ordered Juan Pérez de Guevara to depart with twenty Spaniards to[6] attack those who refused peace. They were warned by the very Indians who were with the Christians and who advised them not to wait for those who were sent against them because they were furious. They feared the enterprise, and because they realized that they were close to the sword's edge, they abandoned their own houses and with great cowardice fled from only twenty Christians who came against them. Not finding any Indians although they diligently searched for
fol. 119 them, they returned to inform the captain. He departed at once for a village called Charrasmal, where the natives came out in peace, rejoicing to have an alliance with the Spaniards.

After a few days, Alvarado explored as much as he could of those eastern territories, passing through a cold paramo. Below it was a small place where he learned that inland there were large and very populous towns that had made a league to wage war against him. When Alvarado heard this, he tried first to gently persuade them to surrender to the Spaniards. Therefore, he immediately sent messengers and set out with the Spaniards until he arrived in the village of Cocoso,[7] from which the inhabitants had fled in fear of the horses. Alvarado learned about it; he ordered[8] three Spaniards to assault them on a road and try to seize as many Indians as they could to be guides. They kept watch during the night, but were unable to capture any, so they returned to the camp.

That land is very populated, and the Incas always kept a garrison there because the people are spirited. When they saw that the Spaniards were there against their wishes and were making themselves absolute lords of everything, as if it were theirs by inheritance, they roared with anger. Furious, they assembled to attack them, armed according to their custom, disparaging the promised peace. They were confident because of the multitude of them and the small number of Christians, and because the highway [the Spaniards] were taking passed through slopes and high mountains and some deep valleys. They set up guards everywhere in order to attack when they were near. Alvarado was informed about all of this. He marched in good order. He learned that the road led to where the Indians had positioned themselves in a very high mountain in order to dominate the heights. When he arrived at the foot of the mountain, he ordered[9] Pedro de Samaniego to take the western side of the mountain with thirty Spaniards, and Juan Pérez de Guevara the other side with another thirty. He distributed in other parts the allied friends, who numbered more than three thousand and whose principal captain was named Gueymaquemulos,[10] to attack the enemy. The horsemen proceeded on the royal highway; Varela[11] with certain crossbowmen went in the vanguard. The enemy learned about the division of the Spaniards. One of their captains, named Yngocometa,[12] began to rouse his people, encouraging them in a loud voice to fight. When they heard him, a large number of them began to descend against our men. With the first shots, they wounded the horse of Gómez de Alva- *fol. 119v* rado,[13] and they penetrated his back saddle bow through and through with a dart of palm, which had no iron. But the captain and the horsemen who were with him were already pursuing them so that they killed several of them, and the rest began to flee in great confusion, as did those who were in those highland places where Juan Pérez de Guevara and Pedro de Samaniego had gone.

The way secured, the Spaniards united. The [Indian] friends brought provisions that they found in the region, destroying whatever they came across, even burning the houses, which caused such great despair among the natives that they themselves lay waste to their own fields and villages, complaining to God about the Christians, who had come from such faraway lands to totally destroy them. When Alvarado saw the devastation, it distressed him. He wanted to capture some of those Indians in order to persuade them not to be crazy or wreak such havoc upon themselves. Therefore, he ordered a leader named Camacho[14] to go and attempt it with forty Spaniards and one thousand friends. Four or five thousand warriors had departed from another region named Chillao[15] to reinforce those who had already been defeated. The Christians encountered them and demanded peace many times; it was not enough. For that reason our men moved against them: Antonio de la Serna, Juan de Rojas, Antonio de San Pedro, and Juan Sánchez went in front with crossbows. When they shot some arrows with them, hurting[16] the Indians, they became frightened by such extraordinary novelty and fled because they quickly lose courage if they do not see the game won. The Christians went in pursuit. Some Indians from the region arrived to join the others, and news of it went to the captain. But as soon as he ordered some horsemen to go out to reinforce [the Spaniards], they turned around and in the greatest hurry fled. The Christians slept that night in a secure place, and the next day they joined Alvarado.

Some Spaniards came looking for them from Trujillo in order to take part in that conquest. They left that place, all the land was scorched, lacking provisions. The captain ordered Balboa[17] to go with some Spaniards and Indians to a village called Tonche to collect provisions. In spite of having been offered peace on Alvarado's behalf, the Indian warriors did not want to return to settle in their lands; instead, they went in bands around the hills, abusing the Spaniards, calling them thieves and other ugly names; [Alvarado] decided to go in
fol. 120 person to find them. Forty shield bearers and crossbowmen were put in readiness, and he left with them, taking along the Indian friends, which was advantageous for him.

Marching through a cold and rugged land, they went an entire day without coming across anything. They were forced to pass the night on a river bank in a green meadow; when daylight came, they set out for a great river. But they had not gone more than half a league when they heard loud shouts. Some of the more daring Spaniards went toward them and found that a squadron of the natives at war were having a shouting match with most of their friends and allies on the other side of the river. When the Christians arrived, they fled without daring to wait. They followed them. The captain waited until they returned from the pursuit, which lasted until they chased the enemy into some narrow passages, where fearing[18] to fall into the power of the Spaniards, they rashly chose death because they jumped into the river. With great luck those who knew how to swim came out on the other side; the rest drowned. Among the Christians was one named Prado, who understood something of the language. He admonished those who were on the other side of the river not to be crazy and go from hill to hill like guanacos as they did, deceived by the devil so that he could take their souls; they should put down their arms and come out to the captain as friends, and he would treat them with great benevolence. One captain, called Jodjo, replied that their cacique was not among them and that [the Spaniards] should send their message to him because peace or war was in his hands. With that they rejoined Alvarado, who had remained waiting for them where it has been said. They then departed from there to explore that section of the region. And they were caught in a rainstorm accompanied by thunder and lightning, which caused them great anguish. They had used up what they had taken in their knapsacks. They were hungry, which was relieved when they found a field of yucca, where they managed to pull out and eat those roots. They slept in two deserted straw houses. Alvarado believed that it would be advisable to return to the camp because he had neither encountered the warriors nor attracted them to peace.

He then summoned Pedro de Samaniego to go with forty Spaniards with swords and bucklers and crossbows, along with some friends, to the province of Chillao, which was rebelling, and to wage war on the natives with full force. They left the camp with this goal; they marched through tall mountains covered by forest. The Indians were *fol. 120v* warned that they were coming to their land; it was such frightening news that without daring to wait in the villages, they abandoned them, leaving the houses deserted. The Christians arrived in one of these places, which was of the principal lord named Longlos, where they found many provisions and some herds of sheep and some fowl. The friends, who exceeded two thousand, made loads of what they could to take to the camp, destroying whatever they wanted. Some Indians who had abandoned the village had remained on the summits. When they saw the destruction done to their property, upset and angry, they notified their captains. They collected more than four thousand warriors,[19] and stationed in familiar places that they chose, they awaited the Christians and their friends, who were already coming after them. The Indians who were loaded with provisions fled like hares, leaving the Christians alone, who attacked the enemy when they heard their loud clamor and noise. They killed and wounded many of them with crossbows and swords, and the rest fled, leaving our men exhausted and with no more harm than a wound that one received in the arm. And as best they could, they returned and joined Alvarado.

Notes

1 A helmet without a visor that looks like a hat with a crest; it was popular among Spanish soldiers of that period.

2 Cieza spells it "Longia"; it is located approximately twenty kilometers south of modern Chachapoyas in the province of Luya.

3 Capital of Bongará, about sixty kilometers north of modern Chachapoyas. Cieza spells it "Xunbia."

4 Ruy Barba Cabeza de Vaca y Coronado was born in Seville about 1512. After the Quita incident, he went with Alonso de Alvarado to Lima, then to Cuzco to defend it during the native uprising. He received the encomienda of Jayanca and became a vecino of Lima in 1537. He died in 1589. See Busto, *Diccionario,* 1:201–3.

5 the Indians

6 that land

7 Cieza spells it "Cocoxo."

8 Juan Pérez el chequito

9 Captain

10 Busto spells it "Guaquemila"; *Diccionario,* 1:94.

11 Luis Varela.

12 Busto spells it "Igametá"; *Diccionario,* 1:94.

13 Gómez de Alvarado, Pedro de Alvarado's brother, had served in Cuba, New Spain, and Guatemala before coming to Peru in 1534. He joined Almagro and was involved in the initial Chilean expedition. He was taken prisoner at the Battle of Salinas, but Hernando Pizarro allowed him to escort Diego de Almagro the Younger to Lima. Although an Almagrist, he ultimately fought against them at the Battle of Chupas. He became ill and died shortly afterward. See Busto, *Diccionario,* 1:106–8.

14 Alonso Camacho.

15 An ethnic group that lived in what is today the province of Luya; Stiglich, *Diccionario geográfico,* p. 375.

16 wounding

17 Busto lists five Balboas of the period, but none seems to be this Balboa. *Diccionario,* 1:191–92.

18 death

19 Indians

XC

About how while Juan Pizarro was lieutenant and captain in Cuzco, King Manco Inca Yupanqui, detesting the rule the Christians had over them, attempted to leave the city in order to begin a war against them and was seized twice and placed in chains

At this time there occurred what the story should deal with now. While Juan Pizarro, the governor's brother, was lieutenant and chief justice of Cuzco, King Manco Inca Yupanqui—son of Huayna Capac and supported by Pizarro to don the fringe—was in the city. The natives respected and feared him as their true lord, the legitimate[1] heir of the great kingdom that the Incas, his fathers, had won. And before Almagro had left Cuzco, this Manco and Villac Umu and Paullu and other leaders discussed what I have already related. Several days
fol. 121 after Almagro had departed, the Inca secretly summoned many of the legitimate lords of the provinces of Condesuyu, Antisuyu, Collasuyu, and Chinchasuyu, all of whom surreptitiously answered his call, and great festivities were celebrated between them and the orejones. And when they were all assembled, Manco Inca offered them this address:

Manco's Speech

I have sent for you in order to tell you in the presence of our kin and attendants how I feel about what these foreigners strive to do with us, so that in time and before more join them we can make arrangements that in general would benefit everyone. Remember that the Incas, my fathers, who rest in the heaven with the Sun, ruled from Quito to Chile, treating those whom they received as vassals[2] so well that it seemed they were children who had emerged from their own entrails. They did not steal and killed only when it served justice; they kept order and reason in the provinces that you know. The rich did not succumb to pride; the poor were not destitute, and they enjoyed tranquility and perpetual peace. Our sins made us unworthy of such lords; rather, they were the

21. Manco Capac. Felipe Guaman Poma de Ayala, *El primer nueva corónica y buen gobierno,* 3 vols., ed. Rolena Adorno and John V. Murra (Mexico City: Siglo Veintiuno, 1980), f. 398. Courtesy of Siglo Veintiuno Editores.

cause that these bearded ones entered our land, theirs being so far away from here. They preach one thing and do another, and they give us so many admonitions, yet they do the opposite. They have no fear of God or shame, and treating us like dogs, they call us no other names. Their greed has been such that there is no temple or palace left that they have not looted. Furthermore, even if all the snow turned to gold and silver, it would not satiate them. They keep the daughters of my father and other ladies, your sisters and kin, as concubines, behaving bestially in this. They want to divide, as they began to, all the provinces, giving one to each of them so that as lords they can pillage them. They strive to have us so subjugated and enslaved that we have no other care than to find them metals and to provide them with our women and livestock. Furthermore, they have drawn the yanaconas and many mitimaes to them. These traitors did not wear fine clothing before or an opulent llautu.[3] Since they joined these foreigners, they act like Incas, and before long they will divest me of the fringe. They do not honor me when they see me, and they speak loosely because they learn from the thieves with whom they associate. What justice and reason did they have to do these things, and what will these Christians do? Look, I ask you! Where did we meet them, what do we owe them, or which one of them have we injured that they would make such cruel war on us with these horses and weapons of iron? They killed Atahualpa without cause. They did the same with his captain-general, Chalcuchima, and they have also killed Rumiñavi and Zope-Zopahua in Quito in the fire *fol. 121v* so that the souls would burn with the bodies and could not go to enjoy heaven.[4] I believe that it would not be just or honest for us to consent to this; rather, we should strive with full determination either to all die, or to kill these cruel enemies. Do not pay attention to those who have gone with the other usurper, Almagro, because Paullu and Villac Umu are encharged to effect an uprising to kill them.

Alimache—who was Manco Inca's attendant and now is Juan Ortiz de Zárate's—related to me what I have written, among other things that he told me, and he has a good memory and a sharp judgment. Those who were listening to Manco Inca began to weep, replying:[5] "You are the son of Huayna Capac, our very powerful king; the Sun and all the gods are supporting you so that you may free us from the captivity that we fell into unexpectedly; we will all die in order to serve you."

After these and other words were uttered, it was decided by all who were present there that Manco Inca himself, surreptitiously without the Christians knowing, would try to leave Cuzco in order to establish himself in a safe and convenient place where all of them would assemble. But, although they tried to keep these discussions very secret, they were hardly so because they came to the notice of certain yanaconas who revealed them to Juan Pizarro and the other Christians. Juan Pizarro did not entirely believe what was being affirmed by those who had found out about this issue, but for better or worse he ordered the yanaconas who were considered most faithful to watch Manco Inca day and night, unnoticed, so that if he truly wanted to abandon the city, they would inform him.

Several days later the Inca, unable to rest, abandoned his house, and with the orejones and servants that he needed he left the city in an opulent litter in accordance with his royal rank. Many of his wives went with him, and many remained in their houses or palaces, and they took the highway to Mohina, which is the one they call of Chinchasuyu. When the watchmen woke up, he was already gone, but as soon as they found out, they told Juan Pizarro, who was playing cards. Furthermore, a Christian named Martín de Florencia,[6] who also learned of it, came to tell him. Juan Pizarro took his sword and cape and accompanied by some Christians went to the Inca's house where he verified what they had told him. And although he had not ordered it, nor could it be prevented, they plundered the great riches of gold and silver and fine cloth that the Inca had in his house, which was a notable loot. The yanaconas watched much of this. Juan Pizarro returned to his lodgings where he ordered his brother, Gonzalo Pizarro, to go swiftly in pursuit of the Inca even if the night were wretched, dark, and fearful— providing that Alonso *fol. 122*
de Toro,[7] Pedro Alonso Carrasco,[8] Beltrán del Conde,[9] Francisco de Solar,[10] Francisco Peces,[11] Diego Rodríguez Hidalgo, and Francisco de Villafuerte should ride with him. They left on horseback at full speed, and thus they rode to Salinas, which is one-half league from the city, where they began to catch up with the people who were going with the Inca. They asked them about him, and they replied that he had

gone another way and not that one. In the litter that he was traveling in, [Manco Inca] heard the noise. He feared the enemy and cursed a great deal those who had informed them that he had left. In the meantime, Gonzalo Pizarro and the others arrived at some narrow passes formed by small mountain ridges, where they reached a principal orejón, one of those guarding the king's person. They threatened him to tell them where he was or which way was he going. He faithfully denied the truth in order not to be a traitor to his lord. Gonzalo Pizarro, furious, alighted from his horse, and with help from the others they tied a rope to his genitals to torture him, which they indeed did so that the poor orejón screamed loudly, declaring that the Inca was not traveling on that highway. Beltrán del Conde, Francisco de Villafuerte, and Diego Rodríguez Hidalgo continued on the road to Mohina, and as they passed those that they had reached, they asked after the lord, who had reached some marshes. Because those who walked with him were making noise, they did not sense[12] the horses who were already very close to the litter, and being afraid, he got out of it and hid among some small rushes. The Spaniards loudly asked for him, and one of the horsemen approached the place where he was hiding. Believing that he had been discovered, he came out, saying that it was he and that they should not kill him, and he told a great lie, which was that Almagro sent him a messenger that he should follow him. He was placed in the litter and treated with honor because not one bad or discourteous word was spoken to him. They shouted to Gonzalo Pizarro, and all together they returned to the city. From there they sent a messenger to Juan Pizarro, who had gone out with other horsemen in the other direction in search of the Inca. And when he returned, he reproached him for leaving in that manner, saying how badly he repaid Pizarro the love that he had for him and the Christians for always treating him with honor. He excused himself, saying that Almagro had sent him messengers to come and join him and that he wanted to leave in that way because he believed they would not permit it. Juan Pizarro, with benevolance and
fol. 122v genteel civility, admonished him to calm down and take pleasure in the friendship and favor of the Spaniards, and said that he knew very well that Almagro did not send him such message. Afterward, Manco Inca went to his house. Juan Pizarro sent certain yanacona Indians to

keep an eye on him night and day, which they could do because many always lived where he was.

Although he failed to accomplish what he yearned for, and each day he hated and loathed the Christians more—primarily for having plundered his house and taken many of his women—he did not cease contemplating how he could leave again in order to escape. And having informed his household servants and retainers, he once again left the city, intending to go into the nearest snow. And when he left, those who kept watch over him immediately informed Juan Pizarro, and they caught up with him not even two crossbow shots away from Cuzco. Juan Pizarro, furious, ordered that he be put in irons and publicly guarded by the Christians. In this manner, Manco Inca was imprisoned by Juan Pizarro. And I also have to say that some Indians rightfully and with reason excuse [Manco Inca], affirming that Almagro took a great amount of gold from him and that Juan Pizarro asked him for that metal with such vehemence that, desperate, he wanted to get away. There must be something to it, although the principal cause was to form a league or to assemble troops to start a war against the Christians, as has been written.

Notes

1 true

2 Again, Cieza uses European concepts.

3 A headdress of woven bands wrapped around the head. See also chapter 33.

4 Again, the importance of the cult of the ancestors and of the maintenance of the mummified bodies is stressed. Spanish churchmen later searched out and destroyed by fire the ancestor huacas in order to stamp out idolatry.

5 saying

6 See chapter 52.

7 See chapter 36.

8 See chapter 83.

9 Conde came to Peru with Almagro in 1533 and was one of the founders of Cuzco. He later fought at Salinas and Chupas, always against the Almagro faction. Busto, *Diccionario,* 1:391.

10 Probably Francisco de Solares, one of the footmen at Cajamarca. He was

from the area of Trujillo-Cáceres. He was a founder and encomendero of Cuzco. Always loyal to Pizarro, he was jailed by the Almagrists, but he disappears from the record after that. See Lockhart, *Men of Cajamarca,* p. 354.

11 Cieza mistakenly calls him Pérez; see chapter 52.

12 the noise

XCI

About how after killing a Spaniard, those who killed him fortified themselves on a ridgetop with their cacique, and about what happened until the ridgetop was taken

At first, anything that is unfamiliar is believed to be easy and simple, but when one discovers what it is, that which was joyous is detested. Therefore, because the Indians here were accustomed to serving their kings and lords with their persons and property, and although they had heard that the Christians were to divide the provinces among themselves, they were unconcerned because they believed that they would be less burdened and that they would not be mistreated or abused. This contentment lasted only a short time. The cause was not their wickedness or the inferior reason attributed to them by those who want to justify the evil done to them; rather, it was that *fol. 123* our people disparaged them and were hungry for silver and gold, and also because of the novelty of being served, revered, and so venerated that they even gave them their[1] daughters and kinswomen, and many other reasons that became apparent, and which God Almighty as the strict and perfect judge showed [the Indians] because such little care was taken with the conversion of all these people. It sprung from these things that the caciques and kurakas[2] were making great exclamations, secretly praising the government of the Incas and saying that they knew how to preserve peace and maintain justice in many lands. They composed romances and songs about it; they publicly and openly spoke with the demon; and those who were chosen for that religion made sacrifices, killing many sheep and some birds for the offerings. They loathed the Spaniards; they wished to kill them and see them divided so that they could slay them without risk. They did not show their feelings openly because they were afraid, especially when they saw Manco Inca in chains.

One vecino named Pedro Martín de Moguer[3] left Cuzco to go to a village that he had been given, which I believe was called Angocavo,[4] where he came to a terrible misfortune because the cacique with the Indians whom he chose killed him or ordered him killed one night.

And although they tried to keep the death a secret, they could not because some of the very Indians who went with the Christian returned to Cuzco and informed Juan Pizarro about it. He went to talk to Manco, believing that he had ordered it. He denied it because neither did he order it, nor did he know about it.

Gonzalo Pizarro went out with some Spaniards to punish the killers. [The Indians] hid in a safe place on a naturally fortified ridgetop, large and rocky—which, surrounded by its wall, did not have more than one entrance. Inside they made some huts where they put their wives and children. When Gonzalo Pizarro arrived, he tried to lay siege to the stronghold. His large force was not sufficient. They had taken there all the provisions and water they could carry, but Gonzalo Pizarro was on them so many days that they ran out of water, and therefore they were ready for an agreement. But that night so much snow fell that the next day they found themselves with more water than they originally brought. They declared that God sent it to them out of compassion. Gonzalo Pizarro informed Juan Pizarro about the strength of the ridgetop and how he could not win it. He left Cuzco with more people and many orejones to help him; he said that because this was the first Christian whom the Indians had killed,[5] it would be expedient to severely castigate them in order to set an example to the others.

When he arrived, he ordered a mantelet[6] made so that they could climb up. [The Indians] launched so many shots and stones that they broke through it and wounded five Christians and some friends and yanaconas. Those of the ridgetop had their watchmen. With huge effort they closed the entrance, using enormous rocks and thick, *fol. 123v* strong ropes. Juan Pizarro admonished them to surrender. They would not trust his word, and as he saw the time go by without anything happening, he spoke secretly with the orejones, asking them to negotiate with those of the ridgetop so that he could have them in his power. The orejones had come by the command of the Inca, and they wished for those of the ridgetop to succeed. But they showed no sign of it; instead, they replied that they would do it. And they say that their captain was able to speak to the Indians of the ridgetop, encouraging and animating them not to weaken. He made a pact with them that on a certain day, during the night, they [the orejones] would kill the horses of the Christians, and they would descend to do the same to them [the Christians]. He told Juan Pizarro, on the other hand, that they had asked him for a six-day term to decide what they should do. A yanacona[7] found out about this agreement. He informed Juan Pizarro, who angrily ordered the chief orejón burned. He sent word to Cuzco to Gabriel de Rojas,[8] who had remained there in his place, to threaten Manco Inca for the treachery planned by his captain and retainer. Gabriel de Rojas did it. Manco defended himself from the blame being laid on him, and fearing that the Christians, his enemies, might kill him, he ordered a brave orejón captain called Paucar Inca[9] to go and join the Christians and help them in anything they commanded. And that is what he did. Juan Pizarro reminded him of the punishment that he gave the other. Indeed, this one spoke with those at the top with much pretense, complaining about the Christians because they had Manco imprisoned in chains and saying that he came by his command to support them against the Christians. They rejoiced when they heard this, and even more when he said that he brought the sacred axe of the Sun to make an oath. They agreed that he would return the next night with only four Indians, his closest friends, in order to discuss the manner in which they could kill the Christians who had them surrounded.

Paucar Inca secretly returned. He saw that there were three entrances among the crags and the rocks of the strong ridgetop, which they closed at night with boulders[10] tied with ropes. He told Juan Pizarro that in order to satisfy Manco Inca he would have to perform a great deed, from which he would be lucky to come out alive. Also, he should order four Christians to shave their beards and dress in shirts and mantas, and smear themselves with a type of mixture, so that after they put it on, whether they were black or white, they would all look like Indians, and they could go with him, secretly carrying their swords. And he with the rest of the Christians and yanaconas should follow after them. Because he had the Inca imprisoned, Juan Pizarro trusted the words of the orejón and ordered Mancio Sierra,[11] Pedro del Barco,[12] Francisco de Villafuerte, and Juan Flores to go with the Indian to help him. He advised the rest of the Christians to be prepared with their arms to immediately follow with him in the night. The orejón and the four Spaniards had already left the camp, climbing *fol. 124* below the mountain ridges toward the ridgetop with great hardship because of its ruggedness. Juan Pizarro and the Spaniards left within moments in order to provide support for Paucar Colla.

Those who were on the ridgetop had discussed this business, and they suspected that the orejón might be involved in some double dealing. They regretted that they had told him to come to see them the following night. They decided that because they had told him to come with only four Indians, they should see if he did, and if more came, they would kill all of them. But if they did not surpass that number, they would open the first entrance of their great stronghold, where they would make the four coming with the orejón stay, and opening the second gateway, they would keep him until they could see the sacred axe and while the oaths were being made. And they carried out what they decided. They sent their spies to the highway, who returned to say that no more than Paucar Inca and the four Indians were coming and that they were already approaching the height of the ridgetop. The orejón was carrying a small copper axe with a short stick as a handle, used for the solemn oaths to the sacred Sun, and underneath the manta he carried a club. He shouted so that they would know he was there. Some armed men came out from the top, and after they entered the gate, they left the four beardless Christians, not allowing them to go ahead, and opening the other gate, they wanted to let in the orejón. The Spaniards were frightened and believed that they would be betrayed. They feared death and complained about the orejón without reason because when he realized that they wanted to detain him and close the gate, he threw off the manta, took his club, and loudly exclaimed: "Viracochas, udcaxamo!"—which means, "Christians, come quickly!" They did that. The orejón had wounded several Indians with the club. Many others arrived, saying that they had been betrayed, and they struck and wounded Paucar Colla Inca so much that, imploring the Spaniards to avenge him, he fell dead to the ground. With their swords, the four courageously fought against the power of the Indians. Their lives were saved because it was night and such a narrow place. Juan Pizarro and the rest arrived to reinforce them. When daylight came and those of the ridgetop saw their enemies in control of their impenetrable fortress, it is not easy to describe the clamor, wails, shouts, and fearful cries of the men and women, young and old, and the youth and children. And when they saw the luster of the swords, many chose a voluntary death, and jumped down from those precipices, leaving their brains among the snow-covered points of the rocks. And many tender-aged children, unaware of the misfortune while they played with the nipples of their mothers' breasts, bravely threw themselves over, their bodies without souls arriving below. The Spaniards had begun to wound and kill without any restraint, cutting legs and arms, and not sparing anyone's life. The yanaconas were doing the same. The clamor on both sides was great, and greater still the killing. In *fol. 124v* desperation, many of the Indians took their wives and children, and making them close their eyes, plunged down the cliffs with them, exclaiming: "It is better to die in freedom than to live in servitude of such cruel people." Among those who threw themselves, the deed of a principal of good appearance and countenance was noted. He shed abundant tears from his eyes, naming Huayna Capac many times, and he took a strong and very long rope with which he tied his wife and two children, and five or six sheep, and three loads of their clothing and furnishings. He wrapped the rope two or three times around his arm, closed his eyes, and they saw him falling down those large cliffs, bringing behind him his company, which was very painful to watch. And all of them were crushed to pieces. Tired of killing men, the Spaniards turned to pillaging, and they found—according to what they say—a little more than five thousand castellanos. By the consent of all, they were given for the maintenance of the church of Cuzco, and they turned them over to a cleric who was there. This punishment finished, Juan Pizarro went to settle those who had remained in the village. A notice came that in Condesuyu one Juan de Becerril[13] was killed by his Indians. With this news he decided to set out to punish them, without regard that the Indians were killing their enemies and that if they did not kill all of them, it was because they lacked the power for it.

Notes

1 women
2 The Quechua term for cacique.
3 See chapter 48.

4 According to Busto (*Diccionario,* 1:231), it was Angocagua.

5 The first Christian killed by his encomienda Indians.

6 A screen used in siege warfare to protect those who are climbing the walls from below.

7 a yanacona woman (una yanacona)

8 See chapter 71.

9 Paucar Colla Inca.

10 brought

11 Mancio Sierra de Leguízamo, one of the founders of Cuzco, was a councilman and received an encomienda. He was later alcalde and distinguished himself in defense of the city. See Lockhart, *Men of Cajamarca,* pp. 469–70, and Mendiburu, *Diccionario,* 10:215–16.

12 Born in Lobón, Extremadura, around 1505, Barco came to the Indies with Gil González Dávila and participated in the conquest of Nicaragua and Guatemala. He reached Panama in 1532 and went to Peru with Diego de Almagro. He settled in Cuzco, was a town councilman, and received the encomienda of Paria in Charcas. He was executed by the rebels during the Gonzalo Pizarro revolt. See Busto, *Diccionario,* 1:207–209.

13 According to Busto (*Diccionario,* 1:231), Antonio de Becerril, "and some say Rodríguez Becerril."

XCII

About how a founding was done in the City of the Kings and Hernando Pizarro procured that the said donation be offered to His Majesty, and about his parting for Cuzco and the governor's departure to inspect the northern cities

Hernando Pizarro was already in the City of the Kings, as has been told before. He was very eager to serve the emperor, and he pointed out his large expenses and how from all parts of his realm they made donations to him. Furthermore, because it pleased God that during the time of his sovereign reign such a wealthy kingdom as that of Peru had been discovered by them, they were obligated to present him with a large gift. Some who heard it murmured about these statements, saying that Hernando Pizarro wanted to win the king's favor at the cost of their possessions when it sufficed to give him the fifth because it was so large and was obtained without spending one single real. They also complained that Hernando Pizarro had told them he would bring great freedoms and liberties for the conquistadors and settlers, and they saw nothing other than the Order of Santiago on his chest. This was not discussed in his presence because *fol. 125* in exchange for money they did not want to displease him. And when [Francisco] Pizarro ordered the start of the founding, they began to throw in large amounts of gold and silver. He told his friends not to refuse what Hernando suggested, assuring them that the king would give grants to all of them and perhaps might even give them the Indians in perpetuity.[1] In the founding itself, each gave, not counting the fifth, one thousand five hundred or one thousand or less, according to the metal that each one put in, and most of the cities of the kingdom were notified to do likewise. In Trujillo they murmured more because [Hernando Pizarro] was not present. They said that he negotiated nothing other than his encomienda, making them commoners. The officials who were in charge of the royal treasury had an account of what the sum collected for this donation amounted to.

News arrived at this time how an uncle of Manco Inca, called

Tiso, left Jauja and devastated Tarma and Bombón, most of which the treasurer Alonso Riquelme[2] held in encomienda. Because it concerned him, he fervently asked Pizarro to order that he be captured and punished. Without hearing Tiso's excuse and in order to humor Riquelme, Pizarro ordered a vecino called Cervantes[3] to go and capture him. Tiso learned of it and departed for the Andes to hide in the thickness of the forests. He first sent[4] messengers to Manco, his nephew, that as soon as he escaped from the hands of the Christians, he should assemble troops to wage war on them. Because in the City of the Kings the donation had been made to the emperor, as has been told, Hernando Pizarro asked the governor to give him permission to go to the city of Cuzco to procure the same. He replied that he would be glad, and so that [Hernando] would have more influence in the enterprise, he ordered his secretary, Antonio Picado, to arrange a provision to make him lieutenant and chief justice. He wrote to Juan Pizarro the reason why he had removed him from the post, begging him to accept it. He wrote the same to the town council. And although this was the main reason that Hernando Pizarro went to Cuzco with this commission, I believe that the most important was the fear that Almagro might return to the city, claiming that it fell within his governance. And Pizarro believed that the possession of it would be safer with Hernando than with Juan because he was older and had more authority. With him went Pedro de Hinojosa,[5] Cervantes, Tapia,[6] and other knights among those noble young men from Extremadura who had left Spain with him, and others remained in the City of the Kings, where they were well treated and favored by Pizarro.

After Hernando departed for Cuzco, Pizarro decided to leave Lima[7] in order to inspect the cities of Trujillo and San Miguel to see how his lieutenants were excercising their positions and if the natives were being treated well and their conversion being procured, as His Majesty had ordered. And leaving Francisco de Godoy,[8] a knight from *fol. 125v* Cáceres, as his lieutenant, he embarked on a ship in order to go faster, accompanied by some of his retainers. And he left from Callao, which is the port, on the fourteenth day of the month of February of the year fifteen hundred and thirty-six. He personally inspected those cities, hearing some complaints and remedying the grievances, aiding the Indians, honoring the caciques, and admonishing everyone to become Christian. He made them understand the foolishness of believing in gods of rock and stick and in the sayings of the demon, who—he assured them—was such a powerless coward that he fled from fear of only a small cross. And, they should test it, and they would see that he was telling them the truth. Furthermore, he told them through the interpreters that the sun and the moon were neither gods nor demons, but resplendent luminaries that God created so that they would always serve and give light to the world, and thus, fulfilling his command, they never stopped day and night. And the Christians who were evil went with the infidels to hell and the good ones to glory. Pizarro said these things with affection and good will because the time had not yet arrived when due to his sins and those who were in Peru, these good beginnings were lost, and other times commenced when they waged war on each other, consuming themselves in miserable battles caused by envy, with no other people participating but brothers against brothers, cousins against cousins, and friends against friends. And there was so much impiety among all that I would not want to be a witness in such a grave case.

The kurakas and the Indians were delighted to hear such lofty words, and had [the Spaniards] preached[9] to them truthfully with Christian fervor in the beginning and given a good example of themselves, many who are now in hell crying into God's ears could have been saved. Although it is also true that in those beginnings there was never the order that existed afterwards because things cannot be truly understood then. [Pizarro] wrote letters to Quito, Puerto Viejo, and Guayaquil, encharging all in the service of God and the king and the good treatment of the natives. Diego Pizarro de Carvajal[10] asked him for the expedition to Lupalupa, which is where the famous Captain Ancoalli, a native Chanca, entered the east via Moyobamba. He graciously granted it to him, but for lack of supplies the expedition was abandoned at that time.

After this, Pizarro returned by land to the City of the Kings, where he was well received, and he hurried to order the building of the church.

Notes

1 The debate over perpetuity would be a major cause of the Peruvian civil wars and would continue almost to the end of the century. In 1536 Charles V issued a decree whereby the grant of Indians lasted only two generations. Soon a commission was established to review the question. The deliberations led to a severely restricted institution under the New Laws of 1542. Hemming provides some analysis of the subject in *Conquest,* pp. 266, 385–90.

2 See chapter 54.

3 Cieza spells it "Carvantes." It is unclear who this might be.

4 writing first

5 Hinojosa was born in Trujillo and came to Peru with Hernando Pizarro. He became a town councillor in the mining district of Chuquisaca. He joined Vaca de Castro and fought at Chupas against the Almagrists. During the Gonzalo Pizarro revolt, he became his captain of the guard and commanded his naval forces. Ultimately, he shifted to Gasca and was rewarded with a rich encomienda in Charcas. He was corregidor of La Plata, then Potosí. He was assassinated in 1553 during the uprising of Sebastián de Castilla. See Mendiburu, *Diccionario,* 6:258–67.

6 Gonzalo de Tapia was a relative of Francisco Pizarro.

7 This is the first time Cieza uses the name Lima in this text.

8 See chapter 47.

9 the preachers

10 Another kinsman of Pizarro.

XCIII

About what happened to Captain Alonso de Alvarado in his conquest of the Chachapoyas

When Samaniego joined Alvarado and he learned what had occurred and that the natives of those highlands were persistent in refusing *fol. 126* peace, he did what he was obligated to do as a Christian. He sent them messengers, admonishing them not to abandon their houses or leave the cultivation of their fields because they learned of his presence in the land. It was to their benefit and that of their souls, and it was not harmful. Neither these nor other statements were enough for them to do what he wished, which was the reason that he decided to go with the whole camp in search of them. He then ordered Alonso Camacho[1] to go with twenty Spaniards to explore the countryside, checking if the road was safe. They marched along the skirt of a mountain until they reached an unpopulated place. From there, after they went a little more than a league and a half, they came across an open field, but the road was full of sharp stones, which they call ceburocos,[2] dangerous for the horses and even more for the men who go on foot.

The natives of the region where Alvarado was exploring knew very well of his coming and how many Christians and horses there were. Many had assembled with their captains and leaders, after they first placed their women and possessions in safety, and they discussed what would be most sound for them. They decided to offer a feigned peace to the Christians in order to distract them so that they would come without suspicion to where they would rush out and kill them. With this hoax, five or six Indians went with some sheep to Alvarado. They told him that for God's sake they should have mercy on them and not attack them, nor should the crossbows shoot arrows with the speed that they had personally felt because they wanted peace, and they were appealing for it in the name of all. Alvarado answered them kindly, praising such good resolve. The Indians returned to report what they had done. The Christians marched without stopping. When they arrived to where they awaited them, [the Indians] rushed out with such a cry and frightening clamor that it seemed a roaring of demons. They launched some shots. Our men arranged themselves in order, neither disturbed nor frightened by what they saw, and they wounded and killed many enemies. They pressed them in such a way that although for each Christian there were more than 150 Indians, they did not dare to wait any longer, and instead they began to flee with much cowardice. One Spaniard named Prado went in pursuit of the captain. An Indian shot him with a stone, hitting him on the head with such force that, in spite of the helmet and morion he was wearing, it knocked him off the horse, his brains exposed. Luis Varela[3] found himself in danger because he was alone and surrounded by Indians. He commended himself to God, whose protection miraculously shielded him from them until He made it possible for some companions to come to his aid; and while they had him surrounded, he killed seven Indians.

fol. 126v The Indians who escaped from the skirmish discussed with the others who assembled what would be expedient for them to do in order to be safe and not all die. They did not know which was the soundest advice. There was among them a lord, the highest one, whom they call Guayamamulos.[4] He told them that it was madness to remain at war with men they clearly saw were favored by the Sun and that he had decided to win their goodwill and be in their graces. Some were distressed when they heard this from him; others praised him. And discarding his fine mantas, he put on some plain ones, and with an old woman he went to the camp of our men, where he spoke with Alvarado about what has been told. He received him well and promised to treat him thus. Guaman, who was another lord, an enemy of this one, boldly confident of the Spaniards' friendship, spoke to this one with great anger and threats. Alvarado scolded him for that, declaring that he would keep peace with those who came, even if they had waged war and killed Christians. Following this, Alvarado spoke to this lord [Guayamamulos], begging him to try to make the lords and chieftains of the province of Chillao and the other valleys come to the Spaniards in friendship. He promised to make them come, and he fulfilled it, inducing them with pronouncements delivered by messengers. When they arrived in the captain's presence, he received them well. He learned from them that one of the instigators of the league was one among them named Guandamulos, a usurper and an invader, and with the agreement of all he was seized and executed.

From then on many unarmed Indians began to come to serve our people. Alvarado learned that nearby there was a very populated valley named Bagua.[5] The captain ordered one Francisco Hernández to go with some Spaniards to see it. When he returned with a report about it, Alvarado left that place and explored the villages and rivers throughout those parts. He strove to bring the natives to friendship with the Spaniards and to prevent any pillaging or major harm as much as he could. And thus they place him in the forefront of the captains who are praised for having dealt reasonably with the Indians.

And while he was engaged in this conquest, he came across a large river that flowed northward. On the other side there were[6] many Indians up in arms. He sent messengers to induce them to make peace. They wanted nothing but war. Alvarado commanded construction of balsas to cross the river. They were carefully made because the Spaniards here are handy. But because the river was wild, it carried away one of the balsas, and those traveling the river in it were in danger. Pedro de Samaniego went with some Spaniards to engage the enemy *fol. 127* in every direction. He arrived near a small river that flowed through a valley to a village that they afterwards named De la Cruz. There was a large number of native warriors, who gave a great cry and shot many arrows and darts when they saw the Spaniards so close to them. Without daring to wait, they went downriver. The Spaniards plundered the village, planning to rejoin the captain.

The natives heard from their neighbors that those who formed friendship and alliance with the Christians were treated in a friendly way, but that they waged war on those who did not until they totally destroyed them; therefore, they decided to make peace. And that is what they did: their chiefs went to speak to Alvarado, and he received them as he normally did those who wanted to be friends of the Christians. He announced to all of them that now that he had finished exploring the region, he would establish a Christian settlement, which would be like Cuzco or Lima or San Miguel, where all of them would come to serve the Christians, among whom the villages and caciques were to be divided.

And following this, Alvarado set out to go to the village that I said was called De la Cruz, which Samaniego had reached. And that day he slept outside of it with the whole camp because he did not reach the place, although some did. After they crossed the river, there was a thunderstorm with hail such as they had never seen before. When they arrived in the village, the captain took up lodgings and learned that there were some Indians from that district who did not come to see him as the rest had done. Some horsemen went out. They found that it was true, but the river was in between, which was the reason that they could not harm them. The enemies were laying waste to their countryside, destroying the fields, which distressed the captain, and he sent messengers to the lord of those Indians to ask him to become his friend. He replied that he should send him a sword because he wanted to see with what weapons the Christians fought. With an Indian, Alvarado sent him a sword that had a silver pommel. He was pleased when he saw it. He decided to make peace with the Christians, sending first a gift of feathers and some mantas to the captain, and accompanied by some Indians he went to see [Alvarado], who honored him very much, encouraging him to be kind to the Christians.

Notes

1 Busto (*Diccionario,* 1:306–7) lists several Camachos, including three Alonso Camachos, who were active in the region.

2 See chapter 2.

3 See chapters 59 and 89.

4 Busto (*Diccionario,* 1:94) spells it "Guaquemila."

5 Cieza spells it "Baguan"; Bagua is located in the Utcubamba River valley, about twenty kilometers from where it empties into the Marañon River.

6 large villages

XCIV

About how Almagro sent Captain Salcedo[1] to punish the Indians who had killed the three Christians, and they gave him a gift of more than ninety thousand pesos, and how Villac Umu fled, and what else happened

When Almagro learned about the three Christians who were killed in Jujuy, he became very angry. He ordered Captain Salcedo to set out at once with sixty horsemen and footmen and not to stop until they arrived in that land, where he was to inflict great punishment. Salcedo left[2] as he had been commanded. He took as guides the two Christians who had escaped. Those who had killed the said Christians made great sacrifices to their demons and were arming themselves, apprehensive about what happened. They dug deep pits along the highways, as they normally do, subtly covered with grass to hide the trap. Furthermore, they fortified themselves, building drywalls and bulwarks. Salcedo marched swiftly and arrived where the Indians were, but he could not attack them or harm them because their stronghold was large; he could only surround it so that they could neither enter nor leave. He informed Almagro of all this, asking for succor; when [Almagro] learned about it, he ordered Francisco de Chaves[3] to provide it with some horsemen, and traveling quickly, he joined Salcedo. *fol. 127v*

The Indians learned from their spies that they were coming, and before they ever came together, without making any noise they all abandoned the stronghold whichever way they could. And after Francisco de Chaves passed with the horsemen, the inhabitants came out to the highway and assailed the yanaconas and stole part of the baggage, quickly retreating to flee the fury of the horsemen, who with a battle cry descended on them. When they learned that the enemy had abandoned the village, the Spaniards set up camp in some groves below it. They were very cautious because they were close to the Juris, wild and very brave people, many of whom eat human flesh, and who were so feared by the Incas that not only were they unable to make friends of them, but fearing the devastation they caused, they had placed regular garrisons of warriors on the borders; and they live almost like barbarians. Many describe these people, especially the Spaniards who are involved in the conquest of the Río de la Plata. Salcedo again sent messengers to the adelantado, letting him know what had happened and confirming that the three Christians had been killed in that land and that he had information about three others ahead.

Almagro arrived at Tupiza, where he caught up with Villac Umu[4] and Paullu, who had gone ahead, and the Indians gave him ninety thousand pesos in pure gold, which some say they had brought from Chile from the tributes of the Incas. He had great reports that there were rich veins of metals in Collasuyu, and they even discussed settlement, which was another issue because they had their feet in the *fol. 128* richest land in the world. But to this Almagro replied that it was very little land for the many Spaniards who were with him. The chiefs of the province of Paria[5] and other caciques from the previous villages had come with Almagro because he ordered them to; they were treated with much honor, and most or all of them returned to their lands.

Villac Umu—who had a pact with Manco to stir up the eastern provinces against the Christians who were going to Chile because they believed that this way their destruction would be more certain—quietly and with great dissimulation incited the villages and places through which they marched, saying many blasphemies about the Spaniards so that later they would openly rebel against them. Those who listened did not have the courage, nor did he strive for it out of fear that there were too many horses and Spaniards. But he wished to get away and join Manco, considering it easier to kill those who were in Cuzco than those who were going to Chile. And thus, believing that Almagro was far from Cuzco and that it would not be possible for him to return quickly, he decided to flee. After he planned it, he carried it out one night when they did not expect it, taking with him some Indian men and women. He went toward Collao, on secret roads unknown to our people, receiving wherever he went superb services because they greatly respected him due to his pontifical office of priesthood. In the morning Villac Umu was missed. It was confirmed that he got away. Almagro was incensed and summoned Paullu, whom he angrily asked how Villac Umu could have gone and why he did not warn him about it. Paullu was a boy. He replied fearfully that he knew or understood nothing. Almagro arranged to have him watched from then on so that he would not do what Villac Umu had done, placing him in the care of Martín Cote,[6] a brave soldier and a native Viscayan. [Almagro] spoke with great benevolence to the natives of that land, assuring them of the friendship of the Christians. He left to join captains Salcedo and Francisco de Chaves, leaving a note for Noguerol de Ulloa,[7] who remained with the rearguard, to march quickly and join him. He then marched with his people and arrived in the village of Jujuy, where he spent more than two months waiting for the Spaniards who had remained behind. Among them came Don Alonso de Montemayor,[8] an illustrious knight, native of Seville, whom Almagro received very well.

Almagro continued exploring until he arrived in Chicoana,[9] where *fol. 128v* he found the natives had risen up and were at the point of war. He ordered Francisco de Chaves and Saavedra[10] to go with certain horsemen to survey up the valley. It was very useful because when the natives saw the speed of the horses, they all hid, some in one part, others in another, so that none were seen. But within a few days a larger force had assembled, gaining in strength. They swore on the Sun, high and almighty, that they were going to kill them all or die. When they decided this, they sent people to aggravate and kill the yanaconas, the Blacks, and the servants who, leaving the Christians, would come out of the camp to look for grass, firewood, straw, or other necessary things. After they caused some harm, Almagro and several horsemen ambushed them in order to kill them, but they were not too afflicted and killed his horse. Shortly afterwards he returned with more people. He found the villages deserted and the Indians gone. They appeared only on the edges of the ridges and hills, from where they fervently screamed, and given the hoarse and frightful howls, it seemed as if there were demons among them. After the adelantado returned from searching for the Indians, he decided to leave Chicoana, giving permission to the lords of Paria and the rest to return to their lands.

There were 193 Spaniards, horsemen, and footmen who had joined Almagro. Rodrigo Núñez[11] went as his campmaster and Maldonado[12] as standard bearer. To carry the baggage and for service they took so many Indian men and women that it is painful to say. They were all placed in chains, ropes, and other shackles, and had to endure being guarded by yanacona and Black tyrants, who gave them great blows and whippings if they stopped walking, not allowing them to catch their breath. If anyone complained of being tired or ill, he was not believed, nor did he have another cure than kicks, so that losing their strength and spirit, they left their bodies without souls in the chains and shackles. And they were not only used for that, but when they arrived at the camp, as exhausted as they were, they made them go for firewood, grass, straw, water, and anything else that was needed. They swallowed many bitter pills. When night came, they piled them all up, giving them the ground for bed, even if it were freezing, and for cover the sky, and there they guarded them. And if anyone needed to relieve himself or tried to move from weariness, the nightwatch regardless made him stay still with the pommels of the swords or clubs. Many, many times I have seen with my own eyes these and other more severe things done to these unfortunate people. And those who read it, have patience because I cut short what I am relating, and do make use of reading about it to supplicate Our Lord to pardon such grave sins.

Notes

1 Rodrigo de Salcedo.

2 Then

3 Chaves came to Peru in 1534. When Almagro returned to Cuzco, Chaves was one of the guards of Gonzalo and Hernando Pizarro. He was a founder and town councillor of Chincha. After the Battle of Salinas he was imprisoned by Pizarro, but was later released. Chaves came into conflict with the Almagrists over a concubine, and after insulting Almagro the Younger, he was executed. See Busto, *Diccionario,* 1:417–18.

4 See chapter 49.

5 Encompassing Lake Poopó and the mining district of Oruro, this region held the largest population in Charcas.

6 Cote later fought for the Almagrists in the Battle of Salinas, and after Pizarro's assassination, Almagro the Younger made him captain of the horse. He fought at Chupas, was captured, and hanged the following day. See Busto, *Diccionario,* 1:406.

7 For a biographical study of Francisco Noguerol de Ulloa, see Cook and Cook, *Good Faith and Truthful Ignorance.*

8 Montemayor fought with Almagro at the Battle of Salinas and was taken prisoner. Later, after initially supporting Almagro the Younger, he switched to Vaca de Castro and fought at Chupas. He remained loyal to the Crown, and after Viceroy Blasco Núñez Vela was killed at the Battle of Añaquito, Gonzalo Pizarro ordered Montemayor's execution. The sentence was commuted to exile in Chile, but the ship's captain took him to Guatemala instead. See Mendiburu, *Diccionario*, 7:417–18.

9 About sixty kilometers south of Salta, on one of the tributaries of the Paraná River. They reached the southeastern frontier of the Inca Empire and were near the Chaco Austral. The natives had directed them further east than necessary to reach Chile, perhaps hoping to be rid of them.

10 Juan de Saavedra; see chapter 85.

11 See chapter 32.

12 Lockhart points out there were several Diego Maldonados in Peru during the period. This is not the "Rich" Maldonado who was at Cajamarca; see *Men of Cajamarca*, p. 223.

XCV

About how, while exploring, Almagro arrived at snowy mountain passes where his people suffered great hardship

fol. 129 Almagro left the land where he had been and went toward the south to the place they call Chile. After marching several days and having a great shortage of provisions, he arrived at a small fortress. Even though that region is flat, it is so sterile that it lacks what elsewhere abounds. He ordered some of those who came with him to go out and search in all directions because the camp had not fully arrived, nor did it come until the next day. Because there were so many people together, and they did not find anything to eat and had brought only a little, they were all dejected, knowing that there would be no settlement or any place to find provisions for several days. Almagro ordered that certain pigs[1] they had left be distributed, and sheep, and he begged the Spaniards to bear the hardships with courage, for without them no honor or any profit was ever won. They replied that they would and took steps to safeguard what they had left. They set out and marched for seven days through some saltpeters and a sterile and desolate land. They began to feel the shortage. The reason why they were suffering so much was the large entourage that accompanied them. Climbing up a ravine from below, they came across a small dwelling, where Almagro stationed himself. Not very far ahead they saw large mountains, white from the heavy snow cover. They turned their eyes in all directions and clearly realized that the highlands stretched across a vast territory and that they would be forced to cross them without knowing how far they extended. If the courage of the Spaniards were not as inexhaustible and great as it has been, believe me that in reaching such passes they would have abandoned the course, as any other people in the world would have done. It seems, looking at it carefully, that it is more foolhardiness than fortitude to enter the dense forests and snowy countryside, as they do, without knowing when or where they will end up, or whether they will have provisions.

The Indians said that there was much more snow than what they could see where they were. The adelantado decided to go ahead with some horsemen on the highway[2] itself until they came close to the mountain range. Then, if it seemed possible, he would cross the alps, *fol. 129v* and after arriving at a settlement, he would send provisions to those who remained behind. The scout went ahead with some Spaniards. When they entered the snow, there was so much of it that neither the road nor a rock nor any other thing was visible other than its whiteness, with snowflakes continuously falling. Those who had remained with the camp rested because Almagro had gone ahead; they could then go as quickly as possible, stopping little in the alps. Indeed, the day he left, the adelantado marched with great effort until he reached some small tambos, where he slept, feeling the bitter cold. I believe they told me that he rested there for one day to get news of those who had remained behind, and when some reached him, he proceeded on his journey. The south wind blew so strongly that they did not feel their noses or ears, and their feet turned to icicles. If they raised their eyes, the snow burned them; so much of it was falling that it was astonishing. It was twelve leagues from the top of the mountain pass to the valley of Copiapó.[3] Following a day's march, he slept on a river bank in another small tambo at the foot of an alp. Next day, forging quickly ahead, they went until they emerged from that torment, as tired and weary as the reader can imagine.

They arrived in the valley, where they were very well received by its inhabitants. Almagro spoke to them affectionately, begging them to go and help the Spaniards who were coming and to take them some of the food that they had in the valley because he would do for them whatever they asked in anything that concerned them. The good men said joyfully that they would do it, and many of them went out with sheep, rams, maize, and some roots.[4] With Almagro having gone ahead, as has been told, those who remained behind were in great need of provisions, and when they entered the snow country, their weariness grew. The Indians wept, reproaching those who had taken them from their lands to die in the snow. The Spaniards regretted being there. If they and these service people wanted to walk, they could not from weakness. And if they stopped to rest, they would freeze. The horses were also tired and spent. They encouraged each other by saying that soon they would reach the valley of Copiapó. Many Indian men and women and some Spaniards and Blacks began to die. Some, being hungry, ate the mud that forms in the marshes.

There was no firewood to make fire with, just sheep dung and some roots[5] that they pulled from below the ground. The nights that they spent sleeping in the mountain passes were so full of hardship, so fearful and frightening, that it seemed to them they were all in hell. The
fol. 130 wind did not weaken, and it was so cold that it made them lose their breath. Thirty horses and many Indian men and women and Blacks died; their souls left them while they leaned on the rocks, gasping. In addition to this misfortune, there was such great and ravenous hunger that many of the living Indians ate the dead ones; the Spaniards heartily ate the horses that had frozen, but if they stopped to butcher them, they found themselves like them. And they relate how a Black who was traveling with a bridled horse stopped to listen to some voices that he heard, and he and the horse instantly froze. The Spaniards, distressed and transfigured, marched on, commending themselves to God Almighty and to Our Lady. When night came they set up their tents as best as they could in the vast amount of snow falling on them.[6]

In the meantime, as I have related, Almagro tried to make the natives of Copiapó go to the highway with refreshment to help those who were coming through the snow. When some came out of it, they shouted loudly to one another so that all would learn that they were close to a settlement and flat land, and they could take heart and regain courage, which they indeed did. When they were out of the alps and large snow-covered rocky mountains and in a cheerful land where the sun was shining brightly, and they could see clear sky, they praised God, and it seemed to them as if they were reborn that day. Their pleasure increased with the provisions of meat, maize, and other things that the Indians brought. Because they were starved, they stuffed themselves so much that many became ill, unable to digest, producing obstructions in their bellies. It did not last long because this malady is cured with work and exercise of the body. And after all of them were out of the snow, they reached the valley, where they fully recuperated.

The legitimate lord of [the valley] was a young boy. At the time that his father died, he left his tutelage and the governance of the land in charge of a chieftain from among his kin. When the lord died, [the chieftain] unjustly usurped the rule that did not belong to him for more time than until the minor came of age. Furthermore, he attempted to kill him to ensure his treachery. But some of the natives loyal to him decided to hide him where the usurper could not put his plan into effect. After the Spaniards entered, he came to them to ask for their help and justice from the high God of the heavens. Almagro ordered that testimony be taken about this case, and he learned that the disinherited youth was indeed telling the truth and asking for justice, so he received his support.

But now that his dominion was returned to him, I will also relate here how three Christians, without Pizarro's or Almagro's orders, left Cuzco, preceding the others whom [the Indians] had killed, foolishly *fol. 130v* passing through many lands and far away from where our people were. The Indians were so kind that they did not harm them; instead, they carried them in litters or hammocks from one village to another, giving them the necessary provisions. And when they arrived at the end of the day, they gave testimony, saying: "Look that we give them to you alive, well and healthy!" This was the law of the Incas, so that if one or more went, and they were killed, they would know where it happened, so that if it was punished the innocent ones would not be taken for the sinners. In this manner these three men traveled until they reached a valley whose lord was named Marcandey, who received them well. But having an evil thought, he decided to kill them and the horses they had brought. And while they were asleep, he did it, burying the bodies and the horses in a secret place. Some say that all the chiefs of the district took part in it; others say that they did not, but that after they were dead and they learned about it, they came to celebrate with Marcandey, making great sacrifices and drunken feasts. Almagro always asked about these three Christians, and they would inform him that they had gone ahead.

He left Copiapó, and in three days journey he reached this valley. They received him well with an appearance of peace, supplying his people with provisions. The yanaconas and Christians went in search of some necessities, and finding the remains of the dead, they discovered their deceit. Almagro set out to explore, and he arrived in the valley of Coquimbo,[7] where there were large dwellings of the Incas. He made a report about the death of the three Christians and sent a messenger back to Captain Diego de Vega, who had remained with the rearguard, [ordering] that he should capture Marcandey and his brother on an appointed day, and that some Spaniards should return to Copiapó and seize the previous illegitimate lord and come with them to Coquimbo. There, with great dissimulation, he forced all the chiefs to appear before him. They took twenty-seven of them captive, and with great cruelty and little fear of God he ordered them burned, unwilling to hear the excuses that some offered. Moreover, the Christians deserved what came to them for wanting to go ahead of everyone and rule as lords in a faraway land where they owed them little. They commented to me that [the chiefs] died with great courage, but from what I have seen, I know this comes from savagery. Among those they burned there was an orejón who loudly exclaimed: "*Viracocha, ancha misque nina,*" which means, "Oh Christian, how very sweet is the fire to me."

Notes

1 When possible, the Spaniards drove with them hogs that could be used as a source of food.

2 The royal highway of the Incas extended southward; the eastern wing ran through Tucumán; and the western continued toward the central valley of Chile. See John Hyslop, *The Inka Road System* (Orlando: Academic Press, 1984).

3 They may have marched through the Pass of San Francisco (4,726 meters) just north of the towering Nevado Ojos del Salado (6,880 meters). Copiapó, at the southern boundaries of the Atacama Desert, is only fifty kilometers from the Pacific Coast.

4 Tubers.

5 Dried llama dung and stored dry chunks of a large Andean lichen were the traditional combustible materials in the barren highland sectors of the Andes and continue to be used there.

6 The chronology is unclear, probably because it must have seemed an eternity to those who made the march and later described it to Cieza. The distance that they had to travel at elevations more than 4,500 meters, at or above the snowline at this latitude, suggests several days.

7 Three hundred kilometers south of Copiapó and roughly half distant between that city and present-day Valparaíso. Here, they were approaching the southern border of the vast Inca domain.

XCVI

About how Rodrigo Orgoños left Cuzco and what happened to him until he reached the valley of Copiapó

I remember that I wrote earlier that when the adelantado set out from the city of Cuzco, he left behind his general, Rodrigo Orgoños, to follow him with the people who were coming from everywhere to participate in the expedition. And when it was time, he left—along with Cristóbal de Sotelo,[1] Oñate,[2] Pérez, and other vecinos. They took good horses with good equipment and Blacks for service, as well as other things that are useful in an exploration. They marched each day until they entered the large province[3] of Collao. The Indians served them well and provided them with what was needed, without receiving any payment for it because here it is customary to eat at the will of others. Although these natives were very restless because of what Villac Umu had admonished them to do, they waited to learn that Manco was out of prison before they would clearly and openly act against the Christians and attack them. [The Spaniards] went through these villages, and after they left them, they arrived within a few days in the province of Tupiza. They needed provisions, which was the reason why it was expedient for some horsemen and service people to search for them throughout the region. *fol. 131*

After they went eight leagues, in a gorge they found a large herd of sheep and other provisions, but the Indians to whom these belonged were armed to defend them from anyone wanting to take them. They had placed many boulders on the top of the precipices to hurl down from the heights, which with their massiveness and speed would kill everything they hit below. Because the Spaniards had come out only to get what they knew was there, and underrating the Indians as well as their huge rocks, they descended into the gorge below. The natives, threatening them maliciously, pushed the boulders, which frightened our people, who tried to[4] escape to avoid being hit. Some were able to save themselves, but most could not flee, nor could two of them avoid being crushed,[5] which delighted the Indians, who exclaimed: "Take it, *fol. 131v* thieves, eat what we have served you!" and other similar taunts. The

Spaniards had left the horses somewhat behind because the terrain was rugged and they were ineffective. But because they found themselves in such danger and unable to assail the Indians, they decided to get to them as quickly as possible. Aware of this weakness, the Indians pressed them dreadfully so that they killed two more Christians. The rest, with great fortune and especially God's favor, seized the horses, and after they returned to the camp, they told Orgoños what had happened to them. He set out from that land, marching on the same route that Almagro was taking, suffering great hardship and necessity because the natives had hidden the provisions, and they were unable to find anything other than some roots and wild herbs.

They arrived in this way to Jujuy, where they found some food, which was a great relief for them. The horses were tired, and therefore they rested four days. From here they went to Chicoana, where they halted for two [days] to provision themselves with food, of which they found plenty. They were informed about the alps of Chicoana. They marched until they reached a river called Bermejo River,[6] where they made carob bread, which is good.[7] Within several days they arrived in view of large snow-capped mountains. They were astonished to see such whiteness, and they feared the cold they would endure. As best as they could, they entered the snow, all of them commending themselves to God our Lord. The wind was strong, and they marched with great hardship. When night fell, the fear increased, and as best as they could, they set up tents. The cold was so great that most of the Blacks and Indian men and women died, and those who escaped lost their fingers or became blind. When Orgoños was setting up his tent, so much snow was falling that when he barely put his hand on a pole to attach it, his fingers burned and his fingernails fell off. For days everyone's skin changed as if it were Saint Anthony's fire.[8] Two Spaniards were in one of these tents, and a strong gust of south wind ripped it down, and so much snow fell that this place became an eternal resting place for the two Spaniards and their Indian men and women, as well as for the horses, which had been tied next to the tent. Sotelo and Castillo (?) [*sic*] also suffered[9] on their hands
fol. 132 the same injury as Orgoños.[10] The Spaniards, frightened to see such a storm, prayed to God to deliver them from it. And with His help, after four days passed, they came out of the snow, leaving behind

the two dead Spaniards and many Indian men and women, Blacks, and twenty-six horses with their saddles and gear, and many leather trunks and bundles of clothing.

The natives of Copiapó learned of their coming. Because of the support that the lord of the valley had received from Almagro when he had placed him in possession of his dominion, he decided to honor the Christians who were coming because Almagro himself asked him to do so. Therefore, he ordered many Indians to set out from the valley with provisions, which delighted Orgoños and his people, and they all returned with the Christians to the valley, where they were well received and housed in common lodgings. Because they had suffered so much hardship in the alps, the Christians decided to rest a few days in that land. They did not cause the natives much trouble.

Notes

1 From Zamora. His brother Gregorio de Sotelo was in Cajamarca. He fought at the Battle of Salinas, was involved in the assassination of Francisco Pizarro, and was himself later assassinated. Lockhart, *Men of Cajamarca,* pp. 241–42.

2 Probably Pedro de Oñate, a staunch Almagrist. He was executed by Vaca de Castro after the Battle of Chupas; see Lockhart, *Men of Cajamarca,* pp. 225–26, 233, 245, 273.

3 and abundant

4 jumped

5 dead

6 Literally the "Red" River, it runs through the Gran Chaco before emptying into the Paraná River.

7 Carob bread, made from the flour of ground seeds of the carob tree, was often eaten by the Europeans in time of hunger. The tree grew in the eastern Mediterranean, and there is also an American variety.

8 *Fuego de San Antón* (Saint Anthony's fire) can refer to erysipelas, an acute infectious disease of the skin caused by streptococcus bacteria, but more accurately it was a form of epidemic gangrene, a deadly disease prevalent throughout the sixteenth century. It was characterized by high fever, sharp pains throughout the body, and blots of reddish eruptions on the arms and legs, which later darkened, produced a burning sensation, and then be-

came gangrenous. See Antonio Hermosilla Molina, *Cien años de la medicina sevillana* (Seville: Diputación Provincial, 1970), pp. 408–9.

9 lost

10 This last folio, recto and verso, seems to be the work of a scribe because the handwriting is clear and elegant.

XCVII

About how Juan de Herrada left Cuzco to take the decrees to Almagro, and what happened to him until he reached the valley of Copiapó, where he joined Orgoños

Juan de Herrada,[1] Almagro's majordomo, was in Lima until Hernando Pizarro arrived. He asked him for the decrees that he was bringing for the adelantado. He replied that because they all were going to Cuzco, he would give them to him there, and he would write to Almagro. Juan de Herrada complained to Pizarro, saying that he was upset that his brother refused to hand over the decrees and that he should order him to immediately give them to him. He replied that he would give them to him without fail in Cuzco. When Hernando Pizarro arrived in Cuzco, Juan de Herrada received the decrees, although some say that he enjoined him to get them.[2]

Lorenzo de Aldana,[3] the auditor Juan de Guzmán, Hernán Gómez, Juan de Larreinaga, Pedro Mateo Picón,[4] Luis de Matos, the Bachelor Enrique, and up to fifty others followed Juan de Herrada, and they joined him in the [blank]. There they found that about eighty Spaniards were going on foot and horseback, provided with people of Peru for their service. From there they marched, suffering great need because the natives had hidden the provisions. When they arrived at Ortopisa, they did not find anything to eat there either, which doubled their dismay. One day's march further ahead, twenty horsemen set out by Juan de Herrada's orders to one part and another of *fol. 132v*
the way to see if by chance they could encounter something. Because the Indians had stored the maize in caves, the yanaconas whom they had brought along discovered some, and they joyfully returned with it. Also, a herd of sheep was found by other Spaniards, which they all shared. They marched on, and because they had consumed this food, Juan de Herrada went out with several horsemen to search for some, and as diligent as he was, he came across a gorge where the Indians had hidden some. There were many Indian warriors at the top of the gorge, and it was necessary for several of our men to go out with sword and buckler to take the summit. But [the Indians] shot

so many stones and darts at them that they thought it safer not to proceed further, but instead to return to where the horsemen were. Juan de Herrada ordered the horsemen to alight and descend below the ravine, from where, in spite of the Indians, they were able to take more than one hundred cargas of good maize, and with that they returned to the camp. From there they went until they reached a fortress. They halted and had to search for provisions because after Almagro and Orgoños had gone through, everything had been pillaged, and the natives, in order not to die of hunger, had hidden in secret places what they had left. The Spaniards and the yanaconas went out in every direction from this place, and with great effort they found some provisions. They rested for fifteen days to restore their emaciated horses to health. They learned about the snowy mountain passes and that Orgoños was in Copiapó. They came across several weary Blacks and Indians who had stayed behind, and they saw that many were dead, which was a pitiful sight. Juan de Herrada decided that the Bachelor Enrique, Luis de Matos, and another two or three horsemen should ride ahead with full speed in order to reach Orgoños so that because he knew of their coming and that they were bringing Almagro's decrees, he would supply them with some provisions. And thus they left, and with much hardship they arrived at Copiapó, where they gave this report to Orgoños. He was pleased and announced that Cuzco and the best of the land fell within [Almagro's] jurisdiction, and he agreed to wait for Juan de Herrada, who, along with the Spaniards accompanying him, was suffering great necessity.

We will leave them there in order to tell about the coming of Hernando Pizarro to Cuzco and what else happened.[5]

Notes

1 Herrada, also known as Rada, was from Navarre and came to Peru in 1534 with Pedro de Alvarado. He joined Almagro and often acted as mediator between him and Pizarro. When Almagro was executed after the Battle of Salinas, Herrada became guardian of his son Diego. He was the principal leader of the group that assassinated Francisco Pizarro in 1541 and was largely in charge of the organization of Almagro the Younger's administra-

tion. See Lockhart, *Men of Cajamarca*, p. 272; Mendiburu, *Diccionario*, 9:288; and Hemming, *Conquest*, pp. 262, 559.

2 These were the royal decrees that extended jurisdiction over the south to Diego de Almagro.

3 Born in Cáceres around 1508, Aldana first went to Santa Marta in 1528, then entered Peru in 1535. Back in Cuzco from Chile he helped imprison Gonzalo and Hernando Pizarro, but later allowed Gonzalo to escape to Lima. He explored in the north and founded Pasto. When Pizarro was assassinated, he marched south, joined Governor Vaca de Castro, and fought at Chupas. He was rewarded with an encomienda in Jauja. He rose up with Gonzalo Pizarro, but when Gonzalo sent him to report to the king, he negotiated with Gasca in Panama and turned the fleet over to him. Gasca sent him back south in command of the small navy and with notice of the king's pardons for the rebels. See Busto, *Diccionario*, 1:48–53.

4 Pedro Picón was from Merida and was later involved in the assassination of Francisco Pizarro; see Pedro de Cieza de León, *Crónica del Perú: Cuarta parte*, vol. 2, *Guerra de Chupas* (Lima: Universidad Católica del Perú, 1994), chapter 30.

5 This is where the extant copy of Cieza's manuscript ends. It is clear from the last sentence of this chapter as well as his introduction in *Part One* that this is not where he planned to end *Part Three*. We will finish the narrative as taken by Antonio de Herrera y Tordesillas.

EDITORS' NOTE

Antonio de Herrera y Tordesillas continues the *Discovery and Conquest of Peru,* using Cieza's text with relatively modest changes. This translation of chapters 98–101 is based on the first edition of Herrera y Tordesillas in the Jay I. Kislak Foundation in Miami Lakes, Florida; the selection is partly guided by Sáenz de Santa María, *Obras completas,* 2:361–68.

XCVIII

(From Herrera, decade V, book 8, chapter IV)

That Hernando Pizarro, upon reaching Cuzco freed Inca Manco, who left the city and started the war

After Juan Pizarro had punished in Condesuyu those who had killed Juan Becerril, he returned to Cuzco, arriving at almost the same time as his brother Hernando Pizarro, who immediately took over the government and informed him about the state of things and made him his lieutenant. He then freed Manco Inca against the will of his brothers. Therefore, it was said that in gratitude for it the Inca gave him a most opulent gift of gold. Because Manco acted so humbly with Hernando Pizarro and continuously manifested to him his goodwill, he wanted to treat him with similar liberality.

[Manco] then began to have secret meetings with his men, who always reminded him of the advice of the great priest Villac Umu regarding the attainment of his freedom. They told him that the division of the Castilians was such an opportune time to escape that terrible servitude and to return to his initial standing, and that he should not miss it. Indeed, many of the Almagrists must have died on the way, and when they wanted to return, there would be so few that there would be no reason to fear them. And in Cuzco there were few people, as one could see, and there were even fewer in the City of the Kings. And discussing the way that they had to proceed, all wanted him to follow what the high priest had counseled—that the Inca should leave. In order to better execute it, and having had his council about it, Manco told Hernando Pizarro that he wanted to go for his father's gold and silver statue to present him with it (which they say Pizarro had asked him for), a distance of four leagues from Cuzco, and he ordered two Castilians to accompany him with his Indian interpreter, Alvarico.

When they learned in Cuzco that the Inca had gone, the natives lamented loudly, saying that he had to attempt to kill the Castilians and all the Indians who were with them. Hernando Pizarro, realizing the mistake he had made, left within eight days with seventy horsemen

22. Title page. Volume three of Antonio de Herrera y Tordesillas, *Historia general de los hechos de los castellanos en las Islas y Tierra Firme del Mar Océano* (Madrid, 1601–15). Courtesy of the Jay I. Kislak Foundation, Miami Lakes, Florida.

in order to bring back the Inca, who was in Calca. He had told the two Castilians to return because they were not needed, and they met Hernando Pizarro and told him that they were returning because they had been dismissed. With all this, he wanted to take a look at Calca, and by ascending a hilltop he discovered a multitude of Indians, who attacked him because even in Cuzco they had many spies. And fighting with them, he took them toward the village, and there it ended. The next morning he decided to return to Cuzco because he did not believe it to be safe in his absence. Countless Indians always followed him and bore down on him until they enclosed him in the city.

The Indians did not retreat after Hernando Pizarro had retreated to Cuzco; instead, so many came that those participating in that siege reached two hundred thousand. In the defense there were no more than 170 Castilians and up to one thousand natives who fought in their company, of whom many were yanaconas. Because the Indians were approaching the houses of the city, Hernando Pizarro decided to set out with horsemen, leaving inside the best force he could. Fighting, [the Indians] allowed him to enter well within their ranks, and when they thought it was time, they attacked his rear. But making haste, they broke out safely, except for one horseman named Francisco Mejía. Seeing his horse fall, they assailed him so quickly that they captured him and then cut off his head and also that of his horse. That day they believed they had such advantage that they came closer to the city, and the high priest Villac Umu entered the fortress.[1] Therefore, each day they fought, gaining advantage in the streets, and as they barricaded them, they made openings like loopholes through which they entered and left.

The Castilians had withdrawn to the plaza, and there they had their tents. Because there was a strong house nearby, and fearing that the Indians might gain it, Hernando Pizarro ordered a captain to get inside with some infantrymen and fortify it as best they could. But the first night that they placed it under guard, the Indians took it, which produced such great pride in them that they had gained almost the entire plaza. Because they shot so many rounds of stones with the slings, there was no respite. The Castilians were confined in two houses facing each other. It seemed to them that it would be better to go out than to perish there, and as dense and continuous as the hail of rocks was, they suddenly came out together with their Indian friends, and they went charging into their enemies in the lower streets, destroying their entrenchment. In order to resist the harm of the horses, the Indians devised a certain type of rope made of sheep's tendons with three strands and on each one a stone, and with these they ensnared and bound the horses and the horsemen in such a way that they were tied up and unable to make use of their weapons. The infantrymen were very useful because with their swords they cut those ties that they called ayllus, although with effort because the cords were very strong.

The Castilians regained the plaza fortress with a great effort, and the captain of the infantry was wounded by a stone blow in his head. The noise of the shell trumpets and the drums and [the Indians'] yelling was frightening. The Castilians were very upset to see that they were so few in such a multitude, although by that point they had already taken the city and expelled the Indians because they knew how to fight with skill and with ingenuity to destroy the machines of the barbarians. Considering the great harm that they were receiving from the fortress, Hernando Pizarro proposed to the Castilians that it would be wise to take it because otherwise it would be difficult to survive. When it was decided to do it, he encharged it to his brother Juan Pizarro, who, with the people that he appointed, went fighting against many squadrons of Indians, who before reaching the barbican had made a trench or pit in order to impede the passage of the horses. But Alonso de Mesa valiantly launched forward, passed with his horse, and fighting with the Indians, made it possible for the rest to pass. Thus, they were able to get closer to the barbican of the fortress, which had two entrances. And pushed by raging force, one was gained with a great Indian mortality, although with one stone blow they killed Juan Pizarro's page.

Meanwhile, there was also fighting within the city, and the Indians set fire to it. Because all the houses were covered with straw, in one moment all was ablaze. This placed the Castilians in such straits that in addition to the anguish of having their houses and possessions burned, they were being choked by the smoke. Yet the fact that one part of the plaza was unobstructed, and that they had gained the fortress that was there, was a great relief to them. Yet with all this they felt so upset and anguished that they were on the verge of abandoning the city and going by way of Arequipa and the coastal plains to the City of the Kings, where [the Castilians] were not resting either: because the uprising was general throughout all the land, a large army of Indians had come to lay siege to it. But because [the Castilians] could come there by sea, and the land was flat, where the horses could do much harm to them, the Indians could not linger on as in Cuzco.

Because the Castilians of this city were miserable and without hope of assistance, they judged that in the City of the Kings they would be also in difficulty. The Indians tossed out the heads of some Castilians who had died, of those who resided in their encomiendas, and in addition they killed as many as they could on the roadways. They again discussed abandoning the city, and the regiment asked for it and advised it, believing that it was impossible to defend it because of the great tenacity of the Indians in a siege that had already lasted nine months. But Juan Pizarro, Gonzalo Pizarro, Gabriel de Rojas, and Hernando Ponce argued against it, considering it a shameful thing and that one should rather die there.

Note

1 Sacsahuaman.

XCIX

(From Herrera V, 8, V)

That the fortress of Cuzco was won and Juan Pizarro died then; Hernando Pizarro marched on Tambo

Juan Pizarro persisted valiantly in battling the fortress of Cuzco and pressed down on it, intending not to withdraw until totally winning it because even after they entered it, the towers remained to be taken. It was already very late, and being tired from the exertion of the whole day, he took off his helmet, and at that very instant they hit him so hard with a stone in the head that they stunned him, and he died within fifteen days. The next day it seemed to Hernando Pizarro that because of the continuous Indian assaults against the city, they would be lost if they did not take the fortress. He went himself with no more than twelve horsemen to assist those engaged in that enterprise, leaving in his place Gabriel de Rojas to defend the city. One of the twelve was Hernán Sánchez de Badajoz, who attached a ladder to a tower, although with obvious danger, and covered with his shield and with great agility and even more luck because God wished that he not be knocked down by the many hurled stones, he climbed to the top and jumped in, and fighting with the Indians, he took the tower. Immediately, others climbed up, and the other tower was taken. More than a thousand Indians died in this enterprise. In the city there was also fighting, and they had wounded Gabriel de Rojas with an arrow shot through the nostrils all the way to the palate. They felled Alonso de Toro with two rock launches. With the fortress taken, Juan Ortiz was placed there as guard, with fifty Castilians, so that another negligent loss of it would not happen.

When Don Francisco Pizarro found himself besieged in the City of the Kings, and because he was getting news from all parts of the deaths of the Castilians and of other such misfortunes, and realizing that the uprising was general and that there was no news from Cuzco, he became very distressed. Fearful of losing the land, he notified Don Hernando Cortés in New Spain—as well as the audiencia of Hispaniola, Tierra Firme, Guatemala, and Nicaragua—of the condition in which he found himself, stressing the danger and asking for quick help. Although they came from everywhere, it was late, and the need had already passed. And seeing himself extricated, he sent out at diverse times four captains with some troops of Castilian soldiers. The Indians killed all of them, except for eight or nine Manco had with him, using them as slaves. And along with these people he took horses, arms, and some muskets, and a lot of merchandise and preserves, and the Indians used the weapons and fought with them.

While those of Cuzco were thus engaged, Hernando Pizarro proposed to march on Tambo in the Yucay Valley, six leagues from Cuzco, where the Inca resided. And leaving the city in charge of Gabriel de Rojas, he went with seventy horsemen, some infantry, and a good throng of Indian friends. Arriving near Tambo, he broke through Indian squadrons that all fled—except two from Chachapoyas, who launched two great rocks from the wall and hit the leg of a horse and broke it. He gave so many jumps that he excited the rest of [the horses] so much that it became expedient to retreat to a flat plain near the gate of the place. The Indians were so encouraged by this that such an excessive number converged on the Castilians, they believed they would die on that day. In addition to this, at one point [the Indians] shifted the riverbed that passed through the place and flooded it on top of them so that the horses were mired down. And in addition to this, the Carib Indians were overloaded, and there was great mortality among them and their friends, and also muskets were discharged against the Castilians. With the arrival of night, Hernando Pizarro decided to retreat, which he did with great difficulty because of obstacles they encountered at each step: people and also the many thorns and prickles of a thistle they call *cabuya,*[1] which they had placed in their way and which hamstrung the horses. With the siege already underway for ten months, they resolved to go out for supplies, and they had a fierce battle in which they captured two captains, from whom they learned that the Inca was awaiting the summer in order to amass a more powerful army and finish expelling the Castilians. And because more than three hundred Castilians were killed in this war, in order to please the Inca they brought him their heads. One Castilian from among those whom he had imprisoned said to him that if he sent some of these heads to Cuzco, it would cause the Castilians to lose courage. He did this: in one sack there were seven or eight of them, as well as many letters, and among them a papal brief regarding a jubilee[2] for the city of Cuzco. The Castilian used this ploy so that the benefit of the jubilee would not be lost. And thus Manco, at the advice of the Castilian, ordered the heads thrown out to where those of Cuzco could see them. And coming across the sack, they discovered them and the brief, and they profited from it.

Notes

1 Agave.

2 Jubilee year, a time of special indulgences, was originally instituted in 1300 by Pope Boniface VIII and was to be repeated every one hundred years, though that interval was soon reduced to fifty years or less.

C

(From Herrera V, 8, VI/VII)

That the war with the Indians continues and Gabriel de Rojas routs an enemy army

While this siege lasted, it was customary for six horsemen to go to reconnoiter the countryside each week and to find out if any help from the City of the Kings was coming. Indeed, it seemed impossible that after so much time a message had not reached Don Francisco Pizarro about the trouble that they found themselves in in Cuzco. And going out at one time or another, Gonzalo Pizarro with six well-chosen and most trustworthy horsemen—who were Alonso de Mesa, Tomás Vázquez, Pedro Pizarro, Juan de Pancorbo, Miguel Cornejo, and Castañeda[1]—went reconnoitering in the direction of Jaquijahuana, along the way lancing some small troops of Indians that were passing through the countryside. Arriving at Jaquijahuana, he found such a large number of Indians that because it was already the custom of warfare of the Castilians that no matter how few or many there might be who went to engage the Indians, no matter how large the number [of Indians], and although they understood the obvious danger, they engaged them in order not to allow them to become arrogant. [The Indians] acted with such spirit with their shower of arrows, slingwork, and lancework that many times they were able to take hold of the tails of the horses without being frightened by seeing the irons of lances pierce their chests. Thus, a long time went by when Gonzalo Pizarro was at times retreating and at times attacking, in order to keep gaining ground in this way. Indeed, the effort of the horsemen was diminishing, and the anger and rage of the Indians was increasing, joined by the multitude. It was expedient for these seven valiant men, realizing their obvious perdition, to do more than they had ever done on many other occasions. Gonzalo Pizarro, who was already in position, thought that six were worth as much as seven and decided to send one to let his brother know about the danger he was in. Meanwhile, he felt it was expedient to keep retreating rapidly to a level plain where they could take advantage of the horses. And there,

23. Manco Capac sets fire to Cuzco. Felipe Guaman Poma de Ayala, *El primer nueva corónica y buen gobierno,* 3 vols., ed. Rolena Adorno and John V. Murra (Mexico City: Siglo Veintiuno, 1980), f. 400. Courtesy of Siglo Veintiuno Editores.

recuperating, he waited for the Indians to fight them. In this manner, gaining ground and maintaining their reputation and doing what they should do as brave soldiers, they went on defending themselves until the notice of his difficulties reached his brother, who went out galloping with some horsemen and encountered his brother and his men one league from Cuzco. They were in such a position that they could not move, regardless that these horses, who had already been born in Peru of the best breed of those of Castile, sallied forth very spirited and vigorous, and were very skilled in this engagement.

With the succor of Hernando Pizarro the six horsemen shook off tiredness and danger, but the Indians—who pursued them very closely in order to capture and kill them at each step—lost spirit and retreated in order not to be caught by the fresh and rested horses, who furiously charged into them. There was a great shortage of food, especially meat, in Cuzco, so Hernando Pizarro ordered Gabriel de Rojas, a knight in whom he had great confidence because he was very experienced and prudent in warfare, to go with seventy horsemen toward Pomacanche, a province fourteen leagues from Cuzco, and try to collect all the livestock he could and quickly return. Within twenty days he brought two thousand head. And although many Indian troops appeared in the mountains, they contented themselves with a lot of yelling because Gabriel de Rojas went so well ordered and in such tight formation that they could gain nothing by assaulting him. Having safely entered Cuzco with the livestock, Hernán Ponce de León left for Condesuyu to collect food and to punish some villages because in that province they had killed the first Castilians of this turmoil—calling on Simón Juárez, who had Indians there, under pretense of paying their tributes, and then on eight or nine more because they always knew how to employ these and many other stratagems for their benefit. Hernán Ponce found no people to punish and hence returned swiftly with supplies. Gonzalo Pizarro then set out to survey the field with six horsemen, who were Alonso de Mesa, Alonso de Toro, Beltrán del Conde, Cárdenas,[2] Juan López, and Castañeda.[3] He discovered that in the direction of Jaquijahuana a good force of Indians was passing from one mountain to another, and spurring the horses to take them on the open field because they were already about to go up into a village called Circo, they blocked them on the slope and forced them back to the plain. More than a thousand Indians died, and that could have been the greater part of them. These races of men are very fierce with victory, but they are pitiful and fainthearted when they are in defeat. After this victory they returned to Cuzco with some prisoners, and it was ordered that some have a hand cut off; then they released them all. With this punishment and others, they were so frightened that they did not dare to descend to the plains. The level country was thus liberated so that the Indian friends could go out to do whatever was necessary, and the siege of Cuzco was expanded.

Food again became scarce, so Hernando Pizarro ordered Gabriel de Rojas to go with seventy horsemen to Jaquijahuana, where there was plenty of maize, and to remain there, and he sent him with an escort halfway there. Gabriel de Rojas sent Indians with six horses to a post, where another six horses came from Cuzco, and received them. In this fashion, Cuzco was provisioned within a few days. Gabriel de Rojas was returning to the city, and because they knew in the district that he was there retiring in Tambo, many Indians descended upon him with Castilian weapons and horses, and equipped with some muskets taken from the Castilians that they had killed; the Inca had made those eight or nine whom he held prisoner refine powder and condition the weapons. And one, so that they would not kill him, had gone over to serve him and was very trusted and favored. Descending then on Gabriel de Rojas as he was retreating, the [Indian] musketeers revealed their weapons, and the order of the Indians was different and much tighter than usual: they came out in a much more orderly way and more frequently to discharge their slings, darts, and arrows. They then retired, with others taking their places, as they had learned from the Castilians. He did not allow the horses to grow tired as they normally did; rather, in making their retreat in good order, they defended themselves. In the meantime, he sent a message to Hernando Pizarro about what was happening, asking him for some crossbowmen and to send him fifteen or twenty pikemen with an equal number of shield bearers because the arquebuses were useless from a lack of gunpowder and because the multitude of Indians was growing along with their arrogance and audacity. There was no other way by which to save themselves except by fleeing, which was not expedient because the Indians would then become so haughty that one could imagine that another day he could have two hundred thousand on top of him.

Hernando Pizarro did not tarry in sending succor to Gabriel de

Rojas — who, after discharging several rounds with the crossbows into the Indians, was able to keep them at a greater distance. But because they saw that the horses were not as fast as usual, they still did not lose their valor and daring. Gabriel de Rojas did not allow [his men] to get weary and ordered them to pick up their spirit because he intended to give [the Indians] a good thrashing and be done with them once and for all. And thus, setting up two companies with crossbows, bucklers, and pikes, and another two with horses, he approached the largest squadron of Indians from two sides so that the crossbows could do it much harm. After they sent two or three rounds into the Indians, and when it seemed that they had been effective and that the squadron here had become somewhat weakened because of the dead and injured, he attacked on two sides with the horses in a closed and tight throng. Trampling and killing with the lances, they opened up the squadron, and passing through from opposite sides, the two companies united in one body, as Gabriel de Rojas had ordered it. In one moment they again closed and trampled so that the Indians were defeated and dispersed. And then the Castilians began their killing, which was not little, and it would have been worse if Gabriel de Rojas, a calm and prudent man, had not prevented it. It seemed to him that it was not worth it anymore to shed the blood of those barbarians, saying that it was unnecessary to further employ the victorious spirit over the fallen and diminished one of the vanquished. He took the three mounted muskets that were fired four or five times in this engagement. Many Indians were seen on this occasion with swords and bucklers and halberds and some on horseback with lances, making great demonstrations and shows of bravery and some, as they assailed the Castilians, did deeds in which they showed greater courage than barbarians and skill that they learned from our people.[4]

Those of Cuzco continued their sallies, and Hernando Pizarro — wishing to give the Inca a good lesson in Tambo, and thinking that because the armies had withdrawn, not as many people would come — went out from Cuzco as secretly as he could with eighty horsemen and a few infantrymen. He left the city in charge of Gabriel de Rojas because he could not have commended it to a person of greater caution, experience, and authority. So that arriving at daybreak over Tambo, Hernando Pizarro found the situation very different from what he had expected because there were many corps of guards and many sentries posted in the countryside and on the walls. Sounding the alarm with loud yelling, as the Indians are accustomed, and with great clamor of their shell trumpets and drums, more than thirty thousand men assembled. Without disbanding, they waited for the opportunity to assail the Castilians and were very cautious not to be overtaken or trampled. It was remarkable to watch some come out ferociously with Castilian swords, bucklers, and morions, and it was not unusual to see an Indian who, armed in this fashion, highly esteeming the mastery of the lance, dared to attack a horseman. In order to be regarded as valiant, the Inca appeared on horseback among his people with lance in hand. The army was gathered and stationed in one place, which was very well fortified with a wall and by a river with good trenches and strong ramparts, at intervals and in good order.

Hernando Pizarro, considering that nothing could be gained there, decided to retreat. While a great number of Indians weighed heavily on them with slings, darts, and arrows, he found that in the Yucay River they had made a dam in the ford. But Hernando Pizarro made a swift retreat because the equipage went ahead of him, escorted by some footsoldiers and horsemen, and he followed with a troop of horsemen, and his brother, Gonzalo Pizarro, led the rearguard with another smaller one. The enemies came down hard, and with flaming torches that they carried they killed some Indian friends, without anyone being able to help them because of the difficulty and narrowness of the pass. It was a good decision to retreat to Maras, the site of a settlement that lies in the highest part of the descend, from where the road is level to Cuzco. Before leaving the narrow pass, Alonso de Mesa returned with two arquebusiers, and between them, with his lance and shield, he made a stand so that the Indians were delayed, leaving the Castilians exhausted and many of them injured, and those returned to Tambo, and the Indians to Cuzco.

It must have seemed to the Inca that it would be worth it to repay this action of Hernando Pizarro with another, and he ordered twenty-five thousand Indians to take a look at Cuzco so that when there was an opportunity, they could carry out something. At daybreak they attacked the quarter of Antisuyu, under Gabriel de Rojas, who was prepared to fight with ten horsemen. The Indians came so close to the city that they injured Alonso de Toro, Francisco de la Fuente, and

Juan Clemente. They came down so hard on Gabriel de Rojas that he had his hands full, but Hernán Ponce, Maldonado, Alonso de Mesa, and Pedro Pizarro came to his assistance and resisted the assault of the Indians, holding them off valiantly until more people arrived. Had this help been delayed in coming, the Indians might have entered the city on this day. And as they stubbornly fought each other, Pedro Pizarro's horse fell, and while [Pizarro] was on the ground, an Indian came and with great boldness led him away by the reins, but getting up quickly, he went after the Indian and stabbed him to death and collected his horse. But so many Indians assaulted Pizarro and his horse with rocks that he let it loose, and him they surrounded, and he defended himself valiantly with his sword and shield. Two horsemen came to assist him, and taking him between them, although with great effort, they got him out of the fray. In order to get away from them it was necessary to run, and being exhausted, Pedro Pizarro gasped for air, and he begged his companions to wait for him because he would rather die fighting than running away and asphyxiating. Although they returned to help him, he could not keep away the Indians, who were obsessed with capturing him, and believing that they already had him in their grasp, they let loose a great cry, something that they always did when they captured a man or a knight. And Gabriel de Rojas, turning to see what that yelling was about, assisted Pedro Pizarro with eight horsemen, and with that he was freed from that great peril, although mauled and wounded.

Garcí-Martínez was hit with a stone in one eye, which he lost. They killed Cisneros's horse and then cut off all its feet, and Juan Vázquez de Osuna valiantly retrieved Cisneros. They also took the horse of Mancio Sierra and cut off its feet. When the Indians retired from this skirmish, another of their squadrons returned above Carmenga, and some horsemen sallied forth at them. They learned from an Indian they captured that on the road to the City of the Kings, [the Indians] had killed Captains Huete and Diego Pizarro, whom Don Francisco Pizarro had sent along with some available people for the relief of Cuzco.

Among the other things that occurred in this siege, which were many, it happened that the Indians were filled with a great desire to burn the church because they believed that if they burned it down, it was certain that all the Castilians would die. They shot many red-hot stones with their slings and fire with some arrows. They persisted until it caught fire because the roof covering was of straw, as are those of most buildings of those parts. And it is a certain thing that once it is lighted, it does not cease until it consumes all the straw, and there is no effort great enough to extinguish it, and so they leave it. But this fire—and they all saw it—put itself out, a thing that the Castilians and the Indians took for a miracle. And from then on their spirit was broken so that they never again showed courage or the accustomed fierceness against Cuzco. Thus, they were weakening, leaving the Castilians with more rest and tranquility.

Notes

1 Francisco de Castañeda, a soldier not to be confused with the licentiate.

2 Francisco de Cárdenas.

3 Francisco de Castañeda.

4 The end of Herrera's chapter 5. The next paragraph picks up Herrera's chapter 6 about halfway into it.

CI

(From Herrera VI, 2, I)

That the Adelantado Don Diego de Almagro gives up the Chilean enterprise and returns to Cuzco, and what happened with Manco Inca Yupanqui

Don Diego de Almagro rested in Copiapó because it had many provisions and then continued on to another valley, called Huasco,[1] where, as well as in the third valley called Coquimbo,[2] they found all that was necessary. They departed for the provinces of Chile that lie one hundred leagues beyond. They arrived at the principal town that was then called Concomicagua, where many local people were waiting and with them one Castilian, who prodded by honor had gone to where no one knew him because Pizarro had insulted him. And well informed of the quality of the land, [Almagro] regretted having made the journey, and if he had not been minding his reputation, he would have returned from there to Peru. But wishing to fulfill his service to the king and Don Francisco Pizarro, and to satisfy the soldiers, he sent a captain with eighty horsemen and twenty infantrymen to explore all the land that he could. He returned with ruinous news, and others who also went on discoveries confirmed the first report. And because they had not found the riches that they expected, they all persuaded the adelantado to return to Peru to enjoy the governance the king had given him and to establish its boundaries with that of Don Francisco Pizarro. And one told him that if he should happen to die there, his son would be left with nothing but the name of Don Diego. And the people, desirous of returning to the comforts and riches of Peru, insisted so much that it made him very perplexed. Although he wished to stay for a time in Chile, and at the very least establish two settlements, they pressed him so much that he had to return, with great harm done to the people of those regions.

And in order to further move the adelantado's spirit to the return to Peru, his friends, favorites, and advisers told him that because the king had made him the grant of New Toledo, and he had in his possession the royal provisions, he should head there and let it be known that Cuzco fell within his jurisdiction. Because they wanted to live in that city and enjoy its delights and abundance — this is how much individual convenience, which they call reason of state, can influence — they forgot the common good and served only their own interests. And beginning the journey, they returned by another route in order not to go through the snowy passes, and they discovered the Atacama Desert. It is a sandy flat of ninety leagues, with little water or anything green in all of it, except in four or five spots. Because of this, men and horses perished, and while passing through this uninhabited place, they learned of Manco's war against Cuzco and that all the land was in turmoil. This moved further the adelantado's spirit to hasten the return in order to help those of Cuzco, and he supported the reasons of those who had persuaded him, which further encouraged them to press him for it. And thus they did not stop until Arequipa, seventy leagues from Cuzco, where they were well received and rested for a few days. . . .

Having rested several days in Arequipa, the army of the Adelantado Almagro set out for Cuzco. Some days before, because he had a great friendship with Manco, he sent him a message that he was amazed at the trouble he had caused and that he begged him to desist. Shortly he would be with him in order to favor him in all that he could, and [Manco] should inform him what reasons he had to make such displays. The Inca responded that he was pleased with his return, and using various messengers, he let him know the reasons for his movement. He complained about the little respect with which he was treated by those of Cuzco. And of Hernando Pizarro he said that he had given him a large quantity of gold, and he had left in order not to have to give him any more, considering how much he kept harassing him. And that he [Manco] wanted peace with [Almagro] because he considered him a friend, and that he should send him some trustworthy Castilian to negotiate about these matters. [Almagro] sent him two, with a good interpreter, and having received them well, and after having said that it was Hernando Pizarro's avarice that had moved him to take up arms, he would suspend them until he met the adelantado. And that is what he ordered all the Indians.

At the same time, the scouts of Cuzco captured an Indian from whom they learned that there was an army of Castilians in Jauja, which they found out later was Alonso de Alvarado's.[3] Another day they learned that the adelantado was marching back to Cuzco and that he had an understanding with Manco, and that because of his inducements [Manco] was not conducting hostilities as before, which at first amazed them, not knowing how this novelty originated. But on finding out what had happened, they sent a Mulatto youth to the Inca with a letter in which they asked him not to make peace with Don Diego de Almagro because he was not the lord, but rather with Don Francisco Pizarro. And they ordered that he should also verbally tell that to [Manco], and that was the beginning of sedition. The Inca gave this letter to Almagro's two Castilians so that they would see it, saying that he knew well that those of Cuzco were lying because the true lord was and had to be Don Diego de Almagro. Also, because of that, he wanted to have the hand of that lying messenger cut off. But because they argued so much against it, he contented himself with just cutting off his finger. And later he allowed the Castilians to return and to ask the adelantado on his behalf to meet him in the Yucay Valley, to which he would set out. In order to confirm it, the adelantado sent captain Ruy Díaz, with two or three Castilians, because [Manco] had said that he wanted only the adelantado as a friend. The Castilians affirmed that they did not believe that the Inca had good intentions, and so it seemed because he did not allow Ruy Díaz or his companions to return again. The army of the adelantado reached Urcos, six leagues from Cuzco.

This Manco began his rule at the age of eighteen and at first showed signs of being a man of good disposition, but later he turned out to be very cruel. When the war started, all the Indians who had been serving the Castilians went to serve him. But when it became known that he ordered them to be hanged, they returned, and they became extremely useful for many things. And there are opinions that without them [the Castilians] could not have defended themselves because (among other things) they were great enemies of Manco. Not one of his brothers escaped alive from his hands because he feared that in some way they might take the empire from him. Thus, his brother Paullu always stayed with Almagro to save his life. And when [Manco] was angry, he killed the Indians with a sword that he carried in his hands, which was one of the reasons why the land was pacified earlier. Paullu governed very well in all parts because he had a good mind, and he had suffered the hardships of the Chilean journey with great prudence. And when Almagro entered Cuzco, along with a good repartimiento, he gave him the houses of his brother Huascar to live in, which were the most important ones. And he was always highly esteemed and respected by the Indians as a person of royal blood, and he died a Christian. Long before his death he built a sumptuous chapel in Cuzco, where he was buried. And when he died, he was mourned throughout the entire land because there were no other Incas left. And although it is not its place, this has been said here because if it had not been, it would remain unsaid.[4]

Notes

1 About 160 kilometers south of Copiapó.

2 About 180 kilometers south of Huasco.

3 Alvarado came in response to Francisco Pizarro's call for help.

4 Manco Inca's hold on Cuzco was over, and he withdrew, though he would continue to cause trouble for years to come. He was murdered by a group of Spaniards at Vitcos in 1545. Diego de Almagro and his companions entered Cuzco in April 1537. He immediately reasserted his claim on the city, and following a brief skirmish, imprisoned Hernando and Gonzalo Pizarro. It is at this point that the civil wars begin in earnest. See Hemming, *Conquest*, pp. 227–79.

MAPS

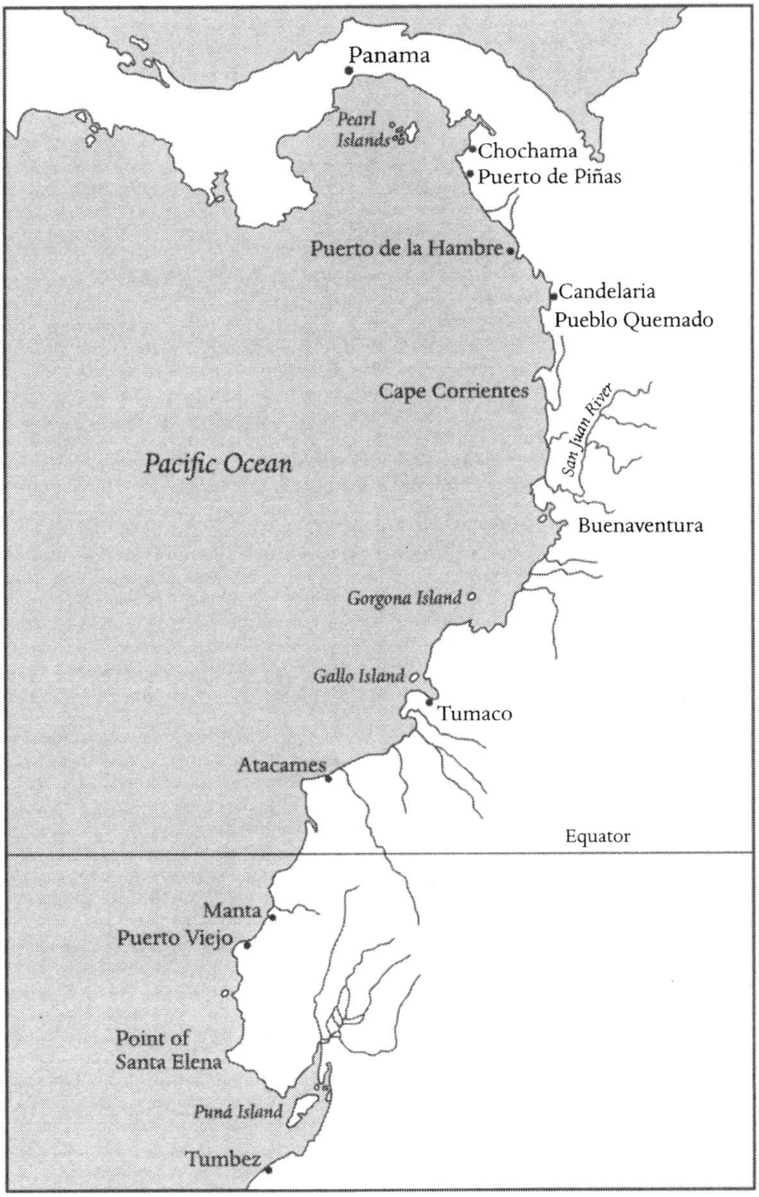
Panama
Pearl Islands
Chochama
Puerto de Piñas
Puerto de la Hambre
Candelaria
Pueblo Quemado
Cape Corrientes
San Juan River
Pacific Ocean
Buenaventura
Gorgona Island
Gallo Island
Tumaco
Atacames
Equator
Manta
Puerto Viejo
Point of Santa Elena
Puná Island
Tumbez

1. The First Voyage

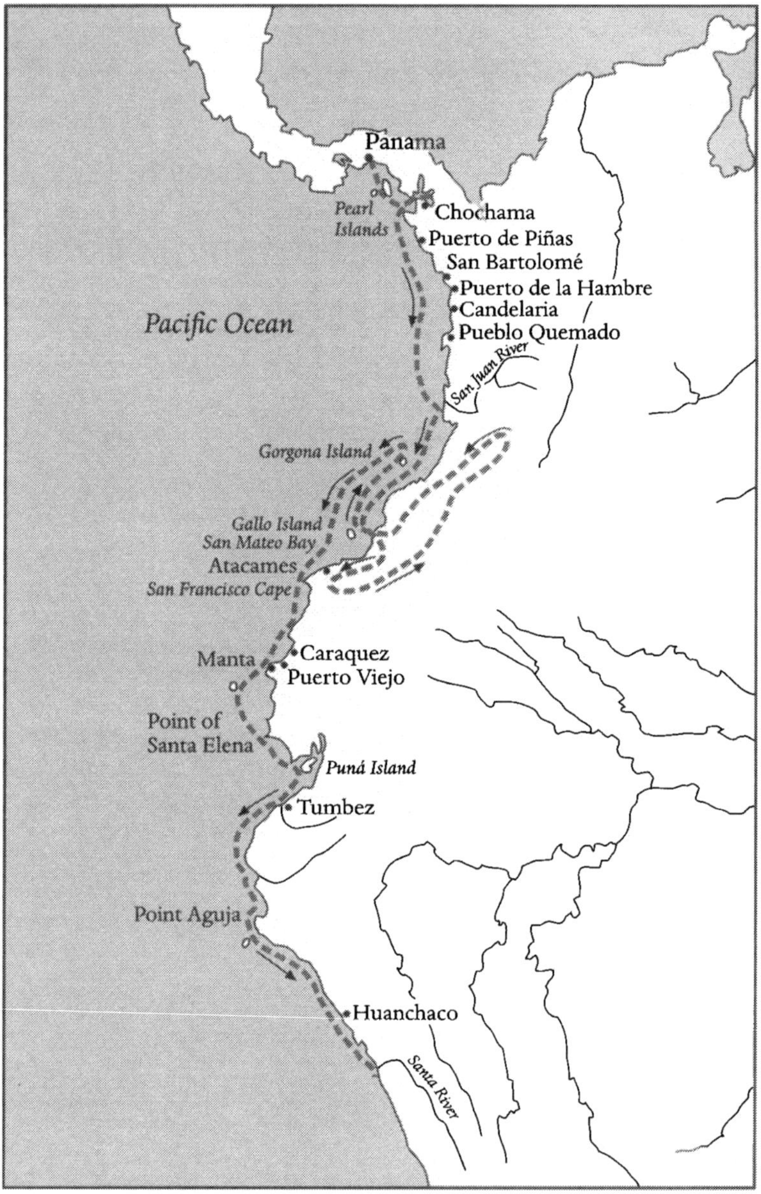
Panama
Pearl Islands
Chochama
Puerto de Piñas
San Bartolomé
Puerto de la Hambre
Candelaria
Pueblo Quemado
Pacific Ocean
San Juan River
Gorgona Island
Gallo Island
San Mateo Bay
Atacames
San Francisco Cape
Manta
Caraquez
Puerto Viejo
Point of Santa Elena
Puná Island
Tumbez
Point Aguja
Huanchaco
Santa River

2. The Second Voyage

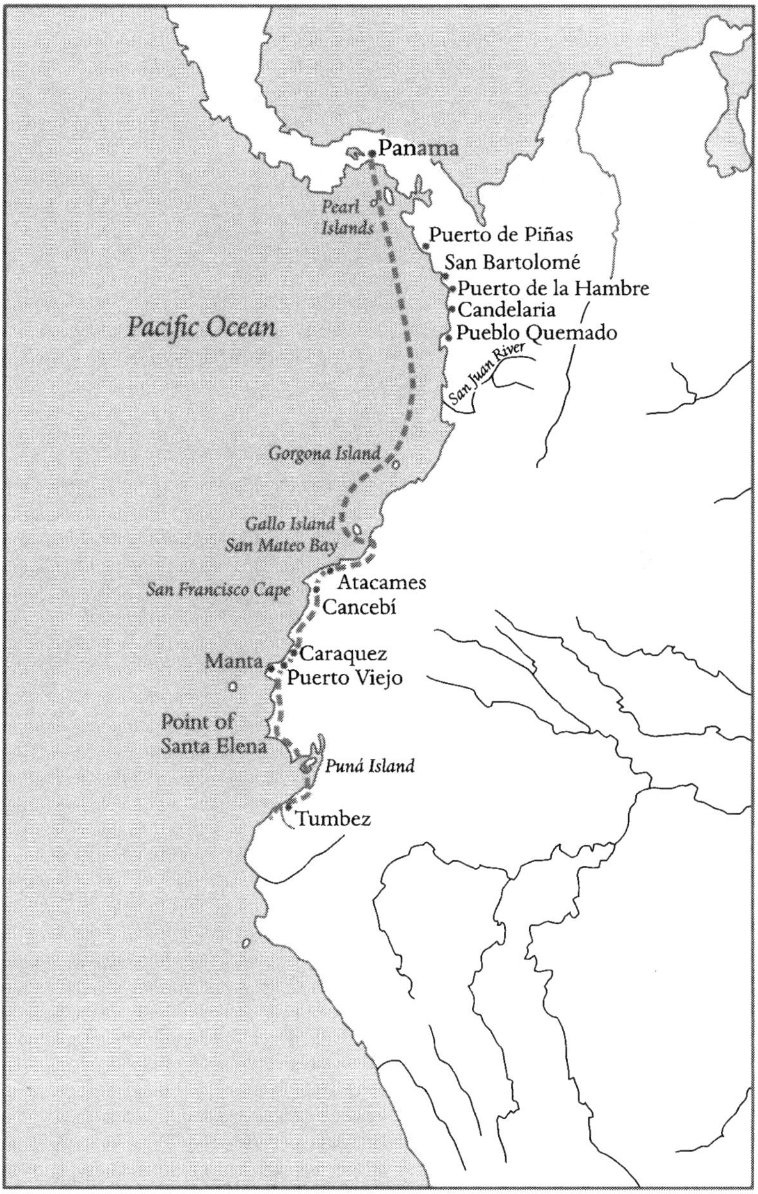

3. The Third Voyage

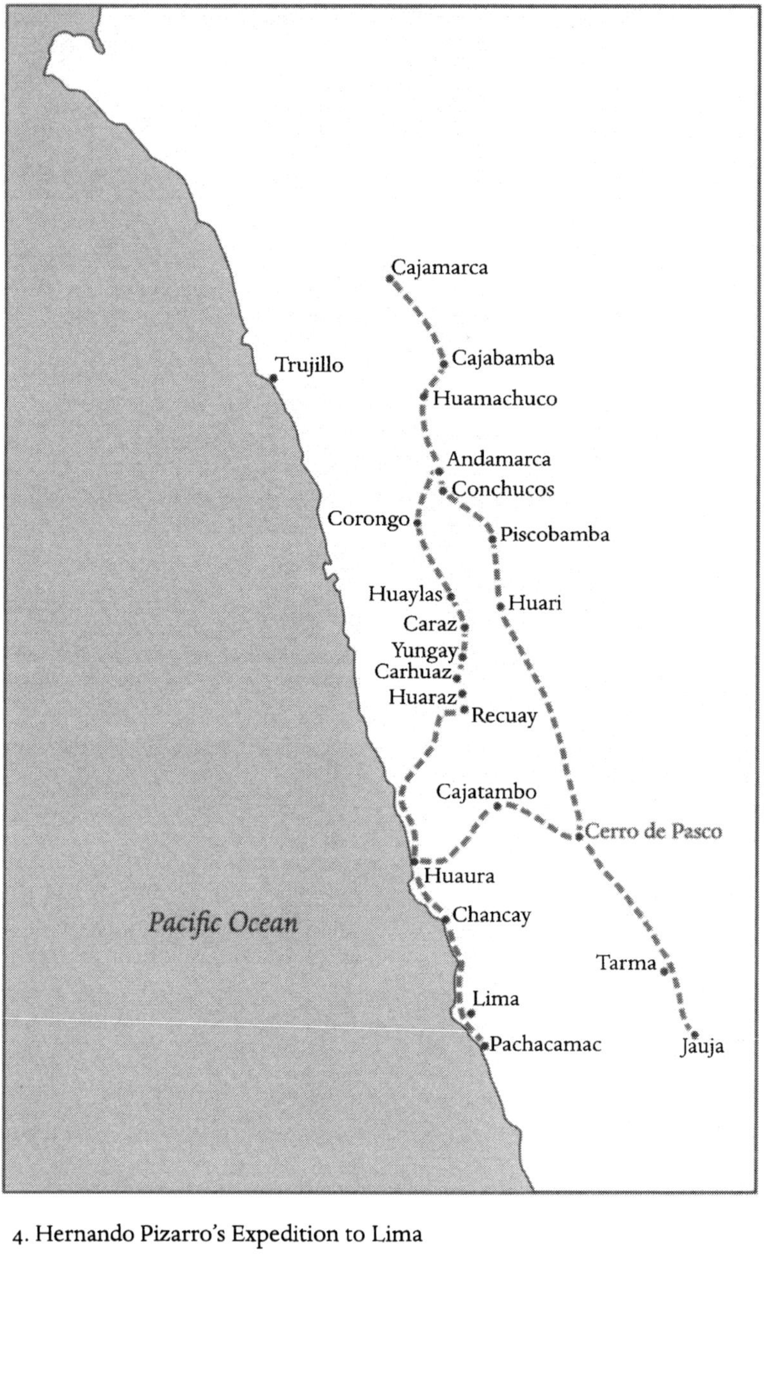

4. Hernando Pizarro's Expedition to Lima

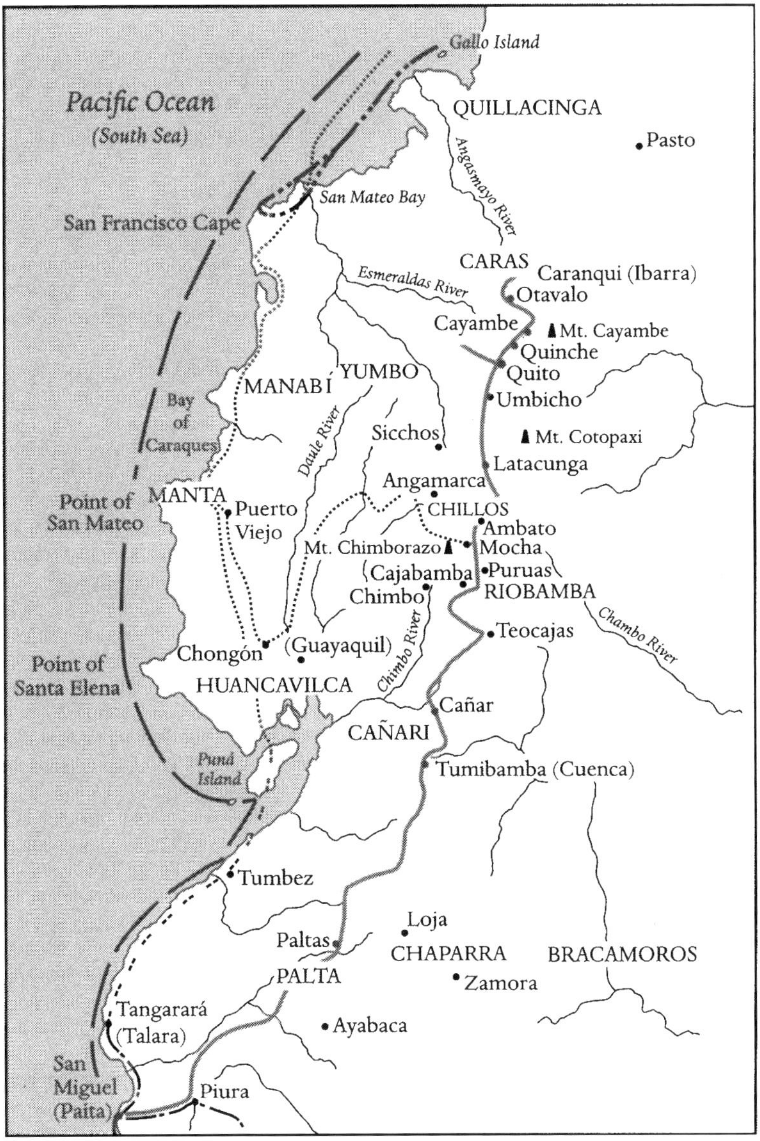

5. Exploration in the Quito Region

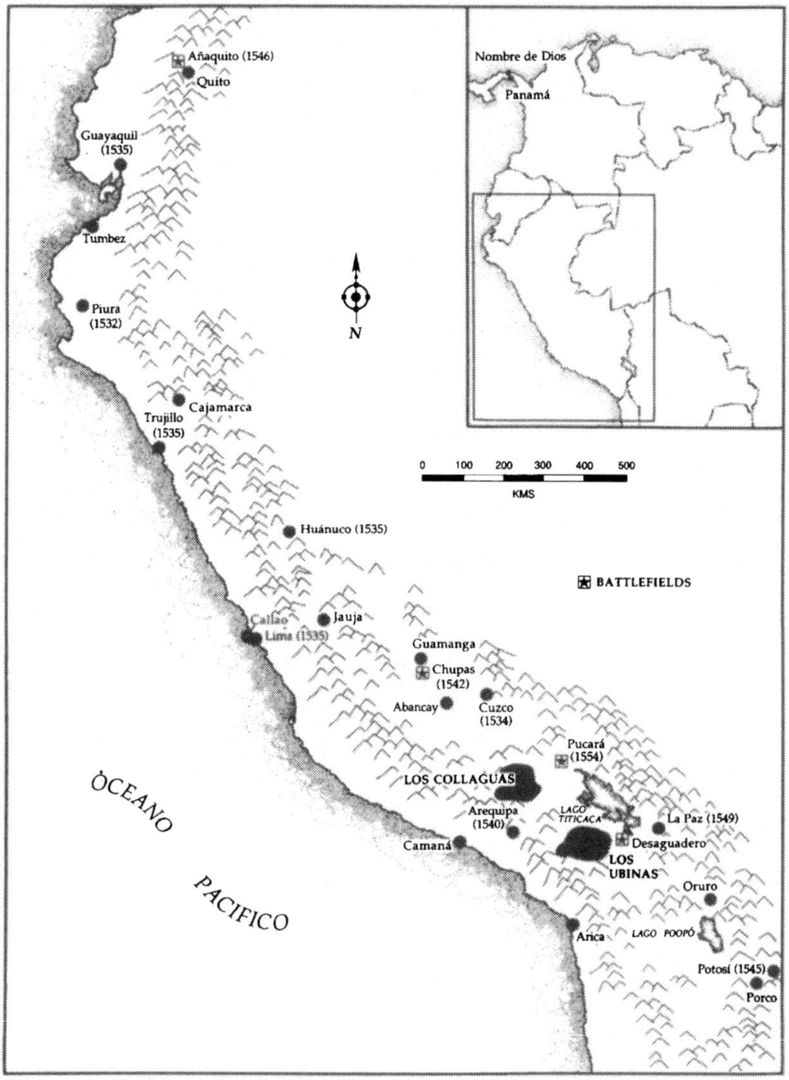

6. The Central Andes

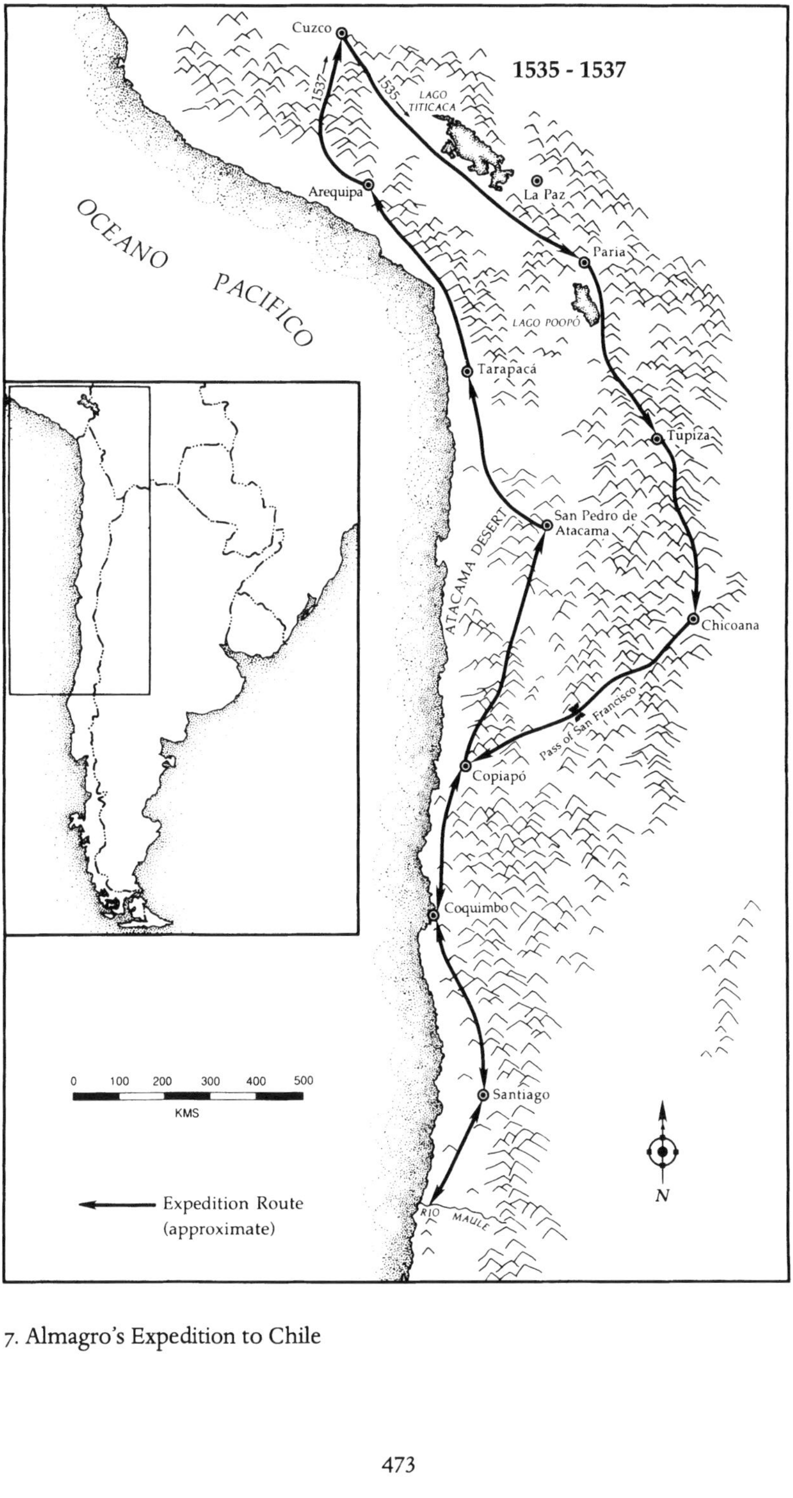

7. Almagro's Expedition to Chile

GLOSSARY

alcalde: town official, mayor
alférez: military official, standard bearer
arras: equivalent of dowry, owed by the groom to the bride
arroyo: a ravine, small valley
audiencia: the high court, which could also have executive functions
ayllu: Andean kin unit; weapon of balls attached to three cords
balsa: South American log or reed vessel
cacique: Amerindian official, chieftain
censo: a type of loan on property, also a census
chaquira: Andean stringed beads made of reed shell, or stone
chasqui: Inca runner, or messenger
converso: a "new" Christian of Jewish ancestry
corregidor: a Spanish official, usually in charge of a province
encomendero: the recipient of an Indian grant
encomienda: an Indian grant
entrada: initial expedition of exploration
huaca: Andean word signifying any object of veneration
kuraka: Andean cacique, or chieftain
maestrescuela: teaching post in Church hierarchy
mamaconas: "chosen" women associated with Inca cult
mandón: [Spanish] local political leader, literally one who orders
manta: unit of wool or cotton cloth
mitimaes: migrant Indians in districts beyond own ethnic cores
naboría: in the Caribbean context a slave or dependent
orejón: "big ear" from ear plugs, Spanish term for Inca leader
paramo: high-elevation, cool, flat grasslands
perulero: return migrant to Spain from Peru
rancho: hut, elsewhere modest agricultural holding
residencia: inquiry, or review of official's tour of duty at end
quinto: the fifth, a royal tax on mineral wealth
quipu: knotted-string mnemonic device used largely for quantities
quipucamayo: Andean specialist trained to use quipu records
repartimiento: a grant of Indians, or any objects
tambo: Inca way station for travelers
Tawantinsuyu: land of the four quarters, Inca realm
Tierra Firme: roughly the mainland coast of northern South America
vecino: city resident with legal rights
veedor: treasury official, inspector
yanaconas: Andean servants, or retainers

WEIGHTS, MEASURES, AND CURRENCY

Weights, measures, and currency units varied by time and place. The following values are only approximations.

Weights and Measures

arroba: weight, about 25.3 pounds, or 11.5 kilograms
fanega: about 1.5 bushels, or 58 liters
carga: volume, about 3 to 4 fanegas
estado: a vertical measure about 5.5 feet, or 1.7 meters
legua: league, about 3.5 miles, or 5.57 kilometers
quintal: weight, about 101.5 pounds, or 46 kilograms

Currency

castellano: worth about 490 maravedies
ducat: value about 375 maravedies
doblón: roughly double a castellano, 2 castellanos
mark: worth 50 castellanos
pesos de oro: American gold coin worth about 450 maravedies
real: silver coin worth about 34 maravedies

BIBLIOGRAPHY

Select Editions of Pedro de Cieza de León

PART ONE

Cieza de León, Pedro de. *Parte primera de la Chrónica del Perú. Que tracta la demarcación de sus provincias: La descripción dellas. Las fundaciones de las nuevas ciudades . . . .* Seville: Martín de Montesdoca, 1553.

———. *Parte primera de la Chrónica del Perú. Que tracta la demarcación de sus provincias: La descripción dellas. Las fundaciones de las nuevas ciudades . . . .* Anvers: Casa de Iuan Steelfio, 1554.

———. *The Seventeen Years of Travel of Pedro de Cieza, through the Mighty Kingdom of Peru . . . ,* trans. John Stevens. London, 1709.

———. *The Travels of Pedro de Cieza de León . . . ,* trans. Clements R. Markham. Hakluyt Society, 1st ser., vol. 33. London, 1864.

———. *Crónica del Perú: Primera parte,* 2d rev. ed., ed. Franklin Pease G.Y. Lima: Universidad Católica del Perú, 1986.

PART TWO

Cieza de León, Pedro de. *Segunda parte de la Crónica del Perú, que trata del Señorio de los Incas . . . ,* ed. Marcos Jiménez de la Espada. Madrid, 1880.

———. *The Second Part of the Chronicle of Peru,* trans. Clements R. Markham. Hakluyt Society, 1st ser., vol. 68. London, 1883.

———. *El señorio de los Incas,* ed. Carlos Araníbar. Lima: Instituto de Estudios Peruanos, 1967.

———. *Crónica del Perú: Segunda parte,* ed. Francesca Cantù. Lima: Universidad Católica del Perú, 1985.

PART THREE

Cieza de León, Pedro de. *Pedro de Cieza de León e il "Descubrimiento y conquista del Perú,"* ed. Francesca Cantù. Rome: Instituto Storico Italiano, 1979.

———. *Descubrimiento y conquista del Perú,* ed. Mario A. Valotta. Madrid: Grupo Cultural Zero, 1984.

———. *Crónica del Perú: Tercera parte,* ed. Francesca Cantù. Lima: Universidad Católica del Perú, 1989.

PART FOUR: THE CIVIL WARS

I. Salinas

Cieza de León, Pedro de. *Guerras civiles del Perú, por Pedro de Cieza de León,* vol. 1, *Guerra de las Salinas,* ed. José Sancho Rayón. Madrid: Viuda de Rico, 1877.

———. *Civil Wars of Peru: The War of Las Salinas,* trans. Clements R. Markham. Hakluyt Society, 2d ser., vol. 54. London, 1923.

———. *Crónica del Perú: Cuarta parte,* vol. 1, *Guerra de las Salinas,* ed. Pedro Guibovich Pérez. Lima: Universidad Católica del Perú, 1991.

II. Chupas

Cieza de León, Pedro de. *Guerras civiles del Perú, por Pedro de Cieza de León, natural de Llerena,* vol. 2, *Guerra de Chupas,* ed. José Sancho Rayón. Madrid: *Colección de documentos inéditos para la historia de España,* vol. 76, 1881.

———. *Civil Wars in Peru, Part Four: The War of Chupas,* trans. Clements R. Markham. Hakluyt Society, 2d ser., vol. 42. London, 1918.

———. *Crónica del Perú: Cuarta parte,* vol. 2, *Guerra de Chupas,* ed. Gabriela Benavides de Rivero. Lima: Universidad Católica del Perú, 1994.

III. Quito

Cieza de León, Pedro de. *Tercero libro de las guerras civiles del Perú, el cual se llama la Guerra de Quito,* ed. Marcos Jiménez de la Espada. Madrid: Biblioteca Hispano-Ultramarina, 1877.

———. *The War of Quito . . . ,* trans. Clements R. Markham. Hakluyt Society, 2d ser., vol. 31. London, 1913.

———. *Crónica del Perú: Cuarta parte,* vol. 3, *Guerra de Quito,* 2 vols., ed. Laura Gutiérrez Arbulú. Lima: Universidad Católica del Perú, 1994.

COMBINED

Cieza de León, Pedro de. *Pedro de Cieza de León: Obras completas,* 3 vols., ed. Carmelo Sáenz de Santa María. Madrid: CSIC, 1984.

———. *The Incas of Pedro Cieza de León,* trans. Harriet de Onis, ed. Victor Wolfgang von Hagen. Norman: University of Oklahoma Press, 1959. [Selections from *Part One* and *Part Two.*]

General References

Armas Medina, Fernando de. *Cristianización del Perú (1532–1600)*. Seville: Escuela de Estudios Hispano-americanos, 1953.

Atlas básico de Colombia. Bogotá: Instituto Geográfico "Agustín Codazzi," 1978.

Bakewell, Peter. "Mining in Colonial Spanish America." In *The Cambridge History of Latin America*, 11 vols., ed. Leslie Bethell, 2:105–52. New York: Cambridge University Press, 1984.

Barba, Francisco Esteve. *Historiografía indiana*. Madrid: Editorial Gredos, 1964.

Barnadas, Joseph M. *Descripción del Perú, 1553* [1553]. Caracas: Universidad Católica Andrés Bello, 1976.

Barriga, Víctor M. *Los Mercedarios en el Perú en el siglo XVI*. Arequipa: La Colmena, 1942.

Bernstein, Harry, and Bailey W. Diffie. "Sir Clements R. Markham as a Translator." *Hispanic American Historical Review* 17 (1937): 546–57.

Bowser, Frederick P. *The African Slave in Colonial Peru, 1524–1650*. Stanford: Stanford University Press, 1974.

Brading, David A. *The First America: The Spanish Monarchy, Creole Patriots, and the Liberal State, 1492–1867*. New York: Cambridge University Press, 1991.

Bromley, Juan. *La fundación de la ciudad de los Reyes*. Lima: Excelsior, 1935.

Burga, Manuel. *Nacimiento de una utopía: Muerte y resurrección de los Incas*. Lima: Instituto de Apoyo Agrario, 1988.

Burkholder, Mark A., and Lyman L. Johnson. *Colonial Latin America*, 2d ed. New York: Oxford University Press, 1994.

Busto Duthurburu, José Antonio del. *El capitán, el trompeta y otros hombres de caballería*. Lima: Editorial Universitaria, 1969.

———. *Diccionario histórico biográfico de los conquistadores del Perú*, 2 vols. Lima: Studium, 1986.

———. *Francisco Pizarro: El Marqués Gobernador*. Madrid: Ediciones Rialp, 1966.

———. *Historia general del Perú: Descubrimiento y conquista*. Lima: Studium, 1978.

———. *La hueste perulera*. Lima: Universidad Católica del Perú, 1981.

Conrad, Geoffrey W., and Arthur A. Demarest. *Religion and Empire: The Dynamics of Aztec and Inca Expansionism*. New York: Cambridge University Press, 1984.

Cook, Alexandra Parma, and Noble David Cook. *Good Faith and Truthful Ignorance: A Case of Transatlantic Bigamy*. Durham, N.C.: Duke University Press, 1991.

Cook, Noble David. *Demographic Collapse: Indian Peru, 1520–1620*. New York: Cambridge University Press, 1981.

———. "Los libros de cargo del tesorero Alonso Riquelme con el rescate de Atahualpa." *Humanidades* (Lima) 2 (1968): 41–88.

———, ed. *Tasa de la visita general de Francisco de Toledo*. Lima: San Marcos, 1975.

Cook, Noble David, and W. George Lovell, eds. *"Secret Judgments of God": Old World Disease in Colonial Spanish America*. Norman: University of Oklahoma Press, 1992.

Covarrubias Orozco, Sebastián de. *Tesoro de la lengua castellana o española* [1611]. Madrid: Editorial Castalia, 1994.

Crosby, Alfred W. *The Columbian Exchange: Biological and Cultural Consequences of 1492*. Westport: Greenwood Press, 1972.

Denevan, William M., ed. *The Native Population of the Americas in 1492*, 2d ed. Madison: University of Wisconsin Press, 1992.

D'Harcourt, Raoul. *Textiles of Ancient Peru and Their Techniques*. Seattle: University of Washington Press, 1977.

Diffie, Bailey W. *Latin-American Civilization: Colonial Period*. Harrisburg, Pa.: Stackpole Sons, 1945.

———. "A Markham Contribution to the 'Leyenda Negra.'" *Hispanic American Historical Review* 16 (1936): 96–103.

Enríquez de Guzmán, Alonso. *Vida y aventuras de un caballero noble desbaratado*. Lima: Cantuta, 1970.

Fernández-Carrión, Mercedes, and José Luis Valverde. *Farmacia y sociedad en Sevilla en el siglo XVI*. Seville: Biblioteca de Temas Sevillanos, 1985.

Freile Granizo, Juan, and Julio Estrada Ycaza. "Descripción del Perú." *Revista del Archivo Histórico de Guayas* 9 (1976): 35–58.

Garcilaso de la Vega, El Inca. *Royal Commentaries of the Incas and General History of Peru*, 2 vols., trans. Harold V. Livermore. Austin: University of Texas Press, 1966.

———. *Los comentarios reales de los Incas*, 4 vols., ed. Horacio H. Urteaga. Lima: Imprenta Gil, 1941–44.

Garrain Villa, Luis José. "Algunos apuntes sobre el testamento de Pedro Cieza de León." *Coloquios Históricos de Extremadura*, no. 18. Cáceres: Institución Cultural "el Broncense," 1991.

———. *Llerena en el siglo XVI: La emigración a las Indias*. Madrid: Junta de Extremadura, 1991.

Guaman Poma de Ayala, Felipe. *Nueva corónica y buen gobierno* [1613], facs. ed. Paris: Musée de l'Homme, 1936.

Hamilton, Earl Jefferson. *American Treasure and the Price Revolution in Spain, 1501–1650*. Cambridge: Harvard University Press, 1934.

Haring, C. H. *The Spanish Empire in America*. New York: Oxford University Press, 1947.

Helms, Mary W. *Ancient Panama: Chiefs in Search of Power*. Austin: University of Texas Press, 1979.

Hemming, John. *The Conquest of the Incas*. London: Sphere Books, 1972.

Hermosilla Molina, Antonio. *Cien años de la medicina sevillana*. Seville: Diputación Provincial, 1970.

Herrera y Tordesillas, Antonio de. *Historia general de los hechos de los castellanos en las Islas y Tierra Firme del Mar Océano* [1601–15], 17 vols. Madrid: Real Academia de la Historia, 1934–57.

Hudson, Charles. *Knights of Spain, Warriors of the Sun: Hernando de Soto and the South's Ancient Chiefdoms*. Athens: University of Georgia Press, 1997.

Hyslop, John. *The Inka Road System*. Orlando: Academic Press, 1984.

Jiménez de la Espada, Marcos, ed. *Relaciones geográficas de Indias: Perú*, 3 vols., rev. ed. Madrid: Atlas, 1965.

Kauffmann Doig, Federico. *Manual de arqueología peruana*. Lima: Iberia, 1983.

Keatinge, Richard W., ed. *Peruvian Prehistory*. New York: Cambridge University Press, 1988.

Kosok, Paul. *Life, Land, and Water in Ancient Peru*. New York: Long Island University Press, 1965.

Kramer, Wendy. *Encomienda Politics in Early Colonial Guatemala, 1524–1544: Dividing the Spoils*. Boulder: Westview Press, 1994.

Lanning, Edward P. *Peru before the Incas*. Englewood Cliffs, N.J.: Prentice-Hall, 1967.

Las Casas, Bartolomé de. *Historia de las Indias*, 3 vols. Mexico City: Fondo de Cultura Económica, 1951.

Lee, Bertram T., and Juan Bromley, eds. *Libros de cabildos de Lima*, 23 vols. Lima, 1935–.

León, Pedro R. *Algunas observaciones sobre Pedro de Cieza de León y la* Crónica del Perú. Madrid: Gredos, 1973.

———. "Pedro Cieza de León 'Principe maltrado': Breve estudio de las traducciones inglesas de la *Crónica del Perú*." *Revista de Indias* 31 (1971): 125–26, 199–219.

Lockhart, James. *Men of Cajamarca*. Austin: University of Texas Press, 1972.

———. *Spanish Peru, 1532–1560: A Colonial Society*. Madison: University of Wisconsin Press, 1968.

Lopéz de Gómara, Francisco. *Cortés: The Life of the Conqueror by His Secretary* [1552], trans. Lesley Byrd Simpson. Berkeley: University of California Press, 1964.

Loredo, Rafael. "Tercera parte del la *Crónica del Perú*." *Mercurio Peruano* (Lima), 340 (1955): 467–71.

Lynch, John. *Spain under the Habsburgs,* 2 vols. New York: Oxford University Press, 1964.

MacCormack, Sabine. *Religion in the Andes: Vision and Imagination in Early Colonial Peru.* Princeton: Princeton University Press, 1991.

Martín, Luis. *Daughters of the Conquistadores: Women of the Viceroyalty of Peru.* Albuquerque: University of New Mexico Press, 1983.

Maticorena Estrada, Miguel. "Cieza de León en Sevilla y su muerte en 1554: Documentos." *Anuario de Estudios Americanos* 12 (1955): 615–74.

———. "Contrato para la primera edición de Sevilla." In Pedro de Cieza de León, *Crónica del Perú: Primera parte,* ed. Franklin Pease G.Y., pp. xlv–li. Lima: Universidad Católica del Perú, 1986.

Means, Philip Ainsworth. *Biblioteca Andina.* Detroit: Blaine Ethridge Books, 1973.

Mendiburu, Manuel de. *Diccionario histórico biográfico del Perú,* 2d ed., 11 vols. Lima: Imprenta Gil, 1931–36.

Monardes, Nicolás. *Historia medicinal de las cosas que traen de nuestras Indias occidentales que sirven en medicina* [1574], facs. ed. Seville: Padilla Libros, 1988.

Morris, Craig, and D. E. Thompson. *Huánuco Pampa—An Inca City and Its Hinterland.* London: Thames and Hudson, 1985.

Murra, John V. "The Cayapa and Colorado." In *Handbook of South American Indians,* 7 vols., ed. Julian H. Steward, 4:277–91. Bureau of American Ethnology Bulletins, no. 143. Washington, D.C., 1946–59.

———. *The Economic Organization of the Inka State.* Greenwich: JAI Press, 1980.

———. "Review of *The Incas of Pedro de Cieza de León.*" *Hispanic American Historical Review* 40 (1960): 281–82.

Murray, James C. *Spanish Chroniclers of the Indies: Sixteenth Century.* New York: Twayne Publishers, 1994.

Newson, Linda A. *Life and Death in Early Colonial Ecuador.* Norman: University of Oklahoma Press, 1995.

———. "Old World Epidemics in Early Colonial Ecuador." In *"Secret Judgments of God": Old World Disease in Colonial Spanish America,* ed. Noble David Cook and W. George Lovell, pp. 84–112. Norman: University of Oklahoma Press, 1992.

Ortiz de la Tabla Ducasse, Javier. *Los encomenderos de Quito, 1534–1660: Origen y evolución de una elite colonial.* Seville: Escuela de Estudios Hispano-americanos, 1993.

Oviedo y Valdés, Gonzalo Fernández de. *Sumario de la natural historia de las Indias.* Toledo, 1526.

———. *Primera parte de la historia natural y general de las Indias, yslas y Tierra Firme del Mar Océano . . . .* Seville: Juan Cromberger, 1535.

———. *Historia general y natural de las Indias,* 5 vols., ed. Juan Pérez de Tudela Bueso. Madrid: Atlas, 1959.

———. *Natural History of the West Indies,* trans. Sterling A. Stoudemire. Chapel Hill: University of North Carolina Press, 1959.

Pease G.Y., Franklin. "Notas sobre Wiraqocha y sus itinerarios." *Histórica* 10 (1986): 227–35.

———. *Los últimos Incas del Cuzco.* Madrid: Alianza América, 1991.

Perry, Mary Elizabeth. *Crime and Society in Early Modern Seville.* Hanover: University Press of New England, 1980.

———. *Gender and Disorder in Early Modern Seville.* Princeton: Princeton University Press, 1990.

Pike, Ruth. *Aristocrats and Traders: Sevillian Society in the Sixteenth Century.* Ithaca: Cornell University Press, 1972.

Pizarro, Pedro. *Relación del descubrimiento y conquista del Perú* [1571], ed. Guillermo Lohmann Villena. Lima: Universidad Católica del Perú, 1978.

Porras Barrenechea, Raúl, ed. *Cartas del Perú (1524–1543).* Lima: Sociedad de Bibliofilos Peruanos, 1959.

———, ed. *Cedulario del Perú, siglos XVI, XVII, y XVIII,* 2 vols. Lima: Torres Aguirre, 1948.

———. *Crónicas perdidas, presuntas y olvidadas sobre la conquista del Perú.* Lima: Biblioteca de la Sociedad Peruana de Historia, 1951.

———. *Los cronistas del Perú (1528–1650) y otros ensayos,* ed. Franklin Pease G.Y. Lima: Banco de Crédito del Perú, 1986.

———. "Dos documentos esenciales sobre Francisco Pizarro y la conquista del Perú." *Revista Histórica* 17 (1948): 9–95.

Puente Brunke, José de la. *Encomienda y encomenderos en el Perú.* Seville: Diputación Provincial, 1992.

Radell, David R. "The Indian Slave Trade and Population of Nicaragua during the Sixteenth Century." In *The Native Population of the Americas in 1492,* 2d ed., ed. William M. Denevan, pp. 67–76. Madison: University of Wisconsin Press, 1992.

Ravines, Rogger, ed. *Chanchan, metropoli chimu.* Lima: Instituto de Estudios Peruanos, 1980.

Recinos, Adrián. *Pedro de Alvarado, conquistador de México y Guatemala,* 2d ed. Mexico City: CENALTEX, 1986.

Ringrose, David R. *Madrid and the Spanish Economy, 1560–1850.* Berkeley: University of California Press, 1983.

Riva Agüero, José de la. *El primer alcalde de Lima Nicolás de Ribera el Viejo y su posteridad.* Lima: Imprenta Gil, 1935.

Rostworowski de Diez Canseco, María. *Doña Francisca Pizarro: Una ilustre mestiza 1534–1598.* Lima: Instituto de Estudios Peruanos, 1989.

———. *Historia del Tahuantinsuyu*. Lima: Instituto de Estudios Peruanos, 1988.

Rowe, John Howland. "La fecha de la muerte de Wayna Qhapaq." *Histórica* 2(1) (1978): 83–88.

———. "Inca Culture at the Time of the Spanish Conquest." In *Handbook of South American Indians*, 7 vols., ed. Julian H. Steward, 2: 183–330. Bureau of American Ethnology Bulletins, no. 143. Washington, D.C., 1946–59.

Sáenz de Santa María, Carmelo. "Los capítulos finales de la Tercera Parte de la *Crónica del Perú* de Pedro de Cieza de León." *Boletín del Instituto Riva-Agüero* 9 (1972–74): 35–67.

———. "Introducción General." In *Pedro de Cieza de León: Obras completas*, 3 vols. Madrid: CSIC, 1984.

Santo Tomás, Domingo de. *Grammática o arte de la lengua general de los indios de los reynos del Perú* [1560], facs. ed., ed. Rodolfo Cerrón-Palomino. Madrid: Ediciones de Cultura Hispánica, 1994.

Sauer, Carl Ortwin. *The Early Spanish Main*. Berkeley: University of California Press, 1966.

Seed, Patricia. *Ceremonies of Possession in Europe's Conquest of the New World, 1492–1640*. Cambridge: Cambridge University Press, 1995.

Sherman, William L. *Forced Native Labor in Sixteenth-Century Central America*. Lincoln: University of Nebraska Press, 1979.

Silverblatt, Irene. *Moon, Sun, and Witches: Gender Ideologies and Class in Inca and Colonial Peru*. Princeton: Princeton University Press, 1987.

Stern, Steve. *Peru's Indian Peoples and the Challenge of Spanish Conquest: Huamanga to 1640*. Madison: University of Wisconsin Press, 1982.

Steward, Julian H., ed. *Handbook of South American Indians*, 7 vols. Bureau of American Ethnology Bulletins, no. 143. Washington, D.C., 1946–59.

Steward, Julian H., and Louis C. Faron. *Native Peoples of South America*. New York: McGraw-Hill, 1959.

Stiglich, Germán. *Diccionario geográfico del Perú*, 3 vols. Lima: Torres Aguirre, 1922.

Stout, David B. "The Choco." In *Handbook of South American Indians*, 7 vols., ed. Julian H. Steward, 4: 269–76. Bureau of American Ethnology Bulletins, no. 143. Washington, D.C., 1946–59.

Tibesar, Antonine. *Franciscan Beginnings in Colonial Peru*. Washington, D.C.: Academy of American Franciscan History, 1953.

Trelles Arestegui, Efraín. *Lucas Martínez Vegazo: Funcionamiento de una encomienda peruana inicial*. Lima: Universidad Católica del Perú, 1982.

Urton, Gary. *The History of a Myth: Pacariqtambo and the Origin of the Inkas*. Austin: University of Texas Press, 1990.

Vargas Ugarte, Rubén. *Historia de la iglesia en el Perú (1511–1568)*. Lima: Imprenta Santa María, 1953.

Varón Gabai, Rafael. *Francisco Pizarro and His Brothers: The Illusion of Power in Sixteenth-Century Peru*, trans. Javier Flores Espinosa. Norman: University of Oklahoma Press, 1997.

Wood, Robert D. *"Teach Them Good Customs": Colonial Indian Education and Acculturation in the Andes.* Culver City, Calif.: Labyrinthos, 1986.

Ziolkowski, Mariusz S. "Las cometas de Atawallpa: Acerca del papel de las profecías en la política del estado Inca." *Anthropologica* 6(6) (1988): 85–110.

Zuidema, R. Tom. *Inca Civilization in Cuzco.* Austin: University of Texas Press, 1990.

INDEX

ABOUT THE AUTHORS

Noble David Cook is professor of history at Florida International University; Alexandra Parma Cook is an independent scholar. They co-authored *Good Faith and Truthful Ignorance: A Case of Transatlantic Bigamy* (Duke University Press, 1991). Noble David Cook is also author of *Demographic Collapse: Indian Peru, 1520–1620* (Cambridge University Press, 1981), and *"Born to Die": Disease and New World Conquest, 1492–1650* (Cambridge University Press, 1998).

Library of Congress Cataloging-in-Publication Data

Cieza de León, Pedro de, 1518–1554.
[Descubrimiento y conquista del Perú. English]
The discovery and conquest of Peru : chronicles of the New World encounter / Pedro de Cieza de León ; edited and translated by Alexandra Parma Cook and Noble David Cook.
p. cm. — (Latin America in translation/en traducción/em tradução)
Includes bibliographical references and index.
ISBN 0-8223-2127-0 (cloth : alk. paper). — ISBN 0-8223-2146-7 (pbk. : alk. paper)
1. Peru—Discovery and exploration. 2. Peru—History—Conquest, 1522–1548.
I. Cook, Alexandra Parma. II. Cook, David Noble. III. Title. IV. Series.
F3442.C66313 1998
985'.01—dc21

98-20158
CIP

Printed in Great Britain
by Amazon

43685564R00310